A Mirror for Modern Scholars

A Mirror for Modern Scholars

Essays in Methods of Research in Literature

Edited by

LESTER A. BEAURLINE

The Odyssey Press

The Bobbs-Merrill Company, Inc., Publisher

Indianapolis · New York

THE ODYSSEY PRESS
A DIVISION OF
THE BOBBS-MERRILL COMPANY, INC.

Printed in the United States of America
Library of Congress Catalog Card Number 65-26779
ISBN 0-672-63064-8 (pbk)
Third Printing

ACKNOWLEDGMENTS

Don Cameron Allen, STYLE AND CERTITUDE, reprinted from *ELH: A Journal of English Literary History,* XV (1948), 167–175, by permission of The Johns Hopkins Press.

William Arrowsmith, A GREEK THEATRE OF IDEAS, reprinted from *Ideas in the Drama: Selected Papers from the English Institute,* ed. John Gassner, pp. 1–41, copyright © 1964, Columbia University Press, by permission.

Donald C. Baker, THE DATE OF *MANKIND,* reprinted from *Philological Quarterly,* XLII (1963), 90–91, by permission of the State University of Iowa and the author.

R. C. Bald, EVIDENCE AND INFERENCE IN BIBLIOGRAPHY, reprinted from *English Institute Annual, 1941,* pp. 159–183, copyright 1942, Columbia University Press, New York, by permission.

G. E. Bentley, Jr., THE DATE OF BLAKE'S *VALA* OR *THE FOUR ZOAS,* reprinted from *Modern Language Notes,* LXXI (1956), 487–491, by permission of The Johns Hopkins Press.

Morton W. Bloomfield, SYMBOLISM IN MEDIEVAL LITERATURE, reprinted from *Modern Philology,* LVI (1958), 73–81, by permission of The University of Chicago Press, copyright 1958 by The University of Chicago Press.

Wayne C. Booth, CONTROL OF DISTANCE IN JANE AUSTIN'S *EMMA*, reprinted from *The Rhetoric of Fiction* by Wayne C. Booth by permission of The University of Chicago Press, © 1961, The University of Chicago Press.

Fredson Bowers, SOME RELATIONS OF BIBLIOGRAPHY TO EDITORIAL PROBLEMS, reprinted from *Studies in Bibliography,* III (1950–51), 37–62, by permission of the author.

James B. Colvert, THE ORIGINS OF STEPHEN CRANE'S LITERARY CREED, reprinted from *The University of Texas Studies in English,* XXXIV (1955), 179–188, by permission of the University of Texas Press and the author.

R. S. Crane, THE HOUYHNHNMS, THE YAHOOS, AND THE HISTORY OF IDEAS, reprinted from *Reason and the Imagination: Studies in the History of Ideas, 1600-1800,* ed. J. A. Mazzeo, pp. 231–253, copyright © 1962, Columbia University Press, by permission.

Leon Edel, PSYCHOANALYSIS [and Literary Biography], reprinted from *Literary Biography* by permission of the author, copyright © 1959 by Leon Edel.

Richard Ellmann, THE BACKGROUNDS OF '*THE DEAD,*' from *James Joyce* by Richard Ellmann, copyright © 1959 by Richard Ellmann, reprinted with permission from the Oxford University Press, Inc.

W. W. Greg, THE RATIONALE OF COPY-TEXT, reprinted from *Studies in Bibliography,* III (1950–51), 19–36, by permission of Lady Greg.

Bruce Harkness, BIBLIOGRAPHY AND THE NOVELISTIC FALLACY, reprinted from *Studies in Bibliography,* XII (1959), 59–73, by permission of the author.

Harrison Hayford, MELVILLE'S FREUDIAN SLIP, reprinted from *American Literature,* XXX (1958), 366–368, by permission of the Duke University Press.

Graham Hough, GEORGE MOORE AND THE NINETIES, reprinted from *Edwardians and Late Victorians: English Institute Essays, 1959,* ed. Richard Ellmann, pp. 1–27, copyright © 1960, Columbia University Press, by permission.

Frank Kermode, 'DISSOCIATION OF SENSIBILITY': MODERN SYMBOLIST READINGS OF LITERARY HISTORY, reprinted from *The Romantic Image,* copyright 1957 by the Chilmark Press, by permission.

F. O. Matthiessen, METHOD AND SCOPE [of *American Renaissance*], from *American Renaissance* by F. O. Matthiessen, copyright 1941 by Oxford University Press, Inc., reprinted by permission.

R. B. McKerrow, FORM AND MATTER IN THE PUBLICATION OF RESEARCH, reprinted from *Review of English Studies,* XVI (1940), 116–121, by permission of The Clarendon Press, Oxford.

S. Schoenbaum, INTERNAL EVIDENCE AND THE ATTRIBUTION OF ELIZABETHAN PLAYS, reprinted from the *Bulletin of the New York Public Library,* LXV (1961), 102–124, by permission.

A. J. Smith, THE METAPHYSIC OF LOVE, reprinted from *Review of English Studies,* n. s. IX (1958), 362–375, by permission of The Clarendon Press, Oxford.

Hallett Smith, PASTORAL POETRY: THE VITALITY AND VERSATILITY OF A CONVENTION, reprinted by permission of the publishers from Hallett Smith, *Elizabethan Poetry,* Cambridge, Mass.: Harvard University Press, copyright, 1952, by the President and Fellows of Harvard College.

Ernest Tuveson, THE IMPORTANCE OF SHAFTESBURY, reprinted from *ELH: A Journal of English Literary History,* XX (1963), 267–299, by permission of The Johns Hopkins Press.

F. P. Wilson, SHAKESPEARE AND THE DICTION OF COMMON LIFE, reprinted from *Proceedings of the British Academy,* XXVII (1941), 167–197, by permission of The British Academy.

Preface

"The scholar is the guardian of memories . . . The choice is *not* between knowledge of the past and the concern for the future; if it were that it would be a hard choice. It is between the search for truth and the acceptance of falsehood. For every community insists on . . . 'the Story that must be told' about its own past, and where scholarship decays myth will crowd in."[1] An art historian, E. H. Gombrich, made these remarks, but they are just as appropriate to literary studies. Each of the following essays attempts to show that the truth really matters. Literary interpretation is not just the endeavour of a generation to read its own preoccupations into the documents of the past. When scholarship is at its worst, we create new myths out of our memories; when it is at its best, we recover a part of the lost or forgotten.

There is a factual substratum beneath every poem or play, a substratum about which assertions can be made, and the assertions are open to investigation of their truth or falsity. Karl Popper suggested that the difference between knowledge and pseudo-knowledge lies in the possibility of refutation—if a theory may possibly be disproved, it may also be verifiable; but a theory that seems to explain everything, such as Freudian pyschology or Marxian historicism, can never be refuted: it is a faith, a pseudo-science.[2] So, in literary study, we might ask what interpretations are more or less verifiable, and what theories such as the nearly universal appeal to irony or symbolism may never be refuted because they are permanently insulated from attack, perfectly self-fulfilling. Most scholars' assertions try to go back to the facts, the primary sources, and most of their assertions are in the form of narrative propositions concerning causes, influences, sources, or corruptions of a work or a tradition, and most of them lead to a scholar's

[1] E. H. Gombrich, *Meditations on a Hobby Horse* (London, 1963), p. 107.
[2] K. R. Popper, *Conjectures and Refutations* (New York, 1962), pp. 33-37.

attempt at reconstruction. He assumes that a work was written by an author with certain determinate purposes, within certain literary conventions, for a certain audience. And although he may never know the full truth, he tries to recover as much as he can.

The selections here do not attempt to represent various periods or genres but to show the methods or problems that scholars must consider. Thus it is no accident that many of these have been read before the English Institute, an organization that takes a special interest in method. Most of the essays address a particular problem, but often they enunciate general principles along the way. Most of these pieces have never been reprinted, and, so far as I know, are not available in a form suitable for a text in advanced literature courses.

A word about the obvious imbalance in the choice of essays. If a clear distinction between scholarship and criticism ever existed, recent writers have blurred and nearly obliterated it, much to the benefit of all concerned. Consequently it has seemed neither desirable nor possible to choose only examples of "pure scholarship" (a species about as rare as "pure poetry"). According to the cliché, criticism depends upon sound scholarship, but we have come to see that good scholarship presupposes good criticism. The articles in sections VI-X illustrate this truth clearly enough. I have nevertheless put emphasis on the factual side of the study of English and American literature, and I was especially generous in the inclusion of elementary problems. Writings of this kind are usually buried in learned journals, an awkward place to inter a large class of students. The standard books on method are old; even R. B. McKerrow's *Introduction to Bibliography* is outdated. Various fields have changed radically since the 1920's, and since most students of literature at one time or another try to edit a text, identify an author, or claim a literary source, and since they all must evaluate the performance of writers who pretend to do these things, they should study some precepts and examples. When, as in sections IV-X, the articles are more reticent concerning theory, I have tried to include contrasting pairs that will provoke thought about their methods, but when pairing was not possible, I settled for two good examples. Several essays could just as easily have fitted in some other section of the book because they illustrate two or three problems, but I was satisfied to place them where they seemed most significant. A special effort was made to secure readable prose, clear exposition, and apt use of detail, so that students may see how some of the best writers present their arguments. All the articles are complete except for the exclusion of the last half of Hallett Smith's chapter on pastoral poetry.

Styles of footnotes remain the same as in their original publications, since it is useful to see the various conventions; footnotes appear at the end of each article.

I am grateful to my students in English 297 at the University of Virginia, whose reactions to many of these essays helped me decide upon their worth, and to my colleagues who suggested several of the pieces to be included. I thank each of the distinguished authors for their kind permission to print their work.

L. A. B.

Charlottesville, 1965

Contents

I BIBLIOGRAPHY

II TEXTUAL STUDIES

III AUTHORSHIP AND DATING

IV BIOGRAPHY

V SOURCES AND ANALOGUES

VI STYLE

VII HISTORICAL PERIODS

VIII HISTORY OF IDEAS

IX HISTORICAL INTERPRETATION

X FORM AND CONVENTION

APPENDIX

A Mirror for Modern Scholars

Evidence and Inference in Bibliography

R. C. Bald

An important branch of the law, especially for the courtroom lawyer, is the law of evidence. Legislators and judges have decided that evidence must be presented to the courts in strict accordance with certain principles which they have laid down and that there are certain types of evidence which they will refuse to accept. Hearsay evidence is rejected, not because it is necessarily untrue, but because it is unreliable; the chances against its being accurate are too great for the courts to allow it to influence their decisions. Again, there are certain crimes for which a man cannot be condemned by the unsupported evidence of one person alone, and the definition of what constitutes corroboration has been worked out by lawyers with extraordinary care and thoroughness.

I have no doubt that many readers of so-called scholarly papers have often wished that a body of law of evidence had been drawn up for scholarship. However, I have no intention of advocating any such course of action. Hearsay is inadmissible in the courtroom, but it may be invaluable to the criminal investigator and may put him on a line of investigation that will produce evidence that can be presented in court. But the legal analogy can be pressed no further, for if there is insufficient evidence of the right kind, the case for the prosecution will lapse. Scholarship, on the other hand, refuses to be thus circumscribed. Scholars are curious people who will not let a problem rest; if a murder has been committed, and there is not enough evidence to send anyone to the gallows, they still preserve the right to speculate on the identity of the murderer.

Yet there is no doubt that scholarship should examine its procedures and question the bases for its conclusions more frequently than it does. My own complacence was rudely jolted some time ago by a classroom incident which I shall relate even at the risk of exposing myself as a teacher. I had asked an unusually good and experienced graduate student to prepare a paper on a minor seventeenth-century figure. He was to make the best use of all the material he could find in our library, though that, as I well knew, was scanty, for I had spent some time in London trying to see what I could add to it. In due course we met in class; he read his paper, and then I went over the ground again to show what fresh light new facts could throw on the old material. My victim's paper was good—and exceedingly plausible—but practically every time he attempted to interpret the facts he had collected or to fill in a gap with a reasonable conjecture he was wrong; I was able to produce facts unknown to him which disproved his interpretations. Yet I felt sure that almost any learned journal would have printed his paper; its conjectures and conclusions would have been generally accepted, and it would unquestionably have been regarded as the most authoritative treatment of the subject. If this were so, it was inevitable that I should feel that the limitations of this particular paper, of which I was aware, should be shared by dozens of others, of whose limitations I was unaware.

It has sometimes been stated, and by the highest authorities, that bibliography is a study not subject to such shortcomings. "Such discoveries as we may make are real discoveries, not mere matters of opinion, provable things that no amount of after-investigation can shake," says McKerrow at the end of the first chapter of his *Introduction to Bibliography,* and Greg, in that genuinely epoch-making address of his in 1912, entitled "What Is Bibliography?"[1], claims for the study the rank of a science. "Critical bibliography is the *science* of the material transmission of literary texts," he asserts, and one of its aims is "the construction of a *calculus* for the determination of textual problems."[2] "Science" is a word with a variety of meanings, more or less precise, but Greg is one who habitually uses words with precision, and the appearance of "calculus" in his next sentence removes any doubt that he is using it loosely or that he would at that time have refused to endorse McKerrow's statement.

Yet, whatever bibliography may or may not be, it is not an exact science, if one understands by an "exact" science a branch of study which arrives at its conclusions through experiment and observation and can reproduce the conditions of an experiment so that the results can be repeated and checked at any time. The making of books is a human activity, and the human factor is the incalculable with which we must always reckon. We might conceivably be able to reproduce a seventeenth-century printing house down to the last detail. But we could not reproduce its probably unwritten "Manual of Style," much less a harassed author, a testy master printer, a stupid proofreader, a love-sick compositor, a drunken pressman, or a newly-articled apprentice—all in the states of mind which affected their relations to a book on, let us say, the first of April, 1625.

Bibliography, therefore, cannot claim for its conclusions the same universal validity as belongs to those of the exact sciences. If it could, then some of its rules, such as McKerrow's rules for determining the order of editions, would have the same force as scientific laws.[3] One of those rules, you will remember, is that an edition of a given book "in which the signatures are all of one alphabet, beginning with A and proceeding regularly, is likely to be later than an edition in which the preliminary leaves have a separate signature."[4] Yet the collation of the first edition of Sir William Berkeley's play *The Lost Lady*, a small folio in 2's, is A-O^2, with the title-page on [A]1 and the beginning of the text on A2; in the second edition, on the other hand, the text beings on B1 and is preceded by the title page on a single unsigned leaf. What happened can be explained easily enough. The first edition was published without the author's consent, and the printer knew when he started printing that there would be no preliminaries after the title page. Then the author interposed, and a corrected edition was published with his authorization; in setting to work the printer decided he ought to allow for preliminaries, although none were actually forthcoming.[5] This example shows, as McKerrow realized when he formulated it in the terms he did, that the rule cannot be expected to hold for every case.

It is clear, then, that if bibliography is the study of "the material transmission of literary texts," it is concerned both with the material objects by which they are transmitted—printers' tools as well as books and their components—and with the human activities which transmit them. This is obvious, because the material objects could not have existed without the relevant human activities, which must accordingly be regarded as basic. Now the studies which deal with the various types of organized human activities *per se* are the group loosely known as "history and the social sciences," and it is to them that bibliography belongs. As Greg himself has stated, in a later address than that which has already been quoted from, "Bibliography is an historical study, or perhaps I should rather say a method of historical investigation."[6]

Without embarking on any profitless arguments as to how far the social sciences are sciences and whether history is a science or an art, we can all agree, I fancy, that the procedures of these studies cannot be identical with those of the exact sciences. Writers on historical methodology have made a distinction, which indicates how their study differs from the exact sciences, between two classes of sources, namely, between remains, or "monuments," as they rather clumsily call them, and documents. The distinction is between material objects, used for instance as indexes of culture or civilization, on the one hand, and written records on the other. The latter, they aver, are subject to all the defects of human inaccuracy—of which imperfections of observation or recollection are the least—in a way that the first class is not. A similar tendency can be observed in criminal jurisprudence to prefer the concrete evidence (fingerprints, the rifling on a bullet, and such like) to the inevitable conflicts and inaccuracies of oral testimony. Bibliography is concerned with the interpretation of material "remains," or books, and this is why Greg referred to it as "a method of historical investigation," but in its task of interpretation it cannot base its conclusions solely on books as material objects—it will make use of any other relevant evidence as well. For this reason the determination of printing-house practice in the sixteenth and seventeenth centuries is a historical enquiry and will be conducted according to the recognized principles of historical investigation.

I do not deny that bibliography, owing to the richness of its "remains," can often achieve a far greater measure of certainty than many other branches of study. We can prove beyond any reasonable doubt that certain Shakespearian quartos dated 1600 and 1608 were actually printed in 1619 and that there was an interruption in the printing of the First Folio. The evidence for these statements is stronger than that for many a "fact" in the history books.

I should not deny, either, that bibliography offers opportunities for thinking and reasoning of a kind that have distinguished much of the best scientific work, though I should hesitate to affirm that such thinking and reasoning are exclusively scientific. One of the most illuminating bibliographical papers ever written is McKerrow's article on "The Elizabethan Printer and Dramatic Manuscripts."[7] It is a paper which can legitimately be compared to the one in which Darwin first formulated the theory of evolution, even though it is admittedly not of equal importance in the history of human thought. Both were the fruit of long and patient observation; both reveal a remarkable capacity for sound generalization; both achieve hypotheses of far-reaching scope. Above all, both have that touch of greatness which expresses itself by asking a question about something which had always seemed a commonplace; as Whitehead says, "It requires a very unusual mind to undertake the analysis of the obvious." McKerrow pointed out that Elizabethan dramatic texts as a class are far worse than any other class of texts in the period. We had all known in a vague way that dramatic quartos, especially Shakespeare's, contained an unusual number of obscurities and cruxes, to say nothing of lesser errors, but no one had demonstrated the fact before so clearly or attached any special significance to it. McKerrow then went on to argue that the printer's copy for plays must have been much worse than for other kinds of printed matter. But the manuscripts used in the theaters were, and had to be, both reasonably correct and legible. Therefore, except when we can show, as we sometimes can, that the prompt copy came into the printer's hands, it is likely that he usually set up his text from the only other manuscript available—the author's "foul papers." A brilliant and illuminating hypothesis, and the more likely to win acceptance from its simplicity! Yet alongside a scientific hypothesis it has one grave disadvantage: it cannot be proved. Einstein's theory inaugurated series after series of experiments, and for years sent expeditions to remote parts of the world to observe each fresh eclipse. But how can confirmation of McKerrow's theory be secured? Scholarship can investigate the premisses, but cannot finally test the conclusion. The past is an experiment that cannot be repeated.

Another weakness of bibliography, from the point of view of the exact sciences, is the use which it has to make of analogy. Argument from analogy is not necessarily unscientific, but some of the so-called social sciences rely on it to such a degree as to make a chemist or physicist doubt their right to be called sciences at all. Anthropology, for instance, is founded almost entirely on the assumption that human behavior under certain circumstances at one time and place is related to somewhat similar behavior under altered circumstances at other times and places. Such an assumption is not unknown in bibliography, but fortunately its use is not so extensive.

"An argument from analogy," it has been said, "is an argument based upon *untested* resemblances,"[8] but, as we have already emphasized, the past cannot be reproduced for testing. Thus our analogies can never be complete; all we can maintain is that their strength depends upon their closeness, and that the nearer similarity approaches identity, the nearer are the conditions of scientific experiment approximated. In his monograph on the printing of the Shakespeare First Folio Dr. E. E. Willoughby found it necessary to estimate the rate at which the type was composed. Suppose that such things as compositors' time sheets for work in Jaggard's shop on books other than the Folio were extant for 1621 and 1622; they would furnish as close an analogy as anyone could hope to find. Actually, Dr. Willoughby had to rely for his estimate on two sorts of evidence: the amount of type a present-day compositor is expected to be able to set by hand, and a number of statements definitely mentioning the rates at which certain seventeenth-century books were set up.[9] Anyone will feel that the second analogy is stronger, or closer, than the first. It is valuable as a check to know what a modern compositor can do, so that there will be no danger of crediting the seventeenth-century compositor with physical impossibilities; but it is more convincing to know what seventeenth-century compositors actually performed under the conditions in which they worked. In this particular case the two analogies led to virtually the same conclusions; nonetheless the distinction between them is not to be ignored.

One of the drawbacks of arguing by analogy is that the validity of the analogy may be challenged. Suppose, for instance, that it is essential to a hypothesis to show that seventeenth-century compositors were accustomed at the end of a day's work to distribute the formes that had been in the press during the day; and suppose, further, that the only available evidence is a passage in Benjamin Franklin's *Autobiography:*

> Breintnal particularly procured us from the Quakers the printing of forty sheets of their history, the rest being done by Keimer, and upon these we worked exceedingly hard, for the price was low. It was a folio, *pro patria* size, in pica, with long primer notes. I composed a sheet a day and Meredith worked it off at press. It was often eleven at night, and sometimes later, before I had finished my distribution for the next day's work; for the little jobs sent in by our other friends now and then put us back. But so determined I was to continue doing a sheet a day of the folio that one night, when having imposed my formes I thought my day's work over, one of them by accident was broken and two pages reduced to *pi.* I immediately distributed and completed it over again before I went to bed; and this industry, visible to our neighbors, began to give us character and credit.[10]

The bibliographer who relied on this anecdote might try to strengthen it as evidence by pointing out that: (1) this incident occurred fairly early in the eighteenth century, namely, in 1728; (2) Franklin had received part of his training in one of the best London printing houses; (3) most of the practices in force there would almost certainly go back to the seventeenth century; and (4) Franklin was a methodical man who would unquestionably have been industrious in following the best practices of his trade. An opponent, however, might well counter such arguments by asserting that (1) Franklin was a methodical man to the extent of being able to improve on the London trade practices if they were capable of improvement; (2) at the time of the incident Franklin by his own admission was working under pressure, and trying to give proof of his industry, so he is not describing normal practice; and (3) to suppose that there would be a regular amount of type ready for distribution every evening is to take no account of accidents (such as the one Franklin describes), human frailties, and the varying sizes of editions.

Such argumentation, I fear, is to be found in almost every scholarly journal, and the extent to which it is beside the point in our hypothetical case is shown by the relevant passage from Moxon:

> The *Compositor,* if conveniences suit, chuses to *Destribute* his *Letter* over Night, that he may have a *dry Case* (as he calls it) to work at in the Morning, because Wet *Letters* are not so ready and pleasant to pick up as Dry; and besides are apt to make the Fingers sore, especially if the *Ly* be not so well *Rinc'd* from the *Letter* as it should be.[11]

After reading Moxon the iconoclast would probably press for a law of evidence to exclude from scholarship anything resembling the previous discussion. But unhappily there is not always a Moxon to fall back on; gaps in historical evidence are inevitable. To fill them the scholar may be driven to all sorts of shifts: he will be forced to extract the last drop of implication from the merest hint or to press a conjecture to extremes. An unfounded assumption or a rough working hypothesis is probably necessary at some stage of every investigation, but it must be judged by the results it can produce, that is, by the extent to which it actually works. And if it seems capable of opening up new possibilities of knowledge it will need to be tested before progress can be assured.

An example of what I have in mind is to be found in Greg's study of *The Variants in the First Quarto of "King Lear."* In that quarto, it will be remembered, an exceptional number of variants has been found, and Greg has made a minute examination of the twelve surviving copies. Twelve out of any number between five and fifteen hundred is a very small proportion, and the problem first to be settled is whether any generalizations can be hazarded from these copies, even though they are liable to differ from one another in the number of corrected and uncorrected sheets they contain. Greg decides that certain propositions are significant: (1) At least 50 percent of the pulls from formes in which variants occur were from the corrected forme. (2) Though it cannot be assumed when a sheet is found in only one state that no other state ever existed, it can be assumed that the corrected, not the uncorrected, state has survived. (3) Variants usually appear on only one side, not on both sides, of a sheet. These are largely *a priori* assumptions, based in part on mathematical probabilities and confirmed by the existing copies of the First Quarto of *Lear*, but they are extraordinarily fruitful and enable Greg, with the aid of the variants themselves, to work out more thoroughly than anyone has done previously the way in which proofs were corrected and revised in an early seventeenth-century printing house. In other words, the assumptions work. Greg's *a priori* case is essentially reasonable, and, as I have said, it is supported by the twelve copies of the Quarto. But twelve out of even five hundred is a distressingly small number on which to lean for support; and, well—we all know what erratic things bridge hands can sometimes be.

Anyone who has read this part of Greg's study will admire the brilliance and cogency of his reasoning, but will, I think, also wish to find some way of checking his assumptions. Of *Lear* itself there is not much left to be said; but would it not be possible to fall back on analogy and to study variants over a much larger number of copies in order to obtain results that might have something approaching experimental validity? Of course, it is quite unlikely that the complete edition of any Elizabethan book has survived, and even if it had there would still be the fantastic task of finding all the copies. Yet if only a quarter of the edition had survived and the copies could be located, some survey of the variants would be of real value. The only book of the period of which such a proportion of copies could be located is unquestionably the Shakespeare First Folio. I am not suggesting that someone should spend his whole life collating the two-hundred-odd known copies—Heaven forbid!—but at most that a few sheets in which variants are known to occur should be concentrated upon. Professor R. M. Smith might undertake the task in connection with his revised census of Folios. Even a review on such lines of the 79 Folger copies might well be profitable.

But to return to the main argument. Conjecture and assumption obviously have their place in building a hypothesis, and it would be foolish to plead for their suppression in scholarship. I do, however, plead for a clearer recognition in each instance of the foundations on which such speculations and assumptions rest, and to that end I propose to present for rigorous examination some bibliographical speculations.

Once again the First Quarto of *King Lear* will furnish a convenient point of departure. In his Introduction to the facsimile of the Folio text of the play Dover Wilson drew attention to an interesting feature of the Quarto:

> while one third of the play is printed in lines 3¼ inches broad, with words tucked in, above, below the end of the line whenever they would otherwise cause it to exceed this breadth; the rest of the play runs between 3¾ inch limits and pays no attention to the narrower restrictions. In other words, the printer of the Q must originally have assumed that the whole copy was in verse (which would naturally fall into a 3¼ inch setting), and only later have discovered his mistake. What this betokens I have no notion, never having had occasion to examine the Q closely; but assuredly it has some bearing upon the provenance and character of the copy used in 1608.

This is inaccurate, because, though it does not state it in so many words, it gives the impression that the 3¼-inch line was used for the first third of the play and the longer line for the rest of it; whereas the play actually begins with the longer line, and the two of them alternate all the way through for passages of varying length. This is not as important at the moment, however, as the attitude of the investigator, who produces a clue with a great flourish and then blandly tells us he has no idea what it means.

The significance of the clue was indicated, not by Dover Wilson, but by Greg, in an article entitled "*King Lear*—Mislineation and Stenography,"[12] in which he politely remarked:

> The other cause of mislining . . . is more complicated and has puzzled some careful observers a good deal. It is found only in quartos, and is particularly common in *Lear*. . . . This is the use of two distinct measures (i. e. line-lengths); the wider being usually reserved for prose, and another narrower one for verse. That the composi-

> tor actually used two composing-sticks of different lengths is clear from the fact that he frequently turned over long lines of verse although there was plenty of room to print them out in the width of the page. . . . The compositor, when he came to a passage of verse in a play, sometimes took a shorter stick, thus producing a column of type narrower than the full measure of the page, and made up the difference in the galley with furniture.[13] Moreover, it is not always whole pages that are in wider or narrower measure: the width of the column of type sometimes alters within the page.

This is final as far as it goes. Greg here shows that there is a bibliographical cause for mislineation in quartos; and he goes on to show that there is another bibliographical cause for mislineation in folios, when it occurs at the beginning of speeches. This part of the article is incontrovertible, but at the risk of seeming to digress I wish to demur against an assumption underlying the rest of it. Greg is engaged in replying to a paper in which it had been suggested that much of the mislineation in the Quarto was due, not to shorthand reporting, but to the compositor's attempts to save space. He shows that this is not an entirely satisfactory explanation, and suggests that the mislining arose from the attempts of "two or more compositors of different ability making what they could of copy that presented no metrical division at all." In other words, both Greg and his opponent assume that the compositor was not following his copy—was, in fact, departing from it fairly extensively. Such studies as have been made—and there is plenty of material extant for a thorough investigation of the topic—scarcely suggest that compositors were liable to modify their copy to this extent. A great deal of the most fruitful textual and bibliographical research of the last twenty years rests on the assumption that compositors *did* follow copy, and the assumption has abundantly justified itself. To depart from it now would merely reinstate the old belief that Shakespeare's texts had, as Dr. Johnson put it, "suffered depravation from the ignorance and negligence of the printers."

To return to *Lear*. Greg's explanation of the reason for the two lengths of line still leaves room for the discussion of two relevant topics. In the first place, can we, knowing the reason for the use of the two measures, make any inference, as Dover Wilson hoped, about the nature and source of the copy for the Quarto? Very little, I fear; merely, perhaps, that the compositor used the shorter length when he thought he had a longish stretch of verse ahead of him, and the longer one when there was a fair admixure of prose to be expected. Conceivably one might suggest that the use of the two lengths argues that the compositor was more than usually interested in distinguishing verse and prose and that therefore his treatment of the two throughout the play reflects pretty accurately his impressions of his copy. But even this would be speculative. Argue if you will that it is a compositor's business to follow his copy and that confusion occurs in the printed text because it occurred in copy too, but do not argue that he had special reasons for following his copy more closely than usual.

Secondly, if careful measurements are made throughout the Quarto of the lengths of the two measures it will be found that each varies to the extent of about three millimeters. This fact might suggest that more than one composing stick of each length had been used and therefore that more than one compositor was at work on the book. Greg, it will be recalled, allowed for this possibility, though he made no attempt to prove it. But an attempt to prove by such means that there was more than one compositor involves two assumptions: first, that composing sticks would be likely to vary in this way and, second, that a different composing stick means a different compositor, or, in other words, that each workman had his own tools.

As to the first, there is some uncertainty as to the exact form of composing stick in use in 1608, but we know from Moxon that in 1683 composing sticks were still made individually by hand,[14] so that minor variations in size would be almost bound to occur. The second is also no difficulty. It is unnecessary to argue that in many trades down to the present day the workman is expected to supply his tools; Moxon specifically states that journeyman compositors had to provide their own composing sticks.[15]

As far as the assumptions are concerned the hypothesis that there was more than one compositor is still a possible one, but alternative hypotheses will doubtless have already occurred to the reader. The variations may be due to the fact that the type worked loose during printing, and on one or two pages this has probably happened, though I doubt if it would have been likely to affect more than one or two pages. They may also be due, as a printer has suggested to me, to deliberate action on the part of a compositor if he happened to find it easier on certain pages to justify the lines by lengthening them by an en or even by a mere hairspace. The variations may also be due to the shrinkage of the paper during drying. Actually, the last is the most probable explanation of the majority of the variations in the *Lear* quarto, since vertical, as well as horizontal, measurements reveal proportionate variations.

I should like to point out, however, that theoretically shrinkage and one of the other explanations are not mutually exclusive. The principle of the forme-unit should be operative here, too. If the variations occurred within the same forme, where one would be justified in presuming fairly uniform conditions of damping and drying, it would seem necessary to have recourse to one of the other explanations as well.

It is unlikely that much progress could be made with an investigation along the lines we have just been considering; there are too many possibilities, and they are too difficult to isolate.[16] On the other hand, in speaking a moment ago about the shrinkage of paper a presumption about damping and drying was made, and it is interesting to find that there is apparently some uncertainty as to the early printers' practice in these matters. "The drying of the sheets," says McKerrow, "*between the printing of the first and second side*, and after the second, was done by hanging them on strings or wooden battens across the room."[17] But this by no means tallies with Moxon's account. Moxon first describes how the paper was dampened and continues:

> having Wet his first *Token* [or half-ream] he doubles down a great corner of the upper sheet of it . . . This Sheet is called the *Token-Sheet*, as being a mark for the *Pressman* when he is at Work to know how many *Tokens* of the *Heap* is *Wrought-off*.[18]

Then, describing the pressman at work, he tells in detail how he takes a sheet from the top of the heap, puts it on the tympan, makes the pull, and removes it from the press

> and so successively every Sheet till the whole *Heap* of *White-paper* be *Wrought off*.
>
> As he comes to a *Token-sheet* , he un-doubles that, and smoothes out the Crease . . . that the *Face* of the *Letter* may Print upon smooth Paper. And being Printed off, he folds it again, as before, for a *Token-sheet* when he works the Reiteration.
>
> Having *Wrought off* the *White-paper*, he turns the *Heap*. . . .
>
> Having now turned the *Heap*, and made *Register* on the *Reteration Form* . . . he Works off the *Reteration*. . . . Only, the *Token-sheets*, as he meets with them, he Folds not down again, as he did the *White Paper*.[19]

McKerrow, then, asserts that as the first side was being printed the damp and freshly-inked sheets were taken off to dry; that they were damped again before being perfected and dried again before folding. Moxon plainly states that the pressman made a pile of the damp and freshly-inked sheets as they came off the press, turned the heap upside down, and, as soon as the new forme was in the bed of the press, proceeded to perfect. In face of this conflict of authority further information seemed necessary, so I consulted *The Printer's Grammar,* by C. Stower, Printer (London, 1808); *Typographia; or, The Printer's Instructor,* by J. Johnson, Printer (London, 1824); *Typographia; or, The Printer's Instructor; second edition with numerous emendations and additions,* by Thomas F. Adams, Typographer (Philadelphia, 1844); and *The American Printer: a Manual of Typography,* by Thomas Mackeller (Philadelphia, 1867). I found with ever-growing surprise that one and all they repeated Moxon's words verbatim. By then the resources of our library were exhausted, but I was still unsatisfied, although I could not help feeling that these good gentlemen, who boasted of their credentials on their title pages, would not have carried their plagiarism so far as to incorporate uncorrected all Moxon's errors. There was only one thing left to do—ask a present-day printer; and I was fortunate enough to find one who had had experience of printing on dampened paper. I put the problem to him and asked him who was right; he laughed and said "Both," but went on to explain, "It depends on the quality of the ink." A cheap ink, he said, dries quickly and will not offset unless under heavy pressure; the very best inks take a long time to dry, and offset easily. McKerrow must have had in mind the practice of printing houses such as the Kelmscott Press, and probably some of the famous fifteenth-century presses. Moxon, however, complains that the usual quality of English ink was bad and describes how much better it was made in Holland in his day.[20] But even the seventeenth-century Dutch methods of manufacturing ink arouse the contempt of De Vinne in his reprint of Moxon,[21] so we can take it that English ink throughout the seventeenth century was far from good, as anyone familiar with the cheaply printed quartos of the period will not hesitate to admit. Ink of better quality was doubtless used sometimes for other classes of books, but very rarely, I should say, in those that are of most interest to the student of literature. Hence we need have no hesitation in accepting Moxon in preference to McKerrow if we wish to know the normal practice of seventeenth-century English printing houses.

Now, if this practice can be regarded as established, one consequence follows: sheets were perfected in exactly the same order as that in which the first side had been printed. This fact is of some importance, for instance, in relation to variants in the forme, and Greg is forced to presume it in a general way on *a priori* grounds, even though he accepts McKerrow's account instead of Moxon's. It also strengthens considerably his contention that when one variant forme appears, the other must, except under abnormal circumstances, be invariant; since if this were not so we should expect to find two uncorrected states or two corrected states appearing together on the same sheet in a large majority of copies.[22]

Earlier in this paper I animadverted on an indiscretion of Professor Dover Wilson in printing what he might better have kept to himself, so I hope no one will make the mistake of supposing that the foregoing discussions are examples of the sort of thing I consider should adorn the pages of our learned journals. Far from it; they are meant as an attempt to bring into the light some of the processes that, fortunately, are generally concealed from the public view—to illustrate, in other words, the processes of testing and elimination that must go on behind the scenes rather than to emphasize the one positive conclusion eventually reached. Perhaps this paper should have been entitled "Some Suggestions towards a Methodology for Bibliography." Yet the title is better as it is; there has been enough pedantry here already without emphasizing it. Methodology is at best a short cut for the inexperienced. The great historians, for instance, have in most cases left such academic trifling to lesser men. In bibliography, as in all other studies, what counts is the trained, alert, and ingenious mind which can cope with its difficulties as it meets them. And the vitality of bibliography today lies not so much in its having, except incidentally, formulated for itself a methodology as in having been guided by practitioners of consummate skill. If in this paper I have seemed here and there to take issue with Greg and McKerrow, it is not from any sense of disrespect; it is rather from a sense of wonder that it should be possible to disagree with them. For bibliography owes its present status almost entirely to their efforts; and one's most earnest hope can only be that a generation of comparable caliber will rise to succeed them. To the bibliographer of the new generation, experienced or still inexperienced, there is but one word of advice to give, and that is "Follow them."

NOTES

[1] *Transactions of the Bibliographical Society*, XII (1911-13), 39-53.

[2] In fairness to Dr. Greg it should be added that in his later writings he has shown a tendency to recede from the more extreme implications of these statements. See especially, "The Present Position of Bibliography," *The Library*, XI (1930-31), 256-58.

[3] The nearest approximation to a scientific law in bibliography is prob-

ably the principle of the forme-unit, and the apparent exceptions to it, due to single-page or two-color printing, are apparent only, not real.

[4] *Introduction to Bibliography for Literary Students,* p. 188.

[5] R. C. Bald, "Sir William Berkeley's *The Lost Lady,*" *The Library,* XVII (1936-37), 395-426, at 402-4.

[6] "The Present Position of Bibliography," at p. 256.

[7] *The Library,* XII (1931-32), 253-75.

[8] L. S. Stebbing, *A Modern Introduction to Logic,* p. 255.

[9] *The Printing of the First Folio of Shakespeare,* pp. 54-55.

[10] *The Writings of Benjamin Franklin,* ed. by A. H. Smith, I, 300-301.

[11] *Moxon's Mechanick Exercises,* ed. by T. L. De Vinne, II, 210.

[12] *The Library,* XVI (1936-37), 181-82.

[13] But see Greg in *The Variants in the First Quarto of "King Lear,"* p. 56*n,* where this is somewhat modified.

[14] *Op. cit.,* I, 32-33.

[15] *Ibid.,* I, 32.

[16] Another, and somewhat different, example of the use of two different measures is worth recording. In *The Knave in Graine,* a play published in 1640, a measure of 92 millimeters is used until the end of sheet H; in the remaining three-and-a-half gatherings one of 97 millimeters is used and the normal number of lines to the page is increased from thirty-seven to thirty-nine. The change comes too soon to assert that there was a definite attempt to get the rest of the play into any specific number of pages, and the increase in the number of lines to the page was probably as much for aesthetic reasons as for economy; that is, thirty-seven lines of the shorter measure and thirty-nine of the longer gave a properly balanced quarto page and represented the normal practice of the printing house. The change, incidentally, has nothing whatever to do with the difference between prose and verse. It looks as if a different compositor took over at the beginning of sheet I and that he simply went on using the stick he had been using for another quarto without realizing that a shorter measure had been used for the part of the play already set up.

[17] *Introduction to Bibliography,* p. 23.

[18] *Op. cit.,* II, 305.

[19] *Ibid.,* II, 325-27.

[20] *Ibid.,* I, 76-77.

[21] *Ibid.,* II, 412-13.

[22] Apparently these combinations do occur in folios, and it seems likely that what has been said above is applicable only to quartos and to books of smaller size. Greg's assertion that one forme is invariable rests on the postulate that both formes of the sheet were made up at about the same time and that one was in the press while the other was waiting and still available for corrections. In a folio, however, printing could begin as soon as the inner forme of the inner sheet had been set up, and thus it might be in the press before the composition of the outer forme was complete. Hence the printing of the outer forme might also have to be interrupted so that the final corrections could be made. This, rather than exceptional care, would explain the combination of corrected or uncorrected formes in the 1616 edition of Ben Jonson's *Works* to which Greg draws attention on pp. 46-47.

Some Relations of Bibliography to Editorial Problems

Fredson Bowers

Bibliography concerns itself with editorial problems not as a usurper of the functions of legitimate criticism, but instead as the necessary foundation on which, in certain investigations, textual criticism must be based and to which criticism must constantly refer for more or less definitive judgments. Bibliography, in W. W. Greg's acute phrase, is the grammar of literary investigation. This position was strikingly advanced in Greg's classic address on the relations of bibliography to literature which appeared some time ago in *Neophilologus*, and, again, in his "Bibliography—An Apologia" (*The Library*, 4th ser. XIII [1932], 113 ff.). Any attempt merely to restate Greg's views here would be quite superfluous. For some years, at least among scholars, the inferential identification of bibliography with textual criticism has been so firmly established that to talk about the contribution of one to the other might appear to be like a solemn discussion of the usefulness of the arm to the hand.

Nevertheless, it is possible to suspect that, as more and more scholars have come to deal with these twin methods, the popularizing of their disciplines may have led, by subtle degrees, to a rather over-simplified view of the basic provinces of bibliography and textual criticism, especially as applied to editorial problems. Certainly the theory that every bibliographer is professionally qualified to be a full-fledged textual critic and editor is quite wrong. Correspondingly, there are a number of distinguished textual critics whom, according to any strict accounting, we might hesitate to call bibliographers.

Some fortunate scholars like Pollard, McKerrow, Greg, and Percy Simpson may happily combine in themselves both functions, although perhaps in unequal proportions; but this two souls in body one is certainly the exception rather than the rule. On the other hand, the most prominent Elizabethan textual critic now living—I refer to Mr. Dover Wilson—often operates in that dark region of the ur-state of a text which McKerrow rightly hesitated to identify with bibliography. One should comment, however, that not all of Wilson's readers—or his critics—are completely aware of the distinction. It is somewhat perturbing, for example, in Hereward Price's admirable "Towards a Scientific Method of Textual Criticism in the Elizabethan Drama"[1] to find his chief whipping boy, Dover Wilson, consistently referred to as representing the bibliographical school. Save for his impatience at various of Wilson's well-known aberrations, Mr. Price—no more than the rest of us—would, I should think, completely discount such investigations. But we may agree with McKerrow and Greg that this scholarship is not usually bibliographical in any sense in which we should be prepared to use the term.

Bibliography is likely to be a vague and misused word because it has come to be employed for too many different purposes. For the present discussion we may rule out enumerative bibliography—the making-up of finding or reference lists of books on various subjects—and use the term to mean analytical bibliography, the investigation and explanation of a book as a material object. Yet even within this narrower limitation there are various strata and subdivisions of research. For example, we have such forms of bibliographical spadework as the identification and recording of type-faces as by Haebler, or of *STC* printers' ornaments as is now in progress by F. S. Ferguson, with their dates and history.

But when we move from such essential preliminary investigation, and from the recording of material data as a part of publishing history, to another sort of bibliography, more specifically of the kind we designate as *analytical*, we come to a field in which all our accumulated knowledge of printing practice and history is devoted to the examination of individual or related books as material objects, with a view to determining the facts of their production. Is there or is there not a cancel in a certain gathering; were the various sheets of a book printed *seriatim* or simultaneously in two or more sections; did one or two compositors, one or more presses, work on this book, and if so which parts did they do; was a cancel title-page or a cancel in the text printed later or as a part of the continuous printing of the book. Are variants in the sheets of the book the result of different impressions, or do they result from different typesettings or from simple correction at the press. If some of the sheets are of a single impression but certain others exhibit variant typesettings, which setting is the original, and why was the resetting made. If there are variant imprints, which was first through the press. And so on. It will be seen that correct answers to some of these questions depend not only on the simple discovery of the facts themselves, but more particularly on the satisfactory explanation of the ascertained facts. From specific analyses of this kind, some speculatively minded bibliographers may endeavor to evolve new techniques for bringing to light yet further secrets in printed books, techniques which may enable us to attack successfully some general problems which have heretofore been thought insoluble.

Such technical examinations of individual books for their own sake are proceeding very swiftly these days, and they are being matched step by step by the parallel development of techniques for determining with greater precision the relation of the printed book to its underlying manuscript.[2] No textual critic can afford to ignore the results of these investigations. From Willoughby's and Hinman's explorations of spelling tests,[3] assisted in certain cases by evidence from the varying length of the compositor's stick,[4] we are now able to distinguish with some certainty in the *STC* period and the following years the precise pages of a book set by different compositors. By an equation of these compositors' habits we can thereupon make certain assumptions about the characteristics of the manuscript from which they were setting. The cooperative efforts which have been made in the analysis of the evidence of headlines[5] have opened up possibilities, in combination with this compositor evidence, for determining sometimes quite minute but necessary questions of the presswork and proofreading. To these may be added—among many other investigations—the classic Carter and Pollard examination of paper and type which exposed the Wise forgeries, Hazen's use of identified paper to detect Strawberry Hill forgeries, and Stevenson's technique for aligning watermarks with presswork.[6] The unexpected uses of bibliography have been demonstrated in Bond's assignment of authorship to certain doubtful *Spectator* papers, the whole argument resting ultimately on type left standing in advertisements and headings.[7]

Astonishing results have recently accrued from certain research on eighteenth-century press figures, which had been earlier dismissed by McKerrow as of little bibliographical significance. Knotts[8] has added a chapter to the work of Sale, Chapman, and others; and W. B. Todd's latest interpretation of the evidence of these figures in a number of books demonstrates some most exciting things one can learn of printing.[9] From this evidence a whole new area of research has been opened up of such importance for distinguishing impressions, partial re-impressions, and editions, as well as various other important textual matters, that we may well believe in many cases press figures alone will come to be the most valuable tool for penetrating the extreme difficulties of textual problems in frequently reprinted popular eighteenth-century authors.

I should be less than candid if I tried to pretend that the immediate or even the chief aim of these and of many other bibliographical scholars was to serve as the sons of Martha to textual criticism. Without question, a number of bibliographical investigations which eventually proved invaluable to textual criticism were not undertaken with this end immediately in view and almost by accident arrived at their textual applications. Thus a real difference from textual criticism must always be felt, I suspect, in bibliographical research in its purest aspect. To defend themselves against doubters, bibliographers are accustomed to argue that the ultimate aim of all bibliographical research, and therefore its justification, is the definitive account of books in a descriptive bibliography, or the direct application of their findings to textual criticism. But I make bold to say that—at least as I view it—the *immediate* end of a great deal of research is no such thing. Although I believe that the conventional justification is valid for the ultimate aims, and that this rationale is deeply felt by almost every bibliographical student, nevertheless, even though eventual application is the ideal, ordinarily textual criticism has not provided the immediate spur to the investigation and no specific textual use is often anticipated, at least in the early stages of the work. This attitude develops, in part, because many technical studies that are absolutely necessary yet require no interest in textual criticism on the part of the investigator. In part, because various of these studies are concerned only with a fragment of some total problem, the whole of which must be unraveled before any of it can be made of practical use to textual criticism.

Nonetheless, in spite of the various legitimate reasons which may be advanced to explain the rationale for much technical work in bibliography, the point of view does in fact serve to separate many bibliographers from textual critics; indeed, it would be tempting to say *most* bibliographers were it not an increasing tendency for a number of analysts, with or without due training, to cross over the line and to concern themselves directly with the editing of texts. Others, though not editors, may develop so great an interest in textual questions that they direct their research specifically towards bibliographical problems which do have an immediate textual application and thus underlie accurate criticism. The record, while respectable, has not been one of unalloyed success, perhaps, and when bibliographers have concerned themselves with matters of textual criticism that were not primarily bibliographical, they have sometimes floundered pitifully if they lacked the training and the qualities of mind which are necessary for textual criticism in *its* purest state.

I use this statement of a point too often overlooked, in our current tendency to exalt the bibliographer, as an aid towards a cursory glance at the nature of textual criticism, a subject on which I can speak with little authority and on which I shall anticipate correction. It is perhaps absurd to set up too sharp a distinction between textual critics and textual bibliographers. Anyone, we may suppose, who is concerned with the origin, derivation, authority, and correctness of a text, in whole or in part, is a textual critic, no matter what his method of approach. Some scholars tackle problems through bibliography, some through what Greg has called metacriticism, some through an attempted or actual combination of bibliography and criticism. For purposes of distinction I must deal in blacks and whites more starkly than is perhaps realistic. Nevertheless, I am sure that when we distinguish between a McKerrow and a Dover Wilson, both brilliant examples of different schools, we are in fact implying a greater fundamental difference than exists between the conservative and speculative wings of the same method.

Greg—and in this he is frequently misunderstood—insists that the bibliographer must view a book only as a material object.[10] This is a far cry from the aims of a textual critic. Historically, textual criticism developed long before analytical bibliography; and it evolved its own rules, especially for dealing with manuscripts, both classical and vernacular, according to certain principles which are outside the strictly bibliographical range, if for our purposes we continue to limit the definition of bibliography to analytical bibliography. These principles, or something like them, were also applied to printed books, again before bibliography was more than a gleam in the eye, and—as Greg has shown in his paper for this series—they are still in part applicable to certain problems. Thus there has been established in the past a firm tradition for dealing with texts; and it would be foolish for us to believe that analytical bibliography has displaced this tradition, or even that in many cases it could. Nevertheless, analytical bibliography has demonstrated that in some circumstances the classical tradition is not completely self-sufficient. We may put it, therefore, that bibliography is neither a usurper nor a poor relation in the field of textual criticism, but rather its foundation, the grammar of the subject.

If, in the interests of brevity, we pass over the important field of manuscript texts and concern ourselves with textual criticism based chiefly on printed books, we may, perhaps, discern three main but by no means mutually exclusive lines of endeavor. The first concerns itself with the authorship, origin, and characteristics of the lost manuscript behind a printed book both in whole and in part. I am thinking first of various studies in the attribution of anonymous works, or of the solution of problems in multiple authorship as in the Beaumont and Fletcher plays, Massinger, and Dekker; and secondly of such studies as Mr. Duthie has made in the bad quarto of *Hamlet* and more recently in the Pide Bull *King Lear*. Dover Wilson's reconstructions of the manuscript copy for *Hamlet* and other texts should be placed here, as also various studies such as Hoppe's of *Romeo and Juliet* but especially Greg's of *Doctor Faustus*. As with the *Faustus* and *Lear* investigations, according to the circumstances this division may merge imperceptibly with the second, which I take to be concerned with the critical analysis of texts in known manuscripts or printed exempla. Here we might place studies like Grierson's on the text of Donne, Wolf's on commonplace books, Shaaber's on *2 Henry IV*. The determination of the order and authority of printed texts after the first also applies, and we must certainly include the very difficult task of separating from compositor's, proof-reader's, and printing-house editor's alterations those true revisions from an authoritatively corrected copy used as the basis for a later edition. The relation of the variants in the Quarto and Folio of *King Lear* or *Troilus and Cressida* is such a problem. In all of these divisions various special studies may enter in one form or another. I list as examples a few of the inquiries which Mr. Price sets up as among the subjects for textual criticism: vocabulary tests of authorship, and also of plagiarism, metrical tests including study of broken lines, deficient lines, redundant syllables, feminine endings, prose as blank verse, and so on, applied to form an opinion of a text.

Finally, perhaps we may assign as a third general division the orderly bringing together of all this information in an editorial capacity, and the consequent evolution of a modern critical text designed to represent the intentions of the author more faithfully than any single preserved manuscript or printed copy. Whereas the findings of analytical bibliography may or may not be applicable in the first two divisions, the claims of analysis enter full force in the editorial third.

In the first two divisions, it is true, the investigations lead hopefully towards the ideal of a definitive text, but, as with pure bibliography, much textual criticism is undertaken either for its own sake or else to attack only a fragment of the total problem, so that the immediate end of the research may not be the formation of a text. For example, Mr. Duthie did not edit *Hamlet* after he had solved the problem of the bad quarto. It will be convenient, however, to treat textual criticism and its relations to bibliography in its narrower application to the evolution of an edited text and to the various delicate problems that arise before this text can eventually be fixed. Moreover, the limitation may be extended to cover only the specific problem of old-spelling critical texts, for—as Greg's paper has shown—these are subject to certain criteria which do not always apply to modernized versions, even though the basic problems are shared in common.

At the start one should distinguish certain editorial problems that have no necessary connection with bibliography. An editor of the literature of the past must have considerable linguistic attainments, or ready access to professional advice. Through long familiarity he must grow to be a native in the characteristic thought, usage, speech patterns, and customs of his period. Although bibliography may occasionally assist in the solution of some problems, or offer a convincing after-the-event confirmation, much emendation—or refusal to emend—much estimate of authenticity, must be made quite independently of bibliographical considerations and instead on a philological basis. This aspect has no relation to bibliography, and it requires a discipline and study which leave little time for bibliographical investigations not concerning the problem immediately at hand. Moreover, if we speak of only one characteristic, the great emendations have been inspired art and not systematic science. One can give a rational palaeographical explanation to derive "a table of green fields" set in type from the crabbed script of "a' babld of green fields," but I beg leave to doubt that this famous emendation would to the present day ever have been arrived at by strictly palaeographic reasoning. Greg, I believe, has no very high opinion of palaeography as giving more than a hint for emendations,[11] although its confirmation is often most valuable. Usually, I suspect, one arrives at an emendation of any subtlety by inspiration, memory, and a strong sense of analogy, and then one brings in palaeography if possible to justify one's conclusions.

Many other considerations of text are too frequently confused as soluble by bibliography. For example, bibliography can establish that edition *B.* was printed from edition *A.*, and not from an independent manuscript; but if revisions appear in *B.*, there is no bibliographical technique for determining except in isolated cases whether they derive from the author himself, a scribe revising the text of *A.* from a manuscript, or an editor of some kind. Such problems in one way or another involving emendation or the acceptance of variant readings fall to the lot of the textual critic once bibliography has cleared his way to the limit of its ability.

This critical acumen, which we cannot value too highly as applied to text, is, of course, the product of a keen and imaginative mind; but, again, it is materially aided by a very close acquaintance with one's period in general philological considerations. This acquaintance gradually develops an opinion about speech and imagery which, in mature and thoughtful hands, has its own authority not only in questions of emendation but in any division of textual criticism. We may note that even the conservative, bibliographical McKerrow does not disdain in certain circumstances to write about the authority of variants between editions which best seem to have the greatest internal harmony with an author.[12]

This strong and subtle imagination necessary for close inquiries into texts may apply itself to studies in attribution, plagiarism, or multiple authorship, or to studies in an author's speech and metrical characteristics, or it may be found in Dover Wilson's various attempts—whether rightly or wrongly—to discover layers of revision in the pre-printing history of a manuscript, or it may be utilized in the scrupulous examination of the sources and methods of corruption in a text which Duthie has demonstrated in *Hamlet* and in *King Lear.* Such striking deductions as those Duthie makes about the composition of memorial texts from tag ends of general recollections exhibit a critical virtuosity which has its own discipline and rigorous training.

If I were a textual critic concerned with such matters as I have been sketching, problems involving my total powers as a critic, I fancy I should be rather impatient with a bibliographer who insisted that I should be all this and McKerrow too. And I should be strongly inclined to reply: you are a technician—you do the technical part of this business and I shall apply your findings, taking care that I have studied the principles and general methods of your craft seriously enough so that I can follow your arguments and understand the applicability of what you are saying.

This is roughly what has happened, and as a consequence something like the following rationale is commonly accepted. The bibliographer's function is to prepare the general material of the texts, when bibliographical investigation is necessarily involved; and the textual critic, in the light of bibliographical findings, can then proceed to apply the discovered relationships, and to add his own art, to achieve the finished, definitive result.

Since we are an age of specialists, this separation of function seems reasonable to us. Indeed, in various cases it may work very well, and in some it may even be positively necessary. Yet I must confess it is a position I held with more conviction in the past than I do today, and I anticipate holding it with even less conviction in the future, especially if certain far-reaching bibliographical speculations and experimental techniques for dealing with the accidentals in an old-spelling text ever reach success. This change in attitude, I am conscious, may have been dictated too much by various experiences with amateur editors, from whom the good Lord deliver us, by a tendency to over-emphasize the importance of a close reconstruction of accidentals, and by allowing the special problems of distinctly unusual texts to bulk too large in my mind so that the uncomplicated, run-of-the-mill variety is obscured.

Whatever the cause, I have here what is only a selection of examples to illustrate that a textual critic, when he is himself incapable of applying advanced bibliographical techniques to every detail of an old-spelling text, can seldom achieve absolute authority in his results, and may indeed be led into serious error through the false confidence induced in him by the notion that bibliography has sufficiently prepared the way before his labors have begun.

This hypothetical critic can ordinarily be prepared only to follow and apply bibliographical arguments: his training has not prepared him to evaluate their correctness on technical grounds. A small but rather interesting example occurs in Thomas Southerne's *Disappointment* of 1684. Here the case for a cancel to abridge a censored scene was very plausibly advanced in 1933, and in 1946 was vetted by a good bibliographer who made some necessary modifications but in no way questioned the central thesis. Yet in the last sixteen years if any textual critic had treated the scene in the light of this apparently authoritative evidence, without testing it bibliographically for himself, he would have been quite wrong, for no cancel exists and the scene is not abridged.[13]

Secondly, this critic may often be forced to enter upon subjects where rigorous bibliographical investigation has not yet been made, although he may not be aware of that fact. A really egregious case of false bibliography has only recently been corrected by W. B. Todd's study of *The Monk.*[14] The full story is very involved, but the point is brief. If between 1935 and 1949 any critic had blindly relied on the accepted ordering of the publishing history which pseudo-bibliography had set up, he would have been led to evolve a text which treated Lewis's revisions as the original readings, and the readings which Lewis had discarded as in fact his later revisions. *Q. E. D.* Don't trust all the bibliographers.

This is a pretty fix for a textual critic, since he is damned if he does and damned if he doesn't. And in fact, in many cases no solution for his dilemma is possible unless he is himself also a trained bibliographer who is capable of re-examining technically a fouled-up problem. Yet he must do something. One course is to trust only *some* bibliographers. The very best butter. Nonetheless we may well remember in this connection Curt Bühler's favorite quotation of the observation made by A. W. Pollard on his colleague Robert Proctor, a great pioneer in incunabula studies, "that in matters of bibliography he would not have taken the results of an archangel upon trust." As an example we may survey two specific but fortunately minor instances in which Mr. Duthie in his new edition of *King Lear* was misled by untested bibliography. A small part of his arguments concerning certain peculiarities of the quarto rests on Greg's speculation that two compositors with different habits might have been engaged with the book. Now in this case Greg was not speaking *ex cathedra* as the result of a detailed bibliographical examination, but only in terms of possibilities. Fortunately the point was of no very great consequence for Duthie's conclusions, because he accepted the speculation on trust and did not test it. We know now, however, from a recent bibliographical study, which can be confirmed by even stricter bibliographical evidence,[15] that only one compositor set the book. These peculiarities, therefore require another explanation.

In the second instance the point of discussion is the mislining of the verse at the opening of Act III, Scene 2, the great storm scene. Greg took the view that the early part is mislined because the compositor was setting the text as prose, and it was not until he reached a certain point that he recognized he was dealing with verse and thereafter proceeded to line correctly. Duthie, naturally, accepted Greg's explanation as 'bibliographical,' and quite properly added that of course the compositor must have gone back to insert capitals at the beginning of each line in the prose section to give it the appearance of verse that it assumes in the printing. However, a single piece of bibliographical evidence demonstrates the mechanical impossibility of such a procedure. Throughout *Lear* the compositor of the quarto used a short stick for verse and a longer stick for prose; and he never sets prose in his short or verse measure. Since the opening lines of this scene were set in the verse measure, not the prose, the explanation for the mislineation must be sought elsewhere, for from the start the compositor intended to set verse. But other consequences resulted from this failure to see the bibliographical evidence. Because the implications of the short measure were not recognized, in these lines Duthie over-conservatively retained a corrupt lack of punctuation which succeeds in destroying, almost completely, not only a successful flower of rhetoric but also one of the mightiest images of this great storm scene.[16]

If the critic finding himself thus abused hurls a curse on this treacherous science of bibliography and betakes himself to his own estimates —to what Greg calls metacritical evidence—he may find himself in a rather vulnerable position. A simple, though typical, case occurs in *The Dumbe Knight* of 1608 which is preserved with either one of two title-pages, the major difference between them being that one gives the author's name whereas the other does not. Metacritics worked up a pretty romance about this play, conjecturing that Gervase Markham, the author, was so disgusted when he found his play printed with an inferior underplot by another hand that he withdrew his name from the title. On the contrary, bibliography demonstrates that the title with the name is the true cancel leaf so that the name was added rather than excised.[17]

Vulnerability increases when the problem is one of any complexity. Here is a small problem yet one in which an old-spelling editor must make a decision. The inner forme of text sheet A of George Sandys's *Christs Passion,* a translation in 1640 from Grotius, was reset in the course of enlarging the edition. One typesetting of this inner forme agrees largely with the invariant outer forme in making up capital W's from two V's, whereas the other uses regular W's. Aha, says the critic, I'm not so bad at bibliography myself: obviously the setting of inner A which is consistent with outer A must be the original for me to reprint. The only trouble is, he is wrong. A rather technical interpretation of the evidence of the headlines demonstrates that this setting must have been printed a sheet or so later.[18] The inconsistent forme is the authoritative original which must be taken for the copy-text, and it is probably inconsistent because we may be dealing with two compositors casting off copy and setting by formes in order to get the book started in a hurry.

We do not need the example of nineteenth-century editors basing

Shakespeare texts on the Pavier Quartos to indicate some of the larger dangers of inferences about the relations of texts made on purely metacritical grounds. But lest we feel too confident about our present abilities to cope with matters more properly the province of textual criticism, such as our ability to construct a correct family tree of editions on the basis of their readings alone, we may consider the case of the ninth edition of Dryden's *Indian Emperour* in 1694. Certain of its readings are drawn apparently at random from those which are unique in the seventh edition and are not found in the eighth. Others derive from equally random readings unique in the eighth and not found in the seventh. There are three reputable critical interpretations of this phenomenon: (1) the ninth edition comes from an independent manuscript; (2) the seventh and eighth editions were collated at the printing house and the conflation of readings thus results from editorial intervention—or one might even introduce collation of one of these editions against a prompt copy or other manuscript; (3) the ninth is set from a lost edition which may be placed in between the seventh and eighth and on which the eighth is also based. This last would be a favorite with critics accustomed to dealing with manuscripts, and it is certainly the most plausible.

At least the first two of these quite reputable explanations might cause some critical perturbation, since fresh authority could have been introduced into the text, and the various new readings in the ninth not found in either the seventh or eighth might demand critical acceptance on their merits. However, when analytical techniques are applied, the answer is not hard to find. Two compositors were employed on the ninth edition, but—perhaps because only one press was available—instead of chopping the reprint up into two sections to be set and printed simultaneously, they set the book *seriatim* but working in relay. One would compose from four to five type-pages, or only one or two, and then be relieved by the other while he distributed this type, and so on in turn. Since the eighth edition was a paginal reprint of the seventh, what actually happened was that one compositor set from a copy of the seventh, and the other from a copy of the eighth, and so they worked merrily along in relay to the confusion of scholarship, conflating the two editions to form the ninth. The answer is very easy after bibliographical analysis.[19]

I do not wish to infer that in all cases bibliographical evidence is applicable. To be properly bibliographical, evidence must concern itself with only certain relations between preserved printed or inscribed pieces of paper. For example, a form of textual criticism linked with bibliography can usually decide on an over-all basis whether variations in a later edition are compositors' variants or editorial revisions; and pure bibliography can demonstrate whether or not this later edition was otherwise set from a copy of an earlier. But whether these revisions were the author's or someone else's can never be decided by bibliography under ordinary circumstances; that is for textual criticism pure and simple. The case is usually not demonstrable by any form of bibliographical evidence. Some critics may deal extensively with evidence which is probably bibliographical at bottom because it is founded on the peculiarities of printed inscriptions on paper; but the inferences they draw may have no relation to the laws of bibliographical evidence. As I shall indicate in a moment, strictly bibliographical deduction is not always possible from bibliographical facts. It is this common confusion about the difference between the strictly bibliographical and the metacritical interpretation of the evidence offered by a book as a material object which places, wrongly I believe, a number of Dover Wilson's ingenious arguments in the field of bibliography. Larger examples may be cited. The *Taming of the Shrew* problem can have no bibliographical basis, for whatever relation existed between *A Shrew* and *The Shrew* antedates their printing, and the manuscripts behind the printed copy of each have no bibliographical relation. Somewhat less clearly, perhaps, the formation of a critical text of *Hamlet* is not, basically, a bibliographical investigation. There is no direct relationship between the three printed texts.

But when pure textual criticism concerns itself with problems in which bibliographical investigation is possible, it can seldom be equally definitive as in this other field, for critical interpretation of evidence is at best inferential, and the logic of the argument is frequently reversible. Until the problem was directly tackled by bibliographical methods, the question of whether *Troilus and Cressida* in the Folio was set from an annotated copy of the quarto or from an independent manuscript had yielded no convincing answer from the critical approach. Yet Mr. Williams has made the problem seem like child's play,[20] and we may find his study very illuminating for the relative validity of bibliographical and critical methods in such situations. Similarly, Mr. Hinman's authoritative study of *Othello* and its second quarto contains a most ingenious bibliographical solution of another long-vexed critical problem.[21]

There are other problems involving the relations between editions. Greg, I think, has remarked that given two editions only, the critical method could never satisfactorily establish their relationship or indeed, if they are similarly dated, as with certain of the Pavier quartos, their priority. I may be making this more positive or detailed than his original statement, but when we realize that Greg is not thinking in terms of inferences establishing high probability but instead of absolute proof, then we must admit that true demonstration is impossible because of the reversibility of the critical evidence. Is a variant a correction or rationalization in one edition, or a corruption in the other—frequently the case may be argued either way.

An example is Dryden's *Wild Gallant,* which has two editions in 1669, the year of its first appearance in print. One is clearly a paginal reprint of the other, but the question is—which? On the one side we have Macdonald setting up his number 72a as the first edition, whereas Griffith, backed by Osborn, argues for 72b, or Macdonald's second edition. As a part of a fresh bibliographical examination of this play I have elsewhere tried to show in detail too lengthy to be summarized here that while the basic fact on which each hinges his argument is bibliographical, the arguments from this fact are only inferential and therefore do not conform to the strictest requirements of bibliographical reasoning, that is, to a mechanical demonstration for which there is no possible alternative save in the realm of purest fantasy.[22]

It will be pertinent, however, to consider more fully in this play certain kinds of evidence which, for a very good reason, have not been published. The exposé, I hope, will offer an enlightening example, though at my own expense, of what bibliographical evidence is and what it is not. I can speak very feelingly on the subject because when I came to the problem as an editor I was completely booby-trapped, and at first I arrived at certain conclusions on grounds which I gullibly persuaded myself were bibliographical only to have the whole argument blow up in my face when at length the true evidence became apparent.

A textual collation of the two editions quickly established that there had been no real rewriting between them, but that in a score of places —if 72a were first—corrections, possibly even revisions, had certainly been made in 72b, a few of which could have come only from the author himself. On the other hand, if 72b were first, in various readings the text had undergone a corruption rather more serious than one might expect in a first reprint. Mr Osborn in his notes to Griffith's argument had confidently pronounced *B.* the first on the evidence of this textual degeneration in *A.*[23] This is a critical touchstone which experience has shown to be sound, provided the further inference is made that the author had no part in producing the reprint. However, I approached the *Gallant* fresh from a study of *The Indian Emperour,* in which without question Dryden had directly concerned himself with revising not only the second but also the third edition, the year before and after *The Wild Gallant* respectively. With this example before me, I felt hesitant to accept Osborn's conclusions without further inquiry, for the second inference could not be automatically applied. Indeed, I came to feel that there was just about as much chance that the careless errors of *A.* had been rectified in *B.* by an errata list sent to the printer as that *A.* represented a careless and unauthoritative reprint of *B.* And I still do not think that the priority of one or other edition can be positively demonstrated on the readings alone. Whether one is corruption or the other correction is not demonstrable in the very strictest sense once we know that Dryden had concerned himself at this date with correcting reprints of at least one other play.

I approached the two editions, therefore, not on the basis of the respective 'goodness' of their readings, but in search of some material evidence that one had been printed from the other. Here are some of the highlights of the preliminary case I evolved for the priority of *A.*

In the *A.* edition, the shortened name *Will* is almost invariably followed by a period to indicate that it is an abbreviation for *William,* and this period substitutes for other necessary punctuation such as commas, semi-colons, or even question marks. In *B., Will* is treated as a simple familiar name and no period is ever found except once—and significantly this once is the first time the name appears. Inadvertent following of copy by *B.* in this single initial instance seemed the best answer.[24] Given this hint, I continued looking for what one might describe as fossils in *B.* of strong characteristics present in *A.* but not in *B.* Twice in *A.* one compositor set the extreme contraction *h's* for *he's,* and, once later, *h'll* for *he'll.* In *B.* the two *h's* are normalized to the conventional *he's,* but the fossil *h'll* retained. More evidence appeared of what was apparently inadvertent following of copy. For example, the two compositors of *A.* spelled the conjunctive adverb *than* indifferently as *then* or as *than.* In *B.* the invariable spelling is *than,* even when *then* appears in *A.,* except for two cases, and one of these turned out to be in the uncorrected state of a press-variant forme in *B.* where the *A.* spelling *then* originally appeared in *B.* but was changed by the proof-reader to *than.* There were various other instances in which the isolated appearance in *B.* of marked characteristics in *A.* seemed significant, especially since the two pairs of compositors were different in each edition. Moreover, on the textual principle that the 'harder' reading is the original, there were at least two cases which seemed to point to the priority of *A*. In the first, the form *wall* in the phrase in *A*. "she wall write" seemed to derive more plausibly from a manuscript colloquialism *wall* or *wull* than from a misprint of the *B*. "she shall write." In the second, Constance is deceiving Lord Nonsuch that she is with child, and when he demands the name of the father she responds that she does not know. He exclaims, "Not know! went there so many to't?" and in *A*. she answers, "So far from that, that there were none at all, to my best knowledge, Sir." In *B*. the repetition *went* substitutes for *were*, and it seemed a plausible hypothesis that the 'harder' reading was *were*, and that memorial failure in the *B*. compositor carried over the repetition of *went* from Nonsuch's line. That the *A*. compositor in such a circumstance, where the repetition seems most natural, saw *went* in his *B*. copy and set *were* seemed more difficult to believe.

There is not time to go into this next evidence, but in the light of general experience that irregularities between catchword and following word in an original edition usually tend to be normalized in reprints, it seemed to me at first highly probable that certain irregularities in the *A*. catchwords were much better explained on the belief that it was the first edition rather than the second.

Finally, I attacked the gap of eight pages in the pagination which appears between sheets G and H in both editions. In one edition this identical error could have resulted only from slavish following of copy. Hence if I could establish a reason for the gap in one edition, but no reason in the other, I felt I should have my original. Analysis disclosed that edition *A*. was set by two compositors in sections of one or more full sheets and that their respective sections can be identified not only by the different lengths of their sticks but also by the difference in the use of skeleton-formes which is associated with each.[25] In *B*. there is no evidence for any interruption in the presswork between sheets G and H, and indeed it seems likely that one compositor set the last pages of G and continued over into the first pages of H as part of his stint. On the contrary, in *A*. the gap in pagination occurs between one of the clearly marked sections where the compositors shifted, and it seemed a reasonable inference that when the compositor of sheet H returned to duty and came to make his first impositions, he forgot the system under which he was working and miscalculated the pagination.

I had, then, among various other pieces of evidence, the apparent survival in unique forms in *B*. of strongly marked compositorial habits manifested in *A*., among such fossils being the abbreviation of *Will*, the survival of the form *h'll* and of a random *then* spelling. I may also mention a few cases in *B.* of the very common practice in *A.* of using a semi-colon for a question mark, the setting in *A.* of a period in over a dozen cases where a necessary question mark was used in *B.*, and a very odd but marked use of the full *-ed* ending in *A.* for the elided form *apostrophe d* in *B.*, an expansion difficult to account for with such frequency in a reprint. Then there were such cases as this. The colloquial form *u'm* for *them* is absolutely consistent throughout both editions except for one single late use of *them* in *A.* where *u'm* appears in *B.* The probability seemed much higher that *B.* had normalized *A.* than that *A.* had wilfully departed from its copy *B.* There were also two cases where proper names were found in italic in *B.*, as customary, but in roman in *A.*, a reversal hard to account for. Finally, the evidence of the catchwords possibly, but almost certainly that of the mispagination, seemed to point to *A.* as the original.

I hope I have made this case reasonably convincing, even in an incomplete and digested form, because I am ashamed to confess that initially—before I began to prepare the text for an edition—it had me thoroughly convinced. Yet I hasten to point out that all these conclusions are quite wrong, that Griffith and Osborn are right. Edition *B.* indeed precedes *A.;* and this case I have presented for Macdonald's order, though based mostly on 'bibliographical' facts, has been one only of inference and probability but never of true bibliographical demonstration.

This, briefly, is the real evidence for *B.* as the first edition which my subsequent investigation revealed. Only one press-variant forme emerged from collation of eleven copies of *A.*, but from ten copies of *B.* I finally turned up seven formes which had undergone stop-press correction. Of these, two are indifferent since the uncorrected state agrees with *A.* for one, and the other is the variant act-heading noticed by Professor Griffith in the apparently unique Texas copy. Of the remaining five, all—in their significant *B.* readings—have an agreement between the *corrected* state of the formes and *A.* There is no need to elaborate the bibliographical argument here.[26] Almost inevitably, *A.* must have been set from *B.*

Finally, to clinch the case, this evidence developed. On one occasion in *A.* the verb *tells* in the phrase *she tells me* is misprinted as *tel's.* We can demonstrate the source of this misprint in *A.* when we find that in the corresponding place in *B.* the second letter *l* in *tells* inks so very slightly in all observed copies that only its tip is visible without a magnifying glass; and since this inked tip would almost inevitably be taken as an apostrophe, the compositor of *A.* read it as one and faithfully followed what he thought was the spelling of his copy. Correspondingly, in three places in *A.* where rather essential punctuation is missing, we find that the actual commas are so lightly inked in some copies of *B.* as scarcely to be seen. The evidence of the *tel's* alone is sufficient on which to rest one's whole case for the order of the editions; but especially when so powerfully confirmed by the evidence of the press-variant formes in *B.* followed by *A.*, one could take the dispute to a court of law and secure a judgment for the priority of *B.*

From this detailed example I draw a moral which applies to much of what I have been trying to say in this paper. Textual and pseudo-bibliographical evidence can seldom if ever afford more than a high degree of probability, and this is essentially different from positive demonstration. A very plausible chain of inferences can be built up, if the person is as stupid as I seem to have been; and if only the same line of evidence is employed to attack such a case, nothing but an indecisive stalemate can result. On the contrary, strictly bibliographical evidence such as that about the *tel's* and the press variants—evidence which usually appears in texts if one digs deep enough—crosses the line of probability into something close to the field which in science would be regarded as controlled experiment capable of being reproduced. Instead of high probability we have, in fact, practical demonstration on physical evidence of a mechanical nature, demonstrable by a mechanical process, evidence like the prose and verse measures of *King Lear,* and this is what Greg means by bibliography's treatment of a book as a material object. To every point in my construction of the case for 72a as the first edition, alternatives could have been suggested, and therefore any credibility it possessed depended on the cumulative bulk of the inferences. Yet when actual bibliographical evidence enters the scene, one little *tel's* sweeps all before it.

I draw the further moral as this applies to editing. Such minute yet crucial evidence on which the case hinges would normally be discoverable only by an editor. For example, the ordinary tests which a descriptive bibliographer would apply could not determine the truth; hence, if a textual critic, faced with the problem of corruption versus correction, felt that the standard bibliography of Dryden had sufficiently set up the material for him to proceed with 72a as his copy-text (and he could very well do so), he would be most seriously misled if he failed to come upon the bibliographical points which destroy Macdonald's case.

In this paper I seem to have given a considerable number of examples where bibliographers were wrong. I have not intended to cast doubts on the validity of bibliographical findings, or to speak in a way to discourage the faint-hearted from depending upon bibliographical evidence. Quite the reverse. What has been paramount in my mind is, first, that bibliography may sometimes be imperfectly practised; and unless a textual critic is himself enough of a bibliographer to make his own discoveries independently, or else to submit existing bibliographical conclusions about his material to the acid test of his own bibliographical re-evaluation—unless he can do this, in many cases he will be living in a fool's paradise, either believing that there are no bibliographical problems, or else that the bibliographers have authoritatively worked over the material for him and he can go ahead on his own line without further consideration.

Secondly, this principle seeps down from the very top, or the choice and treatment of the copy-text, to the very bottom of the last, minute detail of an old-spelling critical edition which must be exhausted bibliographically before pure criticism can properly operate.

Thus I think we may freely say that the bibliographer's text is by no means always the best that can be contrived if the editor has not got the mind of a true textual critic—only perhaps that such a text does the minimum of harm. On the other hand, as a practising bibliographer I do object mightily to critics who often nullify the brilliance of their substantive text by failing to observe bibliographical principles when they engage themselves to an old-spelling edition. I should be inclined to set up four operations which an old-spelling editor should perform, for the interpretation and application of the evidence discovered by these investigations lie at the heart of a sound edition. It is astonishing to a bibliographer to find how often various of these have been omitted by an editor who otherwise has exhibited every desire to be scrupulous in the details of his work. First, the determination of authority in all early editions and, on this evidence, the proper choice and treatment of the copy-text as we have heard it described by Greg. Second, the collation of multiple copies of each authoritative edition to disclose proof-corrections for analysis. Third, the analysis of running-titles for the interpretation of the presswork, a matter which is closely linked with the fourth, or compositor analysis, this last being positively essential, at least in Elizabethan texts, for any consideration of the variants between two or more authoritative editions in a direct line of derivation.

These few demands are not especially severe and need not require any extraordinary technical training. But I place them as the basis for any bibliographical preparation of an individual text by an editor once the larger questions have been settled. And until they become standard procedure, at least in cases of any complexity where their chief value is found, our old-spelling texts are not going to be definitive in any real sense. Critical brilliance can settle many a substantive crux, although by no means all of them; but if these excellent major substantives are placed in a semi-substantive old-spelling background which is not itself accurate, then the reason for old-spelling texts degenerates into sentimentality or ostentation. Moreover, by an accurate background of accidentals and minor substantives, much more should be implied in many cases than the mechanical ability to copy and then proofread accurately from an old edition. If we are to learn to reconstruct the accidentals and minor substantives of an author's manuscript with as much care as we labor over reconstructing his correct major substantives, a whole new and delicate biblio-critical art is involved in which criticism by itself can never be a sufficiently scientific instrument.

I shall try to summarize the main points at which I have glanced. First, both textual criticism and analytical bibliography in their purest states are, in my opinion, independent arts which have no necessary relation in their disciplines, or frequently in the subjects with which they concern themselves. Textual criticism must deal with words and their meanings, with stylistic and linguistic considerations, and with the basic quesions of authority in texts, both in whole and in part. Pure analytical bibliography, on the other hand, deals with books as material objects formed by the mechanical process of printing. In many investigations it is not concerned with texts as such; but when it does approach texts it endeavors to treat them not from the literary or critical point of view, which is that of the 'goodness' of readings, but instead as pieces of paper mechanically impressed with certain symbols. The mechanical relation between these sets of symbols is thereupon its chief concern.

Second, although the two methods are essentially independent, textual criticism cannot controvert accurate bibliography in its findings when the subject is one on which bibliography can properly operate. However, the two often join in attacking certain problems of texts. These problems are by no means limited to editing, but nevertheless the construction of a critical text is most commonly the point at which the two methods cross.

Third, even though the first and the last approach to a text must be the bibliographical one, neither method can achieve definitive textual results in any detailed manner if utilized without reference to the other. On a broad scale it is bibliography which establishes the physical facts of the derivation of texts from one another and which wrings from a given book every last drop of information about the mechanical process of its printing that may be of service in determining the relation of the printed result to the manuscript or printed copy used by the printer. Still on a broad scale, it is the function of textual criticism to evaluate the authority of this manuscript and then to proceed to the correctness and the authority of the words in the text in the light of the ascertained physical facts which bibliography has furnished. Thereupon, in the process of fixing the text of a modern critical edition in every possible detail, the two methods are often so closely conjoined that an attempt to separate their respective functions would be futile.

When we come to criticize the average edited text produced today, we find that the usual source of error lies in the insufficient bibliographical training of the editor. Either he has little concept of textual problems, and—scornful of the minutiae which sometimes concern the bibliographer—is content to have any kind of a text, because what he really wants is only a peg on which to hang his annotations; or else he is overconfident in his purely critical abilities to solve any problems which may arise. In either case he has ventured on a delicate literary task without knowing his grammar, and hence his results can seldom be definitive. Sometimes even greater harm is caused by a little knowledge than by none. It is enough to make the angels weep to find Saintsbury, for example, throwing out various correct readings in Scott's text of *The Wild Gallant,* derived from edition 72b through the Folio and a later edition, to substitute absolute corruptions from 72a under the illusion he was restoring the purity of the text from the first edition. Or to find Davenport in the new edition of Joseph Hall's *Poems* declining the editorial responsibility to make a choice of readings, and basing his text on the derived reprint of 1598 for the first six books of *Virgidemiarum,* even though it was slightly revised, rather than the purer 1597 first edition.[27] It is really the hardest job in the world for a bibliographer to convince a critic who is beginning to be conscious of old-spelling problems that an author did not set his own type, seldom proof-read his book and if he did cannot be taken as approving every minute detail of its accidentals, and that a printed book is a fallible second-hand report of the author's manuscript, not a facsimile of it set in type.[28] One of the chief functions of textual bibliography is to try to pierce this veil of the printing process and to restore, however imperfectly, the authority of the manuscript, which we know only through its printed and thus secondary form.

On the other hand, a bibliographer who tackles the problems of text with insufficient critical and philological training is also in danger of false judgments in decisions which are not material and are therefore not strictly the business of bibliography. The usual result is that he may retreat to the narrowest conservatism to avoid having to face up to problems which are not wholly factual. And this timidity is as unbalanced as a critic's rashness in proceeding without the counterweight of bibliography. Such critical uncertainty may lead to good reprints of a single authority for a text but by no means to a true edition of the best text of an author.

It seems to me that for an ideally definitive work an editor must combine in himself the knowledge of both methods, and the training to put both into practice, or else he must resort to an almost impossible attempt at collaboration. Collaboration can be effective between a bibliographer and a literary critic who will handle all problems of biography, attribution of authorship, literary estimates, and who will write the critical introductions and illustrative notes. In such a case each has his relatively independent responsibilities; and indeed Greg is inclined to recommend this procedure for many editions. But I find it harder to imagine save in the most exceptional circumstances an effective collaboration of bibliographer and critic on the minutiae of the text.

I disclaim bibliography as the usurper of editorial privilege, and indeed I am concerned to aid the textual critic against the increasing pressure which editor-bibliographers are exerting on him. But if this potentially most valuable kind of an editor is to produce texts which in every detail will stand up under the increasingly exact and rigorous standards which are now being applied to this form of scholarship, he must learn his bibliography with a thoroughness not previously thought necessary. Only by this wider extension of scholarship can texts be achieved which will not need to be done all over again by the next generation.

NOTES

This paper was read before the English Institute on September 9, 1949.

[1] *Journal of English and Germanic Philology*, XXXVI (1937), 151-67.

[2] In this connection one must al-

ways recall W. W. Greg's searching monograph on *Orlando Furioso* and *The Battle of Alcazar.*

[3] E. E. Willoughby, *The Printing of the First Folio of Shakespeare* (1932); C. J. K. Hinman, "Principles Governing the Use of Variant Spellings as Evidence of Alternate Setting by Two Compositors," *The Library,* 4th ser., XXI (1940), 78-94; see also P. Williams, "The Compositor of the Pied-Bull *Lear,*" *Papers Bibl. Soc. Univ. Virginia,* I (1948), 61-68.

[4] *Studies in Bibliography,* II (1949), 153-67.

[5] For a number of references, see J. G. McManaway's footnote in *Standards of Bibliographical Description* (1949), pp. 88-89. See also *The Library,* 4th ser., XIX (1938), 315-38; 5th ser., II (1947), 20-44, 5th ser., III (1948), 124-137; *Papers Bibl. Soc. America,* XLII (1948), 143-48; XLIII (1949), 191-95.

[6] J. Carter and G. Pollard, *An Enquiry into the Nature of Certain Nineteenth Century Pamphlets* (1934); A. T. Hazen, *A Bibliography of the Strawberry Hill Press* (1942); A. H. Stevenson, "New Uses of Watermarks as Bibliographical Evidence," *Papers Bibl. Soc. Univ. Virginia,* I (1948), 151-82.

[7] D. F. Bond, "The First Printing of the *Spectator,*" *Modern Philology,* XLVII (1950), 174-77.

[8] W. E. Knotts, "Press Numbers as a Bibliographical Tool: A Study of Gay's *The Beggars' Opera,* 1728," *Harvard Library Bulletin,* III (1949), 198-212. See also, P. Gaskell, "Eighteenth-century Press Numbers: Their Use and Usefulness," *The Library,* 5th ser., IV (1950), 249-61.

[9] "Observations on the Incidence and Interpretation of Press Figures," *Studies in Bibliography,* III (1950-51), 171-205.

[10] "Bibliography—An Apologia," *op. cit.,* pp. 121 ff.

[11] "Principles of Emendation in Shakespeare," *Proceedings of the British Academy,* XIV (1928), 154-55.

[12] *Prolegomena for the Oxford Shakespeare* (1939), p. 18.

[13] *The Library,* 4th ser., XIII (1933), 395-98; 5th ser., I (1946), 67-69; II (1947), 64; and finally "The Supposed Cancel in Southerne's *Disappointment,*" forthcoming in *The Library,* vol. V (1950).

[14] "The Early Editions and Issues of *The Monk,*" *Studies in Bibliography,* II (1949), 3-24.

[15] P. Williams, *loc. cit.;* see also *Studies in Bibliography,* II (1949), 164.

[16] For a detailed consideration of this passage, see G. W. Williams, "A Note on *King Lear,* III. ii. 1-3," *Studies in Bibliography,* II (1949), 175-82.

[17] W. W. Greg, *A Bibliography of the English Printed Drama to the Restoration,* I (1939), no. 277.

[18] *Papers Bibl. Soc. America,* XLII (1948), 146-48.

[19] J. S. Steck, "Dryden's *Indian Emperour:* The Early Editions and their Relation to the Text," *Studies in Bibliography,* II (1949), 147.

[20] P. Williams, "Shakespeare's *Troilus and Cressida:* The Relationship of Quarto and Folio," *Studies in Bibliography,* III (1950-51), 131-43.

[21] C. J. K. Hinman, "The 'Copy' for the Second Quarto of *Othello,*" *Joseph Quincy Adams: Memorial Studies* (1948), pp. 373-89.

[22] "The First Edition of Dryden's *Wild Gallant,* 1669," *The Library,* 5th ser., V (1950), 51-54.

[23] J. M. Osborn, "Macdonald's Bibliography of Dryden," *Modern Philology,* XXXIX (1941), 83-85.

[24] The reverse seemed, and still seems to me, almost incredible. With A. the reprint, both compositors of A. (for two compositors can be readily established) agreed in treating the name as an abbreviation and in sub-

stituting the abbreviating period for other punctuation found in *B.*, their copy, perhaps rigidly following the single hint of the initial abbreviation of the name in *B.*

[25] One identifiable compositor used only one skeleton to impose both formes of his sheet; the other, seemingly the quicker workman, used two.

[26] The full argument is provided in the article mentioned above in fn. 22, but no bibliographer will need the details. If *B.* were set from *A.*, we should have to believe that in these five corrected formes in *B.* the proof-reader made only changes in minutiae which helped to bring the reprint into conformity with its copy, and no other alterations. Moreover, an error in the uncorrected state of one forme in *B.* could under no circumstances have originated in a misreading of *A.*

[27] Davenport's theory of editing and its contracitory results are touched on in my "Current Theories of Copy-Text, with an Illustration from Dryden," *Modern Philology*, August, 1950.

[28] Apparently this unbibliographical view is held by Richard Flatter, *Shakespeare's Producing Hand* (1948), and the error succeeds very thoroughly in turning his textual criticism into absurdity. For an analysis of his position, see my review in *Modern Philology*, August, 1950.

The Rationale of Copy-Text

W. W. Greg

When, in his edition of Nashe, McKerrow invented the term 'copy-text', he was merely giving a name to a conception already familiar, and he used it in a general sense to indicate that early text of a work which an editor selected as the basis of his own. Later, as we shall see, he gave it a somewhat different and more restricted meaning. It is this change in conception and its implications that I wish to consider.

The idea of treating some one text, usually of course a manuscript, as possessing over-riding authority originated among classical scholars, though something similar may no doubt be traced in the work of biblical critics. So long as purely eclectic methods prevailed, any preference for one manuscript over another, if it showed itself, was of course arbitrary; but when, towards the middle of last century, Lachmann and others introduced the genealogical classification of manuscripts as a principle of textual criticism, this appeared to provide at least some scientific basis for the conception of the most authoritative text. The genealogical method was the greatest advance ever made in this field, but its introduction was not unaccompanied by error. For lack of logical analysis, it led, at the hands of its less discriminating exponents, to an attempt to reduce textual criticism to a code of mechanical rules. There was just this much excuse, that the method did make it possible to sweep away mechanically a great deal of rubbish. What its more hasty devotees failed to understand, or at any rate sufficiently to bear in mind, was that authority is never absolute, but only relative. Thus a school arose, mainly in Germany, that taught that if a manuscript could be shown to be generally more correct than any other and to have descended from the archetype independently of other lines of transmission, it was 'scientific' to follow its readings whenever they were not manifestly impossible. It was this fallacy that Housman exposed with devastating sarcasm. He had only to point out that 'Chance and the common course of nature will not bring it to pass that the readings of a MS are right wherever they are possible and impossible wherever they are wrong'.[1] That if a scribe makes a mistake he will inevitably produce nonsense is the tacit and wholly unwarranted assumption of the school in question,[2] and it is one that naturally commends itself to those who believe themselves capable of distinguishing between sense and nonsense, but who know themelves incapable of distinguishing between right and wrong. Unfortunately the attractions of a mechanical method misled many who were capable of better things.

There is one important respect in which the editing of classical texts differs from that of English. In the former it is the common practice, for fairly obvious reasons, to normalize the spelling, so that (apart from emendation) the function of an editor is limited to choosing between those manuscript readings that offer significant variants. In English it is now usual to preserve the spelling of the earliest or it may be some other selected text. Thus it will be seen that the conception of 'copy-text' does not present itself to the classical and to the English editor in quite the same way; indeed, if I am right in the view I am about to put forward, the classical theory of the 'best' or 'most authoritative' manuscript, whether it be held in a reasonable or in an obviously fallacious form, has really nothing to do with the English theory of 'copy-text' at all.

I do not wish to argue the case of 'old spelling' *versus* 'modern spelling'; I accept the view now prevalent among English scholars. But I cannot avoid some reference to the ground on which present practice is based, since it is intimately connected with my own views on copy-text. The former practice of modernizing the spelling of English works is no longer popular with editors, since spelling is now recognized as an essential characteristic of an author, or at least of his time and locality. So far as my knowledge goes, the alternative of normalization has not been seriously explored, but its philological difficulties are clearly considerable.[3] Whether, with the advance of linguistic science, it will some day be possible to establish a standard spelling for a particular period or district or author, or whether the historical circumstances in which our language has developed must always forbid any attempt of the sort (at any rate before comparatively recent times) I am not competent to say; but I agree with what appears to be the general opinion that such an attempt would at present only result in confusion and misrepresentation. It is therefore the modern editorial practice to choose whatever extant text may be supposed to represent most nearly what the author wrote and to follow it with the least possible alteration. But here we need to draw a distinction between the significant, or as I shall call them 'substantive', readings of the text, those namely that affect the author's meaning or the essence of his expression, and others, such in general as spelling, punctuation, word-division, and the like, affecting mainly its formal presentation, which may be regarded as the accidents, or as I shall call them 'accidentals', of the text.[4] The distinction is not arbitrary or theoretical, but has an immediate bearing on textual criticism, for scribes (or compositors) may in general be expected to react, and experience shows that they generally do react, differently to the two categories. As regards substantive readings their aim may be assumed to be to reproduce exactly those of their copy, though they will doubtless sometimes depart from them accidentally and may even, for one reason or another, do so intentionally: as regards accidentals they will normally follow their own habits or inclination, though they may, for various reasons and to varying degrees, be influenced by their copy. Thus a contemporary manuscript will at least preserve the spelling of the period, and may even retain some of the author's own, while it may at the same time depart frequently from the wording of the original: on the other hand a later transcript of the same original may reproduce the wording with essential accuracy while completely modernizing the spelling. Since, then, it is only on grounds of expediency, and in consequence either of philological ignorance or of linguistic circumstances, that we select a particular original as our copy-text, I suggest that it is only in the matter of accidentals that we are bound (within reason) to follow it, and that in respect of substantive readings we have exactly the same liberty (and obligation) of choice as has a classical editor, or as we should have were it a modernized text that we were preparing.[5]

But the distinction has not been generally recognized, and has never, so far as I am aware, been explicitly drawn.[6] This is not surprising. The battle between 'old spelling' and 'modern spelling' was fought out over works written for the most part between 1550 and 1650, and for which the original authorities are therefore as a rule printed editions. Now printed editions usually form an ancestral series, in which each is derived from its immediate predecessor; whereas the extant manuscripts of any work have usually only a collateral relationship, each being derived from the original independently, or more or less independently, of the others. Thus in the case of printed books, and in the absence of revision in a later edition, it is normally the first edition alone that can claim authority, and this authority naturally extends to substantive readings and accidentals alike. There was, therefore, little to force the distinction upon the notice of editors of works of the sixteenth and seventeenth centuries, and it apparently never occurred to them that some fundamental difference of editorial method might be called for in the rare cases in which a later edition had been revised by the author or in which there existed more than one 'substantive' edition of comparable authority.[7] Had they been more familiar with works transmitted in manuscript, they might possibly have reconsidered their methods and been led to draw the distinction I am suggesting. For although the underlying principles of textual criticism are, of course, the same in the case of works transmitted in manuscripts and in print, particular circumstances differ, and certain aspects of the common principles may emerge more clearly in the one case than in the other. However, since the idea of copy-text originated and has generally been applied in connexion with the editing of printed books, it is such that I shall mainly consider, and in what follows reference may be understood as confined to them unless manuscripts are specifically mentioned.

The distinction I am proposing between substantive readings and accidentals, or at any rate its relevance to the question of copy-text, was clearly not present to McKerrow's mind when in 1904 he published the second volume of his edition of the Works of Thomas Nashe, which included *The Unfortunate Traveller*. Collation of the early editions of this romance led him to the conclusion that the second, advertised on the title as 'Newly corrected and augmented', had in fact been revised by the author, but at the same time that not all the alterations could with certainty be ascribed to him.[8] He nevertheless proceeded to enunciate the rule that 'if an editor has reason to suppose that a certain text embodies later corrections than any other, and at the same time has no ground for disbelieving that these corrections, *or some of them at least*, are the work of the author, he has no choice but to make that text the basis of his reprint'.[9] The italics are mine.[10] This is applying with a vengeance the principle that I once approvingly described as 'maintaining the integrity of the copy-text'. But it must be pointed out that there are in fact two quite distinct principles involved. One, put in more general form, is that if, for whatever reason, a particular authority be on the whole preferred, an editor is bound to accept all its substantive readings (if not manifestly impossible). This is the old fallacy of the 'best text', and may be taken to be now generally rejected. The other principle, also put in general form, is that whatever particular authority be preferred, whether as being revised or as generally preserving the substantive readings more faithfully than any other, it must be taken as copy-text, that is to say that it must also be followed in the matter of accidentals. This is the principle that interests us at the moment, and it is one that McKerrow himself came, at least partly, to question.

In 1939 McKerrow published his *Prolegomena for the Oxford Shakespeare*, and he would not have been the critic he was if his views had not undergone some changes in the course of thirty-five years. One was in respect of revision. He had come to the opinion that to take a reprint, even a revised reprint, as copy-text was indefensible. Whatever may be the relation of a particular substantive edition to the author's manuscript (provided that there is any transcriptional link at all) it stands to reason that the relation of a reprint of that edition must be more remote. If then, putting aside all question of revision, a particular substantive edition has an over-riding claim to be taken as copy-text, to displace it in favour of a reprint, whether revised or not, means receding at least one step further from the author's original in so far as the general form of the text is concerned.[11] Some such considerations must have been in McKerrow's mind when he wrote (*Prolegomena*, pp. 17-18): 'Even if, however, we were to assure ourselves . . . that certain corrections found in a later edition of a play were of Shakespearian authority, it would not by any means follow that that edition should be used as the copy-text of a reprint.[12] It would undoubtedly be necessary to incorporate these corrections in our text, but . . . it seems evident that . . . this later edition will (except for the corrections) deviate more widely than the earliest print from the author's original manuscript. . . . [Thus] the nearest approach to our ideal . . . will be produced by using the earliest "good" print as copy-text and inserting into it, from the first edition which contains them, such corrections as appear to us to be derived from the author.' This is a clear statement of the position, and in it he draws exactly the distinction between substantive readings (in the form of corrections) and accidentals (or general texture) on which I am insisting. He then, however, relapsed into heresy in the matter of the substantive readings. Having spoken, as above, of the need to introduce 'such corrections as appear to us to be derived from the author', he seems to have feared conceding too much to eclecticism, and he proceeded: 'We are not to regard the "goodness" of a reading in and by itself, or to consider whether it appeals to our aesthetic sensibilities or not; we are to consider whether a particular edition taken *as a whole* contains variants from the edition from which it was otherwise printed which could not reasonably be attributed to an ordinary press-corrector, but by reason of their style, point, and what we may call inner harmony with the spirit of the play as a whole, seem likely to be the work of the author: and once having decided this to our satisfaction we must accept *all* the alterations of that edition, saving any which seem obvious blunders or misprints.' We can see clearly enough what he had in mind, namely that the evidence of correction (under which head he presumably intended to include revision) must be considered *as a whole;* but he failed to add the equally important proviso that the alterations must also be *of a piece* (and not, as in *The Unfortunate Traveller,* of apparently disparate origin) before we can be called upon to accept them *all.* As he states it his canon is open to exactly the same objections as the 'most authoritative manuscript' theory in classical editing.

McKerrow was, therefore, in his later work quite conscious of the distinction between substantive readings and accidentals, in so far as the problem of revision is concerned. But he never applied the conception to cases in which we have more than one substantive text, as in *Hamlet* and perhaps in 2 *Henry IV, Troilus and Cressida,* and *Othello.* Presumably he would have argued that since faithfulness to the wording of the author was one of the criteria he laid down for determining the choice of the copy-text, it was an editor's duty to follow its substantive readings with a minimum of interference.

We may assume that neither McKerrow nor other editors of the conservative school imagined that such a procedure would always result in establishing the authentic text of the original; what they believed was that from it less harm would result than from opening the door to individual choice among variants, since it substituted an objective for a subjective method of determination. This is, I think, open to question. It is impossible to exclude individual judgment from editorial procedure: it operates of necessity in the all-important matter of the choice of copy-text and in the minor one of deciding what readings are possible and what not; why, therefore, should the choice between possible readings be withdrawn from its competence? Uniformity of result at the hands of different editors is worth little if it means only uniformity in error; and it may not be too optimistic a belief that the judgment of an editor, fallible as it must necessarily be, is likely to bring us closer to what the author wrote than the enforcement of an arbitrary rule.

The true theory is, I contend, that the copy-text should govern (generally) in the matter of accidentals, but that the choice between substantive readings belongs to the general theory of textual criticism and lies altogether beyond the narrow principle of the copy-text. Thus it may happen that in a critical edition the text rightly chosen as copy may not by any means be the one that supplies most substantive readings in cases of variation. The failure to make this distinction and to apply this principle has naturally led to too close and too general a reliance upon the text chosen as basis for an edition, and there has arisen what may be called the tyranny of the copy-text, a tyranny that has, in my opinion, vitiated much of the best editorial work of the past generation.

I will give a couple of examples of the sort of thing I mean that I have lately come across in the course of my own work. They are all the more suitable as illustrations since they occur in texts edited by scholars of recognized authority, neither of whom is particularly subject to the tyranny in question. One is from the edition of Marlowe's *Doctor Faustus* by Professor F. S. Boas (1932). The editor, rightly I think, took the so-called B-text (1616) as the basis of his own, correcting it where necessary by comparison with the A-text (1604).[13] Now a famous line in Faustus's opening soliloquy runs in 1604,

Bid *Oncaymæon* farewell, *Galen* come

and in 1616,

Bid *Oeconomy* farewell; and *Galen* come . . .

Here *Oncaymæon* is now recognized as standing for *on cay mæ on* or ὂν καί μὴ ὄν: but this was not understood at the time, and *Oeconomy* was substituted in reprints of the A-text in 1609 and 1611, and thence taken over by the B-text. The change, however, produced a rather awkward line, and in 1616 the *and* was introduced as a metrical accommodation. In the first half of the line Boas rightly restored the reading implied in A; but in the second half he retained, out of deference to his copy-text, the *and* whose only object was to accommodate the reading he had rejected in the first. One could hardly find a better example of the contradictions to which a mechanical following of the copy-text may lead.[14]

My other instance is from *The Gipsies Metamorphosed* as edited by Dr. Percy Simpson among the masques of Ben Jonson in 1941. He took as his copy-text the Huntington manuscript, and I entirely agree with his choice. In this, and in Simpson's edition, a line of the ribald Cock Lorel ballad runs (sir-reverence!),

> Allw^{ch} he blewe away with a fart

whereas for *blewe* other authorities have *flirted.* Now, the meaning of *flirted* is not immediately apparent, for no appropriate sense of the word is recorded. There is, however, a rare use of the substantive *flirt* for a sudden gust of wind, and it is impossible to doubt that this is what Jonson had in mind, for no scribe or compositor could have invented the reading *flirted.* It follows that in the manuscript *blewe* is nothing but the conjecture of a scribe who did not understand his original: only the mesmeric influence of the copy-text could obscure so obvious a fact.[15]

I give these examples merely to illustrate the kind of error that, in modern editions of English works, often results from undue deference to the copy-text. This reliance on one particular authority results from the desire for an objective theory of text-construction and a distrust, often no doubt justified, of the operation of individual judgement. The attitude may be explained historically as a natural and largely salutary reaction against the methods of earlier editors. Dissatisfied with the results of eclectic freedom and reliance on personal taste, critics sought to establish some sort of mechanical apparatus for dealing with textual problems that should lead to uniform results independent of the operator. Their efforts were not altogether unattended by success. One result was the recognition of the general worthlessness of reprints. And even in the more difficult field of manuscript transmission it is true that formal rules will carry us part of the way: they can at least effect a preliminary clearing of the ground. This I sought to show in my essay on *The Calculus of Variants* (1927); but in the course of investigation it became clear that there is a definite limit to the field over which formal rules are applicable. Between readings of equal extrinsic authority no rules of the sort can decide, since by their very nature it is only to extrinsic relations that they are relevant. The choice is necessarily a matter for editorial judgement, and an editor who declines or is unable to exercise his judgement and falls back on some arbitrary canon, such as the authority of the copy-text, is in fact abdicating his editorial function. Yet this is what has been frequently commended as 'scientific'—'streng wissenschaftlich' in the prevalent idiom —and the result is that what many editors have done is to produce, not editions of their authors' works at all, but only editions of particular authorities for those works, a course that may be perfectly legitimate in itself, but was not the one they were professedly pursuing.

This by way, more or less, of digression. At the risk of repetition I should like to recapitulate my view of the position of copy-text in editorial procedure. The thesis I am arguing is that the historical circumstances of the English language make it necessary to adopt in formal matters the guidance of some particular early text. If the several extant texts of a work form an ancestral series, the earliest will naturally be selected, and since this will not only come nearest to the author's original in accidentals, but also (revision apart) most faithfully preserve the correct readings where substantive variants are in question, everything is straightforward, and the conservative treatment of the copy-text is justified. But whenever there is more than one substantive text of comparable authority,[16] then although it will still be necessary to choose one of them as copy-text, and to follow it in accidentals, this copy-text can be allowed no over-riding or even preponderant authority so far as substantive readings are concerned. The choice between these, in cases of variation, will be determined partly by the opinion the editor may form respecting the nature of the copy from which each substantive edition was printed, which is a matter of external authority; partly by the intrinsic authority of the several texts as judged by the relative frequency of manifest errors therein; and partly by the editor's judgement of the intrinsic claims of individual readings to originality—in other words their intrinsic merit, so long as by 'merit' we mean the likelihood of their being what the author wrote rather than their appeal to the individual taste of the editor.

Such, as I see it, is the general theory of copy-text. But there remain a number of subsidiary questions that it may be worthwhile to discuss. One is the degree of faithfulness with which the copy-text should be reproduced. Since the adoption of a copy-text is a matter of convenience rather than of principle—being imposed on us either by linguistic circumstance or our own philological ignorance—it follows that there is no reason for treating it as sacrosanct, even apart from the question of substantive variation. Every editor aiming at a critical edition will, of course, correct scribal or typographical errors. He will also correct readings in accordance with any errata included in the edition taken as copy-text. I see no reason why he should not alter misleading or eccentric spellings which he is satisfied emanate from the scribe or compositor and not from the author. If the punctuation is persistently erroneous or defective an editor may prefer to discard it altogether to make way for one of his own. He is, I think, at liberty to do so, provided that he gives due weight to the original in deciding on his own, and that he records the alteration whenever the sense is appreciably affected. Much the same applies to the use of capitals and italics. I should favour expanding contractions (except perhaps when dealing with an author's holograph) so long as ambiguities and abnormalities are recorded. A critical edition does not seem to me a suitable place in which to record the graphic peculiarities of particular texts,[17] and in this respect the copy-text is only one among others. These, however, are all matters within the discretion of an editor: I am only concerned to uphold his liberty of judgement.

Some minor points arise when it becomes necessary to replace a reading of the copy-text by one derived from another source. It need not, I think, be copied in the exact form in which it there appears. Suppose that the copy-text follows the earlier convention in the use of *u* and *v*, and the source from which the reading is taken follows the later. Naturally in transferring the reading from the latter to the former it would be made to conform to the earlier convention. I would go further. Suppose that the copy-text reads 'hazard', but that we have reason to believe that the correct reading is 'venture': suppose further that whenever this word occurs in the copy-text it is in the form 'venter': then 'venter', I maintain, is the form we should adopt. In like manner editorial emendations should be made to conform to the habitual spelling of the copy-text.

In the case of rival substantive editions the choice between substantive variants is, I have explained, generally independent of the copy-text. Perhaps one concession should be made. Suppose that the claims of two readings, one in the copy-text and one in some other authority, appear to be exactly balanced: what then should an editor do? In such a case, while there can be no logical reason for giving preference to the copy-text, in practice, if there is no reason for altering its reading, the obvious thing seems to be to let it stand.[18]

Much more important, and difficult, are the problems that arise in connexion with revision. McKerrow seems only to mention correction, but I think he must have intended to include revision, so long as this falls short of complete rewriting: in any case the principle is the same. I have already considered the practice he advocated (pp. 44–45)—namely that an editor should take the original edition as his copy-text and introduce into it all the substantive variants of the revised reprint, other than manifest errors—and have explained that I regard it as too sweeping and mechanical. The emendation that I proposed (p. 46) is, I think, theoretically sufficient, but from a practical point of view it lacks precision. In a case of revision or correction the normal procedure would be for the author to send the printer either a list of the alterations to be made or else a corrected copy of an earlier edition. In setting up the new edition we may suppose that the printer would incorporate the alterations thus indicated by the author; but it must be assumed that he would also introduce a normal amount of unauthorized variation of his own.[19] The problem that faces the editor is to distinguish between the two categories. I suggest the following frankly subjective procedure. Granting that the fact of revision (or correction) is established, an editor should in every case of variation ask himself (1) whether the original reading is one that can reasonably be attributed to the author, and (2) whether the later reading is one that the author can reasonably be supposed to have substituted for the former. If the answer to the first question is negative, then the later reading should be accepted as at least possibly an authoritative correction (unless, of course, it is itself incredible). If the answer to (1) is affirmative and the answer to (2) is negative, the original reading should be retained. If the answers to both questions are affirmative, then the later reading should be presumed to be due to revision and admitted into the text, whether the editor himself considers it an improvement or not. It will be observed that one implication of this procedure is that a later variant that is either completely indifferent or manifestly inferior, or for the substitution of which no motive can be suggested, should be treated as fortuitous and refused admission to the text—to the scandal of faithful followers of McKerrow. I do not, of course, pretend that my procedure will lead to consistently correct results, but I think that the results, if less uniform, will be on the whole preferable to those achieved through following any mechanical rule. I am, no doubt, presupposing an editor of reasonable competence; but if an editor is really incompetent, I doubt whether it much matters what procedure he adopts: he may indeed do less harm with some than with others, he will do little good with any. And in any case, I consider that it would be disastrous to curb the liberty of competent editors in the hope of preventing fools from behaving after their kind.

I will give one illustration of the procedure in operation, taken again from Jonson's *Masque of Gipsies*, a work that is known to have been extensively revised for a later performance. At one point the text of the original version runs as follows,

> a wise Gypsie . . . is as politicke a piece of Flesh, as most Iustices in the County where he maunds

whereas the texts of the revised version replace *maunds* by *stalkes.* Now, *maund* is a recognized canting term meaning to beg, and there is not the least doubt that it is what Jonson originally wrote. Further, it might well be argued that it is less likely that he should have displaced it in revision by a comparatively commonplace alternative, than that a scribe should have altered a rather unusual word that he failed to understand—just as we know that, in a line already quoted (p. 47), a scribe altered *flirted* to *blewe.* I should myself incline to this view were it not that at another point Jonson in revision added the lines,

And then ye may stalke
The *Gypsies* walke

where *stalk,* in the sense of going stealthily, is used almost as a technical term. In view of this I do not think it unreasonable to suppose that Jonson himself substituted *stalkes* for *maunds* from a desire to avoid the implication that his aristocratic Gipsies were beggars, and I conclude that it must be allowed to pass as (at least possibly) a correction, though no reasonable critic would *prefer* it to the original.

With McKerrow's view that in all normal cases of correction or revision the original edition should still be taken as the copy-text, I am in complete agreement. But not all cases are normal, as McKerrow himself recognized. While advocating, in the passage already quoted (p. 44), that the earliest 'good' edition should be taken as copy-text and corrections incorporated in it, he added the proviso, 'unless we could show that the [revised] edition in question (or the copy from which it had been printed) had been gone over and corrected *throughout* by' the author (my italics). This proviso is not in fact very explicit, but it clearly assumes that there are (or at least may be) cases in which an editor would be justified in taking a revised reprint as his copy-text, and it may be worth inquiring what these supposed cases are. If a work has been entirely rewritten, and is printed from a new manuscript, the question does not arise, since the revised edition will be a substantive one, and as such will presumably be chosen by the editor as his copy-text. But short of this, an author, wishing to make corrections or alterations in his work, may not merely hand the printer a revised copy of an earlier edition, but himself supervise the printing of the new edition and correct the proofs as the sheets go through the press. In such a case it may be argued that even though the earlier edition, if printed from his own manuscript, will preserve the author's individual peculiarities more faithfully than the revised reprint, he must nevertheless be assumed to have taken responsibility for the latter in respect of accidentals no less than substantive readings, and that it is therefore the revised reprint that should be taken as copy-text.

The classical example is afforded by the plays in the 1616 folio of Ben Jonson's Works. In this it appears that even the largely recast *Every Man in his Humour* was not set up from an independent manuscript but from a much corrected copy of the quarto of 1601. That Jonson revised the proofs of the folio has indeed been disputed, but Simpson is most likely correct in supposing that he did so, and he was almost certainly responsible for the numerous corrections made while the sheets were in process of printing. Simpson's consequent decision to take the folio for his copy-text for the plays it contains will doubtless be approved by most critics. I at least have no wish to dispute his choice.[20] Only I would point out—and here I think Dr. Simpson would agree with me—that even in this case the procedure involves some sacrifice of individuality. For example, I notice that in the text of *Sejanus* as printed by him there are twenty-eight instances of the Jonsonian 'Apostrophus' (an apostrophe indicating the elision of a vowel that is nevertheless retained in printing) but of these only half actually appear in the folio, the rest he has introduced from the quarto. This amounts to an admission that in some respects at least the quarto preserves the formal aspect of the author's original more faithfully than the folio.

The fact is that cases of revision differ so greatly in circumstances and character that it seems impossible to lay down any hard and fast rule as to when an editor should take the original edition as his copy-text and when the revised reprint. All that can be said is that if the original be selected, then the author's corrections must be incorporated; and that if the reprint be selected, then the original reading must be restored when that of the reprint is due to unauthorized variation. Thus the editor cannot escape the responsibility of distinguishing to the best of his ability between the two categories. No juggling with copy-text will relieve him of the duty and necessity of exercizing his own judgment.

In conclusion I should like to examine this problem of revision and copy-text a little closer. In the case of a work like *Sejanus,* in which correction or revision has been slight, it would obviously be possible to take the quarto as the copy-text and introduce into it whatever authoritative alterations the folio may supply; and indeed, were one editing the play independently, this would be the natural course to pursue. But a text like that of *Every Man in his Humour* presents an entirely different problem. In the folio revision and reproduction are so blended that it would seem impossible to disentangle intentional from what may be fortuitous variation, and injudicious to make the attempt. An editor of the revised version has no choice but to take the folio as his copy-text. It would appear therefore that a reprint may in practice be forced upon an editor as copy-text by the nature of the revision itself, quite apart from the question whether or not the author exercized any supervision over its printing.

This has a bearing upon another class of texts, in which a reprint was revised, not by the author, but through comparison with some more authoritative manuscript. Instances are Shakespeare's *Richard III* and *King Lear*. Of both much the best text is supplied by the folio of 1623; but this is not a substantive text, but one set up from a copy of an earlier quarto that had been extensively corrected by collation with a manuscript preserved in the playhouse. So great and so detailed appears to have been the revision that it would be an almost impossible task to distinguish between variation due to the corrector and that due to the compositor,[21] and an editor has no choice but to take the folio as copy-text. Indeed, this would in any case be incumbent upon him for a different reason; for the folio texts are in some parts connected by transcriptional continuity with the author's manuscript, whereas the quartos contain only reported texts, whose accidental characteristics can be of no authority whatever. At the same time, analogy with *Every Man in his Humour* suggests that even had the quartos of *Richard III* and *King Lear* possessed higher authority than in fact they do, the choice of copy-text must yet have been the same.

I began this discussion in the hope of clearing my own mind as well as others' on a rather obscure though not unimportant matter of editorial practice. I have done something to sort out my own ideas: others must judge for themselves. If they disagree, it is up to them to maintain some different point of view. My desire is rather to provoke discussion than to lay down the law.

NOTES

This paper was read before the English Institute on September 8, 1949, by Dr. J. M. Osborn for W. W. Greg.

[1] Introduction to Manilius, 1903, p. xxxii.

[2] The more naive the scribe, the more often will the assumption prove

correct; the more sophisticated, the less often. This, no doubt, is why critics of this school tend to reject 'the more correct but the less sincere' manuscript in favor of 'the more corrupt but the less interpolated', as Housman elsewhere observes ('The Application of Thought to Textual Criticism,' *Proceedings of the Classical Association*, 1921, xviii. 75). Still, any reasonable critic will prefer the work of a naive to that of a sophisticated scribe, though he may not regard it as necessarily 'better.'

[3] I believe that an attempt has been made in the case of certain Old and Middle English texts, but how consistently and with what success I cannot judge. In any case I am here concerned chiefly with works of the sixteenth and seventeenth centuries.

[4] It will, no doubt, be objected that punctuation may very seriously 'affect' an author's meaning; still it remains properly a matter of presentation, as spelling does in spite of its use in distinguishing homonyms. The distinction I am trying to draw is practical, not philosophic. It is also true that between substantive readings and spellings there is an intermediate class of word-forms about the assignment of which opinions may differ and which may have to be treated differently in dealing with the work of different scribes.

[5] For the sake of clearness in making the distinction I have above stressed the independence of scribes and compositors in the matter of accidentals: at the same time, when he selects his copy-text, an editor will naturally hope that it retains at least something of the character of the original. Experience, however, shows that while the distribution of substantive variants generally agrees with the genetic relation of the texts, that of accidental variants is comparatively arbitrary.

[6] Some discussion bearing on it will be found in the Prolegomena to my lectures on *The Editorial Problem in Shakespeare* (1942), 'Note on Accidental Characteristics of the Text' (pp. l-lv), particularly the paragraph on pp. liii-liv, and note 1. But at the time of writing I was still a long way from any consistent theory regarding copy-text.

[7] A 'substantive' edition is McKerrow's term for an edition that is not a reprint of any other. I shall use the term in this sense, since I do not think that there should be any danger of confusion between 'substantive editions' and 'substantive readings'.

I have above ignored the practice of some eccentric editors who took as copy-text for a work the latest edition printed in the author's life-time, on the assumption, presumably, that he revised each edition as it appeared. The textual results were naturally deplorable.

[8] He believed, or at least strongly suspected, that some were due to the printer's desire to save space, and that others were 'the work of some person who had not thoroughly considered the sense of the passage which he was altering' (ii.195).

[9] Nashe, ii.197. The word 'reprint' really begs the question. If all an 'editor' aims at is an exact reprint, then obviously he will choose one early edition, on whatever grounds he considers relevant, and reproduce it as it stands. But McKerrow does emend his copy-text where necessary. It is symptomatic that he did not distinguish between a critical edition and a reprint.

[10] Without the italicized phrase the statement would appear much more plausible (though I should still regard it as fallacious, and so would McKerrow himself have done later on) but it would not justify the procedure adopted.

[11] This may, at any rate, be put

forward as a general proposition, leaving possible exceptions to be considered later (pp. 51 ff.).

[12] Again he speaks of a 'reprint' where he evidently had in mind a critical edition on conservative lines.

[13] Boas's text is in fact modernized, so that my theory of copy-text does not strictly apply, but since he definitely accepts the B-text as his authority, the principle is the same.

[14] Or consider the following readings: 1604, 1609 'Consissylogismes', 1611 'subtle sylogismes', 1616 'subtle Sillogisms'. Here 'subtile', an irresponsible guess by the printer of 1611 for a word he did not understand, was taken over in 1616. The correct reading is, of course, 'concise syllogisms'. Boas's refusal to take account of the copy used in 1616 led him here and elsewhere to perpetuate some of its manifest errors. In this particular instance he appears to have been unaware of the reading of 1611.

[15] At another point two lines appear in an unnatural order in the manuscript. The genetic relation of the texts proves the inversion to be an error. But of this relation Simpson seems to have been ignorant. He was again content to rely on the copy-text.

[16] The proviso is inserted to meet the case of the so-called 'bad quartos' of Shakespearian and other Elizabethan plays and of the whole class of 'reported' texts, whose testimony can in general be neglected.

[17] That is, certainly not in the text, and probably not in the general apparatus: they may appropriately form the subject of an appendix.

[18] This is the course I recommended in the Prolegomena to *The Editorial Problem in Shakespeare* (p. xxix), adding that it 'at least saves the trouble of tossing a coin'. What I actually wrote in 1942 was that in such circumstances an editor 'will naturally retain the reading of the copy-text, this being the text which he has already decided is *prima facie* the more correct'. This implies that correctness in respect of substantive readings is one of the criteria in the choice of the copy-text; and indeed I followed McKerrow in laying it down that an editor should select as copy-text the one that 'appears likely to have departed least in wording, spelling, and punctuation from the author's manuscript'. There is a good deal in my Prolegomena that I should now express differently, and on this particular point I have definitely changed my opinion. I should now say that the choice of the copy-text depends solely on its formal features (accidentals) and that fidelity as regards substantive readings is irrelevant—though fortunately in nine cases out of ten the choice will be the same whichever rule we adopt.

[19] I mean substantive variation, such as occurs in all but the most faithful reprints.

[20] Simpson's procedure in taking the 1616 folio as copy-text in the case of most of the masques included, although he admits that in their case Jonson cannot be supposed to have supervised the printing, is much more questionable.

[21] Some variation is certainly due to error on the part of the folio printer, and this it is of course the business of an editor to detect and correct so far as he is able.

Bibliography and the Novelistic Fallacy

Bruce Harkness

It is a truth universally acknowledged, that a critic intent upon analysis and interpretation, must be in want of a good text.[1] It is also universally acknowledged that we live in an age of criticism, indeed of "new criticism"—which means that we as critics are dedicated to a very close reading of the text. Sometimes, it is true, that critical principle leads to abuses. The symbol-hunting, the ambiguity-spinning become wonders to behold. As one objector has put it, "nose to nose, the critic confronts writer and, astonished, discovers himself."[2] Nonetheless, the principle of close reading is held central by us all. Immediately that one contemplates novel criticism, however, an oddity appears: the last thing we find in a discussion by a new critic is some analysis of the actual text.

The modern critic is apt to be entirely indifferent to the textual problems of a novel. He is all too prone to examine rigorously a faulty text. As Gordon Ray and others have pointed out, even the Great Cham of British Criticism errs in this respect. F. R. Leavis defends the early Henry James in *The Great Tradition:* "Let me insist, then, at once, . . . that his [James's] 'first attempt at a novel,' *Roderick Hudson* (1874), in spite of its reputation, is a very distinguished book that deserves permanent currency—much more so than many novels passing as classics." Professor Ray adds that "Mr. Leavis goes on to quote three long paragraphs to illustrate the novel's 'sustained maturity of theme and treatment. . . .' These remarks are amply warranted by the passage that Mr. Leavis cites. But unhappily he has quoted, not the text of the first edition of 1877 [while carefully dating it from the time of composition to make it appear all the more precocious], which is simple enough, but that of the New York edition of 1907, revised in James's intricate later manner. This leaves him," concludes Leavis's critic, "in the position of having proved at length what nobody would think of denying, that James's writing at the age of sixty-four has all the characteristics of maturity."[3]

Unhappily, few of us can afford to laugh at the poor new critic. We all know the truth that we must have a good text, but most of us do not act upon it. A commonplace? Yes, and unfortunately, I have only that commonplace to urge; but I claim good company. Jane Austen, with whom I started, recognized that *Pride and Prejudice* had no profoundly new meaning. She ironically developed upon commonplaces: don't act on first impressions; don't interfere in your best friend's love affair; don't ignore your younger daughters. My point is that, ironically, everyone ignores the bibliographical study of the novel. People who would consider it terribly bad form to slight the textual study of a play or poem—or even doggerel—commit bibliographical nonsense when handed a novel. It seems that the novel just doesn't count. A key error in many studies of the novel is simply this, that the novel is unconsciously considered a different order of thing from poetry—a poem's text must be approached seriously. I shall illustrate by mentioning the sins of editors, reprinters, publishers, scholars, and, alas, bibliographers. Then, after discussing a few of the many reasons for this bibliographical heresy, I shall turn to my main illustration of the need for textual bibliography, *The Great Gatsby*.

II

A list of representative errors, by no means exhaustive, by sound men whom I admire in all other respects will make clear how faulty the texts of novels are, and how little we care. A good editor has put *The Nigger of the "Narcissus"* in *The Portable Conrad,* an excellent volume the introductions to which contain some of the best Conrad criticism. But what, one may wonder, is the copy-text for *The Nigger?* A search through the book discloses two references, the less vague of which reads as follows: "It is from the editions published and copyrighted by the latter [Doubleday and Company] that the texts reproduced in this volume have been drawn" (p. 758).

After a spot of searching the reader can discover for himself that the copy-text for *The Nigger of the "Narcissus"* is not the collected English edition, which as is well known was Conrad's major concern. The copy-text was an early American publication, which Conrad habitually did not supervize. The new critic immediately asks, does it make any difference?

The collected English edition was, as one might suspect with an author who was constantly revising, changed in many ways. This final version cuts down Conrad's intrusive "philosophizing," and corrects Donkin's cockney accent, among other shifts.[4] I yield to no man in my admiration for Conrad, but if he has a fault, it lies in that adjectival "philosophy" which is admired by some, charitably overlooked by others, and condemned by a few as pipe-sucking old seadog-talk. Surely the following, from the early part of Chapter Four, is inappropriate in the mouth of the sailor-narrator: "Through the perfect wisdom of its grace [the sea's] they [seamen] are not permitted to meditate at ease upon the complicated and acrid savour of existence, lest they should remember and, perchance, regret the reward of a cup of inspiring bitterness, tasted so often, and so often withdrawn before their stiffening but reluctant lips. They must without pause justify their life. . . ." Most of this passage, and much similar sententiousness, were cut by Conrad from the collected English text; but they all stand in *The Portable Conrad.*

As for the class of books known loosely as "reprints," I suppose that no one expects a good text for twenty-five or thirty-five cents. These books I am not concerned with, but the more serious paperbacks, obviously intended for use in colleges, are sometimes faulty. For example, Rinehart Editions' copy of *Pride and Prejudice* reprints Chapman's excellent text—but suppresses the indication of three volume construction by numbering the chapters serially throughout.[5] Though three volumes are mentioned in the introduction, this misprinting of such a tightly constructed novel can only be regretted, for the effect on the college reader must be odd.

What of the publisher of more expensive novels? It can easily be seen that errors are not limited to the paperback field. Consider, for example, the one-volume Scribner edition of James's *The Wings of the Dove,* dated 1945 or 1946. Here is no scrimping for paperback costs, but the book is not what one would think. It is not a reprint of the famous New York edition; it is another, unacknowledged impression of the 1902 first American edition, dressed up with a new-set New York preface—an odd procedure the reason for which is not apparent. The publisher nowhere tells the reader that this is like some wines—an old text with a new preface. Yet one line of print would have made the matter clear. It is only by his own efforts of collation of the preface and the text itself that the reader knows where he is.[6]

To turn to the errors of scholarship, take F. O. Matthiessen's lengthy appreciation of Melville's phrase "soiled fish of the sea" in

White Jacket. Melville's narrator says of himself, after he had fallen into the sea, "I wondered whether I was yet dead or still dying. But of a sudden some fashionless form brushed my side—some inert, soiled fish of the sea; the thrill of being alive again tingled. . . ." This section Matthiessen acclaims as being imagery of the "sort that was to become peculiarly Melville's . . . hardly anyone but Melville could have created the shudder that results from calling this frightening vagueness some '*soiled* fish of the sea'!" Then follows a discussion of the metaphysical conceit and its moral and psychological implications.

As has been pointed out, the genius in this shuddering case of imagery is not Melville, who wrote *coiled* fish, not *soiled* fish. "Coiled fish" stands in the first editions of *White Jacket*, and to an unknown Constable printer should go the laurels for soiling the page with a typographical error.[7]

Matthiessen's error does not concern me now, but it does concern me that the scholar who first caught the mistake has a strange but perhaps understandable attitude toward textual matters. Recognizing that such an error "in the proper context" might have promulgated a "false conception," the scholar feels that the slip does not actually matter in Melville's case. Furthermore, he feels that Matthiessen's position is essentially sound—he was merely the victim of "an unlucky error." While sympathizing with common sense and professional etiquette, one may still wonder, however, how many such slips in illustration are allowable. Could the critic, if challenged, produce as many sound illustrations as one would like? Does not Matthiessen, in his categorizing of conceits, virtually admit that this particular kind is rare in *White Jacket*?

When we look at the texts of novels from the other way, how many good editions of novelists do we have? How do they compare with the poets? We know a good bit about the bibliographies of Scott, Trollope, Meredith, but those of Dickens, Thackeray, Conrad, Hawthorne, and many more are completely out of date.[8] How many collected editions can be put on the same shelf with Chapman's 1923 Jane Austen? "We have virtually no edited texts of Victorian novelists," says Mrs. Tillotson in the introduction of *Novels of the Eighteen-Forties* (1954). How slowly we move, if at all.

Take Hardy for example. In 1946 Carl Weber said that "many scholars have apparently made no attempt to gain access to Hardy's definitive texts." In March, 1957, a scholar can complain that "As late as November 1956, sixty full years after the publication of the book, the only edition of *Jude* printed in the United States took no account of either of the two revisions which Hardy gave the novel. . . . The New Harper's Modern Classics edition . . . [however] is *almost* identical with that of the definitive 1912 'Wessex Edition.' "[9] One is hardly surprised that Professor Weber is the editor.

Sixty years is a long time, but American literatue is no better off. *Moby-Dick,* our greatest novel, presents no problem of copy-text. Yet more than 100 years went by after publication before we had what a recent scholar called the "first serious reprint," by Hendricks House. Before that, the careful reader did not even know, for example, the punctuation of the famous "Know ye, now, Bulkington?" passage. But how good is this reprint? The same scholar—not the editor—asks us to consider it a definitive edition. His reasons? It contains only 108 compositor's errors and twenty silent emendations.[10] Would anyone make such a claim for a volume of poems?

So much for editors, publishers, scholars. The sins of the bibliographer are mainly those of omission. For well-known reasons he tends to slight 19th- and 20th-century books in general, and in consequence most novels.[11]

The critic therefore needs convincing that novels should be approached bibliographically. The critic appreciates the sullied-solid-sallied argument about Shakespeare, but not that of 108 typos for *Moby-Dick.* A false word in a sonnet may change a fifth of its meaning; the punctuation at the end of the "Ode on a Grecian Urn" can be considered crucial to the meaning of the whole poem; but who, the critic argues from bulk, can stand the prospect of collating 700 pages of Dickens to find a few dozen misplaced commas? Like the "soiled fish" reading of *White Jacket,* a few mistakes seriously damage neither novel nor criticism. They are swallowed up in the vast bulk of the novel, which by and large (and excepting a few well-known oddities such as *Tender is the Night* in which case one must be sure which text one is attacking) is decently printed and generally trustworthy. The critic feels that a mistake here or there in the text is immaterial. "It doesn't *really* alter my interpretation," is the standard phrase.

This attitude has long since been defeated by bibliographers for all genres except the novel. One wonders indeed, if the critic would be willing to make his plea more logical. Could not the attitude be extended to some formula for trustworthiness versus error? It ought not to be difficult to arrive at a proportion expressing the number of errors per page, exceeding which a novel could be condemned as poorly printed.

Amid bad reasoning, there is some truth to the critic's defence against bibliography. The argument can be shifted from the ground of a novel's size and a reader's energy to the aesthetic nature of the novel. The critic is certainly right in maintaining that novels are more loosely constructed, even the best of them, than poems or short stories. The effects of a novel are built through countless small touches, and the loss of one or two—whether by error in text or inattention in reading—is immaterial. Putting aside the counter claim that this truth is damaging to the critical and crucial premise of close reading, surely all is a matter of degree. And what is more, the theory applies mainly to character portrayal. If we fail to recognize Collins as a fawning ass on one page, we will certainly see him aright on another.

That much must be granted the critic. In other concerns, however, the novel may not be repetitive. To give just one illustration: F. Scott Fitzgerald's *Last Tycoon* as published in unfinished form contains a boy whom the reader should compare to the "villain" of the piece, Brady (or Bradogue as he was called in an earlier draft). In Fitzgerald's directions to himself left in his MSS, he says "Dan [the boy] bears, in some form of speech, a faint resemblance to Bradogue. This must be subtly done and not look too much like a parable or moral lesson, still the impression must be conveyed, but be careful to convey it *once* and not rub it in. If the reader misses it, let it go—don't repeat."[12]

My last and painful reason why virtually no one is concerned with the texts of novels is this: most bibliographers are also university teachers and many of them suffer from schizophrenia. I do not refer to that familiar disease which makes us scholars by day and diaper washers by night, but that split in the man between Graduate Seminar number 520 in Bibliography and Freshman "Intro. to Fic.," 109. How many of us make bibliographical truths part of our daily lives or attempt to inspire our graduate students so to do? In this respect many bibliographers are like socialists and Christians: walking arguments for the weakness of the cause.

Let me give one or two illustrations from experience. Not very long ago I sat in a staff meeting while we worried over a sentence of Conrad's introduction to *Victory* in the Modern Library edition. The sentence contained the odd phrase "adaptable cloth," used about mankind. It made no sense until it was finally pointed out that "adap-table" was divided at the end of the line in both American collected edition and reprint—a domestically minded compositor was talking about a table cloth, while Conrad was saying that Man is "wonderfully adaptable both by his power of endurance and in his capacity for detachment."

And our silly discussion had gone on despite long teaching, and one's natural suspicion of the cheaper reprints that perforce must be used in college classes.

More seriously, consider Dickens' *Great Expectations,* taught to freshmen at many universities, by staffs composed of men nearly all of whom have been required to "take" bibliography. Yet how many of these teachers have turned to the facts of serial publication to explain the figure of Orlick, extremely puzzling by critical standards alone? One immediately sees that Orlick's attack on Mrs. Joe, which ultimately causes her death, is used by Dickens to pep up a three instalment sequence the main purpose of which is simply to let Pip age. This sequence would have been too dull, too insistent on domestic scenes round the hearth while Pip gradually withdraws from Joe, were it not for the Orlick subplot.[13] The novel apparently had to have thirty-six weekly units, and Dickens therefore could not simply skip this period of Pip's life. The figure of Orlick may not be critically acceptable, but he is at least understandable when one views him in the light of publishing history.

I am also indicting myself for not understanding this point; for it was not many months ago that I looked up the weekly issues of *All the Year Round* and now have far more detail than, as the saying goes, "the short space of this article will permit the discussion of." I was derelict in my duty partly because life is short and bibliography is long, but also partly because I unconsciously resented the editor of my paperback *Great Expectations* whose job I was having to do.

For I am more familiar with the schizophrenia than most people, though mine takes a different form. With critics I am apt to claim to be a bibliographer; among bibliographers, I proclaim myself a critic.

The critic, one must recognize, can argue on aesthetic grounds against working on the texts of novels. He can produce the *tu quoque* argument. And he can say that the bibliographer neglects *what* he is working on. Of 244 articles on textual bibliography in the *Studies in Bibliography* list for 1954, only three were related to novels.[14] "What has the bibliographer been doing?" asks the new critic.

It may be that under the aspect of eternity George Sandys' *Ovid* is more important than Conrad's *Nostromo* or Melville's *Moby-Dick,* but it would be hard to convince the novel critic of that.

III

For these reasons I have chosen F. Scott Fitzgerald's *The Great Gatsby* as my main illustration. It brings out nearly all my points: inconsistent editing, an unknown or unidentified text, a publisher who is good but vague, important errors in an important book, schizophrenia in the bibliographer-teacher. Not only is *Gatsby* a fine novel, but it is taught so often because it contains many of the basic themes of American literature: West versus East; the search for value; the American dream; crime and society; and in young Jim Gatz's "General Resolves," it even reaches back to Ben Franklin and Poor Richard.

How many know, however, what they have been teaching?

The Great Gatsby exists in print in three main versions: the first edition, beginning in April, 1925; a new edition in the volume with *The Last Tycoon* and certain stories, beginning in 1941; and a sub-edition of the latter text in the Modern Standard Authors series (*Three Novels)* together with *Tender is the Night* and *The Last Tycoon*, beginning in 1953.[15] Though *Gatsby* in the *Three Novels* version is another impression of *The Last Tycoon* plates I call it a sub-edition because *Gatsby's* position is different, coming first in the volume, and there are many changes in the text.[16]

So far as I know, the only available information about the text of *Gatsby* is buried in the notes to Arthur Mizener's *The Far Side of Paradise*. Mizener says that Fitzgerald found a misprint in the first edition: the future Nick Carraway speaks of at the end of the novel should be "orgiastic," not "orgastic".[17]

> It was one of the few proof errors in the book [adds Mizener], perhaps because Scribner's worked harder over *Gatsby* than over Fitzgerald's earlier books, perhaps because [Ring] Lardner read the final proofs. The only other proof error Fitzgerald found was the reading of "eternal" for "external" on p. 58 [of the first edition]. . . . Edmund Wilson's reprint in his edition of *The Last Tycoon* corrects all it could without access to Fitzgerald's personally corrected copy.[18]

Let us couple these comments with Matthew Bruccoli's interesting article on Fitzgerald's *This Side of Paradise*. Bruccoli is surprised that thirty-one errors are corrected in later impressions of the novel. He concludes that "the first printing was an inexcusably sloppy job," although Fitzgerald was himself in part responsible for the difficulty. We might infer two things, therefore: far fewer errors in *Gatsby's* first edition, and a correction of the word "eternal," in *The Last Tycoon*.

Not so. The correction to "external" is not made in the second impression of the first edition, nor in any impression of *Last Tycoon* (202.2, TN 38.2). Though there are only four changes from the first to second impression of the first edition, there are no less than twenty-seven changes between *First* and *Last Tycoon.* Between *First* and the 1953 *Three Novels,* there are more than 125 changes. Of these changes about fifty are quite meaningless. They change "to-morrow" with a hyphen to "tomorrow," for example. Or they change "Beale Street Blues" to *Beale Street Blues.* This class of change will not be commented upon nor included in statistics, except to add that the publisher was not at all consistent in making such alterations.[19]

There are, in other words, 75 changes of moment between the first edition and *Three Novels*—forty-four more than in *This Side of Paradise.* Many of them are more important. Of the changes the August, 1925, first edition brought, the most important was the substitution of the word "echolalia" for "chatter" in the phrase "the chatter of the garden" (*First* 60 line 16).[20]

But we must remember that *Last Tycoon* and *Three Novels* are both posthumous, and that of the twenty-seven changes from *First* to LT, twelve are clearly errors, seven are dubious improvements, and only eight are clearly better readings. Of them all, the word "orgiastic," apparently, alone has the author's authority. What's more, the sub-edition *Three Novels* retains all but two of these bad changes. An example of an error begun in LT and continued in TN occurs on page 209.6 of *First* (296.8 of LT and 132.8 of TN). The sentence of Nick's, "It just shows you." is dropped from the text, thereby making the punctuation wrong and leading the reader to confuse speakers.

Between *First* and *Three Novels* the changes are of several kinds. In addition to the fifty or so "meaningless" changes, there are (a) fifteen changes of spelling, including six that change the meaning of a word and others that affect dialect; (b) seventeen changes in punctuation, including quotation marks, paragraph indication, and so on; (c) six incorrect omissions of a word or sentence or other details; (d) six proper deletions of a word or more; (e) thirty-one substantive changes—the substitution of a word or the addition of a phrase or sentence. For instance, Gatsby is transferred from the Sixteenth to the Seventh Infantry during the war. (See *First* 57.17, LT 201.12, TN 37.12.)

For when we turn to *Three Novels* we must move out of the camp of strict bibliography into the field of its important ally, publishing history. Fitzgerald's own copy of the first impression, with pencilled notes in the margins, is now located at the Princeton University Library and was used to make the sub-edition.

Of the seventy-five changes between *First* and TN, thirty-eight are with Fitzgerald's sanction and thirty-seven are without. Most of the thirty-seven changes not recommended by Fitzgerald are "corrections" made by a publisher's staff editor or by Malcolm Cowley, who supervized the sub-edition. However, some of this group are clearly errors, many of them having crept into the text by way of the *Last Tycoon* version. The noteworthy thing is that no reader knows the authority for *any* of the changes. The sub-edition itself does not even announce that it takes into account Fitzgerald's marginal comments—which, one would have supposed, would have been good business as well as good scholarship.

Furthermore, some of the thirty-eight "sanctioned" changes were only queried by Fitzgerald: no actual rewording was directed. An example is the phrase "lyric again in." Fitzgerald questioned "again" and the editor dropped it. But in five instances of Fitzgerald's questioning a word, no change was made—as, for example, Fitzgerald was unhappy to note that he had used the word "turbulent" twice in the first chapter.[21] There is also one instance in which Fitzgerald expressly asked for a change that was not made. At *First,* 50.1, Fitzgerald corrected "an amusement park" to "amusement parks," but the later version does not record the request (TN 32.32).

On the whole, one can say this, therefore: that about sixty of the changes from *First* to *Three Novels* are proper. That is, they either have the author's authority or are stylistic or grammatical improvements or are immaterial. I speak just now as a devil's advocate—a critic with a jaundiced eye toward bibliography. He would call the deletion of a comma from a short compound sentence "immaterial," though it was not done by the author.[22] I am trying, in other words, to make the text sound as good as I can. Problems arise, however, from the fact that awkward readings sometimes come from purely typographical errors, sometimes from editor's decision, and sometimes from Fitzgerald's own notes. Everyone would accept such changes as "an Adam study" for "an Adam's study," (*First* 110.26, LT 233.30, TN 69.30); but by the same token few critics will be pleased by a Fitzgerald marginal correction reading "common knowledge to the turgid sub or suppressed journalism of 1902," instead of "common property of the turgid journalism of 1902" *First* 120.11, TN 76.5).

We are left then with fifteen or sixteen errors begun or continued in *Three Novels,* errors which I trust even the newest of new critics would accept as having some degree of importance. That degree of course varies. The dedication "Once again, to Zelda," is left off, for example. Dialectical words are falsely made standard English, or half-doctored-up, as in this sentence where the word in *First* was "appendicitus": "You'd of thought she had my appendicitis out" (*First* 37.4,

LT 188.37, TN 24.37). Sentences start without a capital[23] or end without a period[24] or are dropped altogether.[25] Quotation marks appear or disappear[26] and awkward readings come from nowhere. To illustrate that last: on page 149.10 of *First* Nick says that "the giant eyes of Doctor T. J. Eckleburg kept their vigil, but I perceived, after a moment, that other eyes were regarding us with peculiar intensity from less than twenty feet away." The eyes are Myrtle Wilson's but in *Three Novels* 95.1 (and LT 259.1) the sentence is confused when "the" is added without any reference and "from" and "with peculiar intensity" are dropped: "the giant eyes of Doctor T. J. Eckleburg kept their vigil, but I perceived, after a moment that *the* other eyes were regarding us less than twenty feet away" (italics added). Another dubious change is this: a joking slip or drunken mistake by Daisy is corrected—"Biloxi, Tennessee" becomes academically placed in its proper governmental locality.[27] One hardly needs to add that none of these changes have Fitzgerald's sanction.

The biggest errors, critically speaking, are ones that also occur in *Last Tycoon.* The principle of order in *The Great Gatsby* is a simple one: Nick Carraway, the narrator, tells his story wildly out of chronological order, but *in* the order that he learned it—with one exception.[28] The first half of the book is concerned with the development of the outsiders' illusions about Jay Gatsby—he is "nephew to Von Hindenburg," and so on (TN 47). The second half is a penetration in depth of Gatsby's illusion itself. The shift in the theme of the book is marked by the one major sequence which Nick gives the reader out of the order in which he himself learned it. I refer to the Dan Cody episode from Gatsby's early days.[29]

Now the most important structural unit in the book below the chapter is the intra-chapter break signified by a white space left on the page.[30] In *Last Tycoon* and *Three Novels* four of these important indications of structure are suppressed.[31] Oddly enough, it is the one following the Dan Cody story that is the first one missing. The detail that divides the book into its two structural elements is botched.

In the *Three Novels* version of *Gatsby,* then, we have a book quite well printed—surprisingly so when we look at the galley proofs. They are filled with changes—with page after page added in long hand, with whole galleys deleted or rearranged. (I would estimate that one-fifth of the book was written after the galley stage.) And we have a book that tries to take into account the author's latest stylistic revisions. Unfortunately, it is also a book that has far too many errors.

Perhaps this is the place to mention the third Scribner edition of

Gatsby, the paperback Student's Edition, which uses TN as copy text. Have matters been improved? Some have, but more errors have been added. There are twelve changes from TN to SE: it makes two distinct improvements, including the replacement of the dedication; but it adds three places in which intra-chapter breaks are suppressed.[32] The other changes are "immaterial" typographical errors such as "turned to be," instead of "turned to me" (SE 71.17 and TN 54.20) and "*police*," instead of "pol*ice*" (SE 27.27 and TN 22.19).

I hope it is clear, then, that *Three Novels* represents the best present text of *Gatsby*. No doubt it and the Student's Edition will be the ones most used in colleges for some time. It should also be clear that in *Three Novels*, we have this kind of book:

1. A book which nowhere gives the reader the authority for seventy-five changes, all of them posthumously printed.
2. One which fails to make use of all of Fitzgerald's corrections.
3. One which contains thirty-seven changes which Fitzgerald did not authorize—some of which are of most dubious value.
4. A book which contains at least fifteen quite bad readings, one of which is of the highest structural importance.

So, armed with this mixed blessing, or with the worse one of *Last Tycoon*, or worst of all, with a reprint by another publisher which has none of Fitzgerald's corrections and additions, many students unwittingly face the next semester with their prairie squints. Only a nonexistent, eclectic text, combining the best of the August, 1925 first edition and the *Three Novels* text of *The Great Gatsby* would be proper.[33]

Could we not as critics pay more attention to Bibliography, and we as Bibliographers to criticism? Can not we somehow insist that editing actually be done—instead of the practice of putting a fancy introduction on a poor text? Can not we have sound texts reproduced and publisher's history stated by the editor? Can not we know *what it is* we have in our hands? For it is simply a fallacy that the novel does not count.

NOTES

[1] This article represents an expanded form of a paper read at the Bibliography Section of the 1957 Modern Language Association meetings.

[2] Marvin Mudrick, "Conrad and

the Terms of Modern Criticism," *Hudson Review*, VI (1954), 421.

[3] Gordon N. Ray, "The Importance of Original Editions," in *Nineteenth-Century English Books*, by Gordon N. Ray, Carl Weber, and John Carter (1952), p. 22. See also "Henry James Reprints," *TLS*, Feb. 5, 1949, p. 96.

[4] C. S. Evans of the editorial department of Heinemann wrote Conrad on 2 Sept., 1920, about Donkin's inconsistent dialect: "I have queried spelling of 'Hymposed,'" and so on. (See *Life and Letters* [London: Heinemann, 1927], II, 247-248, for the exchange with Evans.) J. D. Gordon in *Joseph Conrad: The Making of a Novelist* (1940), p. 139, et passim, discusses many of the revisions of the text.

It might be possible to defend the use of an early text for *The Nigger*, but no reason is given in *The Portable Conrad*.

[5] Though I cannot pretend to have examined them all, I know of only one independently produced paperback novel with good textual apparatus. This is Rinehart Editions' *Lord Jim*, which contains a collation of the four main texts. Riverside's *Pride and Prejudice* has a good text, but again Chapman's edition lies behind it. There must be, I am sure, many more good texts beside *Lord Jim* in the higher class of paperbacks, and even in the cheaper ones. But what publishers draw them to our attention, and what publisher doesn't (apparently) feel that a properly edited paperback novel will frighten away the common reader by its appearance?

[6] Furthermore, it would be difficult to defend the choice of first-edition text, as one might for *The Nigger of the "Narcissus,"* or *Roderick Hudson*, since James was writing in his intricate manner by 1902.

[7] See J. W. Nichol, "Melville's 'Soiled Fish of the Sea,'" *AL*, XXI (1949), 338-339.

[8] See John Carter, *op. cit.*, p. 53 et passim; reasons for the lack of bibliographical study are also discussed.

[9] Robert C. Slack, "The Text of Hardy's *Jude the Obscure*," *N-CF*, XI (1957), 275. Italics added.

[10] William T. Hutchinson, "A Definitive Edition of *Moby-Dick*," *AL*, XXV (1954), 472-478.

[11] See Fredson Bowers, *Principles of Bibliographical Description* (1949), p. 356 ff, for a discussion of these reasons on the part of the bibliographer. One should admit, furthermore, that the non-professional bibliographers, the scholarly readers and editors, may have reasons which are indefensible, but are nevertheless *reasons*. I daresay one would be shocked to know how many trained men feel today that novels aren't really "literature"; or that modern printing is either perfect or too complicated ever to be fathomed.

[12] F. Scott Fitzgerald, *The Last Tycoon*, in *Three Novels* (1953), p. 157. Italics added.

[13] See instalments 8, 9, 10 (Chapters XII and XIII, XIV and XV, XVI and XVII). The Pip-Magwitch strand is early developed as much as can be without giving away the plot. Pip loves Estella early, but is apprenticed back to Joe by the beginning of chapter XIII. The glad tidings of Great Expectations don't come until instalment 11. Without Orlick, more than four chapters would have to deal with domestic bliss and withdrawal. Orlick is introduced and attacks Mrs. Joe, all in the ninth instalment.

At the other end of the book a similar situation obtains. The reconciliation with Miss Havisham comes in instalment 30; that with Joe is brief enough not to be needed until after instalment 33. Estella is not brought in until the end. Instalments 31, 32, 33 are needed, therefore, to make the 36 weekly unit structure complete—but they cannot all contain the secret plan to get Magwitch down stream. The reader cannot go boating with Pip, Startop, and Herbert for two entire instalments before the disastrous attempt to get Magwitch out of the country; so instalment 32 is devoted to Orlick's attempt to kill Pip.

In other words, serial publication took Dickens to melodrama, but not quite in the crude form that one's unsubstantiated suspicions would indicate.

[14] There are, it is encouraging to note, signs of change. In the last year or two, one has the feeling that perhaps six or eight articles appeared on the texts of 19th- or 20th-century novels. For example, see Linton Massey, "Notes on the Unrevised Galleys of Faulkner's *Sanctuary*," *SB*, VIII (1956), 195-208 or Matthew J. Bruccoli, "A Collation of F. Scott Fitzgerald's *This Side of Paradise*," *SB*, IX (1957), 263-265. The latter article is especially interesting in pointing out changes between impressions of editions.

Having mentioned Dickens, I must add that Mrs. Tillotson has followed up her remark (*op. cit.*) that we have no Victorian texts, and "no means, short of doing the work ourselves, of discovering how (and why) the original edition differed from the text we read." I refer of course to John Butt and Kathleen Tillotson, *Dickens at Work* (1957); on the importance of part publication, it deals mainly with novels other than *Great Expectations*. While it also illustrates how long it takes for a general appreciation of the importance of bibliographical facts to culminate in a specific study, the book makes my comments on Dickens, so to speak, unspeakable.

[15] The first edition has had three impressions: April, 1925, August, 1925, and August, 1942. I have collated three copies of the first impression, including Fitzgerald's personally corrected volume now located at Princeton. The August, 1942 impression I have not examined. I would like to record here my special thanks to Lawrence D. Stewart of Beverly Hills, California, for most kindly checking my collation against his copy of the rare second impression.

The second edition of *Gatsby* is that printed with *The Last Tycoon* and certain stories, as supervised by Edmund Wilson. It uses as copy-text the August, 1925 first edition. I have collated three impressions, 1941, 1945, 1948.

The sub-edition of *Gatsby*, as printed with *Tender is the Night* and *The Last Tycoon*, in the *Three Novels* volume, has been collated in three impressions, 1953, 1956, 1957.

The parent company, Scribner's, has permitted several reprints, which I have not examined thoroughly. There is also a recent (1957), third edition of *Gatsby*, by Scribner's, a paperback, called "Student's Edition."

I shall refer to these editions of *Gatsby* by the short but obvious forms of *First*, *Last Tycoon* or LT, *Three Novels* or TN, Student's Edition or SE. For convenience I shall give the line in a page reference by a simple decimal; as TN 31.30, for *Three Novels*, p. 31, line 30. [Matthew J. Bruccoli, "A Further Note on the First Printing of *The Great Gatsby*," *SB*, XVI (1963), 244, supplements this information. *Editor's note*.]

[16] My thanks are due to Princeton University Library for permitting me to examine both Fitzgerald's own copy of *Gatsby* and the surviving manuscripts. Doubtless I should add

that since my special concern is the printed texts, I did not rigorously collate the mass of MS, TS, and galleys.

I would like also to thank Wallace O. Meyer of Scribner's, Harold Ober, Edmund Wilson, Malcolm Cowley, and Dan C. Piper for their advice and for patiently answering my queries about the changes in the texts.

[17] The comment is a trifle misleading, because the reading "orgastic" stands in MS, galleys, and first edition. Perhaps this is another example of Fitzgerald's well-known weakness in matters of spelling, grammar, and so on; at any rate, it can hardly be called a "proof error."

[18] Arthur Mizener, *The Far Side of Paradise* (1951), p. 336, n. 22. Mizener points up the generally sad fate of Fitzgerald's texts by mentioning that the reprints of The Modern Library, New Directions, Bantam (first version), and Grosset and Dunlap all have the word "orgastic." One therefore assumes they reprint the first edition, though at least the Modern Library reprints the second impression. The later Bantam edition and *The Portable Fitzgerald* both use the faulty *Last Tycoon* as copy-text.

[19] See, for example, the word "today," in LT, p. 280 line 36 and TN, p. 116 line 36; but "to-day" (as in *First*, p. 184 lines 7 and 10) is kept three lines later—LT p. 281.1, TN p. 117.1. In addition to forty-two such changes, there are six more which are nearly as minor: the word "sombre" is changed to "somber"; "armistice" to "Armistice," as examples. All these, and the change in the spelling of a name (Wolfshiem to Wolfsheim) which was usually but not always wrong in the first edition, are not included in my statistics.

[20] See LT 203.4 and TN 39.4. The other changes in the August, 1925 *First* are as follows:

April, 1925 it's driver p. 165.16
August 1925 its driver
April some distance away p. 165.29
August some distance away.
April sick in tired p. 205. 9 & 10
August sickantired

All four are, presumably, authorial.

[21] See "lyric again in," *First* 62.17, LT 204.12. "lyric in," TN 40.12. Cf. "turbulent," *First* 20.17, LT 178.25, TN 14.25; "turbulence," *First* 7.28, LT 171.3, TN 7.3.

[22] See *First*, 35.21: Her eyebrows had been plucked and then drawn on again at a more rakish angle, but the efforts of nature. . . . LT 188.7 and TN 24.7 remove the comma.

[23] *First* 111.14 and LT 234.5 When I try . . . TN 70.6 when I try . . .

[24] *First* 115.25 generating on the air. So LT 236.33. TN 72.33 generating on the air.

[25] The sentence "It just shows you," mentioned above as an error begun in LT.

[26] *First* 141.6, LT. 253.38, TN 89.38. Tom Buchanan is speaking and by closing a paragraph with quote marks, LT and TN give the reader the momentary impression that the next sentence and paragraph beginning "Come outside . . ." is by someone else.

First 139.26, LT 253.7, TN 89.7 represent the obverse. "The bles-sed pre-cious . . . spoken by Daisy loses the quotation mark in LT and TN.

[27] See *First* 153.8, LT 261.14, TN 97.14. TN alone reads "Biloxi, Mississippi." I realize that the line can be interpreted in other ways, that for example, Fitzgerald wished an obviously fictional town. But I cannot agree that Fitzgerald was so ignorant of Southern geography as to put the city in the wrong state. I am all the more certain that Fitzgerald meant it as a joke because

there is other geographical word-play in the same scene, and it is only four pages earlier that Tom snorts that Gatsby must have been an Oxford man—"Oxford, New Mexico."

[28] The statement is not quite accurate: there are one or two other violations of this order, minor ones very late in the book. For example, the giving of the Michaelis's testimony, p. 124 of TN is apparently after the scene on pp. 119 ff.

[29] The scene was, in the manuscript, at the place where it is referred to in the chapter now numbered VIII, pp. 112 of TN. Fitzgerald then changed it to its present position, ending at TN 76, LT 241, *First* 121—Chapter VI.

[30] Since I have mentioned Conrad so often, it might not be amiss to add Conrad's name to the list of influences mentioned by Cowley in the introduction to *Three Novels.* (See Fitzgerald's introduction to the Modern Library *Gatsby* and *The Crack-Up* for his interest in Conrad.) The time scheme of *Gatsby* is, of course, Conradian, as well as the narrator. And there are quite a few passages that echo Conrad—the closing section on the old Dutch sailors' feelings in New York might be a twist on parts of "Heart of Darkness." "In the abortive sorrows and short-winded elations of men," p. 4 of TN's *Gatsby,* is just one of the verbal echoes of Conrad. More pertinently, the intra-chapter break was a device very much used by the older author. For a detailed examination of this relationship, see R. W. Stallman, "Conrad and *The Great Gatsby,*" *TCL,* I (1955), 5-12.

[31] See *First* 121.26, LT 240 foot, TN 76 foot; *First* 163.26, LT 267 foot, TN 103 foot; *First* 192.16, LT 285 foot, TN 121 foot; *First* 214.21, LT 299.21, TN 135.21. In all but the last of these the break in the page comes at the turn-over of the page and, unfortunately, no space was left for it.

[32] For the suppressed intra-chapter breaks, see TN 126.31 and SE 167.26; TN 132.24 and SE 175.19; TN 136.24 and SE 181.7. The other improvement is at TN 89.7 and SE 117.3, where SE returns to *First* to get the quotation marks of "The bles-sed . . ." as spoken by Daisy, correctly once more. SE 175.1 does not restore Nick's sentence "It just shows you." but it does "correct" the quotation marks that were wrong in the preceding sentence in TN 132.9.

[33] I should add that the collation of these three editions has of course not been reproduced in full here—and there are several places in the text that call for emendation though there are no changes between editions. For example, Tom brings the car to a dusty spot under Wilson's sign. (So in *First* 147 and TN 93.23 and SE 123.7). Should it be a dusty stop?

Internal Evidence and the Attribution of Elizabethan Plays

S. Schoenbaum

In the field of Elizabethan drama, attribution studies based on internal evidence—chiefly the evidence of style—command little respect these days, and present serious inconveniences.[1] They are associated with eccentricity, amateurism, and irresponsibility; with error, contradiction, and wild surmise; with Fleay and the heritage of Fleay. They have added to the burdens of the editor, who must determine which plays to include in his edition; the critic, who must trace the course of a dramatist's development; and the historian, who must evaluate previous scholarship on authenticity and attribution. G. E. Bentley is constrained to write:

> After working painfully through the attributions of an anonymous play like *The Revenger's Tragedy* to Webster and to Tourneur and to Middleton and to Marston, the disgusted historian is tempted to lay down this principle: Any play first published in a contemporary quarto with no author's name on the title page and continuing without definite ascription of authorship for twenty-five years or more should be treated as anonymous world without end Amen.[2]

The almost 1500 pages of volumes III to V of *The Jacobean and Caroline Stage* tell a melancholy story of the fate of a large number of attempted attributions. Yet such studies, which are a necessary part of our discipline, continue to appear regularly in the pages of journals and the appendices of monographs. But certainly they should be better than they are; the same follies are committed again and again. "The problem," Chambers shrewdly observed in his famous British Academy lecture on the disintegration of Shakespeare, "seems to me one which calls for exploration upon a general and disinterested method, rather than along the casual lines of advance opened up by the pursuit of an author for this or that suspected or anonymous play."[3] Few have followed this excellent advice in the thirty-five years since it was offered, and this essay may be regarded, at least in part, as an act of belated homage. In it I shall be concerned necessarily with past errors and illusions, but also, and more important, with first principles and particular tests, and with inherent difficulties and shortcomings of the method. This is broad coverage, perhaps rather too broad for a single paper; but there may be compensatory advantages to a wide-ranging discussion of a topic usually given narrow or perfunctory notice—when it is given notice at all—as a preface to specific authorship investigations.

I

Just half a century ago, in the Golden Age of Attribution Studies, Oliphant could survey the land and find it good. In his essay on "Problems of Authorship in Elizabethan Dramatic Literature," he cited the large number of plays of anonymous, uncertain, or disputed authorship that had survived, and he recommended, with the delicious casualness of a departed era, that "students with time and inclination for such pursuits" make "a selection from amongst the problems that await solution."[4] In the years following, the selection was duly made. Lawrence, Lloyd, Wells, and others urged the merits of their author-candidates; Sykes published the studies later assembled as the *Sidelights;* Oliphant himself turned to the Beaumont and Fletcher canon, *The Revenger's Tragedy,* and other plays. Meanwhile the disintegrators disintegrated Shakespeare.

These men knew and loved the old plays, and were fertile of ideas and intuitions. They ransacked scenes for parallel passages; they counted nouns, adjectives, and interjections, rhymes, end-stopped lines, and double and triple endings; they strained their ears to catch the elusive notes of the "indefinite music" permeating the verse.[5] Yet by 1932 Miss Byrne could remark, in the course of her devastating arraignment of Sykes, that "it is extraordinarily difficult to persuade most people to examine seriously the so-called 'stylistic' attributions of anonymous or acknowledged collaborate plays."[6] Her statement has lost none of its relevance. It is no easier—perhaps, indeed, it is more difficult—to persuade Bentley than it was to convince Chambers.

Why did Oliphant, Sykes, and the rest come to grief? After all, they were not, like Fleay, fantastics unwilling to support their theories with argument, prone to dizzying improvisations and changes of mind, possessed by demons of inaccuracy.[7] Their great failing is revealed inadvertently by Oliphant in the concluding paragraph of his essay of fifty years ago. "As to how the detection of the presence of unknown writers . . . is to be effected and their identity determined," Oliphant writes, "that is a matter which every investigator must settle for himself."[8] It is this astonishing indifference to method that is their fatal weakness, and the source of the anarchy still prevalent in attribution work. These enthusiasts set vigorously to work without troubling about the essential preliminaries. They established no basic principles of procedure. They made no attempt to define the nature of evidence. They applied the various tests indiscriminately. They often ignored relevant external information about the plays they scrutinized so minutely. They failed to grasp the significance of the bibliographical revolution taking place around them: they were indifferent to the fortunes of copy in the printing-house, they did not discuss compositors. Oliphant and his co-workers were essentially literary amateurs unable by training or temperament to subject their investigations to the tedious rigor of scholarly discipline. Their approach—subjective, intuitive, ardent—differs little from that of the impressionist critics with whom they were contemporaneous. But the canonical impressionists were mischievous in a way that the critics were not. For in rationalizing their intuitions and presenting them as evidence, they bequeathed a legacy of confusion and error. Little is to be gained by attempting—as R. H. Barker has recently tried to do—a belated resurrection of Oliphant's reputation, on grounds that the strictures of our most distinguished authorities merely reflect the vagaries of scholarly fashion.[9] The gesture in the direction of Oliphant's memory may have sentimental appeal, but the strictures themselves are not easily dismissed, and indeed Barker makes no effort to refute them. If a case is to be made for the legitimacy of employing internal evidence to determine authorship, it must be made with a full awareness of past failures and present limitations.

II

The limitations are considerable. The investigator's task, as I see it, is to isolate and describe the special character of a literary work of unknown or doubtful authorship, to show the extent to which a known writer's work partakes of that special character, and from this evidence to arrive at an appropriate conclusion. The enterprise is hazardous, for an author's individuality never exists as pure essence, but is subtly alloyed by many interrelated factors: literary conventions and traditions; personal, professional, social, religious influences. And of all writers the dramatist is most elusive, as he appears not in his own persona but in the manifold guises of the personages that are his imaginative creations. All plays, furthermore, are in a sense collaborations, shaped from conception to performance by the author's awareness of the resources of actors and theatre, the wishes of impresario or shareholders, and the tastes and capacities of the audience.

The investigator working with the Elizabethan drama faces additional difficulties. Far removed in time from his materials, he may be easily misled into fancying as original what a contemporary would have instantly recognized as imitation. His task is not eased by the fact that a great many plays of the period have perished, or by the related fact that plays generally were not held in very high literary esteem, expecially before the appearance of the great Jonson Folio in 1616. Artistic individuality is scarcely to be expected in artifacts manufactured for a commercial market. That individuality nevertheless blossomed—that the age produced not only Shakespeare, Marlowe, and Jonson, but also Chapman, Marston, Webster, and a number of other distinctive voices—is a remarkable assertion of the creative principle. But it should not blind the investigator to the parlous conditions of his labor: conditions that favor not the establishment of facts but the proliferation of conjecture.

I cannot then accept Arthur Sherbo's "basic premise" that, in questions of authorship, "internal evidence deals with essentials while external evidence deals with accidentals," and that "short of an unequivocal acknowledgment by the author himself, the value of internal evidence outweighs any other."[10] External evidence can and often does provide incontestable proof; internal evidence can only support hypotheses or corroborate external evidence. So far as the Elizabethan drama is concerned, the justification for the use of internal evidence in determining a canon lies primarily in the inadequacy of the available outward evidence. Our primary sources of information—the title-pages of plays, the Stationers' Register, the Office Book of the Master of the Revels, the seventeenth-century catalogues—are pitifully incomplete, misleading, or inaccurate. Famous "standard" attributions at times rest on remarkably fragile foundations. No record, for example, survives from Kyd's lifetime to connect his name with *The Spanish Tragedy*. The only external evidence that he wrote the age's most sensationally popular melodrama is Heywood's statement in his *Apology for Actors,* which appeared eighteen years after Kyd's death.

Yet *The Spanish Tragedy* is linked inseparably with Kyd's name. Justly so. For we recognize, with the play's most recent editor, that it stands in "a peculiarly intimate relation" to the closet drama *Cornelia,* translated by Kyd from Garnier, and that "the only reasonable way of accounting for the relationship is to say that the same man was responsible for both works."[11] In this case, as in others, the external evidence—by itself hardly overwhelming—is buttressed by the evidence of style. The responsible historian is of course aware of the gaps and contradictions in the records with which he works. Thus it is that Bentley cannot subscribe to his own tempting formula, already quoted, of everlasting anonymity after twenty-five years. Such a principle, he is quick to note, would not only deprive Marlowe of *Tamburlaine* but Beaumont and Fletcher of *The Woman Hater;* it would thrust *The Thracian Wonder* upon Webster and *The London Prodigal* upon Shakespeare.

Internal evidence used in fruitful conjunction with the meagre external facts stirs no controversy but provides, rather, welcome illumination of the obscurity in which we must too often work. But it is another matter to suggest authors where the external evidence is pathetically insufficient, as in the case of *The Bloody Banquet,* with its 1639 title-page ascription to "T.D."; or non-existent, as with *The Fairy Knight, Dick of Devonshire,* and many other plays. It is risky to attempt the allocation of scenes in collaborations, even when all the partners are known—Middleton, Rowley, and Massinger's *The Old Law,* for example, which has come down in a wretched text; riskier still when not all the collaborators are specified, as in the Beaumont and Fletcher corpus, amply dissected by the disintegrators. Fraught with even greater perils are the investigator's attempts to transform into collaborations plays for which the outward evidence points to single jurisdiction: Eberle finding Dekker in *The Family of Love,*[12] Lucas and others seeing Webster in *Anything for a Quiet Life.*[13] But most dangerous of all is the attempt to overthrow, by the weight of internal evidence alone, an attribution for which there is external support; and here we have the famous case of *The Revenger's Tragedy,* to which I shall return at the conclusion of this essay.[13a]

III

The investigator who works without external evidence to bolster his conclusions assumes the full burden of proof; he must anticipate that his assumptions, methods, and claims will undergo the severest scrutiny. It is a measure of the amateurism of Sykes and Lawrence and the rest that they did so little to fortify themselves against this inspection. But even today, when there is less excuse, attribution studies frequently offer little or nothing in the way of description or defense of the methods employed. In some cases apparently no thought *has* been given to methodology, or so one would conclude from the cavalier violations of ordinary principles of logical procedure. Recently one investigator has even, by implication, expressed impatience with the rigors of methodological discipline; but the vague standard of doing "the best one can," offered instead, may seem inadequate to the conscientious student faced with the frustrating complexities of a canon.[14] I cannot, therefore, really apologize for the elementary character of the procedures that I now recommend to canonical investigators. Such interest as these principles may have will lie primarily in the fact that they have to be stated at all. That they do need stating, the illustrations will, I trust, demonstrate.

(1) *External evidence cannot be ignored, no matter how inconvenient such evidence may be for the theories of the investigator.*

The Spanish Gypsy, claimed wholly or in part for Ford by Sykes, Sargeaunt, and others,[15] is credited to Middleton and Rowley on the title pages of the 1653 and 1661 Quartos. There is no reason to suspect fraud on the publisher's part: the flaunting of the names of the dramatists on the title page would not have stimulated sales, if one can judge from their contemporary reputations.[15a] The attribution is, moreover, in keeping with the fact that the play was licensed for acting by the Lady Elizabeth's men (9 July 1623). In the previous year the same company had performed the same authors' *Changeling*, which indeed is advertised by an allusion in the second act of *The Spanish Gypsy*.[16] The outward evidence of authorship is then fairly strong, and the play cannot be dislodged from the Middleton canon on the basis of subjective critical impressions—especially since some Middletonians have no difficulty in reconciling the play, on critical grounds, with the dramatist's acknowledged later work. Other instances might easily be cited of the too casual treatment of relevant external facts. Most striking perhaps is Lucas's work on *The Fair Maid of the Inn*, which was licensed by Herbert in 1626 as Fletcher's composition and printed in the 1647 Beaumont and Fletcher Folio. Lucas includes the play in his standard edition of Webster, and divides it among Webster, Ford, and Massinger—thus eliminating Fletcher entirely.[17] It is Bentley's painful duty to point out that, contrary to Lucas's theories, the Master of the

Revels was not an advertising agent, and the King's men, who produced the play and took a direct part in the preparation of the 1647 Folio, knew their business.[18]

(2) *If stylistic criteria are to have any meaning, the play must be written in a style.*

"Very few writers," remarks Miss Byrne (22-23), "are capable of anything so distinguished as a recognizable style, and the minor Elizabethan dramatists are definitely not among that happy band. Men like Munday and Chettle used blank verse as quickly, as slickly, and in as unremarkable a manner as the modern journalist uses his so-called prose." The editors of the Oxford *Jonson* make much the same point about Jacobean prose dialogue.[19] Collaborations (which prompted the foregoing observations) and revisions are less likely to have stylistic individuality than the unrevised work of a single author. The partners may adjust their styles to one another; the reviser may imitate his predecessor. In *Eastward Ho,* Jonson, Marston, and Chapman—three of the age's most individualistic writers—pooled their talents to produce a play with remarkable consistency of texture. Whoever added to *The Spanish Tragedy* acquired, as Prior points out, mannerisms and characteristic images of the original author.[20] I do not envy the future investigator who attempts, on the basis of style, to distinguish between the work of William Faulkner and his collaborators on the screen play of *Land of the Pharaohs.*

Yet a recognizable style, and hence one that may be described, is perhaps rather less rare than Miss Byrne would have us believe. Even hacks like Chettle and Munday, with whom she is concerned, may have occasional strange quirks of individuality. And when she suggests that style is likely to answer our question only when we are dealing with genius, Miss Byrne overlooks the startling distinctiveness that really bad writing can have. Marston at his worst, for example.

The principle holds, however: no style, no stylistic evidence. A collection of stylistic commonplaces isolates nothing and persuades only the gullible or those already convinced. Such collections—Sykes's stock in trade—have unfortunately been the rule rather than the exception (*vide* Bentley). As preposterous as any are the attribution studies of William Wells who, after expressing learned disagreement with Sykes, goes on to use similar "evidence" to assign *King Leir, Alphonsus Emperor of Germany, The Troublesome Reign of King John, Edward II,* and other plays to Thomas Kyd.[21] The number of curious additions to the Kyd canon is, Wells grants, "large enough to evoke hilarious incredulity among leading authorities with a too conservative bent."[22] With this point I hesitate to quarrel.

(3) *The investigator must always work with reliable texts, preferably directly with the early editions or manuscripts.*

As in canonical investigations the closest and most scrupulous study of texts is required, the validity of this principle should be apparent. Yet Sykes evidently trusted to whichever edition came first to hand. He used Hazlitt's *Webster* for *Appius and Virginia* and *The Fair Maid of the Inn,* and the same editor's *Dodsley* for *The Second Maiden's Tragedy, Lust's Dominion,* and other plays. He relied on Dyce's *Middleton* for *Anything for a Quiet Life,* Pearson's reprint of Chapman for *Alphonsus,* and (not without amply justified misgivings) the Mermaid *Webster and Tourneur* for *The Revenger's Tragedy.* Of these editions one, the Dyce *Middleton,* was an admirable achievement for its own time; but that time was 1840. Yet T. S. Eliot defers to Sykes as "perhaps our greatest authority on the texts of Tourneur and Middleton."[23] So much for our greatest. Investigators continue, however, to rely upon unsuitable texts. In two recent books concerned with the Dekker canon, the data—often involving small details of style—are taken from the miserable Shepherd reprint of Dekker's plays, despite the fact that the first volumes of the superb Bowers edition have for several years been readily available.[24]

(4) *Textual analysis logically precedes canonical analysis.*

The wise investigator knows his own text and what evidence it may afford of corruption, revision, or collaboration. Apparently Lawrence did not know the Quarto of *Eastward Ho* when he proposed that before publication the play underwent authorial revision, presumably by Jonson, so that offensive passages might be deleted and the gaps "neatly" closed.[25] The editors of the Oxford *Jonson* have since shown that the cuts were almost certainly the work of the publisher, and that, with the exception of the notorious passage on the Scots in Act III, they were in fact not closed.[26]

Thus the canonical question bears an intimate relation to the textual problem. Further, an apparent matter of style may conceivably be an actual matter of text. Because the only extant early edition of Shakespeare's *Pericles* falls into sections of unequal merit, some authorities have assumed that the play is a collaboration. According to this view, the second author took over with the third act, when the style suddenly improves. But if Edwards is correct in suggesting that the 1609 Quarto represents a memorial reconstruction by a pair of reporters—

the first responsible for the first two acts; the second, better skilled, for the last three—then we have no basis for regarding the original play of *Pericles* as anything but the work of a single dramatist.[27] Edwards' suggestion is of course only one hypothesis of many that have been offered to explain a particularly difficult problem. But it illustrates a possibility that other canonical investigators have failed even to consider.

In dealing with the minute features of a dramatic text—spelling, linguistic forms, punctuation, and the like—the investigator has a special problem. He must recognize the possibility of compositorial intervention in the case of printed texts, and scribal intervention in the case of manuscripts. We know that compositors and scribes were capable of exercising considerable autonomy over certain features of the manuscripts they were reproducing. The impressionists—as I shall refer hereafter to the school of Oliphant and Sykes—do not often trouble themselves with considerations so hostile to romance, and it is not surprising that the skeptical reader should trouble himself as little with data gathered in a vacuum. On the other hand, an investigator like Cyrus Hoy, aware of the relevant bibliographical considerations, disarms us at the outset of his study of the Beaumont and Fletcher canon by forthrightly discussing the role of compositors and scribes.[28] Hoy's criteria for authorship—the presence or absence of certain pronominal and verbal forms and contractions—are simple enough and have been employed by previous students. Certainly they are not equally serviceable for all the collaborators traced in the Beaumont and Fletcher corpus. But these tests have never been handled with the like judgment and discretion, and for this reason Hoy's monograph has from the first commanded respect.[29]

(5) *For any author proposed, a reasonable amount of unquestioned dramatic writing, apart from collaborations, must be extant.*

The more plays the better; better yet if some precede and others follow the work under consideration, as a theory of imitation is then with more difficulty maintained. Oliphant suggests the possibility that Thomas Watson had a hand in *Thorney Abbey* (printed in 1662 as by "T. W."), and he goes on to advise that "Anyone who wants a quite new field of Elizabethan study might first steep himself in a knowledge of Watson's poetry and then read the dramas (and especially the unattached dramas) of the period prior to the middle of 1592, with an eye to determining his presence."[30] The value of the advice is lessened by the fact that not a single play survives that is known to be the work, in whole or in part, of Thomas Watson. Thus a whole new field of study remains unexplored.[31]

(6) *Intuitions, convictions, and subjective judgments generally, carry no weight as evidence.* This no matter how learned, perceptive, respected, or confident the authority.

An anonymous reviewer in *The Times Literary Supplement* writes: "Tourneur's case [for *The Revenger's Tragedy*] has rested partly on historical evidence (admittedly flimsy), but far more upon the judgment of critics such as Mr. Eliot or Professor Ellis-Fermor or Professor Nicoll, who write with a special sensibility for such matters as the poetic style of the two authors, their range of characterization and their dramatic idiom and texture. 'Middleton,' says Mr. Eliot, 'has a different feel of the relation of the tragic and the comic.' This is of course the kind of view which a critic may hold with an instinct bordering on certainty, but which is quite unsusceptible of proof."[32] But a case cannot rest upon "judgment," and a view "unsusceptible of proof" has no binding authority. The keenest sensibility may go astray. To show that Middleton is at times "a great master of versification," our greatest living man of letters, T. S. Eliot, singles out the passage beginning, "I that am of your blood was taken from you / For your better health. . . ."[33] The speech occurs in the last scene of *The Changeling*—a scene which, according to all the evidence and all the reputable authorities, is the unaided work of William Rowley.

The value of intuitions is that they are sometimes right. Their correctness is determined by the evidence. Nothing else counts.

(7) *Wherever possible, stylistic evidence should be supplemented by textual evidence.*

A playwright's individuality may find expression in a number of accidentals: his idiosyncrasies with regard to speech prefixes, stage directions, act divisions, the recording of entrances, etc; his peculiarities of spelling, punctuation, and abbreviation. As with linguistic preferences, the usefulness of the data depends entirely upon the fidelity with which scribe or compositors have followed the author's manuscript—provided they worked from author's manuscript. Because so little autograph dramatic manuscript has survived from the Elizabethan period, it is often impossible to do more than theorize about a playwright's habits with regard to these minutiae. Yet bibliographical evidence may at times provide a valuable corroboration of an attribution already probable on critical grounds. This is demonstrated in Bowers' textual introduction to Dekker and Massinger's *The Virgin Martyr*.[34]

For Massinger there survives the holograph manuscript of *Believe As You List;* for Dekker we have only a single scene from *Sir Thomas More,* but valid inferences can be made from Dekker's printed texts. The 1642 Quarto was set by a single compositor, probably from the holograph papers of the two authors. Guided by such minute features of the text as the spellings *Cesarea* and *Cæsarea* and the use of hyphens in compounds, Bowers effectively supplements the stylistic evidence for scene allocation.

Such textual evidence has not often enough been brought to bear on canonical problems. *The Puritan,* to cite but one example, has for long puzzled scholars. Printed in 1607 as by "W. S.," it is certainly not by Shakespeare. A number of authorities feel it may be a Middleton work. The play is a comedy of London life acted by the Children of Paul's about 1606; at that time Middleton was the chief Paul's dramatist, and he was writing London comedies. There is some stylistic evidence for Middleton. No other plausible candidate for authorship has been proposed. But the case, as it stands, is inconclusive; further evidence is badly needed if the play is to be given even a conjectural place in the Middleton canon. Yet, although a number of investigators have made pronouncements about *The Puritan,* and although we have a sufficient quantity of dramatic manuscript in Middleton's hand, the 1607 Quarto has never been studied for spelling, punctuation, and other textual clues to authorship. Nor, for that matter, has it been studied for the related evidence of linguistic preferences.

The seven principles I have outlined do not exhaust the possibilities for cautionary advice to canonical investigators. Other strictures, at least equally wholesome, will no doubt occur to readers who have concerned themselves with attribution questions. The principles I have suggested derive from my own experience with particular problems and with the literature of attribution, which I have had to explore rather systematically in revising Alfred Harbage's *Annals of English Drama.* All seven reflect my dissatisfaction with the casual methodlessness of stylistic impressionism, the dominant mode of investigation during the past half century. That methodlessness is, I feel, largely responsible for the disesteem in which authorship studies are now held, at least in the area of Elizabethan drama.

IV

It is not possible, in the compass of a single essay, to deal with very many—let alone all—of the tests by which investigators in their wisdom or folly have sought to prove authorship by style. Some of the criteria that have been employed are, in any case, too feeble even to require citation. But one or two tests, particularly that of parallel passages, certainly call for serious discussion, while still others, such as metrical investigations, may for present purposes be briefly considered.

"The danger of metrical evidence is that it is too often believed." So wrote Lucas some years back in his edition of Webster (IV 250). After giving entirely persuasive reasons for regarding the tests with profound distrust, he goes on to apply them himself to *Anything for a Quiet Life* and *The Fair Maid of the Inn*, with results no happier than those of his predecessors. Today little danger exists of metrical statistics being too easily believed, except perhaps by their compilers. If the use of such evidence can be justified at all, it is only as corroboration for the assignment of scenes of collaborate plays in which the partners have been identified, and are known to have widely differing metrical habits (e.g., Middleton and Rowley's *Fair Quarrel* and *The Changeling*). But even with such cases previous results testify to the need for extreme caution.[35]

Imagery studies have also yielded much dubious evidence. The hazards are nicely illustrated in the work of Marco Mincoff and the late Una Ellis-Fermor. Each made, unaware of the other, a detailed study of the imagery of *The Revenger's Tragedy*.[36] Mincoff concluded that the play was Middleton's; Ellis-Fermor, that it must be Tourneur's. Mincoff avoids certain pitfalls: he does not use imagery as the basis for pseudo-biographical reconstructions, which must be reckoned as evidentially worthless. But skeptical readers will hardly be persuaded by his data, and the conflicting results achieved by two well-known scholars working on the same play and concerned with the narrowest possible field of author-candidates do not inspire confidence in the method. The strictures (discussed below) relevant to the test for parallels may be held to apply to image tests as well, and may provide some discipline. But the image-hunter faces special difficulties. The need for selection—few words do not convey an image of some kind—and classification inevitably enlarges the subjective factor in attribution work. The investigator is, moreover, hampered by our very limited knowledge of the images and image-patterns favored by the various minor Elizabethan dramatists. Detailed study of imagery is a relatively recent critical preoccupation, and misgivings about applying its techniques prematurely to authorship problems would seem to be fully warranted.[37]

The foundation of most stylistic attributions during the past fifty years has not, however, been imagery or metrics, but the testimony of parallels: unusual correspondences of language and thought, generally in brief passages, between the doubtful play and the acknowledged works of the suggested dramatist. This test too has occasioned doubts and skeptical protests. "There is nothing more dangerous," Chambers declared, "than the attempt to determine authorship by the citation of parallels."[38] More recently, the editors of the Oxford *Jonson* have remarked upon "the illusory test of parallel passages" (IX 636), and Bentley has deprecated, with customary vigor, the "parallel-passage 'evidence' of modern enthusiasts."[39] But in this instance the difficulties are, I feel, different in character and significance from those presented by the tests I have already touched upon. Most conservative editors, the Simpsons included, are able to use the evidence of parallels, and most conservative historians, Bentley included, can accept attributions based chiefly on such evidence.

In his account of the disintegration of Middleton's *Anything for a Quiet Life* by the impressionist quartet of Sykes, Oliphant, Lucas, and Dunkel, Bentley provides (IV 859-860) an at times almost farcical but essentially sad chronicle of the misuse of stylistic evidence. That evidence consists mainly of parallel passages. Bentley's chief complaint is that "Most of the passages are not parallel, and the words and phrases are by no means peculiar to Webster [Middleton's proposed collaborator]." The objection to commonplace or unparallel parallels occurs often in *The Jacobean and Caroline Stage*. It is a legitimate objection, but applies less to a method than to its abuses. For if the parallels are not parallel and the words and phrases are commonplace, the test, in a very real sense, has not been employed.

The abuses that Bentley properly deplores did not pass with the impressionists of the Roaring Twenties. In 1948 G. J. Eberle published a study of *The Family of Love*, a comedy issued anonymously in 1608 and assigned to Middleton in Archer's 1656 playlist. The aim of the study is to demonstrate that the play "is a revision by Dekker and Middleton of an early play written by Middleton with considerable help from Dekker."[40] A thesis as complicated as this is difficult either to prove or disprove; unfortunately for Eberle, the burden of proof rests upon him. To support his argument, he assembles a number of parallels, or "touchstones," as he calls them. "Even distant echoes in Middleton" are cited. "Commonplaces and proverbial expressions" are "included as confirmatory evidence if Dekker uses them often and Middleton never" (725). Thus Middleton's collaborator—if he had one—is from the outset presumed to be Dekker. Eberle assumes also that *The Puritan* and *The Revenger's Tragedy* are Middleton's, and he gives to

Dekker all or part of *Blurt, Master Constable; The Weakest Goeth to the Wall; The Bloody Banquet; The Merry Devil of Edmonton;* and *The Black Book.* All these ascriptions are the proposals of modern critics, and all are controversial. To parallels from these works, Eberle adds others from collaborations: *The Changeling; The Honest Whore, Part I* (a Dekker-Middleton collaboration!); *The Roaring Girl* (also by Dekker and Middleton); *The Old Law* (where the authorities disagree on the assignment of some scenes); and *A Fair Quarrel* (where an episode almost certainly by Rowley is cited as evidence for Middleton). Despite the catholic variety of sources Eberle has to draw upon, many of his parallels are not parallel. The entire essay is, indeed, a fine illustration of the inadequacy of good intentions alone. "This study," Eberle had assured his readers at the beginning, "attempts to approach the ideal set down by Bentley for studies in attribution" (725).

If Eberle's study falls short of his own ideal, it is because he has set up no *a priori* rules of procedure for his own guidance in collecting data, and has made no effort to classify and evaluate the evidence once gathered. Rather he has amassed ungraded parallels. The amassing of ungraded parallels proves nothing. This truth was stated almost three decades ago by Miss Byrne.[41] At the same time she offered five Golden Rules, as she reasonably described them, for the improvement of parallel hunting. Miss Byrne observed that parallels vary in quality, and that correspondences of thought and phraseology are greatly superior to simple verbal parallels. She reasoned that parallel collectors may pass logically from the known to the anonymous or from the known to the collaborate play, but less securely from the collaborate to the anonymous work. She did not skirt the problem that even striking parallels may admit of more than one explanation: they may testify to common authorship, but they may also be the result of coincidence or of imitation, conscious or unconscious. Above all, Miss Byrne stressed the necessity for the careful grading of parallels, and for submitting them to negative checks to show that they cannot be duplicated as a body in acknowledged plays of the period.

The impressionists have not questioned the validity of any of Miss Byrne's tenets. Instead they have left her article severely alone. Although in my work of revising the *Annals of English Drama,* I have had occasion to examine a number of attribution studies involving the citation of parallels, I cannot recall one that referred to Miss Byrne's paper. Eberle's study of *The Family of Love* does not stand alone as an unhappy reminder of the dangers faced by the investigator unacquainted with her untarnished Rules.

Allied to verbal parallels, and subject to some of the same strictures governing the admissability of evidence, are the larger correspondences of thought and theme, characterization and dramatic technique. But parallels of this kind—which for convenience I shall call literary correspondences—also make special demands of their own. Their usefulness depends closely upon the investigator's capacities for literary analysis, and the precision with which he can formulate critical distinctions. In practice the canonical impressionists have been, as we might expect, critical impressionists, and the subjective element present in all criticism has been in their work pervasive and detrimental. Their inclination, insufficiently resisted, is to make oversimplified descriptive pronouncements and pass oversimplified value judgments. A scene is by Jonson because it is "masterful," by Middleton because "it has his irony," by Peele or Greene or Heywood because it is not very good. As evidence for Dekker's authorship of *Blurt, Master Constable*, Lawrence suggests that two songs in the play "have a good deal of that careless grace of style, what one might characterise artful artlessness, which marks Dekker's lyrics."[42] Apparently it did not occur to Lawrence that precisely the same observations might be made about any tolerable Elizabethan lyric, and the age produced a number of tolerable lyrics. The limited critical value of this kind of impressionism is sufficiently obvious. As evidence its value is nil.

Yet verbal parallels and literary correspondences—defined correspondences, not mere impressions—may provide a basis for attributions acceptable to the responsible historian, critic, and editor. The evidence of style—largely of parallels—for the assignment of *The Queen* to Ford is most impressive.[43] Archer surely erred in assigning the play to Fletcher in his 1656 playlist, and the error is satisfactorily explained by Greg. The attribution has gone unchallenged since Bang proposed it over half a century ago. An equally successful argument for attribution was made by Cyrus Day, who pointed out striking resemblances of phraseology, dramatic situation, and character portrayal between an anonymous seventeenth-century comedy, *The Drinking Academy*, and the known writings of Thomas Randolph, a distinctly minor dramatist who habitually pillaged his own works.[44] The literary correspondences are in this case satisfyingly concrete: the characters of Worldly, Knowlittle, and Cavaliero Whiffe in *The Drinking Academy* are equivalent to Simo, Asotus, and Ballio in *The Jealous Lovers*. The verbal parallels with nine of Randolph's acknowledged pieces are numerous and often unusual. There are no external facts to contradict the evidence of style, and Randolph's authorship of the play has been accepted by (among others) Hyder Rollins, Fredson Bowers, and G. E. Bentley.

V

The results of any single test of authorship have to be viewed, of course, as part of a larger design. An investigator like Hoy, applying a limited number of linguistic criteria to the Beaumont and Fletcher canon, must at times supplement his findings with other kinds of evidence, and he recognizes fully that his own work depends in part upon the work of others before him. A case for attribution may well represent the patient efforts of a number of scholars over a long period of time. Each contributes his particular bits of evidence. The ultimate effect sought is a cumulative one, in which all the internal evidence—stylistic, bibliographical, and linguistic—converges inexorably upon a single possible author-identification: an identification compatible with the known external information.

This cumulative effect no doubt is, as Sherbo and others have urged, something apart from and greater than the individual pieces of testimony of which it is composed, just as a building transcends the materials—the steel, concrete, wood, and plaster—that have gone into its making. But the architect of attributions must beware lest his materials be merely of the air, airy—the formulas of style and expression that are the common currency of an age. Thus the word "dilling," as the Simpsons complain with understandable irritation, "is not 'a Marston word' because it occurs once in the text of Marston . . . and 'well-parted' . . . is not exclusively a Jonson phrase when it is found in Shakespeare, Webster and Rowley, and Field."[45] Zeros, Ephim Fogel neatly puts it, no matter how great their number, add up to zero.[46]

Yet proper methods, employed by disinterested seekers after truth, may yield inconclusive results. Attribution proposals as firmly supported as those for *The Queen* or *The Drinking Academy* are after all rare, and the successful identification of the authors of collaborate plays rarer still. The investigator may find himself, sooner than he anticipated, at the frontiers of ignorance, which after so much expenditure of sweat and ink, remains a spacious domain. The words with which Baldwin Maxwell concludes his study of *A Yorkshire Tragedy* apply equally well to a number of other plays of anonymous or doubtful authorship. "A convincing identification of the author or authors . . . ," Maxwell writes, "if it is ever to be accomplished, must await our clearer knowledge of what were the peculiar characteristics of the various Jacobean dramatists."[47] The trend away from simple impressionism to a more analytical criticism (well exemplified by such recent work as Jonas Barish's *Ben Jonson and the Language of Prose Comedy*) may help to provide that knowledge with regard to the larger aspects of dramatic art. Electronic calculating machines will make possible on a wide scale the compilation of valuable statistical data—information about spelling, linguistic preferences, and other accidentals of style. They will also facilitate work on concordances. The few such tools now readily available—the Shakespeare, Kyd, and Marlowe concordances—have demonstrated how vulnerable is some of the vocabulary evidence put forward by the impressionists. Further shocks will no doubt be felt as the stock of source materials for negative checks is increased. Cornell University has led the way in the pioneering application of electronic computers to literary research; others may be expected to follow.

But it would be excessively hopeful to assume that, even with better tools and more refined methods, students will be able to find answers—plausible explanations, I should say—for the majority of our vexing attribution problems. The investigator may be halted by unbridgeable gaps in his evidence; he may find himself faced with the stubborn reluctance of facts to dispose themselves conveniently in support of hypotheses. This brings us to the extraordinary question of *The Revenger's Tragedy*. The most important Elizabethan play of disputed authorship, it may serve as an object lesson in the perplexities and frustrations of canonical research.

Printed anonymously in 1607 and assigned to Cyril Tourneur by the early cataloguers, *The Revenger's Tragedy* has become in the present century the subject of an exasperatingly protracted controversy. In 1926 Oliphant, in what was probably his best performance, made a detailed argument for attributing the play to Middleton, whom he had tentatively proposed some years earlier.[48] Since then the literature on the subject has reached staggering dimensions, as scholars have supported or rejected Oliphant's contention.[49] In 1955 I summarized the case for Middleton in my book on the tragedies, and I concluded then that, while the evidence was not definitive, it justified a provisional assignment of the play to Middleton. This conclusion received, it is fair to say, a mixed reception. Against this background, Barker's announcement in 1958, in the Preface to his *Thomas Middleton*, has more than ordinary interest. "I have given new evidence," he writes, "that will, I think, settle the controversy about authorship once and for all." The new evidence is a literary correspondence, supported by a verbal parallel, between *The Revenger's Tragedy* and Middleton's *A Mad World, my Masters*. Barker suggests that the two plays are companion pieces: Vindice and Follywit, their protagonists, are examples of "the clever man who is blinded by his own cleverness, the self-satisfied hero who turns out to be anything but a hero in the end."[50] This is of course the classic peripeteia of drama, tragedy and comedy alike. The fate that overtakes Vindice and Follywit, as one reviewer was quick to note, also overtakes the clever and self-satisfied Volpone, and the list of complacent heroes thus undone might be indefinitely extended. Several articles on the authorship of *The Revenger's Tragedy* have followed upon Barker's book. Two (by one student) support Tourneur; a third favors Middleton.[51] Thus the deadlock continues.

The view to which my concern with attribution problems during the past five years has led me is that the question remains unanswered because it is unanswerable. This despite the considerable labors of a number of scholars—labors that have yielded a rather massive accumulation of evidence. A full review of that evidence here is not feasible, but the chief issues may be stated briefly.

First, the external evidence. It is not very satisfactory—if it were, the controversy would not have arisen—but such information as we have favors Tourneur. The lists of Archer and Kirkman do not command respect for their accuracy, but it is more difficult to account for a mistake in the assignment of *The Revenger's Tragedy* to an obscure figure like Tourneur than it is to explain the erroneous ascription of, say, *The Queen* to Fletcher or *A Trick to Catch the Old One* to Shakespeare. The play was, moreover, printed "*As it hath beene ſundry times Acted, by the Kings Maiesties Seruants*."[52] There is no evidence to contradict this title-page statement which, as Miss Ekeblad points out, is supported by the use in Act V of a blazing star, a stage effect for which the Globe theatre was noted.[53] Nor is there any evidence that Middleton had a connection with the King's men at the time, about 1604-1606, that *The Revenger's Tragedy* was written. He was then the leading playwright for Paul's boys, providing them almost singlehandedly with a comic repertory. He is not likely to have undermined his own efforts by contributing plays to the powerful company with whom his own troupe was waging an increasingly desperate competitive struggle. A possible explanation—if Middleton wrote the play—is that *The Revenger's Tragedy* was originally performed by the children, and somehow afterwards passed, like Marston's *The Malcontent*, into the repertory of the adult company; but this is merely speculation.

The internal evidence is more complicated. In some ways *The Revenger's Tragedy* is a unique product of the Jacobean stage, and hence unlike either Tourneur or Middleton. It bears, however, enough general resemblance of theme and dramatic technique to *The Atheist's Tragedy*, Tourneur's only unquestioned extant play, for the attribution to Tourneur to be acceptable to many. But on the basis of other considerations, involving minute details of style and linguistic preferences, it is difficult to accommodate the two works with one another as the achievement of a single author. Indeed, our severest authorities have expressed their qualms: Chambers was skeptical enough about Tourneur's claim to *The Revenger's Tragedy* to classify the play as an anonymous work in *The Elizabethan Stage;* Greg doubted that it would have been assigned to Tourneur at all were it not for the seventeenth-century catalogues.[54] On the other hand, the stylistic evidence for Middleton is extensive and varied, and it has recently been supplemented by George R. Price's very welcome bibliographical study of *The Revenger's Tragedy.*[55]

Still the internal evidence does not sweep all before it, and the situation, as it stands, is that neither Middleton's nor Tourneur's advocates have been able to bring forward the kind of proof to which one party or the other must submit. Hence the seemingly endless exchanges of replies and counter-replies in our journals. Whatever his own personal *feeling* about the attribution may be, the task of the historian is, as I see it, to record the fact of uncertainty, which is in this case the only certainty. In the "Authors" column of the revised *Annals of English Drama*, the entry for *The Revenger's Tragedy* will read: Anonymous (Tourneur, C.? Middleton, T.?).

Does this inconclusive conclusion mean that the efforts of a number of scholars over the past thirty-five years represent so much wasted labor? I think not. By focusing intensively on so many manifestations of style, the work on *The Revenger's Tragedy* has fostered a more sensitive awareness of the distinctive characteristics of two dramatists, one of whom is a major dramatist. It has raised questions that needed raising. Less than a century ago, Churton Collins could edit Tourneur without any sense of the limitations of the evidence for the authenticity of the play on which the dramatist's fame chiefly rests. This uncritical certainty has been superseded by a reasonable doubt, and a serious hypothesis of alternative attribution has been proposed—an hypothesis that the responsible historian cannot safely ignore. Our understanding of the nature of a particular problem has been to some extent modified. That is a legitimate accomplishment of scholarship. However much we may yearn for certainties, and for grander and more romantic achievements, we recognize—or we should recognize—that the scholarly process usually proceeds by the slight modification of already existing knowledge.

There is a place for hypothesis as well as for demonstration, and in the field of Elizabethan drama, where the factual records are far from satisfactory, hypothesis assumes an especially important role. We want to know; something there is that doesn't love an anonymous play. And so scholars use internal evidence as a basis for attribution. Some of their hypotheses are much better supported than others; some, and I have noted one or two in this paper, are almost certainly correct. But all of them remain hypotheses. Despite the safeguards devised, a subjective element resides in all attribution work, and even the utilization of electronic computers will not eliminate the need for the exercise of scholarly judgment. Bentley, in including *The Queen* in his section on Ford, judiciously adds the proviso that the play "may be accepted as his until evidence of its composition by a very clever imitator is forthcoming."[56] The proviso is justified. Still we would be the poorer without Bang's hypothesis, as indeed we would without a number of others.

But if hypothesis is to be accorded its full value it must be recognized and presented as such. Not only in authorship studies but in almost every specialty, we have encountered studies in which the evidence does not support the claims which the scholar's enthusiasm has led him to make. No doubt many a worthwhile speculation has been too easily dismissed because of the impatience that undue partisanship arouses. It is good, I believe, that we pay tribute now and then to the virtue of recognizing our limitations.

"Several things dove-tailed in my mind," writes John Keats in perhaps the most famous passage of his correspondence, "and at once it struck me what quality went to form a Man of Achievement, especially in Literature, and which Shakespeare possessed so enormously—I mean *Negative Capability,* that is, when a man is capable of being in uncertainties, mysteries, doubts, without any irritable reaching after fact and reason. . . ."[57] The scholar no less than the poet must have his own kind of negative capability. He must know and accept the often frustrating limitations of the methods available to him if, in his quest to dispel illusions and errors, he is not to create new ones in their place.[58]

NOTES

This paper was read, in a somewhat different form, at the English Institute in New York on September 8, 1960.

[1] I use the term *Elizabethan* loosely, but conveniently, to include the period until the closing of the theatres in 1642.

[2] G. E. Bentley, "Authenticity and Attribution in the Jacobean and Caroline Drama," *English Institute Annual 1942* (New York 1943) 102.

[3] E. K. Chambers, "The Disintegration of Shakespeare," *Shakespeare Gleanings* (Oxford 1944) 12.

[4] E. H. C. Oliphant, "Problems of Authorship in Elizabethan Dramatic Literature," *MP* VIII (1911) 413.

[5] Oliphant, *The Plays of Beaumont and Fletcher* (New Haven 1927) 31.

[6] M. St. C. Byrne, "Bibliographical Clues in Collaborate Plays," *The Library* 4th ser XIII (1932) 23.

[7] On Fleay, see Chambers, "Disintegration of Shakespeare," 4-5.

[8] Oliphant, "Problems of Authorship," 459. It is true that years later, when the reaction had begun to set in, Oliphant prefaced his study of the Beaumont and Fletcher canon with an account of the way in which he approached the task of disintegration; but the account breaks down into rationalization and emotional self-justification, and is further marred by an ill-conceived and intemperate attack on Chambers, in the course of which Oliphant offers the quaint suggestion that Chambers was not a scholar (*Plays of Beaumont and Fletcher* 10-12).

[9] Richard Hindry Barker, *Thomas Middleton* (New York 1958) 166. On attribution procedures I am sorry to have to differ with Mr. Barker, the virtues of whose stimulating book I have elsewhere much commended. When Mr. Barker discusses Middleton's plays, his enthusiasm—readily communicated—has a positive value of its own.

[10] Arthur Sherbo, "The Uses and Abuses of Internal Evidence," *Bulletin of The New York Public Library* LXIII (1959) 6.

[11] Philip Edwards, ed, Thomas Kyd, *The Spanish Tragedy* (London 1959) xvii.

[12] Gerald J. Eberle, "Dekker's Part in *The Familie of Love*," *Joseph Quincy Adams Memorial Studies*, ed McManaway, Dawson, and Willoughby (Washington, D.C. 1948) 723-738.

[13] F. L. Lucas, ed, John Webster, *Works* (London 1927) IV 66-68; H. Dugdale Sykes, *Sidelights on Elizabethan Drama* (Oxford 1924) 159-172; Barker, *Thomas Middleton* 191-192.

[13a] For a balanced view of the whole problem of attribution, whether by internal or external evidence, see W. W. Greg's brief, disinterested statement in *A Bibliography of the English Printed Drama to the Restoration* (London 1939-1959) IV xxi-xxii.

[14] Barker writes: "I have avoided enumerating Middleton's 'characteristics,' partly because this has often been done before, and partly because I feel that to do so here would be to misrepresent the process of determining authorship, which is anything but deductive. One just does the best one can. One reads and forms, or tries to form, impressions; finally a play or a scene or a passage gets to 'sound like' Middleton or Dekker or Rowley. Then one looks for somewhat more objective evidence that can be used

to convince other readers" (*Thomas Middleton* 155). Oliphant, on the other hand, thus describes the same process: "However strong the internal evidence may be, it is after all only a matter of deduction: because the style of a play, the literary form, the vocabulary, the phraseology, the dramatic technique, the characterization, the philosophy, the outlook on life, are characteristic of a certain writer, we assume his authorship" (*Plays of Beaumont and Fletcher* 13). Yet Barker, as noted, pays tribute to Oliphant, and both men approach attribution study in essentially the same way. That they should disagree on so fundamental a matter as whether the method they employ is inductive or deductive would seem to indicate that they have not fully considered the nature of their own assumptions and procedures.

[15] Sykes, *Sidelights* 183-199; Oliphant *Shakespeare and His Fellow Dramatists* (New York 1929) II 18; M. Joan Sargeaunt, *John Ford* (Oxford 1935) 41-57; Barker, *Thomas Middleton* 208-209. I have myself in the past accepted too easily the arguments for Ford (Schoenbaum, *Middleton's Tragedies: A Critical Study*, New York 1955, 202, 247).

[15a] It should be noted, however, that the same publisher, Richard Marriott, is responsible for the attribution of *Revenge for Honor* to George Chapman on the title page of the 1654 Quarto—although he had previously entered the play on the Stationers' Register as the work of Henry Glapthorne. The most plausible explanation *is*, in this instance, a dishonest commercial intention on the part of Marriott: the name of the famous translator of Homer, thus displayed, might well have been expected to spur the play's sales. But Middleton and Rowley are another matter.

[16] This point is made by Bentley, *The Jacobean and Caroline Stage* (Oxford 1956) IV 894.

[17] Lucas, Webster's *Works* IV 148-152.

[18] *Jacobean and Caroline Stage* III 338; V 1252-53.

[19] "From the beginning of the seventeenth century there was a tendency for individual dramatic styles in prose dialogue to converge on one more or less established type; somewhat as a modern journal acquires a distinctive style to which all who write for it tend to conform" (C. H. Herford and Percy and Evelyn Simpson, eds, Ben Jonson, *Works*, Oxford 1925-52, IX 637). And Jonas Barish, who has studied Elizabethan dramatic prose more closely than most students, similarly finds that "Elizabethan style, in the theatre particularly, tends toward anonymity" (*Ben Jonson and the Language of Prose Comedy*, Cambridge, Mass 1960, 281).

[20] Moody E. Prior, "Imagery As a Test of Authorship," *SQ* VI (1955) 383.

[21] William Wells, "The Authorship of 'King Leir,'" *N&Q* CLXXVII (1939) 434-438; "Thomas Kyd and the Chronicle-History," *N&Q* CLXXVIII (1940) 218-224 and 238-243; and "'Alphonsus, Emperor of Germany,'" *N&O* CLXXIX (1940) 218-223 and 236-240.

[22] "Thomas Kyd and the Chronicle-History" 219.

[23] T. S. Eliot, "Cyril Tourneur," *Selected Essays* (London 1951) 186.

[24] M. T. Jones-Davies, *Un peintre de la vie londonienne, Thomas Dekker* (Paris 1958) 2 vols; Barker, *Thomas Middleton*.

[25] W. J. Lawrence, *Pre-Restoration Stage Studies* (Cambridge, Mass 1927) 363-364.

[26] Herford and Simpson, Jonson's *Works* IV 495-498; IX 637.

[27] Edwards, "An Approach to the Problems of *Pericles*," *Shakespeare Survey 5* (Cambridge 1952) 25-49. In his New Cambridge edition of *Pericles*, J. C. Maxwell considers and rejects the arguments in Edwards' "important article" (1956 xvi-xviii). Greg, however, regards them more favorably (*The Shakespeare First Folio* [Oxford 1955] 98).

[28] Cyrus Hoy, "The Shares of Fletcher and His Collaborators in the Beaumont and Fletcher Canon," *Studies in Bibliography* VIII (1956) 137-142. Installments of Hoy's study have appeared in *Studies in Bibliography* VIII (1956) 129-146; IX (1957) 143-162; XI (1958) 85-106; XII (1959) 91-116; XIII (1960) 77-108.

[29] It must be said, however, that Hoy is most effective when he relies upon linguistic criteria. When he turns (as indeed he must) to other kinds of evidence to supplement inconclusive linguistic findings, he drifts into stylistic impressionism. See, for example, Hoy's discussion of *The Laws of Candy* (XIII 97-100), which he gives entirely to Ford. Hoy goes on to assign Ford a share in Act II, Sc. 1, of *The Fair Maid of the Inn*, on the very doubtful basis that "one passage therein echoes fairly closely a passage of similar import from III, 2 of *The Laws of Candy* . . ." (102-103). Thus, as so often in the work of Oliphant and company, one inference leads to another, supposition is based upon supposition.

[30] "Problems of Authorship" 439.

[31] The next—and ultimate—step is to attribute plays to persons for whom we have no literary remains whatsoever. That step has, indeed, been taken more than once. Several students have proposed Sebastian Westcott as the author of various extant and lost Tudor plays; see H. N. Hillebrand, "Sebastian Westcote, Dramatist and Master of the Children of Paul's," *JEGP* XIV (1915) 568-584; C. W. Roberts, "The Authorship of *Gammer Gurton's Needle*," *PQ* XIX (1940) 97-113; and James Paul Brawner, "Early Classical Narrative Plays by Sebastian Westcott and Richard Mulcaster," *MLQ* IV (1943) 455-464. But, as Arthur Brown points out, "there is neither music nor literature extant which can with certainty be attributed to him [Westcott]," and "until we know a good deal more about Master Sebastian, we must continue to treat his claim to any of these plays as *not proved*" ("A Note on Sebastian Westcott and the Plays Presented by the Children of Paul's," *MLQ* XII [1951] 134-136). Marjorie L. Reyburn has recently suggested that Owen Gwyn—for whom, similarly, we have no surviving writings of any kind—collaborated in the Parnassus trilogy ("New Facts and Theories about the Parnassus Plays," *PMLA* LXXIV [1959] 325-335).

[32] Review of Schoenbaum, *Middleton's Tragedies*, *TLS* LV (1956) 102.

[33] Eliot, "Thomas Middleton," *Selected Essays* 169.

[34] Fredson Bowers, ed, Thomas Dekker, *Dramatic Works* (Cambridge 1958) III 368-374.

[35] Metrical statistics for Rowley's plays have been derived from texts in which printers and editors have misdivided lines and printed prose as verse and verse as prose; see Dewar M. Robb, "The Canon of William Rowley's Plays," *MLR* XLV (1950) 9-10. Robb justly concludes that "Metrical tests based upon such texts are worse than useless."

[36] U. M. Ellis-Fermor, "The Imagery of 'The Revengers Tragedie' and 'The Atheists Tragedie,'" *MLR* XXX (1935) 289-301; Marco K. Min-

coff, "The Authorship of *The Revenger's Tragedy*," *Studia Historico-Philologica Serdicensia* II (1939) 1-87.

[37] Certain of the pitfalls are usefully discussed by Prior in "Imagery As a Test of Authorship" 381-386. The complexities of definition and classification are ably surveyed by Edward B. Partridge in *The Broken Compass: A Study of the Major Comedies of Ben Jonson* (London 1958) 19-36. Partridge believes that "imagery cannot be safely used to settle questions about the canon of an author" (p 14).

[38] Chambers, *William Shakespeare: A Study of Facts and Problems* (Oxford 1930) I 222.

[39] *Jacobean and Caroline Stage* IV 860.

[40] Eberle, "Dekker's Part in *The Familie of Love*" 726.

[41] Byrne, "Bibliographical Clues" 24.

[42] Lawrence, "Dekker's Theatrical Allusiveness," *Speeding Up Shakespeare* (London 1937) 118.

[43] See W. Bang, ed, *The Queen, Materialien* (Louvain 1906) vii-ix, 41-57; also Sargeaunt, *John Ford*, Appendix I; Sykes, *Sidelights* 173-182; and Bentley, *Jacobean and Caroline Stage* III 457-458.

[44] Cyrus L. Day, "Thomas Randolph and *The Drinking Academy*," *PMLA* XLIII (1928) 800-809.

[45] Jonson's *Works* IX 636-637.

[46] Ephim G. Fogel, "Salmons in Both, or Some Caveats for Canonical Scholars," *Bulletin of The New York Public Library* LXIII (1959) 304.

[47] Baldwin Maxwell, *Studies in the Shakespeare Apocrypha* (New York 1956) 196.

[48] Oliphant, "The Authorship of *The Revenger's Tragedy*," *SP* XXIII (1926) 157-168.

[49] The discussion up to 1954 is summarized in Schoenbaum, *Middleton's Tragedies* 153-182.

[50] Barker, *Thomas Middleton* 70-71.

[51] I.-S. Ekeblad, "An Approach to Tourneur's Imagery," *MLR* LIV (1959) 489-498, and "On the Authorship of *The Revenger's Tragedy*," *ES* XLI (1960) 225-240; George R. Price, "The Authorship and the Bibliography of *The Revenger's Tragedy*," *Library* 5th ser XV (1960) 262-277.

[52] R. A. Foakes makes this point in his important article, "On the Authorship of *The Revenger's Tragedy*," *MLR* XLVIII (1953) 129-138. I have previously dismissed Mr. Foakes's paper too lightly, and I am pleased to have an opportunity to comment upon it again.

[53] Ekeblad, "A Note on 'The Revenger's Tragedy,'" *N&Q* CC (1955) 98.

[54] Greg, "Authorship Attributions in the Early Play-lists, 1656-1671," *Edinburgh Bibliographical Society Transactions* II (1946) 317-318.

[55] See note 51.

[56] *Jacobean and Caroline Stage* III 457.

[57] John Keats, *Letters*, ed M. B. Forman (Oxford 1947) 72.

[58] I wish to thank Mr. J. H. P. Pafford, the Goldsmiths' Librarian, for generously permitting me to make use of the facilities of the Library of the University of London during the summer of 1960, when this essay was written. I also owe a debt of gratitude to his very capable staff.

The Date of Blake's *Vala* or *The Four Zoas*

G. E. Bentley, Jr.

Blake's long manuscript poem, which he first entitled *Vala* and later altered in pencil to *The Four Zoas,* was never published by him even in the limited sense in which most of his prophecies were published. Blake left the poem in manuscript, and the first attempt at a published transcript was in the late nineteenth century. Consequently the dating of the poem is extremely difficult, since there are no contemporary references to it. Blake himself wrote after his first title "by William Blake 1797," but it is difficult to be sure just what this means. The first part of the poem (about thirty-four pages) is written in an elegant large hand which must be a fair copy of Blake's rough draft. However, eighty-six percent of the poem is in a distinctly different hand, and to this have been added about eight hundred lines of corrections. It is impossible to be certain which stage of the poem the date 1797 refers to, though it is generally assumed that since the date is written in Blake's copperplate hand it refers to his fair copy.

Several of Blake's engraved prophecies are dated 1795. His next public literary productions, *Milton* and *Jerusalem,* are dated 1804 on the engraved titlepages, but, largely on the evidence of the paper used in the only surviving copies, the usually accepted dates for these are about 1808 and 1820 respectively. It seems likely that Blake was engaged during much of the interim from 1795 to 1808 on *Vala,* though there has never been any definite evidence relating to its date other than the 1797 on the titlepage.

There is now definite evidence to prove at least that Blake took the poem with him to Felpham, and there is every reason to believe that he worked on it while he was there from September 1800 until September 1803. On the second page of the fourth Night of *Vala*[1] there is a very faint impression of printing, which has not been commented on before. It is mirror-printing, every letter backwards, and the type gets fainter towards the left-hand side of the page. The type must have been transfered when the print was still fresh,[2] probably when the page with the print was laid on the *Vala* page.

The print transfered is from page nine (the last page) of the first of the Ballads about animals which were written by Hayley and for which Blake made engravings in 1802.[3] Hayley wrote at some length of these Ballads in his letters to Lady Hesketh, who was collaborating with him, more or less, on his biography of Cowper. On May 24th, 1802 Hayley warned her:

> Do not be surprised if you receive in about a Fortnight a Bundle of Ballads, for I have a wicked project of turning your Ladyship into a Ballad Monger for the sake of serving the excellent friendly artist, who has been working so long & so patiently by my side on our Portraits of Cowper.—He has drawn & engraved some very ingenious designs of his own to a series of singular Ballads, one of which He proposes to publish every Month with three prints annexed to it.—for the moderate price of half a Crown.—His first number will be ready in a week or two, delicately printed on a fine quarto paper, & if I send you one dozen to dispose of among yr friends I know you will not think yrself overloaded by
>
> your sincere &
> affectionate Hermit[4]

All the engravings for this first Ballad are actually dated June 1, 1802, and they were evidently published by about this date, for, according to his letter of June 10th, Hayley expected them to have reached Lady Hesketh by the second week of June.

Seagrave, the Chichester printer who was printing Hayley's biography, was responsible for the text of the Ballads, but Blake himself printed the engravings. As Hayley explained in his June 10th letter to Lady Hesketh,

> you receive a *smaller number,* than I led you to expect: not from our apprehension that you might find it difficult to metamorphose them into Half Crowns for the ingenious Artist . . . but in Truth, because the busy artist had not Time to furnish a larger number of these interesting animals for his distant Friends *immediately*—He & his excellent Wife (a true Helpmate!) pass the plates thro' a rolling press in their own Cottage together; & of course it is a work of some Time to collect a Number of Impressions.—But if you find, that you are likely to have *many Customers* in *your new Trade of*

Ballad Monger, He will take care that you shall not want *a stock in Hand. . . .*

Probably Blake collected a large number of printed sheets from Seagrave and took them home to put the engravings in the spaces left empty on the appropriate sheets. Evidently he laid a freshly printed sheet on a page which is now part of the *Vala* manuscript.

This page which transfered print to the *Vala* manuscript has, in the published form, an engraving of an elephant at the foot. There is no trace of this engraving transfered to the manuscript page, but instead there is an indentation in the *Vala* paper of the size and in the position of the engraving which appears in the published Ballad.[5] Hayley does not say so directly, but Blake must have added the engravings to the already printed page rather than vice versa.[6] It seems probable that Seagrave printed up all the necessary copies of the first Ballad, and delivered them fresh from the press to Blake in late May.[7] If so, we can, I think, safely assume that the impression in question was transfered in late May of 1802;[8] the demand for this Ballad was certainly not such as to require Seagrave to make a second printing.

The crucial question is, however, whether the writing is on top of the print, or vice versa. I can give no satisfactory clear-cut solution to this problem; the print itself is so extremely faint that it is impossible to be certain which was added last. However, a minute examination of the manuscript leads me to believe that the writing is on top of the printing.

A number of other probabilities support this conclusion. In the first place, it seems highly unlikely that Blake would have been so careless as to leave a freshly printed page on his carefully written manuscript. Secondly, the pages of the manuscript have tiny holes in the margin, as if they had been stitched, and if they were stitched in 1802 it would be most surprising to find Blake putting a sheet or stack of sheets into his manuscript which he had bound with such care. Thirdly, it is very likely that Blake kept a large number of proofs of his *Night Thoughts* engravings, on which *Vala* is largely written, as scratch paper.[9] Some of the engravings exist in at least three states, and consequently Blake had a considerable number of sheets which, because of the space left in the center for the type, were unsaleable as separate engravings, and which were useful and usable only for scratch paper. It seems likely that the clean *Night Thoughts* engravings were among the "Sixteen heavy & portfolios full of prints"[10] which Blake took with him to Felpham.

I believe that all the evidence points toward the conclusion that the print is underneath the handwriting, and consequently that all of *Vala* from the fourth Night on was written or transcribed in its present state after May, 1802. The least that the evidence indicates, if the print must have been wet when transfered, is that Blake had his *Vala* manuscript with him at Felpham, and that he could have been making additions to it during those years.

NOTES

[1] This page is written in Blake's usual letter-writing hand on the back of a proof of his engraving for Young's *Night Thoughts* which was published in 1797. On the fourth page of the eighth Night (which is also a *Night Thoughts* verso) is a faint impression similar to that described above. It was transfered from the engraving which appeared as page twenty-three of the published *Night Thoughts;* the figure transfered is a sitting cherub or angel.

[2] I think the possibility that the paper was later accidentally moistened, and the print transfered then, is negligible.

[3] These Ballads about animals appeared in two sets; the first was issued in the summer of 1802, every Ballad (to the number of four) being sold separately; and the second was published as a small book in 1805.

[4] Quoted from an article, soon to appear in *Review of English Studies,* in which are transcribed the references to Blake in the correspondence of William Hayley and Harriet Lady Hesketh, now in the British Museum, Adds 30,803.

[5] The Ballad page was laid neatly in the center of the *Night Thoughts* proof, leaving an even border of about two inches all around it. The indentation of the *Vala* page is one quarter inch lower than the engraving on the Ballad page (British Museum copy), but presumably there was a significant variation in every print. The left margin of the indentation is quite firm, but the right margin made several ridges, as if Blake were positioning the copperplate on the Ballad page. Perhaps the *Night Thoughts* proof was used as a backing cushion when the Ballad engravings were printed. Creases on this page of *Vala,* and on the one preceding it, but on no others in the manuscript, lend credit to this suggestion.

[6] Some reasons why one would expect the engravings to have been added to the printed Ballad page are: engraving is more expensive than type; wear on engraving is more significant than wear on type; it would be easy for Blake to run as few sheets through his press as desired, but uneconomical for Seagrave to print off sheets as demand called for them; and Hayley suggests that the production of more copies of the Ballads depends on Blake alone.

[7] Later in these letters Hayley mentions frequently going to a friend who lived nearer Chichester, so he could meet and correct the proofs of his Cowper biography. Blake usually went with him, and perhaps in late May he took, as a

piece of stray paper to protect the Ballad proofs or final printing, the proof of his *Night Thoughts* engraving on which the second page of the fourth Night of *Vala* was later written.

[8] Therefore, whether or no Blake later printed off more engravings for this first Ballad after the first week in June, that fact would not relate to the date at which the printing was transfered to the *Vala* manuscript, as the print can only have been fresh in May.

[9] Forty-seven proofs of these engravings were used in *Vala,* and twenty more are in the possession of Philip Hofer. An examination of these trial proofs reveals that Blake must have made hundreds of proofs of his *Night Thoughts* engravings.

[10] *Poetry and Prose of William Blake,* ed. G. Keynes (London, 1948), p. 844.

The Date of *Mankind*

Donald C. Baker

No great mystery surrounds the date of the so-called "Macro" morality play *Mankind.* It has long been assigned to "around" 1475 on linguistic evidence and because of a rather clear reference in the play to "Edward" as a reigning monarch. Thus scholars have with some confidence placed the play in the reign of Edward IV, the date "around" 1475 being in the second reign of the Yorkist king.

I believe, however, that attention to other internal evidence can improve upon the accuracy of the date, giving a very precise *terminus a quo* and a very likely *terminus ad quem.* This internal evidence consists of the many references to current money found in the play. This example of an early professional play abounds with references to coin, in keeping with the spirit of the later moralities.

In line 458 occurs the sentence "Gyf us rede reyallys, yf ye wyll see hys abhomynabull presens."[1] The phrase "rede reyallys" is, of course, a reference to the "royal" or "ryal," the gold coin valued at ten shillings which Edward IV caused to be coined to replace the traditional noble. It was also called the "rose-noble" because of the institution of the York rose in the reverse design of the coin. This coin was first issued in Edward's second coinage of 1464/5.[2] No previous coin bore this popular name, and therefore the reference in the play is clearly of a date later than 1464/5, probably at least two years later, giving the term some time to gain popular currency.

The second piece of evidence is negative. It begins with the observation that every piece of coin current in England in the second half of the fifteenth century is mentioned in the play with a lone exception. That one exception is rather glaring in view of the fact that this coin, the angel, was first minted in Edward IV's reign, and furthermore, judging from popular and literary references, quickly became the most popular of the gold coins.[3] Literary references to the angel abound, as every student of the field knows, and, after having made a study of its uses in literary works, I feel that it is quite inconceivable that, considering the profuse allusions to current coin found in *Mankind,* a reference to, or pun upon the name of the angel would not have appeared in the play if the coin had indeed been current at the time of its composition.

The angel made its appearance in the last two years of the first reign of Edward IV (1468-69 or 69-70). Its popularity with the people was so great and its value as a symbol of royal authority was so impressive,[4] that, when Henry VI was restored, the only gold coin issued in his short six-month reign (1470-71) was the angel, and upon Edward's regaining the throne, he once again minted the angel, and, as a matter of fact, minted no other gold for the remainder of his reign. The angel, then, quickly became the standard gold of England (ca. 1468) and was the only gold minted until the reign of Henry VII.

To sum up the evidence presented, I feel that a *terminus a quo* of 1464/65 because of the "royal" reference is unquestionably established. Further, I feel that a date for *Mankind* in the second reign of Edward IV (1471-83) is highly unlikely because of the absence of references to the most popular gold coin, the angel, in the midst of a profusion of allusions to current coin. Clearly, the reference to Edward in the play itself rules out the period 1470-71, at least for the six months in which Henry VI had regained the throne. This reference, considering the dependence of the professional players upon popular sympathy, was not likely, further, to have been written in a period of extreme uncertainty as to which of the contestants would win out. Therefore I would rule out on general grounds the period 1469-71. For these reasons, I would argue that *Mankind* is very likely a product of the years 1464-69. Giving the name "royals" time to gain acceptance, and setting the date before the introduction of the angel, and before the restoration of Henry VI would have made a reference to Edward as king impossible, I would assign a tentative date of 1466, being reasonably confident that the date could not be at the most more than a year or two off either way.

NOTES

[1] F. J. Furnivall and A. W. Pollard, *The Macro Plays*, *EETSES* (London, 1904), XCI, 17.

[2] J. J. North, *English Hammered Coinage* (London, 1960), II, 63-68.

[3] See my essay, "The Angel in English Renaissance Literature," *Studies in the Renaissance*, VI (1959), 85-93.

[4] *Ibid.*, p. 87.

Psychoanalysis and Literary Biography*

Leon Edel

I

In these discourses I have tried to suggest that modern biography—and in particular the biography of imaginative writers—has undergone a marked development in our century. From the undocumented life, speculatively erected around a few meagre facts, more straw than bricks, we have come to the life of documentary surfeit, and the biographer has had to learn how to keep from putting up biographical skyscrapers. I have shown how his quest has been altered as a result of man's growing consciousness of himself as a figure in a continuum of history, and the strange and even macabre duel that can occur between subject and biographer—a matching of wits in an unequal battle between the dead and the living. We have looked into the relations between biography and criticism and seen that the biographer is committed at every turn to the act of criticism. And now I should like to examine the newest and most significant of all the biographer's relationships: his as yet uneasy flirtation with psychology.

It would be somewhat more accurate to speak of it as psychoanalysis rather than psychology, formidable and forbidding though that sounds. Psychology is the study of human behaviour: it is an all-inclusive term. Psychoanalysis is the term applied to the special techniques developed by Sigmund Freud and elaborated by his successors for the study of the symbols evoked by man which can explain his behavior.

* Retitled here. The author's chapter heading is "Psychoanalysis."

Neither term is altogether satisfactory for our purposes; the one is too large and the other too narrow. In the psychoanalytic process the analyst has constant access to the symbol life of his subject—dreams; modes of expression (such as slips of the tongue and the pen); association; the interconnections of experience; rationalization; involuntary memory, the events of everyday life. A biographer also deals in such materials: they are the ones I have pictured to you as cluttering his large table. But what a difference there is between having such inert data on a desk and having the subject in front of you in a chair or on a couch! A biographer can never, in reality, psychoanalyse his documents; and yet he is concerned with the same kinds of symbols as the psychoanalyst.

The many confusions and misunderstandings which arise between literature and psychology begin in the fact that psychoanalysts have found—as Freud did from the beginning—that the life of the imagination, and especially of great figures in literature, is highly illustrative. When they look for archetypes or universals they discover them in such figures as Oedipus or Hamlet. The result is that they venture frequently upon literary ground and sometimes indeed into places where angels fear to tread, leaving (from the point of view of the student of literature) large muddy footprints in their wake. Possessing neither the discipline of criticism nor the methods of biography, they import the atmosphere of the clinic and the consulting room into the library. And what they write is not, in reality, so much a contribution to the study of literature—I do not believe they make any such extravagant claim—but an illustration of this or that aspect of their own technical work.

The other side of the picture has been, inevitably, the venture, on the part of critics and biographers, upon psychoanalytic ground, where they have been no less inexpert than the psychoanalysts on *our* ground. The use of the psychoanalytic tool involves high skills, some quasi-scientific; a deep saturation in the problems of the mind and of the emotions; and a grasp of certain phenomena—such as "projection" or "distortion" or "malevolent transformation." We have thus a common problem: that of certain individuals who are perfectly competent in their proper field but who seem prepared to blazon forth their incompetence on ground where they do not belong.

It is not difficult to understand therefore that there has been, in the academy, a vigorous resistance to "psychologizing" and a tendency to stop up one's ears the moment a psychoanalyst arrives on the scene and tries to explain that what was wrong with Robert Louis Stevenson was that he had a feeding problem; that having as an infant been denied his mother's breast he sought ever after to gratify his oral needs—which was why he dreamed up *Dr. Jekyll and Mr. Hyde* and hinged the story on the swallowing of a potion, or why he could hold his own so splendidly at the prodigious day-long feasts in Hawaii and Samoa. This, they further tell us, meant that he never really became a mature adult. It so happens that they are not entirely wrong. Mrs. Stevenson kept a diary when Louis was an infant; and certain of his problems could be traced in psychoanalytic terms to his infantile difficulties there recorded. But isn't the important thing in all this *not* that Stevenson, for deep reasons about which we can only speculate, retained certain childish elements in his make-up—but that out of these grew the eternally youthful *Treasure Island?* And if there was this duality within him, how admirably equipped he was to trace the double sides of man's nature, as he did in the story of Jekyll and his hideous counterpart! In a word, the process of applying psychoanalysis to literature in a purely diagnostic sense invariably ends up by reducing the artist to a neurosis. Perhaps the artist *was* "neurotic." We are interested, however, in how he not only triumphs over his wound, but acquires, because of it, a kind of second sight. I need not go here into the whole troubled question of art and neurosis, which would take us far afield. Mr. Lionel Trilling has written one of his most measured essays on this subject and we have had Edmund Wilson's book *The Wound and the Bow* before us for almost two decades. The literature is large and important. Indeed, Charles Lamb, as Mr. Trilling reminds us, wrote a penetrating essay "On the Sanity of True Genius" long before the advent of psychoanalysis. Men, Lamb observed, "finding in the raptures of the higher poetry a condition of exaltation, to which they have no parallel in their own experience, besides the spurious resemblance of it in dreams and fevers, impute a state of dreaminess and fever to the poet. But the true poet dreams being awake. He is not possessed by his subject but has dominion over it. . . . Where he seems most to recede from humanity, he will be found the truest to it."

Art is the result not of calm and tranquillity, however much the artist may, on occasion, experience calm in the act of writing. It springs from tension and passion, from a state of disequilibrium in the artist's being. "His art is happy, but who knows his mind?" William Butler Yeats asked in speaking of Keats. The psychoanalyst, reading the pattern of the work, can attempt to tell us what was wrong with the artist's mental or psychic health. The biographer, reading the same pattern in the larger picture of the human condition, seeks to show how the negatives were converted into positives: how Proust translated his allergies and his withdrawal from the pain of experience, into the whole world of Combray, capturing in language the very essences which seemed illusory and evanescent in man's consciousness; how Virginia Woolf, on the margin of her melancholy, pinned the feeling of the moment to the printed page as the hunter of butterflies pins his diaphanous and fluttering prize to his; and how James Joyce, visioning himself as Daedalus, soaring over a world he had mastered, created a language for it, the word-salads of *Finnegans Wake*—but where the schizophrenic patient creates world-salads because of his madness, Joyce created them with that method in madness which Lamb was describing when he spoke of the artist's dominion over his subject. These are the triumphs of art over neurosis, and of literature over life, as I have had occasion to say elsewhere, and they illustrate Henry James's assertion to H. G. Wells that "it is art that *makes* life, makes interest, makes importance . . . and I know of no substitute whatever for the force and beauty of its process."

In one supreme instance in recent times, the psychoanalyst and the biographer have become one. I refer to Dr. Ernest Jones and the three substantial volumes in which he recorded the life of Sigmund Freud. Dr. Jones wrote out of a deep friendship and a Boswellian knowledge of his subject's life; he wrote also from extensive documents made available to him by the Freud family and as a disciple who had himself arrived at a mastery of psychoanalysis. He ran the inevitable biographical risk of apotheosizing his dead leader; but having himself been analyzed he could say at the outset (as he did) that "my own hero-worshiping propensities had been worked through before I encountered [Freud]." Dr. Jones had fewer difficulties in his quest for data than many biographers, although Freud, like Henry James, leveled the approaches to certain areas of his early life by destruction of personal papers. The remaining mass was considerable, however, and more important still, there was available to Dr. Jones in Freud's voluminous writings—the writings of a man with a profound literary sense—much of his subject's self-exploration and his dream life.

The result was a biography of major scope as befitted the luminous mind it celebrated; and a work which uses psychoanalysis constantly while being in itself a partial history of psychoanalysis. *The Life and Work of Sigmund Freud* will probably stand as an archetypal study, illustrating the relation of psychoanalysis to biography—and in negative as well as positive ways. Its shortcomings, for the literary biographer, are fairly obvious: they reside in Dr. Jones's ready use of that language —the concepts, assumptions, conclusions—to which he was accustomed and which had become second nature to him, but which is confusing to the uninitiated reader. The reader without psychoanalytic orientation is asked to make too many leaps and to hurdle ideas that by everyday standards appear strange and inconsistent, and indeed are still open to debate within the psychoanalytic disciplines. One example will suffice. In the first chapter Dr. Jones describes the emotional problems which beset the two-year-old Freud upon the impending birth of another child in the family:

> Darker problems arose when it dawned on him that some man was even more intimate with his mother than he was. Before he was two years old, for the second time another baby was on the way, and soon visibly so. Jealousy of the intruder, and anger for whoever had seduced his mother into such an unfaithful proceeding, were inevitable. Discarding his knowledge of the sleeping conditions in the house, he rejected the unbearable thought that the nefarious person could be his beloved and perfect father.

One needs to be more than merely conversant with Freudian theory to grasp this picture of a childish consciousness told in the terms of adult sexuality. Dr. Jones was inevitably much less concerned with the *translation* of his specialized concepts into the language of everyday life. The literary biographer, when he borrows the psychoanalyst's code, is obliged to decipher it and render it into the language proper to literature and literary discussion.

II

Literature and psychology are not necessarily antogonistic, as they have been made to seem. They meet on common ground. We have for decades used psychology in criticism and in biography. When we study the motivations of Hamlet, is not this psychology? When we try to understand and speculate upon symbols in a work, are we not "psychologizing"? And in our time, when creative writers have been exposed directly to the works of Freud and Jung and their disciples, and use them in their writings, we must treat them for the sources that they are. How can we understand William Faulkner's *Light in August* without at least a glance at certain modern theories of "conditioning" and behavior? Can we deal adequately with *Finnegans Wake* without looking into Jung and his theory of the collective unconscious? What meaning can Eugene O'Neill's *Strange Interlude* and *Mourning Becomes Electra* have if they are divorced from the popular Freudian misconceptions of the 1920's? Freud himself acknowledged that Sophocles and Dostoevsky and Ibsen had those glimpses into the unconscious which were vouchsafed to him in his consulting room. The answer to the misguided use of psychoanalysis is not to close our ears, but to ask ourselves: how are we to handle this difficult material while remaining true to our own disciplines—and avoid making complete fools of ourselves?

Well, it is fairly obvious that we can handle it only after we have studied and mastered that part of psychology useful to us, as we must master any learning. Our success will depend entirely on the extent to which we know what we are about and the way in which we learn to use these shiny new tools. We must not run amuck; above all we must beware of the terminology and jargon of the psychoanalysts. What we must try to do is to translate the terms in a meaningful way and into language proper to our discipline. Critics who babble of the Oedipus complex and who plant psychoanalytical clichés higgledy-piddledy in their writings do a disservice both to literature and to psychoanalysis. Biographers who take certain arbitrary symbols and apply them rigidly to the wholly volatile human personality, inevitably arrive at gross and ludicrous distortions. These are matters highly complex and difficult to explain and I have accordingly devised an illustrative problem in an effort to demonstrate what I would deem to be the use—and the abuse—of psychoanalysis in the writing of biography.

I intend to draw upon certain material presented in the Alexander Lectures of 1949-50 in E. K. Brown's discussion of *Rhythm in the Novel.* I am going to take that portion of the third lecture in which Brown discussed Willa Cather's novel *The Professor's House,* a passage later incorporated into his biography of Miss Cather. The passage in question shows Brown at his best as critic and explicator; he evokes the central symbol of the novel—the house—and illuminates it wholly in the light of his own critical intelligence. I will then try, as fairly as I can, to show how the psychoanalyst would handle this same material in a broad diagnostic sense; and finally I will try to show how the biographer, using the material offered by the critic and the psychoanalyst, can more deeply illuminate the work by seeking to determine what the house symbol meant to Miss Cather herself. First, however, let us look at the story.

III

The Professor's House, published in September 1925, is the story of a professor in a Midwestern university who has achieved success but derives no particular pleasure from it. The novel is a record of his mental depression. With the money received from a prize he has won for a monumental historical work, Professor St. Peter has built a new house, to please his wife and daughters. He would prefer to remain in the rented house in which he has shaped his career for thirty years. Indeed he cannot bring himself to move out of his old study, located in the attic, where still stand the wire forms on which a dressmaker fitted the clothes for his wife and growing daughters. The attic sewing-room is lit by an oil lamp. It is heated by a stove. Professor St. Peter has scorned cushion-comforts. He had a "show" study downstairs and has one in the new house. But the attic room, with its silent dummies, is comfort enough for him. He clings to the old place even after the rest of the house has been emptied and the moving is over. Since the lease still has some months to run, he decides he will keep his former workroom until he has to give it up.

His elder daughter is Rosamond, an attractive girl who has married a suave, fast-talking, pretentious but cultivated young man named Louie Marsellus. Marsellus has, with great practicality, turned to commercial use in aviation a certain discovery made by one of the professor's former students. Tom Outland, who was Rosamond's fiancé but who was killed during the First World War. Outland bequeathed his patent to Rosamond, and since her marriage to Marsellus it has become a source of wealth. The professor loves his daughter very much, but intensely dislikes the upstart qualities of her husband and accordingly feels a certain alienation from her. The professor's wife, however, is extremely fond of her son-in-law and his European affectations. She feels that her husband, in his withdrawal from the entire family, does not sufficiently recognize how materially its fortunes are being altered by Louie Marsellus's business acumen. There is a second daughter who is married to a newspaper columnist named McGregor. They tend to side with the father against the somewhat vulgar *nouveau riche* world of Louie and Rosamond. The latter are also building a house—in the style of a Norwegian manor, set incongruously in this Midwestern community.

The first part of the book, titled "The Family," sketches for us the professor's alienation from those closest to him because of his feeling that his wife and daughters do not really understand his deeper emotional life, and his rebellion against the crass materialism of the college town. He has set himself apart rather successfully over the years. He has made for himself a French garden in this prairie setting, he has cultivated his love for French wines and delicate sauces; he has a beach house on the lake and spends long lonely hours in the water. He is a Gallic epicure isolated, like his garden, in surroundings to which he cannot ever wholly belong. He has had only one student in all the years of his teaching who has meant anything to him—Tom Outland. He dislikes the new generation of students. He dislikes college politics. He has no real friends among his colleagues. He feels himself oppressed by the prosaic, mediocre world of the town of which his wife and daughters are so much a part. Material values have been exalted here over those he cherishes: the rich fabric of art related to the rich fabric of the old religion in which great cathedrals and the drama of Good and Evil exalted men to a high creativity.

The second part of the book is called "Tom Outland's Story." Here Miss Cather attempts a risky technical device, which is nevertheless time-honored in fiction. In the manner of Cervantes or Smollett she interpolates a story within a story: she gives us an autobiographical fragment written by Tom Outland and confided to Professor St. Peter. It describes a crucial episode in the young man's life. Miss Cather explained that in writing this part of the novel she had in mind those Dutch paintings in which interiors are scrupulously rendered; in many of these there was "a square window, open, through which one saw the masts of ships, or a stretch of gray sea"; the effect is that of an inset, a picture within a picture. Having given us the interior of the professor's family life, she directs our attention to the one important window in it—the one that looks out upon Tom Outland's adventure.

The crucial episode had been his discovery of a Cliff Dwellers' village tucked into a wall of rock high in a New Mexico canyon. Here was beauty at once primitive and sophisticated. Here were houses that let in wind and sun and yet sheltered an unfathomable past. Here also was a great tower: "It was still as sculpture. . . . The tower was the fine thing that held all the jumble of houses together and made them mean something. . . .That village sat looking down into the cañon with the calmness of eternity." The Cliff Dwellers' houses are never overtly contrasted with the houses in the professor's town, but they invite contrast. In the modern town the emphasis, as E. K. Brown observes, is on the individual buildings. In the ancient village it is on the architectural as well as the social unity.

Tom made his discovery with the aid of a fellow cowpuncher, Roddy. He travelled to Washington in great excitement to inform the Department of the Interior, bringing with him samples of the ancient pottery he had found in the long-deserted houses. In the capital he is promptly wrapped up in needless red tape; he sits in impersonal outer offices; he is met with general indifference. Civil servants seem to him strange modern cave dwellers living in rows of apartments as if in rabbit warrens; and their careerism and arrogance blot out all his hopes. He turns his back on Washington, disillusioned; he had felt he had done the proper thing as a citizen, but the petty officials did not share his interest in his country's distant past. However, a still greater disappointment awaited him. Roddy, during his prolonged absence, had profited by the arrival of a German anthropologist to sell the entire contents of the cliff town. The ancient relics had been packed and shipped to Europe and Roddy had deposited the money for Tom in a bank thinking he had driven a good bargain. Tom, in anger at what he considered a betrayal, broke with Roddy and then returned to the cliff town to spend a few days in magnificent solitude, hiding in the high tower his notes and records of the entire adventure. Then, descending again, he withdrew the money from the bank and used it to go to college, there meeting the professor who became his guide and mentor.

The final part of the novel is a mere sketch. Titled "The Professor," it returns to the dilemma of St. Peter's isolation in his attic. Lonely and depressed, he remains there while his family is away during the summer, living a monastic dream-life, with the old sewing-woman turning up to act as charwoman. One day, on awakening from a nap, he discovers the room filled with fumes from the stove, but he is incapable of making the effort to arouse himself and to throw open the window. He has lost the will to live. The fortuitous arrival of the sewing-woman saves him, and there the novel ends. We can only speculate that the professor will go on living in isolation amid his family.

IV

What are we to make of this novel—if we can call it a novel? It is a stitching together of two inconclusive fragments about a professor, his family, and his wish for death, and the adventures of a young man alone with the past on a mesa and briefly in touch with the modern urban life of Washington. The two episodes relating to the professor hardly constitute a novel: they convey a picture of his deep depression which nothing in the book really explains. Why does he wish for death at a time when his life has been crowned with success and when his family flourishes as never before; when indeed there is the promise of a grandchild, for Rosamond expects a baby as the book ends? The Tom Outland story fills in the background of Rosamond's wealth and gives us the strange story of the intense young man who altered the whole course of the professor's life; this does not illuminate, however, the professor's final state of mind. His wish to die is at no point sufficiently motivated by the facts of the small-town life, the general hopelessness of the Philistine surroundings. To believe so intensely in art and the religion of art, and to have created so fully, and yet at the same time to be overpowered by a sense of futility and ineffectuality—these are the contradictions we discern within the professor.

E. K. Brown, in his Alexander Lecture, found an inner unity which he explained in terms of the symbolism of houses within the book. It is a striking passage. There are, he points out, the two houses of the professor, and of these the old house is the significant one. The new house is wrong for him. The Marsellus-Rosamond Norwegian manor house is wrong too. It is a product of pretension and materialism, without regard for the style of the town and the essential dignity of human dwellings. The homes of the Cliff Dwellers—for these are houses also—primitive and wind-swept on their high perch, possessed that dignity. In the third portion of the book the link between these houses is established. Brown continues, speaking of this final part:

> The first and second parts of the book which have seemed so boldly unrelated are brought into a profound unity. It is in this third part of the novel that the large background of emotion, which demands rhythmic expression if we are to respond to it as it deserves, becomes predominant. In the first part it was plain that the professor did not wish to live in his new house, and did not wish to enter into the sere phase of his life correlative with it. At the beginning of the third part it becomes plain that he cannot indefinitely continue to make the old attic-study the theatre of his life, that he cannot go on prolonging, or attempting to prolong his prime, the phase of his life correlative with that. The personality of his mature

> years—the personality that had expressed itself powerfully and in the main happily in his teaching, his scholarship, his love for his wife, his domesticity—is now quickly receding, and nothing new is flowing in. What begins to dominate St. Peter is something akin to the Cliff Dwellers, something primitive which had ruled him long ago when he was a boy on a pioneer farm in the rough Solomon valley in northwestern Kansas. To this primitive being not many things were real;. . . what counted was nature, and nature seen as a web of life, and finally of death.

For the professor remembers an old poem he has read, Longfellow's translation of the Anglo-Saxon *Grave.* He doesn't recall it quite accurately (that is, Miss Cather didn't) but this is what is given in the novel:

> For thee a house was built
> Ere thou wast born;
> For thee a mould was made
> Ere thou of woman camest.

And Brown concludes:

> All that had seemed a hanging back from the future—the clinging to the old attic study, the absorption in Tom Outland and the civilization of the Cliff Dwellers, the revival of interest in the occupations of his childhood and its pleasures—was something very unlike what it had seemed. It was profound, unconscious preparation for death, for the last house of the professor.

This seems to me quite admirable literary criticism; the critic has seen the unity of the book created by the central symbol; he has penetrated to the professor's state of mind and grasped that his interest in the occupations of childhood is a stepping backward—or forward—to old age and death. But the story, as told by Miss Cather, in reality leaves the critic helpless in one respect: there is no way to explain why the professor should at this moment of his middle years lose his will to live. We are given no clue. Miss Cather records merely the professor's despair.

V

And now let us apply the tools of psychoanalysis to this material. I want to look at it through the understanding of people and of symbols offered us by Sigmund Freud and, more recently, by Harry Stack Sullivan. The first striking element in the story is the professor's strange attachment to his attic room, high up, old, and cramped, but safely away from the family life in the house below. Now, people do form attachments to rooms and to houses, but the professor's attachment here verges upon the eccentric. He clearly thinks of his attic as a place of—and Miss Cather's words express it—"insulation from the engaging drama of domestic life . . . only a vague sense, generally pleasant, of what went on below came up the narrow stairway." And later he thinks that "on that perilous journey down through the human house, he might lose his mood, his enthusiasm, even his temper."

This is much more than a professor seeking a quiet corner for his working hours. The room is "insulation." The professor withdraws from his family and at the same time makes demands on it, for care, food, attention. There is decidedly something infantile here, the security a baby feels in its possession of the mother and the breast for which it need make no return. In this attic room, tiny and snug as a womb, cradled in a warm and alive household, but safe from any direct contact with the world outside, Professor St. Peter can feel taken care of and as undisturbed as an embryo.

The room, furthermore, is used by one other person—the motherly sewing-woman, Augusta. Adjuncts to this mother figure are the two dressmakers' dummies. Seen as part of the sewing-woman, the mother figure, these two dummies express opposite experiences of the mother: one is described as matronly, of a bulk suggesting warm flesh and reassuring physical possession; the other is of sophisticated line suggesting spirit and sexual awareness and interest. So the professor has in his secluded place the beloved mother, who cares for and protects him but is also of some sexual interest to him. He wants his mother to be both a mother and an erotic stimulus and above all he wants to possess her exclusively.

Willa Cather now weaves a second story, but it is in reality a repetition of the same theme. Her hero, again a man, yearns for a high mesa, a sun-beaten plateau, and when he conquers it he finds a cave city. Caves are feminine sexual symbols. These caves are for him inviolate and untouched, like a seemingly virginal mother preserved from others, a mother of long ago, of the infant years, who belonged only to the child greedy at her breast. There is also beautiful pottery. Pottery is again a feminine symbol. The hero cherishes these artifacts and comes to regret that he has a male companion with whom he must share them. The disinclination to share might be seen as sibling jealousy for the mother, or the kind of rivalry a boy, in his Oedipal phase, has for the father who possesses the mother in the sexual way the boy aspires to have her. The hero is disillusioned first when his mother country, symbolized by Washington, is not interested in his discoveries and, in effect, rejects him, and then when his male friend puts the pottery to some practical use: so that we might say the boy is disillusioned when he first learns that in reality his mother is not a virgin and that his father is the cause of her having been thus despoiled. The hero angrily drives the male friend—father or sibling—away and spends a period among the caves—that is with his mother—as blissful as a babe in full possession of the breast. He preserves a record of his narcissistic-infantile paradise, the paradise of life in the womb, of possessing the mother physically, in a notebook which he carefully secretes in the tower. Like the professor's attic room, the tower is still higher and more secluded than the dwellings, where the mother can be preserved, if not in actuality (the pottery), at least in the diary describing his intimate life with her (Outland's detailed account of the caves and their contents as he first found them). Life, its rude events and passage of time, its insistence on moving forward and routing the infant from the womb and the breast, also disrupts the hero's blissful eternity on his hidden mesa, in his caves, with his pottery. He has been disturbed. He seeks stubbornly at least to preserve the memory of days with mother (the mesa, etc.) even as the professor cannot leave his cubbyhole study and would not want the dressmaker's dummies removed.

But life does move on, and in moving on it demands that we follow. The professor seeks a solution to this problem. The family which sustained him in the house below, while he took attic refuge, moves to the new house. If he follows he must accept a new room, a modern room, a room on a lower floor; he must take his place in the family on a different basis; his daughters are now married; they will have children. He must change and grow too, accept his new role as father-in-law and eventually as grandfather. He must, in other words, meet life in an adult way and recognize the demands which are being made on him to take a more active part in the lives of his grown-up children. But the professor clings as long as he can to the old attic room, and with the life gone from the house beneath he is actually threatened with greater isolation than ever before. He has a choice: he can maintain this state of alienation from his family, or he can emerge from his passive dependency and assume the active life expected of him. Appropriately enough, Willa Cather ends her story with the professor nearly suffocating in his room. To remain in the womb beyond one's time is indeed to suffocate. The tenacity of the professor's—and the writer's—determination to maintain this *status quo ante,* if only in fantasy, is illustrated in the ending of the story. It is the sewing-woman—who, by the way, was sensibly eager to move to her new, bigger sewing-room, to a new life, a new relationship, and cannot understand the professor's infantile attachment to the old room, the old relationship—it is the sewing-woman who rescues the professor from suffocation. A mother figure has once more appeared upon the scene for the professor, who thus hangs on to his fixation even though it has brought him an immense threat. The book ends with the professor's problem unresolved, save in the sense that ultimately Mother Earth will enclose him in her womb.

VI

Psychoanalysis, by singling out certain primal elements in the picture, has illuminated our story and offered answers to some of our questions. The professor's death-wish, undefined by the author, would appear to be due to lingering infantile needs, so strong that this successful adult teacher and writer, otherwise a figure of dignity and maturity, adheres to a pattern of behavior which belongs to his childhood. This he masks by rationalization: a love for the past, a dislike of the present. But how are we to handle this material, so heavy with Freud's ideas about infantile sexuality—its insistence upon the attic as a womb symbol, its incestuous fantasies and Oedipal situation—a kind of "psychologizing" which can have meaning only to those who have worked with these concepts on a clinical level? And does this interpretation, fascinating and incredible though some of it is, tell the layman anything about the novel as novel? Or is he being offered a virtually meaningless diagram, highly speculative, of the unconscious fantasies of the professor, derived though it may be from the overt material placed in the book by the author? We all live in some form of house and doubtless, for some of us, on some unconscious level, caves and attics may be wombs and houses mothers, and the smooth curves of pottery may suggest the curves of women. But houses, and the rooms within them, are also universal facts and a universal reality. They testify to man's need for shelter and warmth. It is true that we are thrust out of the womb into the world and must inevitably acquire some shelter, by stages that start with the basket and the cradle and end in adult dwellings. And it is true that there are certain individuals who, instead of welcoming the shelters of this world, long for the unattainable state of the embryo where one was sheltered from everything, that state which James Joyce, mimicking the cradle-tones of our literature, described as "Before born babe bliss had." Wombs are for blissful embryos; houses for growing children and adults. We juggle, so to speak, with the obvious when we invoke such universal symbols.

And what has become of the fine social criticism in the novel? In tracing such a diagram of the professor's neurosis, it is seen as a mere desire to cling to the past for infantile or infantile-sexual reasons. Yet the social criticism is perhaps the best part of Miss Cather's novels. They record the protest of a gifted woman against the ever increasing conformities and clichés of American life. Her voice is never more resonant than when she shows how the capital of the pioneers was converted into the small change of standardization; and that while the original settlers wrested fom the land the glory of America, the sons of the settlers became real-estate agents parcelling this land out and dealing in mortgages, or front-office men—like Louie Marsellus. The anguish of Tom Outland in Washington (whatever neurotic traits he may thereby reveal) is still the genuine anguish of someone who wants government to meet its responsibilities to the past, to history.

And what of criticism of the novel itself? To label the symbols within it in terms of Freud or to describe the "interpersonal" relations between the professor and his family after the manner of Sullivan, gives us no help in assessing the work as work of art. We have merely used psychoanalytic ideas as instruments of quasi-clinical diagnosis. Has Miss Cather successfully carried out her general intention? What is the explanation of the professor's happiness in the past? Why does he experience malaise in the present—a present in which, even without neurotic motivation, the malaise can certainly be held to be genuine?

I have given you the point of view of one critic about this novel, and a psychoanalytical approach to the material. It is my contention that the method used in this approach leads us to a "diagnosis" which can have little meaning unless it is translated into different terms. And I hold that this translation is possible only by calling upon the resources of biography. Let us therefore pursue our inquiry on this third level.

Psychoanalysis is concerned with what goes on in the unconscious and how this is reflected in conscious thoughts and actions. It deals always with a given consciousness. A dream cannot be truly interpreted, as we have seen, unless it is attached to the dreamer, although it may be a pretty story and have distinct meanings for someone to whom it is narrated. These meanings, however, are not necessarily those of the dreamer, who has put into the dream his personal symbols. The personal symbols can be understood only after a close study of their recurrent use in the weaving of that person's dream structures. As with dreams, so with the work of art. Ernest Jones has significantly said:

> A work of art is too often regarded as a finished thing-in-itself, something almost independent of the creator's personality, as if little would be learned about the one or the other by connecting the two studies. Informed criticism, however, shows that a correlated study of the two sheds light in both directions, on the inner nature of the composition and on the creative impulse of its author. The two can be separated only at the expense of diminished appreciation, whereas to increase our knowledge of either automatically deepens our understanding of the other.

It is true that sometimes we have no alternative but to cling to our shreds of evidence and to speculate endlessly. But with a writer so recently in our midst as Willa Cather, we have abundant biographical material relating to her actual experience. We can try to determine—what she at best may have only glimpsed—how this was incorporated into the imagination by which she created.

VII

Our data are derived from E. K. Brown's biography of Willa Cather and from the valuable memoir written by her friend of four decades, Edith Lewis. In these works we discover how intensely Willa Cather suffered as a little girl from an initial displacement from one house to another. She was born in Virginia and lived in a large house. At ten she was torn from the east and taken to the Divide, to a new house. Here she discovered also the sod houses of the early settlers, even as she was later to observe the cave houses of the Cliff Dwellers in the Southwest. We note that the professor in her novel was "dragged" to Kansas from the east when he was eight, that he "nearly died of it."

In Nebraska Willa Cather discovered that nearly all the inhabitants were displaced from somewhere else, and some had been involved in a transatlantic displacement. Her later novels were to depict with deep emotion the meaning of this displacement of the pioneers from Europe and civilization to the rugged prairie. Willa Cather could show empathy with them; their anguish was hers. Then, in Red Cloud, in Nebraska, where the adolescent girl began to discover the life of the frontier, there was a neighboring house in which lived a childless couple. In her own house there was the clash of temperaments and the rivalries of a large family of boys and girls; in their midst was a refined Southern-bred mother, a gentlewoman somehow strangely aloof and exhausted by repeated pregnancies. And so this other house became a retreat; the cultivated Mrs. Wiener from France served as a kind of second mother to Willa Cather. She provided books and quiet surroundings; the future author could lie for hours on the parlor rug, reading and dreaming. A fairly circumstantial account of the two houses may be found in Miss Cather's late story, "Old Mrs. Harris." From the small town Miss Cather went to Lincoln, Nebraska, to attend the university, and here she discovered still another house. It was filled with robust young men, over whom there presided an Old World mother. Miss Cather had again found a home, this time as an escape from the dreariness of a furnished room. The house was that of the Westermann family, and the late William Lynn Westermann of Columbia University, a distinguished Egyptologist, testified to the accuracy of Willa Cather's picture of life in his early home as portrayed in her novel *One of Ours*.

In 1895 Miss Cather went to Pittsburgh and worked on a newspaper. She lived in a series of depressing boarding houses. The way in which she escaped from these into the world of the theatre and music is reflected in her ever-popular short story, "Paul's Case." After five years of drab existence she met a young woman who changed the course of her life. This was Isabelle McClung, the daughter of a prominent and wealthy Pittsburgh judge, a strikingly handsome woman interested in the arts. So attached did she become to Willa Cather, the radiance of her personality and the promise of her art, that she invited her to come and live in the McClung family mansion. The gesture might be described as protective and motherly, and Isabelle became, indeed, during these years, a patron of Miss Cather's art. Her house was many times more elegant and spacious than the Wiener house or the house of the Westermanns. Here Willa Cather put together her first book of verse, began to publish short stories, and finally her first volume of tales. She was given a quiet room to work in at the rear of the McClung mansion. It had been a sewing room. Still standing in it were some dressmaker's dummies.

Willa Cather remained deeply attached to this house. It represented security and peace. From it she was able to face the world and build her career. Even after she had moved to New York and taken up a new abode in Greenwich Village—thus establishing her own home—and was the successful managing editor of *McClure's Magazine,* she would dash off to Pittsburgh for periodic stays with Isabelle and uninterrupted work in her favorite room.

In the midst of the First World War there came a break. It followed Isabelle McClung's decision to marry a violinist she had known for some years, Jan Hambourg, who with his father and brother had a school of music in Toronto. This happened in 1917 when Miss Cather was in her late forties. Isabelle too was no longer young. Thus a significant change was introduced into the fixed pattern of the years. And it is from this moment that the biographer can date a change in Willa Cather's works. They reflect an increasing tension and deep inner anxiety. Her novel *One of Ours,* written in the early twenties, is an anxious book; on the surface the anxiety is related to the disillusion and malaise that followed the war and to a strong sense of betrayal by the new generation in Nebraska, which was watering down the achievements of the pioneers. For all its defects it won the Pulitzer Prize. The title of the next novel clearly conveys the state of mind of the author: it is the story *A Lost Lady*—and it tells of a woman who clings to a vanished past in a changing world. After this Miss Cather wrote *The Professor's House.*

But just before she set to work on this novel, before she had even had the idea for it, she had gone to France to visit Isabelle and Jan Hambourg. Isabelle, in her French home at Ville-D'Avray, had set aside a study for her friend. The new house would incorporate in it this essential feature of the Pittsburgh mansion. Miss Lewis testifies: "The Hambourgs had hoped that she would make Ville-D'Avray her permanent home. But although the little study was charming, and all the surroundings were attractive, and the Hambourgs themselves devoted and solicitous, she found herself unable to work at Ville-D'Avray. She felt indeed that she would never be able to work there."

Why? Miss Lewis does not tell us. But she does tell us what we already have suspected: that there are some traits of Jan Hambourg in the character of Louie Marsellus. Hambourg was a cultivated musician, deeply read in French literature and apparently as good a conversationalist as Marsellus. Miss Cather had dedicated *A Lost Lady* to him, thereby welcoming him to the circle of her intimate friends. The strange thing is that she dedicated *The Professor's House* as well: "For Jan, because he likes narrative." As we collate the somewhat pretentious figure of Louie with the figure of the real-life musician, we recover so many similarities, or exaggerations, of certain traits that we are prompted to speculate whether the novelist did not find it necessary to write this flattering dedication—the second book in succession to bear his name—to mitigate the effect of the unflattering portrait she had painted. A dedication is by its nature so friendly an act that it is difficult to think of it as masking a concealed animus. It is clear that Miss Cather was charmed by one side of Jan Hambourg; but like the professor, she would have welcomed him as a friend rather than as the husband of Isabelle-Rosamond.

We can now see what life itself contributed to *The Professor's House.* Willa Cather's early uprootings have more meaning in explaining the attachment to a fixed abode than the universal uprooting from the womb; her mother's aloofness, and her search for substitute houses, can also be readily fitted into the novel. The Pittsburgh house with its sewing-room has been transferred into the professor's frame house. Like the professor of her fiction, Miss Cather won a prize during her middle years; like him, she achieved success. The new house at Ville-D'Avray has become the new house built by the professor's family; it too was no substitute for the old one, since in France Isabelle could no longer function for Willa Cather as a maternal figure exclusively possessed by her; she now had to share Isabelle with Jan—as she had had to share her mother with her brothers; as the professor, though he dislikes it, must share Rosamond with Louie; and as Outland shares his caves and pottery with Roddy, only to lose them.

And here we touch the heart of our problem. We can now see what motivated the depression of Willa Cather's middle years when she wrote that "the world broke in two in 1922 or thereabouts," for we know that to her search for inner security, going back to childhood, was added the deeper sense, irrational from an adult point of view, that she had been rejected. Of course this was not so: but our emotions have a way of clinging, in the teeth of adult reality, to patterns fixed at an earlier time. The reality was that Isabelle had moved forward in life, and had married; Willa Cather had not been able to move forward and adapt herself to this situation. In *The Professor's House* Miss Cather had so identified herself with the professor that she could not supply any "rejection motif" for his depression. All she could do was to say that the world was out of joint for him, as it was for herself. This depression of spirit is expressed in her first section, in her account of the professor who cannot keep pace with his family, although his life has been crowned with fame and success.

But such is the nature of our inner fantasies that they persist in seeking expression. In the first part of the novel which emerged from these fantasies, the professor in reality is the one who, by clinging to his attic, has rejected his family. Willa Cather accordingly opens a window into a second theme, after the manner of the Dutch painters, and here she can incorporate her deepest feelings. The Tom Outland story is linked to Isabelle in a curious way. It would seem that in Willa Cather's consciousness the Pittsburgh house, standing on high ground, could be identified with the mesa and the tower. For, some years earlier, when she published *The Song of the Lark,* her first novel to draw upon the southwest, she dedicated it to Isabelle McClung with the following verses:

> On uplands,
> At morning,
> The world was young, the winds were free;
> A garden fair
> In that blue desert air,
> Its guest invited me to be.

Uplands had become Outland. The world in the "blue desert air" of the mesa is a re-creation of the feeling of freedom Willa Cather had experienced in her life with the maternal Isabelle, patroness of the arts, and in the sewing-room sanctuary of the Pittsburgh mansion. But Tom Outland is rejected twice: the maternal-paternal Government rejects him, and when he returns home he finds that Roddy, his boon companion, has denuded his cliff sanctuary of all that was precious to him. The fantasy of rejection is thus incorporated into the novel.

The Tom Outland story is complete. That of the professor is not. By merging the insights gained from psychology with the biographical data that give us clues to the workings of the author's imagination, we are able to render a critical evaluation: we can see the failure of *The*

Professor's House as a work of fiction. The professor lives for us as a man who has given up his good fight and takes the world as preparation for the grave. He has retreated into a vale of misanthropy and despair. He has everything to live for; and for reasons unexplained and unresolved he does not want to live. The materialism of an age, the marrying off of one's children to persons we may like or dislike, the process of growing old—these are not sufficient motives for a depression as deep and as all-consuming as the professor's. The world is never all that we would want it to be, and lives are lived in a constant process of doing, and of ups and downs. The novel is thus incomplete because of Miss Cather's inner problems, which did not permit her to resolve clearly the problems of the character she had projected in her novel. Therefore the professor was not given a clear-cut motivation: his state of mind was described but not explained. The truth was that Willa Cather was incapable of admitting to herself—who can?—that what was troubling her was not the departure of Isabelle but what it symbolized: the re-assertion of an old need to have an "other house" and the security of a mother figure all to herself within it. In the guise of Outland, and with a theme further removed from herself, she could project the deeper anxiety resulting from her sense of rejection. The professor was too close to herself. His story could not be told without emotional involvement on the part of the author. Tom Outland was farther away: and his story is told with complete success.

All Willa Cather's later works can be read in the light of this deep feeling of insecurity: her choice of the Rock as the symbol of endurance, her rigidity in the face of her nation's growth and change, her gradual regression in her writings to childhood situations—these spring from the same overpowering isolation, the same death wish yet struggle to live, acted out in the suffocating attic by the professor. I could find other episodes in her life to amplify what I have said. Not least is the one in which she had to uproot herself from her Bank Street apartment in Greenwich Village because a subway was being run through the area. She took refuge for a few days in a Lower Fifth Avenue hotel, and remained there for several years. Whatever rationalizations might be offered, it was clearly difficult for her to move and a sheltering hotel, ministering to her needs, seems to have made her reluctant to search out an apartment and re-establish her home. I am told that Miss Cather intensely disliked being in the hotel—all the more reason, we might suppose, for her to have left it sooner than she did. The world did break in two for Miss Cather. One part of it moved on; she remained stranded in the other. And *The Professor's House,* in its very structure, contained this break. It is an unsymmetrical and unrealized novel because Willa Cather could not bring the two parts of her broken world together again.

To arrive at this view the biographer has had to unite the qualities of critic and psychoanalyst. By penetrating more deeply into the life it has been possible to penetrate more deeply into the work.

The Backgrounds of 'The Dead'

Richard Ellmann

> The silent cock shall crow at last. The west shall shake the east awake.
> Walk while ye have the night for morn, lightbreakfastbringer. . . .
>
> —*Finnegans Wake* (473)

The stay in Rome had seemed purposeless, but during it Joyce became aware of the change in his attitude toward Ireland and so toward the world. He embodied his new perceptions in 'The Dead.' The story, which was the culmination of a long waiting history, began to take shape in Rome, but was not set down until he left the city. The pressure of hints, sudden insights, and old memories rose in his mind until, like King Midas's barber, he was compelled to speech.

Although the story dealt mainly with three generations of his family in Dublin, it drew also upon an incident in Galway in 1903. There Michael ('Sonny') Bodkin courted Nora Barnacle; but he contracted tuberculosis and had to be confined to bed. Shortly afterwards Nora resolved to go to Dublin, and Bodkin stole out of his sickroom, in spite of the rainy weather, to sing to her under an apple tree and bid her goodbye. In Dublin Nora soon learned that Bodkin was dead, and when she met Joyce she was first attracted to him, as she told a sister, because he resembled Sonny Bodkin.[1]

Joyce's habit of ferreting out details had made him conduct minute interrogations of Nora even before their departure from Dublin. He was disconcerted by the fact that young men before him had interested her. He did not much like to know that her heart was still moved, even in pity, by the recollection of the boy who had loved her. The notion of being in some sense in rivalry with a dead man buried in the little cemetery at Oughterard was one that came easily, and gallingly, to a man of Joyce's jealous disposition. It was one source of his complaint to his Aunt Josephine Murray that Nora persisted in regarding him as quite similar to other men she had known.[2]

A few months after expressing this annoyance, while Joyce and Nora Barnacle were living in Trieste in 1905, Joyce received another impulsion toward 'The Dead.' In a letter Stanislaus happened to mention attending a concert of Plunket Greene, the Irish baritone, which included one of Thomas Moore's *Irish Melodies* called 'O, ye Dead!'[3] The song, a dialogue of living and dead, was eerie enough, but what impressed Stanislaus was that Greene rendered the second stanza, in which the dead answer the living, as if they were whimpering for the bodied existence they could no longer enjoy:

> It is true, it is true, we are shadows cold and wan;
> And the fair and the brave whom we loved on earth are gone;
> But still thus ev'n in death,
> So sweet the living breath
> Of the fields and the flow'rs in our youth we wandered o'er,
> That ere, condemn'd, we go
> To freeze, 'mid Hecla's snow,
> We would taste it awhile, and think we live once more!

James was interested and asked Stanislaus to send the words, which he learned to sing himself. His feelings about his wife's dead lover found a dramatic counterpart in the jealousy of the dead for the living in Moore's song: it would seem that the living and the dead are jealous of each other. Another aspect of the rivalry is suggested in *Ulysses*, where Stephen cries out to his mother's ghost, whose 'glazing eyes, staring out of death, to shake and bend my soul, . . . to strike me down,' he cannot put out of mind: 'No, mother. Let me be and let me live.'[4] That the dead do not stay buried is, in fact, a theme of Joyce from the beginning to the end of his work; Finnegan is not the only corpse to be resurrected.

In Rome the obtrusiveness of the dead affected what he thought of Dublin, the equally Catholic city he had abandoned, a city as prehensile of its ruins, visible and invisible. His head was filled with a sense of the too successful encroachment of the dead upon the living city; there was a disrupting parallel in the way that Dublin, buried behind him, was haunting his thoughts. In *Ulysses* the theme was to be reconstituted, in more horrid form, in the mind of Stephen, who sees corpses rising from their graves like vampires to deprive the living of joy. The bridebed, the childbed, and the bed of death are bound together, and death 'comes, pale vampire, through storm his eyes, his bat sails bloodying the sea, mouth to her mouth's kiss.'[5] We can be at the same time in death as well as in life.*

By February 11, 1907, after six months in Rome, Joyce knew in general what story he must write. Some of his difficulty in beginning it was due, as he said himself,† to the riot in Dublin over *The Playboy of the Western World.* Synge had followed the advice of Yeats that Joyce had rejected, to find his inspiration in the Irish folk, and had gone to the Aran Islands. This old issue finds small echoes in the story. The nationalistic Miss Ivors tries to persuade Gabriel to go to Aran (where Synge's *Riders to the Sea* is set), and when he refuses twits him for his lack of patriotic feeling. Though Gabriel thinks of defending the autonomy of art and its indifference to politics, he knows such a defense would be pretentious, and only musters up the remark that he is sick of his own country. But the issue is far from settled for him.

'The Dead' begins with a party and ends with a corpse, so entwining 'funferal' and 'funeral' as in the wake of Finnegan. That he began with a party was due, at least in part, to Joyce's feeling that the rest of the stories in *Dubliners* had not completed his picture of the city. In a letter of September 25, 1906,‡ he had written his brother from Rome to say that some elements of Dublin had been left out of his stories: 'I have not reproduced its ingenuous insularity and its hospitality, the latter "virtue" so far as I can see does not exist elsewhere in Europe.' He allowed a little of this warmth to enter 'The Dead.' In his speech at the Christmas party Gabriel Conroy explicitly commends Ireland for this very virtue of hospitality, though his expression of the idea is distinctly after-dinner: 'I feel more strongly with every recurring year that our country has no tradition which does it so much honour and which it should guard so jealously as that of its hospitality. It is a tradition that is unique as far as my experience goes (and I have visited not a few places abroad) among the modern nations.' This was Joyce's oblique way, in language that mocked his own, of beginning the task of making amends.

The selection of details for 'The Dead' shows Joyce making those

* The converse of this theme appears in *Ulysses* (113[107]), when Bloom, walking in Glasnevin, thinks 'They are not going to get me this innings. Warm beds: warm fullblooded life.'

† See p. 248 [of Ellmann's book].

‡ See p. 239 [of Ellmann's book].

choices which, while masterly, suggest the preoccupations that mastered him. Once he had determined to represent an Irish party, the choice of the Misses Morkans' as its location was easy enough. He had already reserved for *Stephen Hero* a Christmas party at his own house, a party which was also to be clouded by a discussion of a dead man. The other festive occasions of his childhood were associated with his hospitable great-aunts Mrs. Callanan and Mrs. Lyons, and Mrs. Callanan's daughter Mary Ellen, at their house at 15 Usher's Island, which was also known as the 'Misses Flynn school.'[6] There every year the Joyces who were old enough would go, and John Joyce carved the goose and made the speech. Stanislaus Joyce says that the speech of Gabriel Conroy in 'The Dead' is a good imitation of his father's oratorical style.*

In Joyce's story Mrs. Callanan and Mrs. Lyons, the Misses Flynn, become the spinster ladies, the Misses Morkan, and Mary Ellen Callanan becomes Mary Jane. Most of the other party guests were also reconstituted from Joyce's recollections. Mrs. Lyons had a son Freddy, who kept a Christmas card shop in Grafton Street.[7] Joyce introduces him as Freddy Malins, and situates his shop in the less fashionable Henry Street, perhaps to make him need that sovereign Gabriel lent him. Another relative of Joyce's mother, a first cousin, married a Protestant named Mervyn Archdale Browne, who combined the profession of music teacher with that of agent for a burglary insurance company. Joyce keeps him in 'The Dead' under his own name. Bartell d'Arcy, the hoarse singer in the story, was based upon Barton M'Guckin, the leading tenor in the Carl Rosa Opera Company. There were other tenors, such as John McCormack, whom Joyce might have used, but he needed one who was unsuccessful and uneasy about himself; and his father's often-told anecdote about M'Guckin's lack of confidence† furnished him with just such a singer as he intended Bartell d'Arcy to be.

The making of his hero, Gabriel Conroy, was more complicated. The root situation, of jealousy for his wife's dead lover, was of course Joyce's. The man who is murdered, D. H. Lawrence has one of his characters say, desires to be murdered;[8] some temperaments demand the feeling that their friends and sweethearts will deceive them. Joyce's conversation often returned to the word 'betrayal,'[9] and the entangled innocents whom he uses for his heroes are all aspects of his

* He excepts the quotation from Browning, but even this was quite within the scope of the man who could quote Vergil when lending money to his son.[11]

† See p. 14 [of Ellmann's book].

conception of himself. Though Gabriel is less impressive than Joyce's other heroes, Stephen, Bloom, Richard Rowan, or Earwicker, he belongs to their distinguished, put-upon company.

There are several specific points at which Joyce attributes his own experiences to Gabriel. The letter which Gabriel remembers having written to Gretta Conroy early in their courtship is one of these; from it Gabriel quotes to himself the sentiment, 'Why is it that words like these seem to me so dull and cold? Is it because there is no word tender enough to be your name?' These sentences are taken almost directly from a letter Joyce wrote to Nora in 1904.[10] It was also Joyce, of course, who wrote book reviews, just as Gabriel Conroy does, for the *Daily Express*.[11] Since the *Daily Express* was pro-English, he had probably been teased for writing for it during his frequent visits to the house of David Sheehy, M. P. One of the Sheehy daughters, Kathleen, may well have been the model for Miss Ivors, for she wore that austere bodice and sported the same patriotic pin.[12] In Gretta's old sweetheart, in Gabriel's letter, in the book reviews and the discussion of them, as well as in the physical image of Gabriel with hair parted in the middle and rimmed glasses, Joyce drew directly upon his own life.

His father was also deeply involved in the story. Stanislaus Joyce recalls that when the Joyce children were too young to bring along to the Misses Flynns' party, their father and mother sometimes left them with a governess and stayed at a Dublin hotel overnight instead of returning to their house in Bray.'[13] Gabriel and Gretta do this too. Gabriel's quarrels with his mother also suggest John Joyce's quarrels with his mother, who never accepted her son's marriage to a woman of lower station.[14] But John Joyce's personality was not like Gabriel's; he had no doubts of himself, in the midst of many failures he was full of self-esteem. He had the same unshakable confidence as his son James. For Gabriel's personality there is among Joyce's friends another model.[15] This was Constantine Curran, sometimes nicknamed 'Cautious Con.' He is a more distinguished man than Joyce allows, but Joyce was building upon, and no doubt distorting, his memories of Curran as a very young man. That he has Curran partly in mind is suggested by the fact that he calls Gabriel's brother by Curran's first name Constantine, and makes Gabriel's brother, like Curran's, a priest.[16] Curran has the same high color and nervous, disquieted manner* as Gabriel, and like Gabriel he has traveled to the continent and has cultivated cosmopolitan interests. Curran, like Conroy, mar-

* See Joyce's letter, p. 234 [of Ellmann's book].

ried a woman who was not a Dubliner, though she came from only as far west as Limerick. In other respects he is quite different. Gabriel was made mostly out of Curran, Joyce's father, and Joyce himself. Probably Joyce knew there was a publican on Howth named Gabriel Conroy; or, as Gerhard Friedrich has proposed,[17] he may have borrowed the name from the title of a Bret Harte novel. But the character, if not the name, was of his own compounding.*

Joyce now had his people, his party, and something of its development. In the festive setting, upon which the snow keeps offering a different perspective until, as W. Y. Tindall suggests,[19] the snow itself changes, he develops Gabriel's private tremors, his sense of inadequacy, his uncomfortable insistence on his small pretensions. From the beginning he is vulnerable; his well-meant and even generous overtures are regularly checked. The servant girl punctures his blithe assumption that everyone is happily in love and on the way to the altar. He is not sure enough of himself to put out of his head the slurs he has received long ago; so in spite of his uxorious attitude towards Gretta he is a little ashamed of her having come from the west of Ireland. He cannot bear to think of his dead mother's remark that Gretta was 'country cute,' and when Miss Ivors says of Gretta, 'She's from Connacht, isn't she?' Gabriel answers shortly, 'Her people are.' He has rescued her from that bog. Miss Ivors's suggestion, a true Gaelic Leaguer's, that he spend his holiday in the Irish-speaking Aran Islands (in the west) upsets him; it is the element in his wife's past that he wishes to forget. During most of the story, the west of Ireland is connected in Gabriel's mind with a dark and rather painful primitivism, an aspect of his country which he has steadily abjured by going off to the continent. The west is savagery; to the east and south lie people who drink wine and wear galoshes.

Gabriel has been made uneasy about this attitude, but he clings to it defiantly until the ending. Unknown to him, it is being challenged by the song, 'The Lass of Aughrim.' Aughrim is a little village in the west not far from Galway. The song has a special relevance; in it a woman who has been seduced and abandoned by Lord Gregory comes with her baby in the rain to beg for admission to his house. It brings together the peasant mother and the civilized seducer, but Ga-

* The name of Conroy's wife Gretta was borrowed from another friend, Gretta (actually Margaret) Cousins, the wife of James H. Cousins. Since Joyce mentioned in a letter at the same time that he was meditating 'The Dead,' the danger of becoming 'a patient Cousins,'[18] this family was evidently on his mind.

briel does not listen to the words; he only watches his wife listening. Joyce had heard this ballad from Nora; perhaps he considered also using Tom Moore's 'O,Ye Dead' in the story, but if so he must have seen that 'The Lass of Aughrim' would connect more subtly with the west and with Michael Furey's visit in the rain to Gretta. But the notion of using a song at all may well have come to him as the result of the excitement generated in him by Moore's song.

And now Gabriel and Gretta go to the Hotel Gresham, Gabriel fired by his living wife and Gretta drained by the memory of her dead lover. He learns for the first time of the young man in Galway, whose name Joyce has deftly altered from Sonny or Michael Bodkin to Michael Furey. The new name suggests, like the contrast of the militant Michael and the amiable Gabriel, that violent passion is in her Galway past, not in her Dublin present. Gabriel tries to cut Michael Furey down. 'What was he?' he asks, confident that his own profession of language teacher (which of course he shared with Joyce) is superior; but she replies, 'He was in the gasworks,' as if this profession was as good as any other. Then Gabriel tries again, 'And what did he die of so young, Gretta? Consumption, was it?' He hopes to register the usual expressions of pity, but Gretta silences and terrifies him by her answer, 'I think he died for me.'* Since Joyce has already made clear that Michael Furey was tubercular, this answer of Gretta has a fine ambiguity. It asserts the egoism of passion, and unconsciously defies Gabriel's reasonable question.

Now Gabriel begins to succumb to his wife's dead lover, and becomes a pilgrim to emotional intensities outside of his own experience. From a biographical point of view, these final pages compose one of Joyce's several tributes to his wife's artless integrity. Nora Barnacle, in spite of her defects of education, was independent, unself-conscious, instinctively right. Gabriel acknowledges the same coherence in his own wife, and he recognizes in the west of Ireland, in Michael Furey, a passion he has himself always lacked. 'Better pass boldly into that other world, in the full glory of some passion, than fade and wither dismally with age,' Joyce makes Gabriel think. Then comes that strange sentence in the final paragraph: 'The time had come for him to set out on his journey westward.' The cliché runs that journeys

* Adaline Glasheen has discovered here an echo of Yeats's nationalistic play, *Cathleen ni Houlihan* (1902), where the old woman who symbolizes Ireland sings a song of 'yellow-haired Donough that was hanged in Galway.' When she is asked, 'What was it brought him to his death?' she replies, 'He died for love of me; many a man has died for love of me.'[20]

westward are towards death, but the west has taken on a special meaning in the story. Gretta Conroy's west is the place where life had been lived simply and passionately. The context and phrasing of the sentence suggest that Gabriel is on the edge of sleep, and half-consciously accepts what he has hitherto scorned, the possibility of an actual trip to Connaught. What the sentence affirms, at last, on the level of feeling, is the west, the primitive, untutored, impulsive country from which Gabriel had felt himself alienated before; in the story, the west is paradoxically linked also with the past and the dead. It is like Aunt Julia Morkan who, though ignorant, old, grey-skinned, and stupefied, seizes in her song at the party 'the excitement of swift and secure flight.'

The tone of the sentence, 'The time had come for him to set out on his journey westward,' is somewhat resigned. It suggests a concession, a relinquishment, and Gabriel is conceding and relinquishing a good deal—his sense of the importance of civilized thinking, of continental tastes, of all those tepid but nice distinctions on which he has prided himself. The bubble of his self-possession is pricked; he no longer possesses himself, and not to possess oneself is in a way a kind of death. It is a self-abandonment not unlike Furey's, and through Gabriel's mind runs the imagery of Calvary. He imagines the snow on the cemetery at Oughterard, lying 'thickly drifted on the crooked crosses and headstones, on the spears of the little gate, on the barren thorns.' He thinks of Michael Furey who, Gretta has said, died for her, and envies him his sacrifice for another kind of love than Christ's. To some extent Gabriel too is dying for her, in giving up what he has most valued in himself, all that holds him apart from the simpler people at the party. He feels close to Gretta through sympathy if not through love; now they are both past youth, beauty, and passion; he feels close also to her dead lover, another lamb burnt on her altar, though she too is burnt now; he feels no resentment, only pity. In his own sacrifice of himself he is conscious of a melancholy unity between the living and the dead.

Gabriel, who has been sick of his own country, finds himself drawn inevitably into a silent tribute to it of much more consequence than his spoken tribute to the party. He has had illusions of the rightness of a way of life that should be outside of Ireland; but through this experience with his wife he grants a kind of bondage, of acceptance, even of admiration to a part of the country and a way of life that are most Irish. Ireland is shown to be stronger, more intense than he. At the end of *A Portrait of the Artist*, too, Stephen Dedalus, who has been so resolutely opposed to nationalism, makes a similar concession when he interprets his departure from Ireland as an attempt to forge a conscience for his race.

Joyce did not invent the incidents that conclude his story, the second honeymoon of Gabriel and Gretta which ends so badly. His method of composition was very like T. S. Eliot's, the imaginative absorption of stray material. The method did not please Joyce very much because he considered it not imaginative enough, but it was the only way he could work. He borrowed the ending for 'The Dead' from another book. In that book a bridal couple receive, on their wedding night, a message that a young woman whom the husband jilted has just committed suicide. The news holds them apart, she asks him not to kiss her, and both are tormented by remorse. The wife, her marriage unconsummated, falls off at last to sleep, and her husband goes to the window and looks out at 'the melancholy greyness of the dawn.' For the first time he recognizes, with the force of a revelation, that his life is a failure, and that his wife lacks the passion of the girl who has killed herself. He resolves that, since he is not worthy of any more momentous career, he will try at least to make her happy. Here surely is the situation that Joyce so adroitly recomposed. The dead lover who comes between the lovers, the sense of the husband's failure, the acceptance of mediocrity, the resolve to be at all events sympathetic, all come from the other book. But Joyce transforms them. For example, he allows Gretta to kiss her husband, but without desire, and rarefies the situation by having it arise not from a suicide but from a memory of young love. The book Joyce was borrowing from was one that nobody reads any more, George Moore's *Vain Fortune;* but Joyce read it,* and in his youthful essay, 'The Day of the Rabblement,' overpraised it as 'fine, original work.'[21]

Moore said nothing about snow, however. No one can know how Joyce conceived the joining of Gabriel's final experience with the snow. But his fondness for a background of this kind is also illustrated by his use of the fireplace in 'Ivy Day,' of the streetlamps in 'Two Gallants,' and of the river in *Finnegans Wake.* It does not seem that the snow can be death, as so many have said, for it falls on living and dead alike, and for death to fall on the dead is a simple redundancy of which Joyce would not have been guilty. For snow to be 'general all over Ireland' is of course unusual in that country. The fine description:

* He evidently refreshed his memory of it when writing 'The Dead,' for his copy of *Vain Fortune,* now at Yale, bears the date 'March 1907.'

'It was falling on every part of the dark central plain, on the treeless hills, falling softly upon the Bog of Allen and, farther westward, softly falling into the dark mutinous Shannon waves,' is probably borrowed by Joyce from a famous simile in the twelfth book of the Iliad, which Thoreau translates:[22] 'The snowflakes fall thick and fast on a winter's day. The winds are lulled, and the snow falls incessant, covering the tops of the mountains, and the hills and the plains where the lotus-tree grows, and the cultivated fields, and they are falling by the inlets and shores of the foaming sea, but are silently dissolved by the waves.' But Homer was simply describing the thickness of the arrows in the battle of the Greeks and Trojans; and while Joyce seems to copy his topographical details, he uses the image here chiefly for a similar sense of crowding and quiet pressure. Where Homer speaks of the waves silently dissolving the snow, Joyce adds the final detail of 'the mutinous Shannon waves' which suggest the 'Furey' quality of the west. The snow that falls upon Gabriel, Gretta, and Michael Furey, upon the Misses Morkan, upon the dead singers and the living, is mutuality, a sense of their connection with each other, a sense that none has his being alone. The partygoers prefer dead singers to living ones, the wife prefers a dead lover to a live lover.

The snow does not stand alone in the story. It is part of the complex imagery that includes heat and cold air, fire, and rain, as well as snow. The relations of these are not simple. During the party the living people, their festivities, and all human society seem constrasted with the cold outside, as in the warmth of Gabriel's hand on the cold pane. But this warmth is felt by Gabriel as stuffy and confining, and the cold outside is repeatedly connected with what is fragrant and fresh. The cold, in this sense of piercing intensity, culminates in the picture of Michael Furey in the rain and darkness of the Galway night.

Another warmth is involved in 'The Dead.' In Gabriel's memory of his own love for Gretta, he recalls incidents in his love's history as stars, burning with pure and distant intensity, and recalls moments of his passion for her as having the fire of stars. The irony of this image is that the sharp and beautiful experience was, though he has not known it until this night, incomplete. There is a telling metaphor: he remembers a moment of happiness, standing with Gretta in the cold, looking in through a window at a man making bottles in a roaring furnace, and suddenly calling out to the man, 'Is the fire hot?' The question sums up his naïve deprivation; if the man at the furnace had heard the question, his answer, thinks Gabriel, might have been rude;

so the revelation on this night is rude to Gabriel's whole being. On this night he acknowledges that love must be a feeling which he has never fully had.

Gabriel is not utterly deprived. Throughout the story there is affection for this man who, without the sharpest, most passionate perceptions is yet generous and considerate. The intense and the moderate can meet; intensity bursts out and declines, and the moderated can admire and pity it, and share the fate that moves both types of mankind towards age and death. The furthest point of love of which Gabriel is capable is past. Furey's passion is past because of his sudden death. Gretta is perhaps the most pitiful, in that knowing Furey's passion, and being of his kind, she does not die but lives to wane in Gabriel's way; on this night she too is fatigued, not beautiful, her clothes lie crumpled beside her. The snow seems to share in this decline; viewed from inside at the party, it is desirable, unattainable, just as at his first knowledge of Michael Furey, Gabriel envies him. At the end as the partygoers walk to the cab the snow is slushy and in patches, and then, seen from the window of the hotel room, it belongs to all men, it is general, mutual. Under its canopy, all human beings, whatever their degrees of intensity, fall into union. The mutuality is that all men feel and lose feeling, all interact, all warrant the sympathy that Gabriel now extends to Furey, to Gretta, to himself, even to old Aunt Julia.

In its lyrical, melancholy acceptance of all that life and death offer, 'The Dead' is a linchpin in Joyce's work. There is that basic situation of cuckoldry, real or putative, which is to be found throughout. There is the special Joycean collation of specific detail raised to rhythmical intensity. The final purport of the story, the mutual dependency of living and dead, is something that he meditated a good deal from his early youth. He had expressed it first in his essay on Mangan in 1902, when he spoke already of the union in the great memory of death along with life;[23] even then he had begun to learn like Gabriel that we are all Romes, our new edifices reared beside, and even joined with, ancient monuments. In *Dubliners* he developed this idea. The interrelationship of dead and living is the theme of the first story in *Dubliners* as well as of the last; it is also the theme of 'A Painful Case,' but an even closer parallel to 'The Dead' is the story, 'Ivy Day in the Committee Room.' This was in one sense an answer to his university friends who mocked his remark that death is the most beautiful form of life by saying that absence is the highest form of presence. Joyce did not think either idea absurd. What binds 'Ivy Day' to 'The Dead' is that in both stories the central agitation derives from a character who never appears, who is dead, absent. Joyce wrote Stanislaus that Anatole France had given him the idea for both stories.[24] There may be other sources in France's works, but a possible one is 'The Procurator of Judaea.' In it Pontius Pilate reminisces with a friend about the days when he was procurator in Judaea, and describes the events of his time with Roman reason, calm, and elegance. Never once does he, or his friend, mention the person we expect him to discuss, the founder of Christianity, until at the end the friend asks if Pontius Pilate happens to remember someone of the name of Jesus, from Nazareth, and the veteran administrator replies, 'Jesus? Jesus of Nazareth? I cannot call him to mind.' The story is overshadowed by the person whom Pilate does not recall; without him the story would not exist. Joyce uses a similar method in 'Ivy Day' with Parnell and in 'The Dead' with Michael Furey.

In *Ulysses* the climactic episode, *Circe,* whirls to a sepulchral close in the same juxtaposition of living and dead, the ghost of his mother confronting Stephen, and the ghost of his son confronting Bloom. But Joyce's greatest triumph in asserting the intimacy of living and dead was to be the close of *Finnegans Wake.* Here Anna Livia Plurabelle, the river of life, flows toward the sea, which is death; the fresh water passes into the salt, a bitter ending. Yet it is also a return to her father, the sea, that produces the cloud which makes the river, and her father is also her husband, to whom she gives herself as a bride to her groom. Anna Livia is going back to her father, as Gabriel journeys westward in feeling to the roots of his fatherland; like him, she is sad and weary. To him the Shannon waves are dark and mutinous, and to her the sea is cold and mad. In *Finnegans Wake* Anna Livia's union is not only with love but with death; like Gabriel she seems to swoon away.*

That Joyce at the age of twenty-five and -six should have written this story ought not to seem odd. Young writers reach their greatest eloquence in dwelling upon the horrors of middle age and what follows it. But beyond this proclivity which he shared with others, Joyce had a special reason for writing the story of 'The Dead' in 1906 and 1907. In his own mind he had thoroughly justified his flight from Ireland, but he had not decided the question of where he would fly *to.* In Trieste and Rome he had learned what he had unlearned in Dublin, to be a Dubliner. As he had written his brother from Rome with

* See also pp. 724-6 [of Ellmann's book].

some astonishment, he felt humiliated when anyone attacked his 'impoverished country.'[25] 'The Dead' is his first song of exile.

NOTES

[1] Letter to me from Mrs. Kathleen Barnacle Griffin.

[2] See p. 222 [of Ellmann's book].

[3] S. Joyce, 'The Background to "Dubliners,"' *Listener,* LI (March 25, 1954), 526-7.

[4] *Ulysses,* p. 12 (8).

[5] Ibid. p. 48 (44).

[6] Interview with Mrs. May Joyce Monaghan, 1953.

[7] Idem.

[8] Birkin in *Women in Love.*

[9] Information from Professor Joseph Prescott.

[10] At Cornell.

[11] See p. 116 [of Ellmann's book].

[12] Interview with Mrs. Mary Sheehy Kettle, 1953.

[13] *My Brother's Keeper,* p. 38 (58).

[14] See p. 17 [of Ellmann's book].

[15] Interview with S. Joyce, 1953.

[16] Suggested to me by Professor Vivian Mercier.

[17] Gerhard Friedrich, 'Bret Harte as a Source for James Joyce's "The Dead,"' *Philological Quarterly,* XXXIII (Oct. 1954), pp. 442-4.

[18] Letter to S. Joyce, Feb. 1907.

[19] W. Y. Tindall, *The Literary Symbol* (New York, 1955), p. 227.

[20] I am indebted to Mrs. Glasheen for pointing this out to me.

[21] *Critical Writings,* p. 71.

[22] Professor Walter B. Rideout kindly called my attention to the similarity of these passages.

[23] *Critical Writings,* p. 83.

[24] Letter to S. Joyce, Feb. 11, 1907.

[25] Letter to S. Joyce, Sept. 25, 1906.

Melville's Freudian Slip

Harrison Hayford

In the course of his researches for *The Melville Log,* Jay Leyda discovered an error made in the official birth record of Melville's son Stanwix, in the office of the City Clerk of Pittsfield, Massachusetts. The maiden name of the child's mother was recorded not as Elizabeth Shaw (Melville's wife) but erroneously as Maria G. Melville (his own mother). In the *Log* Mr. Leyda reported this error without attributing it to anybody.[1] But on the assumption that it was Melville himself who filled out the official form or reported the birth and supplied the misinformation, this error has been used by two able biographers to support evidence of a mother-complex of some sort.[2] By them the error is regarded as due to a revealing slip of Melville's pen. Since otherwise Melville's emotional attitudes toward his mother must be mostly inferred from his semi-autobiographical fiction, especially *Pierre,* and since such inferences are pretty hazardous, any authentic external evidence beyond fugitive family traditions would be valuable indeed.[3]

For this reason I wrote some time ago an inquiry to the City Clerk of Pittsfield, Mr. John J. Fitzgerald, explaining the exact bearing of the facts. Mr. Fitzgerald made the following admirably explicit reply, which seems to me to account for the error conclusively upon other grounds than a "Freudian slip" of Melville's own pen. Two points discussed by Mr. Fitzgerald reveal additional errors in the official record: the erroneous birthdate October 25 for October 22, and the misspelling "Stanwicks" for "Stanwix," which certainly cannot be attributed to Melville, however wildly he spelled upon occasion.[4] Finally, in any case, as Mr. Fitzgerald indicates, the birth was reported not at the time of its occurence but at the beginning of the following year, 1852. This fact negates the implied assumption that Melville's emotional distraction at the time of the birth contributed to a slip of his pen. Mr. Fitzgerald's letter follows:

> In Massachusetts city and town clerks receive reports of births from three sources—the parents, the attending physician and the hospital authorities when the birth is in the hospital. The official record of birth is compiled from these three sources and entered in the Register of Births. More often than not the three reports will vary in detail and it is up to the town clerk to do the best he can in ascertaining which of the various versions is the correct one. Oftentimes his final choice is nothing but a blind guess.
>
> Since the original reports for 1851 births have been lost there is no way of determining definitely from what sources the birth record of Stanwicks Melville was compiled. From what knowledge I have of the birth registration system in effect in those days I would say that the particular record in question was based upon the annual "baby census" taken by the town clerk. Each one of the 221 births registered in 1851 bears January 31, 1852, as the date of record (the date when the birth was registered) and that indicates to me that the records all came from one source at one time.
>
> Assuming that Stanwicks Melville's birth record found its way to

our books through the town clerk's annual census, and drawing an analogy between that census and canvasses of a similar nature which I have seen in actual operation in modern times, I would say that the error in the mother's name could be attributed to any one of a dozen causes, the least probable of which would be a mother fixation on the part of Herman Melville. For example, it is known that in one year back in the 1870's the town refused to appropriate any money for the annual baby census, and the birth records for that year were apparently made by the clerk without leaving his office. In the censuses of that nature the information is often given by servants or neighbors or by others not in a position to have accurate knowledge of all the details.

For whatever bearing it may have on the problem I would like to point out that we also have the record of birth of an unnamed daughter of Herman Melville who was born in 1855 (month and date not given) in which the mother's name is given as Eliza. Her birthplace is given as Boston whereas the Maria G. named in the other record was recorded as having been born in Albany, N. Y.

Incidentally the name of Herman Melville's son appears in our books as I have given it above and not as Stanwix. If Stanwix was the spelling favored by Herman Melville it would be hard to resist the conclusion that he had nothing to do with the making of the record that appears on our book. Also our book gives October 25 as the date of birth and not October 22. For whatever interest it may have for you I am pleased to send you herewith certified copies of the complete records of both births.[5]

NOTES

[1] *The Melville Log* (New York, 1951), I, 430.

[2] *Pierre,* ed. Henry A. Murray (New York, 1949), p. xxxvii. Newton Arvin, *Herman Melville* (New York, 1950), p. 204. Leon Howard, *Herman Melville* (Berkeley and Los Angeles, 1951), p. 184, says that the error may have been Melville's but draws no psychological inferences. The supposed slip has been referred to in a number of articles as well.

[3] See William H. Gilman, *Melville's Early Life and Redburn* (New York, 1951), p. 342 note 154, for a mordant comment on the other "evidence" of Melville's relationship to his mother.

[4] Family records fix the birth date as October 22.

[5] Letter dated May 8, 1950. Mr. Fitzgerald has consented to its publication.

The Metaphysic of Love

A. J. Smith

Recent discussions of 'The definition of Love', as Marvell is conceived to have attempted it, turn one's mind back quizzically to the hoary old controversy over a still more sizeable treatment of the theme, never satisfactorily resolved. On Donne's much-teased 'The Extasie' opinion seems nowadays to have settled—out of sheer weariness one supposes. We content our minds with the comforting assumption that Donne in that poem quieted once for all the long tug of war between soul and body in human love, which so exercised Sidney and Spenser, to mention no more. Grierson's taut note is reassuringly behind us:

> This is one of the most important of the lyrics as a statement of Donne's metaphysic of love, of the interconnexion and mutual dependence of body and soul.[1]

'Donne's metaphysic of love.' The poem is significant as the statement of a personal philosophical view; and by implication which we have not failed to draw, a revolutionary view at that. Take this with Grierson's further dicta—'a record of intense, rapid thinking', 'a . . . natural utterance of passion'[2]—and we are but a step from the emotional apprehension of thought. It was the late Professor G. R. Potter who added the indispensable Eliotian trimmings for us, in rebutting Legouis's heretical 'Don Juan' reading:

> It seems to us the poem in which Donne came as close as he ever did to putting in words those subtle relations between the body and the mind of which he was conscious continually, and most keenly when he was most in love.[3]

Now we are given the record of an intense personal experience; and the 'metaphysics' become the product of a keen habit of introspection, the analysis of consciousness at the moment of an emotion which heightens it. How very modern, we all conclude, was Donne, and what a piece of original thinking the poem is! It is true that he expressed quite contrary notions of love elsewhere, at a time when he had much more claim to be considered as a thinker—the very notions he is here supposed to be scouting finally.[4] But that was on a public occasion; and a preacher learns to temper the wind.

Yet Professor Tuve has made it more difficult than it used to be, to consider Donne as a startling revolutionary phenomenon. We are at last becoming aware, in general, that our primary office for this poet is not to invest him with current aims and seek covert reports on his psychological condition, but discarding our determinedly inward-focused modern spectacles, to establish a full technical context, and to trace material sources. And if we seek sources for the attitudes to love set out in 'The Extasie', we shall find them in plenty. Indeed, without the varied setting these provide, we may not hope to read the poem aright.

For the theory of love, as it was developed in sixteenth-century Italian writing, was by no means all of a Neoplatonic piece. As well as the Platonic Florence of Ficino there was the Aristotelian Padua of Sperone Speroni, not a whit less in following; and besides both there was the great synthetic source on which all subsequent sixteenth-century theorists, of all complexions, drew heavily, the *Dialoghi d'Amore* of the Spanish-born Italian Jew, Leone Ebreo (Jehudah Arbabnel). Between these schools (if one can call them anything so definite) there was a good deal of common ground, and where they differed was precisely in the degree of importance assigned to the body in love. Thus they were all agreed that love can be of several kinds, varying enormously in operations and effects. For Ficinians the general division tended, of course, to be between those whose love was a contemplation of the beauty of the soul alone—and ultimately an ascent to, and uniting with, the Divine Beauty—and those who cared for the body only, gross and bestial natures. Usually there was an intermediary condition, that of those who tried to love both body and soul. Some found two further species, making five in all. The Florentine Varchi divided the intermediary into 'courteous, or virtuous', when both are loved but the soul more than the body, and only with the senses of sight and hearing; 'human, or civil', when such lovers pass to the other, less spiritual senses as well; and 'plebeian, or vulgar', when both are loved, but the body more than the soul.[5] Aristotelians, on the other hand, tended to restrict themselves to two broad categories—the vulgar love whose end is simply the enjoyment of the body; and, to quote Tullia d'Aragona,

> honest love, which is proper to noble men, that is those who have a gentle and virtuous soul, whether they are poor or rich; and which is not generated in desire, as the other, but by the reason.[6]

Nevertheless, the two 'schools' were close enough in their overall view to permit a fairly general agreement on characteristics.

The characteristic commonly ascribed to the vulgar love was instability. 'All the things that delight our material sentiments, of their nature, when they are possessed are sooner abhorred than loved', said Leone Ebreo,[7] and Tullia tells us that it was the nature of the lower love in particular to be 'past reason hunted', and then 'past reason hated':

> I say, that the carnal desire gratified, there is no one who does not instantly lose that will and appetite which so tormented and devoured him . . . not only does it put an end to love, but turns it to hate.[8]

There could be no permanency or fidelity, for revulsion immediately followed on attainment of the sole end. In higher conditions, on the other hand, the satisfaction of physical desire actually increased, not destroyed love—'And if the appetite of the lover is quite sated with the copulative union, and that desire, or properly, appetite, continently ceases, in no way is cordial love thereby diminished, rather is the possible union bound the closer.'[9] Some, Tullia among them, held that in good love the very physical appetite might increase by what it fed on, seeking bodily union all the more ardently for the pleasure once proved.

There was general agreement that the chief effect of the higher kinds of human love was the conjoining of the souls of the two lovers to make a perfect union, or unity. Indeed, love itself was commonly defined as a 'desire to unite oneself with the thing esteemed good', which 'would be the soul of the beloved'.[10] Speroni put it neatly when he said that lovers in a perfect love were joined so completely that they lost their proper semblance and became a strange third species, neither male nor female, resembling a hermaphrodite.[11] But the standard conceit was that such lovers' souls, transformed into each other by a kind of miracle, become 'one soul in two bodies',[12] and, as the younger Tasso put it, 'the lovers are not two, but one and four'.[13] This arithmetical juggling originated in Ficino's Commentary on the Symposium, and is elaborated at length by such Neoplatonists as Betussi. In essence it means simply that two souls, 'transformed together, the one into the other',[14] are made one; while each at the same time, having another soul added to it, becomes two, making four in all. Strange to think that so crudely sophistical an idea was quite literally intended! But at least its point was the emphasis on a conjoining of souls so perfect that 'they are united together in every part, and become mixed and intermingled'.[15]

Such a union of souls could not be consummated in a normal state; nor could the lovers, having achieved it, remain as they had been in their singleness. It required what Leone Ebreo called 'the ecstasy, or else alienation, produced by amorous meditation'.[16] This love-ecstasy was sometimes said to be brought on above all when 'we direct our eyes in the face, and in the eyes of the person who so much pleases us . . .', the effect of which was that, 'for the marvel of it we become as persons stupefied'. The spirit, 'almost fomented by the continued power of the fixed cogitation', continues Cattani, whose description this is, 'is no sooner affected by that effluence than it all but changes itself into the nature of the other'.[17] The state of 'privation of sense and movement'[18] thus induced permitted a condition of ecstatic mutual contemplation, in which one's soul left its body and remained 'outside the self, in that which it contemplates and desires':

> For when the lover is in ecstasy, contemplating that which he loves, he has no care or memory of himself, nor does he perform any work in his own benefit, whether natural, sensitive, motive, or else rational. Rather is he quite alien to himself, and belongs to the object of his love and contemplation, into which he is totally converted.[19]

We are presented, in fact, with an analogy often explicitly confessed, and as exact as it could be made, between this secular state and the ecstasy of Divine Contemplation, 'when as the Servants of God were taken up in spirit, separate as it were from the body, and out of the body, that they might see some heavenly mystery revealed unto them'.[20] And as the outcome of the 'divine vision' which temporarily united the soul with the great Fount of Truth, was that 'all things are seen most perfectly',[21] so in a suitably humbler way of this. Sometimes the increase of knowledge was material. Following Ficino, writers describe a general exchange and mixing of the beauties of bodies and souls, in which love either 'levels every inequality, and reduces them to parity, to unite them perfectly, and make not union, but unity',[22] or produces a third thing 'finer than they had been separately made', as in 'a compounding of the voice with the lute, of perfume with perfume'.[23] The virtuous lover, knowing that 'love raises souls to high things',[24] might indeed deliberately seek this condition 'to make himself more perfect in the union with the soul of the beloved', for 'always the lover desires to be made participant in that which he lacks, and knows or believes to abound in the beloved'.[25] But some writers describe as well a superior illumination, produced 'when the superior loves the inferior in all the first semicircle, from God down to the prime material'.[26] Again the necessary step to it was the uniting of loving souls. 'There is no perfection or beauty that does not increase when it is communicated, for the fruitful growth is always more handsome than the sterile', said Leone Ebreo; and he made the essence of his ecstatic intercommunion a mystical sharing of some part of the Divine Beauty and Wisdom:

> And so it happens of man with woman; that knowing her in exemplary fashion he loves and desires her, and from love passes to the unitive cognition, which is the end of desire. . . . This great love and desire causes us to be abstracted in such contemplation that our intellect is raised up; and in such a way that, illuminated by a singular divine grace, it comes to know things above human power and speculation; as happens in such union and copulation with the Highest God. . . .

Moreover, this exalted state achieved, the love was thereby irrefrangibly proof against decline, for 'without end is the perfect desire, which is to enjoy union with the loved person'.[27]

Here was the more important ground, and in the main it was common. Some account of the body's part, and therefore of its relation to the soul, was needed. There were in fact few writers on love who steadily discounted the body. Ficino was one. For him the soul is the whole man, and the body its poor instrument—or as the figure was, its prison. But if this was a rare severity, the Florentine account of the vital linking of two such different essences was generally followed. The linking agent, the 'knot between the soul and the elemental body',[28] was the 'spirit', which was 'a certain extremely subtle and lucid vapour, generated by the heat of the heart from the most subtle part of the blood'.[29] This 'spirit' at once 'transfuses the life' from the soul to the body, and, 'being spread through all the members, takes the *virtu* of the soul, and communicates it to the body'. Conversely, it 'takes again, by the instruments of the senses, the images of outside bodies', which the soul is not gross enough to contact directly, and presents them to it 'as in a mirror', for judgement.[30]

Such spirits were thus necessary intermediary agents between the soul and each of the senses, and each of the faculties of the man. The purer Ficinians drew no corollary which might diminish the essential independence of soul. The limit of their admission concerning the two elements was that 'a powerful alteration of the one' might 'make its way to the other'.[31] With the renewed favour of Aristotle in the sixteenth century, however, and following the strong example of Leone Ebreo, writers tended to be syncretic. Even professing Neoplatonists discarded Ficino's strict separatism. Leone's own view was eccentrically non-Christian, founded in the common notion that the soul is 'mixed of elements, or else principles, discontinuous and separate the one from the other',[32] but affirming this mixture to be of elements of intellect and body, which fitted it to mediate between the two. Christian Aristotelians had Aquinas behind them.

The vital Thomist denial of the position that the body is dross is grounded precisely in the Aristotelian affirmation of the absolute interdependence of soul and body. Man is not 'a combination of the two substances but a complex substance which owes its substantiality to one only of its two consecutive principles'. An intellect without a body would be impotent, cut off from the sensible world, and in order to communicate with matter must 'descend, so to speak, into the material plane'. For these Aristotelian intellects Aquinas substitutes immortal souls, whose imperative need of the co-operation of sense-organs he thus affirms:

> in order to obtain this co-operation they acutalise matter; it is due wholly to them that this matter is a body; and yet they are not themselves save in a body; the man, therefore, is neither his body, since the body subsists only by the soul, nor his soul, since this would remain destitute without the body: he is the unity of a soul which substantialises his body and of the body in which this soul subsists.[33]

To trace the wash of this teaching in sixteen-century writings on love, one need hardly canvass extreme opinions–the heretical Giordano Bruno's denial of the essential contrariety of body and soul,[34] or even Tullia's affirmation that self-evidently, 'all the compound, that is the soul and the body together, is more noble and more perfect than the soul alone'.[35] Equicola, a standard authority, found 'the great friendship and union which is seen between the body and the soul' to be so close that 'while this organic member is in being, one cannot think of the action of the soul apart from the body, much less separate them; nor can that of the body be considered without the soul'.[36] Aristotelian Padua naturally approved a close integration of the hypostatic union, and consequent raising of the status of the flesh. 'I say then', said its spokesman, the revered Speroni, 'that our soul, in understanding, has already used the organs of the external and internal sentiments, nor may it understand without those; but those serve it in understanding, supplying it with the species, without which it does not understand. And therefore it is said, and truly, that the man understands and not the soul.'[37] It is more impressive that writers in the other camp should have concurred to the extent of following this crude empiricism, even if it was 'as philosophers and not as Christians'. Varchi starts from just Speroni's position—'our soul being incapable of understanding anything without the sense'; and his conclusion would have won Locke's applause:

> all those things which sense cannot feel and apprehend, the intellect cannot treat of or understand, for there is never anything at all in the intellect which has not first been in sense.[38]

The part Neoplatonists assigned to the body in love was that described in the famous notion of the steps. One ascended by stages from the lowest to the highest, at each stage seeking the appropriate form of union with the loved object. Pleasure in the physical beauty of one's mistress led to the contemplation of her true beauty—that of her soul—and this, ultimately, to the ecstatic vision of the Eternal Beauty. Every step transcended the previous one, which was then rejected. The body was the lowest step, and only beasts and the vulgar went no higher; nevertheless, it was still initially necessary, 'as prospect of truth',[39] physical beauty in some way shadowing forth the beauty of the soul. This splendidly impossible view was certainly influential, but in Italian writing it could not long remain undiluted, or indeed uncontradicted. Petrarchans, predisposed to the sublimated love of Neoplatonism, yet commonly admitted that in love 'one does not love the soul alone', saving their allegiance by adding 'but principally, and more the soul than the body'.[40] Torquato Tasso himself had maintained as a youth the vanity of the opinion that one could love the soul, or virtue alone, and in his soberer age would say only that if bodily intercourse was not necessary to the union of souls, it could be desired as an accessory and sign of that.[41]

But in fact there was authority as considerable as Ficino's for quite another view than his. Leone Ebreo, owing as little to a celibate as to a courtly tradition, had provided an account which satisfied less rarefied demands. While not conceding in the slightest that physical union might be the final end of a perfect love, he was emphatic that it is for a number of reasons to be sought. Amorous acts bind the knot faster. They are signs that the love is fully reciprocal. They allow the consummation of the union, which is not complete with the fusion of souls but requires the coupling of bodies, 'to the end that no diversity may remain'. Above all, the spiritual condition itself is deficient until the bodies are united, for

> with the correspondence of the bodily union, the spiritual love is augmented and made more perfect, just as the understanding of prudence is perfected when it is answered with due works.[42]

This was not the first time that physical conjunction had been recognized as a means to the higher union. The great Bembo himself had remarked the power of the kiss to draw forth souls by the lips, and in chaste love, to join them.[43] But here, in the most quoted and praised of all sixteenth-century writers on the subject, was the theoretical justification of lovers whose 'every love is desire, and very desire is love',[44] an account of the body's part which held good for the common state of secular love. Ficino had seemed to find no connexion between love and the procreation of kind, and was concerned with human relationships only as a means of achieving mystical states. If later writers had followed him they would never have thought of praising love for its work in drawing mankind to temperate coitus, as did even Betussi,[45] nor of adding with Equicola that abstention is actually bad, and for women in especial.[46] But beyond easing such adjustments in the name of practical sense, Leone's view lent weight to the balance at a decisive point. There was a calculated rejection of Ficino behind subsequent reaffirmations that, together with spiritual union, a lover desires also the union of bodies 'to make himself, to the limit of his power, one selfsame thing with the beloved'.[47] Aristotle in fact now supplanted Plotinus as the philosopher in vogue. It was to be a severe stricture on Leone himself that he 'said many things which were not peripatetic'.[48]

One further step was possible, the making of the perfect love of souls actually inseparable from, or dependent upon, the love of bodies. It was taken; and became as a matter of course the standard Aristotelian teaching. The entire philosophy of 'that prince of philosophers Aristotle', declared Equicola, shows that the man is soul and body together, constituents whose actions are indivisible in love as in all else.

To love truly is necessarily to love both, for 'Love is of soul and body, and the operations of the soul depend on the body'. It follows that 'the one ministers to the other in voluptuousness, and to delight the one without the other is impossible'.[49] Such a view was bound to recommend itself beyond the study walls of Padua and Ferrara. Nothing better shows the syncretism of later writers than that a Florentine Platonist should have recommended it to his own Accademia in expounding Petrarch—though without altogether denying his birthright. Varchi's unusually refined analysis of the types of love enabled him to declare that it was just the human sort, 'when some man loves some woman again, in good love', which could not be perfected unless the union was total, and entire, 'that is, if as one first conjoins the souls, one does not conjoin the bodies too'. But his reason hardly admitted of practical distinction, for it was that body and soul are so united while we live that no entity could be more one.[50]

This being the Aristotelian response to the notion of the stairs, Speroni's adoption of that figure in his assault on spurners of the body is particularly pointed. The senses, he says, provide 'stair and path' to the reason, but all the senses and not just sight and hearing. Moreover, it is a step that you have to take every time you want to get there:

> Whoever is such a fool in love that he has no care of his appetite, but as simple disembodied intelligence seeks solely to satisfy his mind, can be compared to him who, gulping his food without touching it or masticating it, more harms than nourishes himself.

Human beings in love are 'centaurs', their reason and desires inextricably mixed.[51] Love's hermaphrodite, ultimate perfection of human lovers, will not be made with souls, or minds, alone.

Such were the ideas which the Italians passed to the rest of Europe, providing in this field, as in so many others, a varied and malleable body of public material. Donne, whether or not he actually read any of the quoted writers, was patently among their beneficiaries. My concern now is to see how he drew on and handled these common positions in 'The Extasie'—that is to say, taking account of the circumstances of his day in England, by what means he made them into a witty poem.

Donne's individual contribution to the theory of love in this poem is, to all appearances, not great. He confines himself to an eclectic use of sources; and one's attention is on the whole less usefully directed to what he used than to how he used it. In other words, it is in that measure a typical piece of witty writing.

What this meant for Donne's age one sees at once in the first episode, lines 1 to 12. The matter is a treatment of the ecstasy-inducing disposition of the lovers' bodies, as Cattani and others described it; but it is tricked out with every convenient quirk of current poetic wit. It seems that Donne's is here an art of embellishment, no less than that of the courtliest Petrarchist, different in that he preferred another means to the elegances, flowers, harmonies, and the like recommended by the Italian theorists of Imitation. The situation is, of course, stereotyped and emblematic[52]—what the rhetoricians called a *topothesia*—and it serves to introduce the general theme. 'Pillow' and 'Pregnant banke' provide erotic motivation, while the violet, 'pleasing flower dedicated to Venus',[53] is emblem of faithful love. A little play on some stock Petrarchan properties touches off the description of the ecstatic posture in lines 5-8, to the end of showing the depth and fixity of the trance. The sweat of the conventionally-joined hands becomes an immovable cement, and the adaptation of an extravagant form of the old play on eye-beams permits the coupling of the contemplating eyes. One surely need not cavil at this latter figure. It is ridiculous only if treated as an 'image', and quite adequately performs its near-emblematic function, while not being markedly different from those common witty plays of the time in which a figurative account is treated as though it were literally intended:

> So with the course of Nature doth agree,
> That Eies which Beauties Adamant do see
> Should on Affections line tremblying remayne.[54]

At all events, this form of coupling would have satisfied an Aristotelian only as a preliminary, and in concluding his first section Donne unambiguously motivates his latter position. A deft exploitation of the even more familiar Petrarchan play of the picture in the eye enables him to refer to the normal end of physical union, and the whole extent of the present deficiency is shown. Moreover, his 'as yet', in line 9, promises a remedy.

The description of the emanation and coupling of souls properly follows that of the bodies, left vacant, immobile, and dumb, 'like sepulchrall statues'. It is done with what is surely comic literalness—the souls hanging out like the Homeric (and emblematic) scales between the waiting bodies. Donne may perhaps have meant here that so far their souls are like the pans of the scales, joined though not one thing. But at least the following lines show that no element of contention is intended; and the only other meaningful point of the simile would seem to be the clever parenthesis, 'which to advance their state, / Were gone out'. These powers seek to augment themselves by the closest alliance, not at each other's expense. The notion is that of the perfecting power of the ecstatic union.

The orderly development of the figure is now momentarily interrupted by the introduction of a privileged overhearer of the spiritual communion. It is an amusing and also a pointed device. Donne is able at once to claim that there is a kind of arcanum of love, a soul-language for initiates, and, parenthetically, to assert the perfect oneness of these loving souls. But he has another point too, no less neatly made. This bystander is an initiate, and some way advanced in the mystery—besides being 'refin'd' by love, he has by his good love 'growen all minde'. Yet if he listens carefully here he will learn much; will indeed take 'a new concoction' ('the acceleration of anything towards purity and perfection', Johnson says),[55] and 'part farre purer then he came'. But the lovers who grew all mind in the process, spurning the body, were the strict Neoplatonists. Donne is certainly not condemning them. He only suggests pleasantly that they have still a great deal to learn, and that he is about to show them what it is.

With the opening of the chorus of souls, it is plain that the climax in this first half of the poem is to be the enunciation of the knowledge which has been granted to the lovers in their ecstasy—a revelation concerning their love, of course. Firstly, they see the inadequacy of their previous knowledge. What they love, they realize now, is not sex. Theirs is not the vulgar physical love, whose essence is individuality, differences, and instability, but something which brings together, and indissolubly mingles. 'So to one neutrall thing both sexes fit';[56] which thing is precisely Speroni's hermaphrodite. The positive part of the new knowledge is simply their awareness of the fusing of their souls, and realization of its consequences. As the individual soul is already a mixture, so of these two souls Love has made a further mixture and they each become the other—an analogy from Plotinian metaphysics dresses up the 'one and four' of the theorists. Complementing each other, the deficiencies of their singleness are remedied; as a puny solitary violet grows and reproduces when set in company. The analogy this time is Leone Ebreo's, though more apt in service of the common point because Donne has introduced the emblematic violet. Finally, the results of these ameliorations and the core of the revelation, to the new composite soul is granted self-knowledge, the understanding of its own nature. It is, simply, souls; and souls are such as 'no change can invade'. They are assured (albeit by a sleight of wit) of their own eternal fidelity, that unending mutual enjoyment which Leone declared to be the outcome and guerdon of perfect desire.

One is not unprepared for Donne's return to the incompletely united bodies. But his transition is dramatic, and the rhetoric of memorable cadence. His concern now, in this latter part of the poem, is to develop the assertion that the lovers' state cannot be perfect while their bodies remain in unsatisfied singleness. This he does by stages. We are given first a few simple puffs of the body; then the negative claim that the sexual coupling of the bodies does not actually prevent the union of souls; and finally—save for a few small concluding points —the full affirmation. The treatment in lines 51-56 of the notion that the body is ready instrument of the soul is not remarkable. What is curious is to find Donne all but compromising his argument, and certainly reducing its possible effectiveness, by his apparent adoption of the Augustinian—and Ficinian—dichotomy in this section: 'They are ours, though they are not wee.' This is much more like Ficino's 'the soul is the man' than Speroni's figure of the centaur, and Aquinas's assertion that the man is neither body or soul alone, but a complex of both. It is, I suppose, with the analogy of 'intelligences' and 'spheres'[57] capable of bearing a Thomist construction. 'They are not wee'—we are no more bodies alone than we are souls alone. But there would seem a maladroitness in that way of presenting it unlooked for in so accomplished a rhetorician, and it may be thought more likely that Donne simply balked at professing the full Thomist position. If that is so, we have a rare hint of his private metaphysical views.

The analogy of 'heavens influence' in lines 57-58 is alien to the love-theorists, but remote in neither of its possible senses. The planets, influencing man, commonly do so by the grosser medium of air. And heavenly beings in their earthly visitations take up and wear the air, so as to make themselves visible to men: 'Then as an Angell, face, and wings / Of aire, not pure as it, yet pure doth weare. . . .'[58] The implication is that if the stars, and even God and the angels, do not disdain to work their spiritual ends through a less spiritual medium, then these lovers should not either. Certainly its use cannot frustrate such refined motions.

Donne chooses to support his climax with an analogy produced from the odd notion of intermediary spirits; and the claim is less convincingly made than if he had stated it baldly. His metaphysics are ordinary in doctrine as in production.[59] He has merely made a pleasant (or perhaps tendentious) figure of that physiological explanation of the hypostatic union, following the traditional terminology of man-making 'subtile knyttynges',[60] 'most subtle exhalation', and 'knot between the soul and the . . . body'.[61] The blood, personified, 'labours'; material itself, it deliberately strives to produce something nearer the nature of souls; it is its 'fingers' which knit the human knot. By this little quirk of wit, and an ambiguity (which may only be awkwardness) in the construction of the analogy, Donne does in fact suggest another argument than the expected one. He seems to be saying, 'Man's humanity is incomplete unless blood labours to beget spirits as like souls as it can'—does its best, that is, to produce souls. So 'pure lovers are not completely lovers unless their fused souls, inciting and acting through their blood (affections, passions), labour in begetting, doing their best to produce souls.' But this is at most secondary. What his sources teach, and he presumably means in chief, is that as the soul would be impotent and incomplete were it not linked to the material body by an intermediary, and thus put in touch with the outside world of sense, so pure lovers are impotent and incomplete if their souls do not stoop to use an intermediary, by whose means they can reach sense and each other. These intermediaries are 'affections' and 'faculties'—terms, like 'sense', of apt double import. 'Sense' in particular, with its common sixteenth-century overtone 'sensuality', or 'sexual play',[62] would add the useful implication that it needs nothing short of full physical intercourse to liberate the joint souls of lovers.

There is also the famous figure of the 'great Prince in prison'. One wonders if this is intended to be just a fine and pithy confirmation of the claim that while the bodies do not join the souls cannot. Certainly it would be no novelty to speak of the soul as a Prince, nor of the body as its prison. But it is interesting to find Davies, in *Nosce Teipsum,* developing his long discussion of the interaction of soul and body through a similar figure of a great prince in prison, and meaning something more subtle. 'This cunning mistress and this queen', he says, who lies in 'the body's prison', must look through the body's windows to know the world, and can discourse on and judge nothing but what sense reports to her. Yet the senses are only her instruments, which she uses for the humble task of garnering knowledge, while she 'sits and rules within her private bower', her sole function to 'judge and choose':

Even as our great wise *Empresse*, that now raignes,
By *soveraigne* title over sundrie lands,
Borrowes in meane affaires her *subiects* paines,
Sees by their eyes, and writeth by their hands;

But things of waight and consequence indeed,
Her selfe doth in her chamber them debate,
Where all her Counsellers she doth exceed
As farre in iudgement, as she doth in state.[63]

Thus, while the soul delegates only meaner matters to the sense, it cannot function without sense, any more than could a Prince deprived of her ability to act through executives. And the harm suffered by such an imprisoned Prince would be a loss of precisely that which makes her a Prince, her ruling power. So we may feel that Donne had precise attributes in mind when he called the new soul a great Prince. A Prince's chief attribute is ruling power; this she cannot exercise in prison. The chief attribute of a lover's soul is its power to govern the body of the lover; and this it cannot exercise while in the body's prison—until, that is, it is released by physical intercourse. Hence, until the bodies of the lovers are joined, their joint soul has no kingdom to command. The joint soul of these lovers has not attained its full prerogative until their joined bodies release it to rule. This follows smoothly on the earlier situation. The new composite soul, hovering outside bodies which its 'atomies' formerly occupied, cannot have a body to command unless these bodies are also made one. Until the bodies are made one the subtle knot is not tied, joint soul exists without body, bodies exist without souls, and the lovers are not truly lovers in love's hypostasis. Within the terms of the play of figure, the plea for the coexistence of bodily love with the highest degree of spiritual union has been completely justified. But it is the play of figure which is original, not the plea.

What follows is winding-up, chiefly by means of the comic pretence of the arcana of love. The idea that bodily union might be desired 'as sign of the primary conjunction'[64] is deftly dressed, the body becoming love's book wherein he reveals his spiritual mysteries to uninitiates. We have, again, the point that the speech of the loving souls is intelligible only to another lover—with the weak joke added that it has been a 'dialogue of one', a novel and mysterious sort of *dialogo d'amore*. And the somewhat enigmatic conclusion seems to be an assertion that the lovers' resort to their bodies now will mean no debasing of their love, or sundering of their eternally faithful souls.

Thus we see that if Donne's poem is hardly the seduction-piece of Legouis's 'scholastic Don Juan', it contains no individual metaphysic of love, and can only perversely be regarded as introspective. It is difficult to conceive how Mr. Eliot's 'sensuous apprehension of thought' could be a useful description of the processes which produced 'The Extasie'. Whether Donne was passionately in love when he wrote the poem is surely a profitless question—one remarks only that it is neither the analysis, nor in any direct way the expression, of personal passion. Beyond doubt it is the work of a strongly original and variously gifted personality, with a fine dramatic sense and feeling for language. But these gifts appear to be exercised in that dressing-up, re-presenting of received positions, which Italian critics of the Renaissance regarded as the essential poetic process. Only, Donne's chief vivifying resource is what his age called 'wit'. Certainly 'The Extasie' is a remarkably 'witty' poem.

NOTES

[1] *The Poems of John Donne* (Oxford, 1912), ii. 41.

[2] Ibid., p. xxxiii.

[3] 'Donne's *Extasie* Contra Legouis', *P.Q.*, xv (1936), 247-53.

[4] See *The Sermons of John Donne*, ed. Potter and Simpson, i. 134, and Sermon 5, pp. 236-51.

[5] B. Varchi, 'Lezzione sopra l'Amore', in *Lezioni* (Fiorenza, 1590), pp. 326-7.

[6] *Della Infinità di Amore*, in G. Zonta, *Trattati d'Amore del Cinquecento* (Bari, 1912), p. 222.

[7] *Dialoghi d'Amore*, ed. S. Caramella (Bari, 1921), p. 6.

[8] *Infinità*, p. 235.

[9] Leone Ebreo, *Dialoghi*, p. 49.

[10] G. Betussi, *Il Raverta*, in Zonta, *Trattati*, pp. 10-11.

[11] *Dialogo di Amore, Opere* (Venezia, 1740), i. 3.

[12] B. Gottifredi, *Lo Specchio d'Amore*, in Zonta, *Trattati*, p. 297.

[13] T. Tasso, *Conclusioni Amorose*, in *Le Prose Diverse*, ed. C. Guasti (Firenze, 1875), ii. 68.

[14] F. Sansovino, *Ragionamento nel quale brevemente s'insegna a' giovani uomini la Bella Arte d'Amore*, in Zonta, *Trattati*, p. 180.

[15] Betussi, *Raverta*, p. 34.

[16] *Dialoghi*, p. 173.

[17] F. Cattani, *I Tre Libri d'Amore* (Vinegia, 1561), pp. 119-20.

[18] Leone, *Dialoghi*, p. 173.

[19] Ibid., p. 176.

[20] J. Weemes, *A Treatise of the Foure Degenerate Sonnes* (Edinburgh, 1636), pp. 72-73.

[21] Leone, *Dialoghi*, p. 43.

[22] T. Tasso, *Le Considerazioni sopra Tre Canzoni di M. Gio. Battista Pigna*, in Guasti, *Prose*, ii. 92.

[23] S. Speroni, *Opere*, i. 4.

[24] Betussi, *Raverta*, p. 95.

[25] Betussi, *Raverta*, pp. 23, 24.

[26] Leone, *Dialoghi*, p. 383.

[27] Ibid., pp. 384, 43, 51.

[28] Cattani, *Tre Libri*, p. 111.
[29] M. Ficino, *Sopra lo Amore* (Lanciano, 1914), p. 92.
[30] Cattani, *Tre Libri*, p. 111.
[31] Ibid., p. 112.
[32] The phrase is Varchi's, in 'Dell' Anima', *Lezioni*, p. 721.
[33] I am indebted to M. Étienne Gilson's discussion of this point in ch. ix of *The Spirit of Mediaeval Philosophy* (1936), from pp. 186-8 of which the quotations are taken.
[34] *De Gl'Heroici Furori* (Torino, 1928), p. 89.
[35] *Infinità*, p. 197.
[36] M. Equicola, *Libro di Natura d'Amore* (Vinegia, 1526), f. 110.
[37] *Discorso dell' Anima Umana*, *Opere*, iii. 370.
[38] *Lezioni*, pp. 371, 612.
[39] Betussi, *Raverta*, p. 32.
[40] Varchi, *Lezioni*, p. 381.
[41] *Conclusioni, Considerazioni*, in *Prose*, ii. 67, 89.
[42] *Dialoghi*, p. 50.
[43] Cit. G. Toffanin, *Il Cinquecento* (Milano, 1941), p. 141. See also Castiglione, *Il Libro del Cortegiano*, ed. V. Cian (Firenze, 1947), pp. 89-90.
[44] *Dialoghi*, p. 213.
[45] *Raverta*, p. 140.
[46] *Natura*, f. 111r.
[47] Tullia, *Infinità*, p. 223.
[48] Ibid., p. 224.
[49] *Natura*, f. 197r.
[50] *Lezioni*, p. 338.
[51] *Opere*, i. 6, 22-23.
[52] Cf. Sidney's 'In a Grove Most Rich of Shade', and such conventional descriptions of setting as that for the 'amorous monologue' in Scaliger, *Poetices*, i. 4.
[53] Equicola, *Natura*, f. 164r.
[54] 'To his Lady who had vowed virginity.' Anon., in *A Poetical Rapsody* (1602).
[55] *O.E.D.* under *Concoction*, 2, lists contemporary uses in this sense.
[56] 'The Canonisation'.
[57] Grierson prints 'spheare' following all the manuscripts, whereas the editions give 'spheares'. His explanation of the singular form is that the bodies made one are the sphere in which the two Intelligences meet and command. This is attractive, but an anticipation of Donne's argument. John Hayward's adoption of 'spheares' in the Nonesuch Edition (*Complete Poetry and Selected Prose of John Donne*, 1929) seems justified.
[58] 'Aire and Angells'.
[59] The passage which Grierson cites from *Sermons*, 26. 20. 291 (Alford) in elucidation of this analogy is a simple fragment of the common teaching. In English there is a better account in *Nosce Teipsum* ('The passions of sense'), *The Poems of Sir John Davies*, ed. C. Howard (New York, 1941), pp. 160-1.
[60] Chaucer, *Boece*, in *Works*, ed. F. N. Robinson (1933), p. 440b, l. 18.
[61] Cattani. See p. 144 above.
[62] *O.E.D.*, *Sense* sb. 4.
[63] *Poems*, p. 127. Davies and Donne are likely to have moved in the same circle.
[64] Tasso. See p. 143 above.

The Origins of Stephen Crane's Literary Creed

James B. Colvert

Literary source hunters have experienced little difficulty in suggesting influences upon Stephen Crane's early novels and stories. But where such study should ideally throw light upon the genesis and processes of Crane's art, too often the claims and surmises about his literary origins are so general or so tenuous that they serve more to endarken than enlighten. Spiller, in the *Literary History of the United States*, fairly states the whole case:

> The appearance of an original artist, springing without antecedent into life, is always illusion, but the sources of Crane's philosophy and art are as yet undeciphered. Neither the cold-blooded determinism of his belief nor the sensuous awareness of his writing can be without source, but nowhere in the scant record he has left is there evidence that he, like Garland, read widely in the current books on biological science. A direct influence of Darwin, Spencer, Haeckel, or their American popularizers cannot be established. Rather he seems to have absorbed these influences at second hand through Russian and French writers.[1]

The problem of the "cold-blooded determinism of his belief" aside for the moment, how can the literary historian account for the "illusion" of Crane's appearance as an "original" artist and the amazing rapidity of his apparently untutored growth? In the spring of 1891 he was a Sophomore at Syracuse University, ambitiously planning to end his college career in order to become a writer; by the fall of 1892 he had already formulated the creed of art by which he was to be guided for the remaining eight years of his life and was presumably writing his first novel; by the spring of 1893 the author of *Maggie: A Girl of The Streets*[2] had won the attentions of two of the most influential literary men of his time, Hamlin Garland and William Dean Howells.

Two theories are commonly advanced to explain this phenomenal literary development. First is the popular and persistent notion, perhaps inevitable in view of his unusual literary rise, that Crane had no origins at all, that he was a "natural" genius who had no need for a literary situation in which to develop. An informed contemporary, Howells, could only say that the young author of *Maggie* "sprang into life fully armed,"[3] and Garland, Crane's patron for a time after 1893, propagated for almost twenty years the idea that his protégé was an inexplicable genius, a sort of unconscious recorder of whatever came to him from the outer reaches of a ghostly world. This belief is commonly found in history and criticism even today. He was, a critic wrote in 1941, "an artist who was really not conscious at all. He arrived . . . fully equipped. He had no need to improve."[4] And as late as 1952 a historian asserted that Crane was an artist of "amazing, almost miraculous prescience," and thus "that despair of the academic critic, a highly 'original' writer."[5]

The other view, accepted in part at least by Spiller in the *Literary History of the United States,* is that Crane sprang directly from the tradition of the French and Russian naturalists, a thesis extensively argued in Lars Ahnebrink's study of *The Beginnings of Naturalism in American Fiction.*[6] Ahnebrink attributes Crane's basic concept of fiction and the writer to the European naturalists, particularly Zola, whose *L'Assomoir* and *La Débâcle* he regards as important sources for Crane's first three novels, *Maggie, George's Mother,* and *The Red Badge of Courage.* Turgenev's *Fathers and Sons,* Ahnebrink thinks, probably influenced *George's Mother,* and Ibsen's *An Enemy of the People* perhaps suggested Crane's novelette, *The Monster.*

But there are serious objections to both of these views. The notion that Crane had no literary antecedents contradicts the fundamental principle that every writer is at first dependent upon his times and its traditions, however widely he may later deviate from them in the process of creating something new out of the old. Nor is the second theory much more acceptable. The chief difficulty with the idea that Crane adopted the doctrines and methods of the naturalists is that it assumes, without much evidence, that he read and imitated the writers of this school, an assumption which does not at all square with the fact that Crane's work and the naturalists' differ in many important respects. There are reasons to doubt seriously that the American ever read Zola or the Russians. When Ahnebrink asserts that "even before the composition of *Maggie,* he [Crane] was familiar with some of Zola's work," he ignores the fact that Crane read *Nana*—the only novel by Zola he ever commented on—more than five years after he started writing *Maggie.*[7] No evidence exists that he ever read *L'Assomoir,* and *La Débâcle* he threw aside, according to Thomas Beer, after reading only a few pages.[8] There is no external—and no convincing internal evidence that he knew either Turgenev or Ibsen.

On the contrary, there is good reason to believe that Crane was unusually ill-read. John Barry, the editor of *The Forum* who read Crane's *The Black Riders* in manuscript in 1894, referred to the young poet as "woefully ignorant of books,"[9] and Berryman, who thinks Crane's reading has been understimated, can nevertheless assert that "it is not easy to think of another important prose-writer or poet so ignorant of traditional literature in English as Stephen Crane was and remained."[10] All his life he denied, sometimes with considerable irritation, any connection with the naturalists. "They stand me against walls," he complained about his English acquaintances to James Huneker in 1897, "with a teacup in my hand and tell me how I have stolen all my things from de Maupassant, Zola, Loti, and the bloke who wrote—I forget the name."[11] Except for a reference to the brief period in 1891 when, as a student at Syracuse, he was studying intensely with a view to forming his style, there is little evidence that he ever read much at all, an omission he once defended on the ground that in this way he avoided the risk of unconscious imitation.[12] Unlike Frank Norris, who once referred to himself as "Mr. Norris, Esq. (The Boy Zola)!" Crane seems to owe little, if anything, to nineteenth-century French and Russian naturalism.[13]

How, then, can the literary beginnings of this precocious (but, one supposes, hardly supernatural) young writer be accounted for? "Here came a boy," Beer wrote of the twenty-year-old ex-college student who went into the East Side slums in the spring of 1891 for material for Maggie, "whose visual sense was unique in American writing and whose mind by some inner process had stripped itself of all respect for these prevalent theories which have cursed the national fiction. He was already an ironist, already able to plant his impressions with force and reckless of the consequent shock to a public softened by long nursing at the hands of limited men."[14] But what had stimulated to action his natural rebelliousness and what were the "inner processes" that turned him to slums for the subject of his painfully realistic *Maggie?* From whom had he learned the use of irony, and to whom was he indebted for his interest in painting and his characteristic use of color imagery? What was the origin of his belief that direct personal experience is the only valid material for the writer, and what led him to emphasize so strongly his belief that absolute honesty is a prime virtue of the artist? These questions, it would seem, define the problem of Crane's literary origins, and the answers are to be found in the period of his almost incredibly brief apprenticeship to the craft of fiction in the years 1891-92.

Crane left one of the most important clues to his artistic origins in a letter of 1896 to Lily Brandon Munro, a lady he was once in love with in his Syracuse student days. "You know," he wrote, "when I left you [in the fall of 1892] I renounced the clever school in literature. It seemed to me that there must be something more in life than to sit and cudgel one's brains for clever and witty expedients. So I developed all alone a little creed of art which I thought was a good one. . . . If I had kept to my clever Rudyard-Kipling style, the road might have been shorter, but, ah, it wouldn't be the true road."[15] The significant point here is not so much Crane's rejection of Kipling as a literary mentor as his implicit admission that the Englishman had served him as a model sometime between 1891 and 1892. It seems more than likely that the young American owed to Kipling the basic principles of his artistic beliefs, for Crane's theory of literature matches precisely the esthetic credo of Dick Heldar, the young artist-hero of Kipling's *The Light That Failed*, a novel Crane read sometime before 1892, probably during the spring semester of 1891 at Syracuse University.

Few young writers in a rebellious mood were likely to escape the attraction of Kipling in the first years of the nineties. At the time *The Light That Failed* was appearing in *Lippincott's Magazine* in January of 1891, Kipling was already a best-selling author whose fiction was considered new and unorthodox. His amazing popularity had in fact become a subject for reviewer's verse:

> No matter where I go, I hear
> The same old tale of wonder;
> It's some delusion wild, I fear,
> The world is laboring under.
> Why every friend I've met today
> (I couldn't help but note it)
> Has asked me "Have you read 'Mulvaney'
> Rudyard Kipling wrote it."[16]

Immediately following this is a review of *The Light That Failed* which emphasizes the unorthodoxy of his realistic tale of an artist's adventures as a war correspondent and suggests something of the appeal it must have had for the youthful Crane, then a cub reporter for his brother Townley's Asbury Park news agency: "Bohemian and unconventional as the characters are," the reviewer states, "no one who has seen much of the two classes whence they are chiefly drawn—newspaper correspondents and lady art students—can say they are grossly exaggerated."[17]

There is convincing evidence that Crane not only knew this novel before 1892, but that it indeed made a profound impression upon him. S. C. Osborn notes that Crane's famous image at the end of Chapter IX in *The Red Badge of Courage*, "The sun was pasted against the sky like a wafer," occurs in Kipling's *The Light That Failed* and concludes that the younger writer unconsciously incorporated the idea into *The Red Badge*.[18] There are strong reflections, moreover, of Kipling's early manner—the impressionistic "modern" imagery, the sententious, often flippant, dialogue, and a keen sense of the ironic—in Crane's earliest fiction, *The Sullivan County Sketches,* written in the summers of 1891 and 1892. In these pieces, which comprise all that may be properly called apprentice work, if the first drafts of *Maggie* and a story published in the Syracuse school paper are excepted, Crane put into practice the basic theories of Dick Heldar, the rebellious and unorthodox artist in *The Light That Failed.*

Dick Heldar must have been the apotheosis of all that the nineteen-year-old Crane hoped to become. Dick is an Impressionist painter in revolt against the canons of nineteenth-century respectability. He chooses Bohemian life for the freedom it gives him in his enthusiastic pursuit of fame, and with great determination he seeks the truth about life in the slums of London and on the battlegrounds of remote deserts. He is proud, independent, and free in the expression of iconoclastic opinions.

Crane's orientation was remarkably similar. As a boy he was in perpetual revolt against the respectability of his conventional, middle-class Methodist home life, and at Claverack College, Lafayette, and Syracuse, an indifferent student at all three places, he incurred the displeasure of the faculty for expressing "angular" opinions. He was asked to withdraw from Lafayette at the end of his first semester for refusing to conform to academic regimen. "Away with literary fads and canons," he exclaimed to a friend in the late spring of 1891,[19] and about the same time he began making trips to New York to study life on the Bowery and in the slums. In the fall of 1892, after he was dismissed from the *Tribune* for writing an ironic account of an Asbury Park labor parade, Crane moved into the East Side more or less permanently, where he remained, observing and writing in wretched poverty, for more than two years.

This way of life he led by choice like Kipling's Dick Heldar, from whom he probably got the idea that this privation was valuable, perhaps even indispensable, to his development as an artist. "There are few things more edifying unto Art than the actual belly-pinch of hunger," Kipling explains when he puts Dick into the London slums to starve and paint within walking distance of an affluent friend. "I never knew," Dick says in explaining the value of his experience with poverty, "what I had to learn about the human face before."[20] When he is at last paid for some art work, Dick calls upon his friend and explains that he could not have asked for help because "I had a sort of superstition that this temporary starvation—that's what it was, and it hurt—would bring me more luck later."[21] Crane, as his way of life during this period shows, was of the same belief. One of his nieces, recalling her uncle's misery in the New York slums, was puzzled by his conduct: "We still wonder why he went through such experiences when he was always so very welcome at both our house and Uncle Edmund's. Perhaps he was seeking his own 'Experience in Misery' . . . altho doubtless it came also through his desire to make his own way independently."[22] To these views Crane himself assented, but a more significant explanation lies in his persistent notion that great art is born of the "belly-pinch of hunger":

> It was during this period [he wrote to the editor of Leslie's Weekly about November, 1895] that I wrote "The Red Badge of Courage." It was an effort born of pain—despair, almost; and I believe that this made it a better piece of literature than it otherwise would have been. It seems a pity that art should be a child of pain, and yet I think it is. Of course we have fine writers who are prosperous and contented, but in my opinion their work would be greater if this were not so. It lacks the sting it would have if written under the spur of a great need.[23]

The remarkable kinship in temperament and attitude between Kipling's protagonist and Crane strongly suggests that Dick's ideas about art deeply impressed the young writer. Dick may have inspired Crane in the use of color images for special effects, a stylistic feature which blazes forth in the Sullivan County tales of 1892. For *The Light That Failed* bristles with artist talk about color. Heldar exclaims with sensuous enthusiasm about the scenery of Sudan: "What color that was! Opal and amber and claret and brick-red and sulphur—cockatoo-crest sulphur—against brown, with a nigger black rock sticking up in the middle of it all, and a decorative frieze of camels festooning in front of a pure pale turquoise sky."[24] Crane's interest in painting, it is true, probably originated in his associations with his sister, Mary Helen, who taught art in Asbury Park in the late eighties and early nineties, and with Phebe English, a young art student with whom he fell in love when he was a student at Claverack College.[25] But in *The Light That Failed* he had before him not only an enthusiastic appreciation of the expressive potentialities of color, but also a striking example, in Kipling's "wrathful red disk" images, of how color could be used by the writer to evoke mood and emotional atmosphere.

More important in Crane's literary credo, though, are the principles governing the selection of materials, their treatment, and the attitude of the artist toward them. In *The Light That Failed* Kipling advances and defends the position that real life furnishes the only valid materials for art. "How can you do anything," his hero exclaims, "until you have seen everything, or as much as you can?"[26] Like the blind and ruined Heldar, who met his death following wars to the far corners of the earth, Crane, ill with tuberculosis, wandered away his energies—in the West, Mexico, the Florida swamps, Greece, and Cuba—in quest of experience in the world of action. "I decided," he wrote once in reference to his literary creed of 1892, "that the nearer a writer gets to life the greater he becomes as an artist,"[27] and in 1897, when his career was drawing to a close, he wrote from England to his brother William: "I am a wanderer now and I must see enough."[28] Both Crane and Kipling's hero expressed and acted upon the firm belief that the artist's material is necessarily drawn from personal experience.

Important corollaries for the realist are the convictions that all experience, ugly and unpleasant though it may be, must be faithfully and truthfully reported if the artist is to maintain his integrity. Around this idea Kipling builds one of the key scenes in *The Light That Failed.* Heldar, disappointed because one of his realistic war sketches has been rejected by all the magazines, decides to alter it to conform to the conventional idea of what the soldier is like:

> I lured my model, a beautiful rifleman, up here with drink. . . . I made him a flushed dishevelled, bedevilled scallawag, with his helmet at the back of his head, and the living fear of death in his eye, and the blood oozing out of a cut over his ankle-bone. He wasn't pretty, but he was all soldier and very much man. . . . The art-manager of that abandoned paper said that his subscribers wouldn't like it. It was brutal and coarse and violent. . . . I took my "Last Shot" back. . . . I put him into a lovely red coat without a speck on it. That is Art. I cleaned his rifle—rifles are always clean on service—because that is Art. . . . I shaved his chin, I washed his hands,

and gave him an air of fatted peace. . . . Price, thank Heaven! twice as much as for the first sketch.[29]

"If you try to give these people the thing as God gave it," Dick argues when his friend Torpenhow reprimands him for this practice, "keyed down to their comprehension and according to the powers he has given you . . . half a dozen epicene young pagans who haven't even been to Algiers will tell you, first that your notion is borrowed and, secondly, that it isn't Art!"[30] But Torpenhow destroys the repainted picture and delivers Dick an impassioned lecture on truth and integrity in the practice of art, after which the penitent Heldar concludes, "You're so abominably reasonable!"[31]

This idea Crane was expounding as early as the spring of 1891, about the time he read Kipling's novel. "I became involved," he wrote again in reference to his creed of 1892, "in the beautiful war between those who say that art is man's substitute for nature and we are the most successful in art when we approach the nearest to nature and truth, and those who say—well, I don't know what they say. Then they can't say much but they fight villainously."[32] On another occasion he stated Dick's idea more explicitly: "I cannot see why people hate ugliness in art. Ugliness is just a matter of treatment. The scene of Hamlet and his mother and old Polonius behind the curtain is ugly, if you heard it in a police court. Hamlet treats his mother like a drunken carter and his words when he has killed Polonius are disgusting. But who cares?"[33]

Writing in 1898 about his literary aims, Crane reasserted his belief in this principle and showed how largely it had figured in his career: "The one thing that deeply pleases me in my literary life—brief and inglorious as it is—is the fact that men of sense believe me to be sincere. . . . I do the best that is in me, without regard to cheers or damnation."[34] This echoes the principle oratorically preached to Dick upon the occasion of his moral lapse: "For work done without conviction, for power wasted in trivialities, for labor expended with levity for the deliberate purpose of winning the easy applause of a fashion-driven public, there remains but one end,—the oblivion that is preceded by toleration and cenotaphed with contempt."[35]

These striking parallels in the artistic aims and attitudes of Dick Heldar and Crane strongly suggest that Kipling's novel provided the young American with his basic conception of the art of fiction. Since the evidence for the influence of the naturalists upon Crane's literary theory is unconvincing, and since he knew neither Howells, or Garland's theories of realism and veritism until after 1892, before which time he had read *The Light That Failed,* it seems likely indeed that Kipling is Crane's chief literary ancestor. This belief is further strengthened by the fact that Crane read Kipling's book at the most impressionable period of his literary life. As a rank novice, rebellious against social and literary conventions and searching for a rationale for a new fiction, Crane must have found Kipling's ideas immensely stimulating. "For short, scattered periods Crane read curiously," Berryman states, "and instinct or luck or fate led him early to what mattered."[36] Later, it is true, he found support for his creed in the ideas of Howels, Garland, and the Impressionist painters with whom he was in constant association during his Bohemian New York period. But the book which laid the basic principle was *The Light That Failed.* Here is developed explicitly a whole literary credo which exactly parallels Crane's. In advocating and following closely the principles that art is grounded in actual experience, that absolute honesty in the artist is an indispensable virtue, that all experience, including the ugly and the unpleasant, is material for the artist, Crane, through Kipling, anticipated the "cult of experience" in American fiction which reached its full development in the literary renaissance of the twenties.[37]

NOTES

[1] Robert E. Spiller and others, eds., *Literary History of the United States* (3 vols., New York, 1948), II, 1021.

[2] The book, Spiller writes (*ibid.,* 1022), with which "modern American fiction was born."

[3] Thomas Beer, *Stephen Crane: A Study in American Letters* (New York, 1923), 96.

[4] H. E. Bates, *The Modern Short Story* (New York, 1941), 65.

[5] Edward Wagenknecht, *The Cavalcade of the American Novel* (New York, 1952), 212.

[6] University of Uppsala *Essays and Studies on American Language and Literature,* IX (1950).

[7] Beer, *Stephen Crane: A Study in American Letters,* 148.

[8] *Ibid.,* 97.

[9] John D. Barry, "A Note on Stephen Crane," *The Bookman,* XIII (1901), 148.

[10] John Berryman, *Stephen Crane* (New York, 1950), 24.

[11] Robert W. Stallman, ed., *Stephen Crane: An Omnibus* (New York, 1952), 674. All references to Crane's letters are to this source.

[12] Barry, "A Note on Stephen Crane," 148.

[13] This view is in harmony with that of Albert J. Salvan, a student of Zola who concludes in his study of the naturalist's influence in the United States: "Dans la question toujours délicate d'établir un rapport d'influence définie entre Zola et

Stephen Crane, nous sommes forcés de rester sur une note evasive. Il n'est guère douteux que l'auteur de Maggie manquait d'une connaissance très entendue de la littérature française du XIXe siecle en genéral." *Zola aux Etats-Unis* (Providence, 1943), 163.

[14] Beer, *Stephen Crane: A Study in American Letters*, 77.

[15] Stallman, *Stephen Crane: An Omnibus*, 648.

[16] "The Light That Failed," *The Literary News*, XII (1891), 29.

[17] *Ibid.*, 19.

[18] Scott C. Osborn, "Stephen Crane's Imagery: 'Pasted Like a Wafer,'" *AL*, XXIII (1951), 363. Osborn notes only one occurrence: "The fog was driven apart for a moment, and the sun shone, a blood-red wafer, on the water." *The Writings in Prose and Verse of Rudyard Kipling* (New York, 1897), IX, 63. The image occurs in variations twice more: "A puddle far across the mud caught the last rays of the sun and turned it into a wrathful red disc" (p. 13), and again: "The sun caught the steel and turned it into a savage red disc" (p. 31). See n. 37.

[19] Arthur Oliver, "Jersey Memories —Stephen Crane," *New Jersey Historical Society Proceedings*, n.s., XVI (1931), 454-55.

[20] Rudyard Kipling, *The Light That Failed*, in *The Writings in Prose and Verse of Rudyard Kipling* (New York, 1897), IX, 41.

[21] *Loc cit.*

[22] Edna Crane Sidbury, "My Uncle, Stephen Crane, As I Knew Him," *Literary Digest International Book Review*, IV (1926), 249.

[23] Stallman, *Stephen Crane: An Omnibus*, 591.

[24] *The Light That Failed*, 53.

[25] Joseph J. Kwiat, "Stephen Crane and Painting," *The American Quarterly*, IV (1952), 331.

[26] *The Light That Failed*, 105.

[27] Stallman, *Stephen Crane: An Omnibus*, 627.

[28] *Ibid.*, 663.

[29] *The Light That Failed*, 55-56.

[30] *Ibid.*, 49.

[31] *Ibid.*, 56.

[32] Stallman, *Stephen Crane: An Omnibus*, 648.

[33] Berryman, *Stephen Crane*, 21.

[34] Stallman, *Stephen Crane: An Omnibus*, 679-80.

[35] *The Light That Failed*, 67.

[36] Berryman, *Stephen Crane*, 24.

[37] When this article was in page proof, I saw R. W. Stallman's "The Scholar's Net: Literary Sources," *College English*, XVII (1955), 20-27, in which Mr. Stallman states that Scott C. Osborn, who first pointed out the similarity between Kipling and Crane's wafer image, "failed to explore the related images for what they mean and how they are used. . . . Nor is there any other point of correspondence between *The Light That Failed* and *The Red Badge of Courage*—only this single image (p. 20)."

Shakespeare and the Diction of Common Life

F. P. Wilson

We have heard much in recent years of the necessity of making ourselves Shakespeare's contemporaries. We shall understand him better, it is said, be in less danger of misunderstanding him, if we know as much as we can of the stage for which he wrote, of the actors who performed his plays, of the audience which saw them acted, of the psychological theories of the age, of its economic, political, and social life, of its taste in rhetoric, in language, and in criticism; in short, if we make ourselves good Elizabethans, if possible intelligent Elizabethans. I shall not quarrel with this ideal. It is one to which every scholar aspires, and most of this paper is taken up with some of the difficulties. But while it is impossible to exaggerate the difficulties, it is sometimes possible to exaggerate the results. It has been said that nothing but a whole heart and a free mind are needed to understand Shakespeare, and if we interpret this to mean a robust heart and an acute and sensitive mind that is true, and true in an important sense. How little Keats knew of Shakespearian scholarship may be a cooling card for the scholar's fancy. He read Shakespeare not in Malone's edition, but in plain texts without commentary, yet he understood Shakespeare 'to his depths'. If ever man made Shakespeare a part of his life, that man was Keats. He is the great Shakespearian humanist. And if we are ever tempted to forget, his example is a perpetual reminder that while we strive to make ourselves Shakespeare's contemporaries, it is even more important to make Shakespeare our contemporary, to keep him level with life and with our lives.

The title of this lecture was suggested by a man who believed in keeping literature level with life. In the Preface to his *Dictionary* Johnson observes:

> From the authors which rose in the time of Elizabeth, a speech might be formed adequate to all the purposes of use and elegance. If the language of theology were extracted from Hooker and the translation of the Bible; the terms of natural knowledge from Bacon; the phrases of policy, war, and navigation from Raleigh; the dialect of poetry and fiction from Spenser and Sidney; and the diction of common life from Shakespeare, few ideas would be lost to mankind, for want of English words, in which they might be expressed.

Johnson does not say that a lexicographer could find in Shakespeare the diction of common life and nothing else. Shakespeare may have had 'small Latin and less Greek', but he had enough Latin to use English words from that language with confidence. 'With cadent tears fret channels in her cheeks', 'My operant powers their functions leave to do', 'The multitudinous seas incarnadine', these and many other lines contain words or senses of words not yet found earlier than Shakespeare. Within fifteen lines of a speech of Agamemnon's there are four such words.[1] But while he realized the value to his cadence and meaning of the learned word beside the familiar, he was never in danger of becoming an inkhornist. He may use the word 'remuneration' comically in *Love's Labour's Lost* and seriously in *Troilus and Cressida,* or 'festinately' comically in *Love's Labour's Lost* and 'festinate' seriously in *King Lear,* but at no time could the creator of Holofernes have admired the sixteenth-century poet who asked his mistress what thing was 'equipollent to her formosity'.[2] And although he profits from them all, he cannot be attached to any one of the various schemes for enriching the English vocabulary recommended by sixteenth-century grammarians and rhetoricians—whether with inkhorn terms, outlandish terms, archaic words, or dialect. What a Greek writer said of Homer is very true of Spenser but is not in the least true of Shakespeare: 'he did not stop at his own generation, but went back to ancestors; had a word dropped out, he was sure to pick it up, like an old coin out of an unclaimed treasure-house, all for love of words; and again many barbarian terms, sparing no single word which seemed to have in it enjoyment or intensity.'[3] The conditions of Shakespeare's art as a dramatist did not permit him to stray far from popular idiom, but even if they had, his mind was of a cast that would still have found the material upon which it worked mainly in the diction of common life. The best of the Sonnets are evidence of that and all the familiar images in his plays which, as his art matures, flow more and more freely from the less conscious levels of his mind. At the same time his instinct for what was permanent in the colloquial language of his day is stronger than that of any contemporary dramatist. No other Jacobean would have displayed 'a Rogue' with so little use of canting or 'pedlar's French' as does Shakespeare in Autolycus. In the words of Coleridge, his language is that which belongs 'to human nature as *human*, independent of associations and habits from any particular rank of life or mode of employment. . . . It is (to play on Dante's words) in truth the NOBLE *volgare eloquenza*'.[4]

His retentive mind received its stores from books, more still from speech and his own penny of observation. 'It is probable', wrote J. M. Synge, 'that when the Elizabethan dramatist took his inkhorn and sat down to his work he used many phrases that he had just heard, as he sat at dinner, from his mother or his children.'[5] Shakespeare may often have cried 'My tables—meet it is I set it down', as Shaw represents him doing in *The Dark Lady of the Sonnets.* When we find in earlier writers that as in *Love's Labour's Lost* a hat or veil comes over a face 'like a penthouse',[6] that as in *Hamlet* this world is 'a sea of troubles',[7] or even that a man's humour is 'tickle of the sear',[8] we may be in doubt whether these are phrases which Shakespeare had read or overheard, but we cannot doubt that in their boldness and concreteness they are characteristic of what he might have read or heard and of the climate in which his own image-making flourished. So, too, when Sir Thomas Egerton, Lord Keeper, urges the Parliament of 1597 to thank God 'upon the knees of our hearts',[9] we are not surprised at the bold extravagance of the metaphor. Egerton is not clipping the Queen's English: this was the current coinage of the realm. He and his contemporaries did not suffer from 'the Danger of thinking without Images'.[10]

We could not know what wealth Shakespeare had to draw upon or how much by his own invention he added to that wealth until the completion of the great *Oxford Dictionary,* and we shall know more fully if the University of Michigan publishes its Early Modern English Dictionary. Perhaps it is not much of an exaggeration to say that a mere recital of the number of ways in which the Elizabethans could and did refer to their besetting vice of drunkenness would take up the greater part of this hour. Their dictionaries, especially Florio's and Cotgrave's, give us some indication of the wealth of synonym and of the delight these lexicographers took in assembling it. They practised 'copy' (*copia verborum*) even in their dictionaries. Florio calls his second edition 'A New World of Words': it is his voyage of discovery into the land of diction. Watch him exploring the possibilities of two Italian words. Under *tinca:* 'a fish called a Tench. Used also for a fresh-water soldier, or unexpert Captain that will have thirty men with him be it but to dig up a Turnip'; and under *squassapennacchio:* 'a tisty-tosty, a wag-feather, a toss-plume, a swashbuckler'. Shakespeare does not use one of these four words, yet every one is rounded to an actor's palate, every one a moving picture.

Unlike J. M. Synge, Shakespeare needed no 'chink in the floor' to enable him to overhear what was being said in the country-kitchen; he was free of it by birth; but he eavesdropped in the City and at Court and found there talk as fully flavoured. Landor has said that the best language in all countries is that which is spoken by intelligent women, of too high rank for petty affectation, and of too much request in society for deep study.[11] That is the language of Rosaline, of Beatrice, of Rosalind. If Shakespeare ever had a weakness for court affectations, he worked it out of his system in *Love's Labour's Lost.* We hear much of these affectations of speech in Elizabethan literature, of 'Arcadian and Euphuized gentlewomen', but as we should expect there were few affectations in the speech of those who were closest to the Queen. In *Cynthia's Revels* it is not Crites or Arete who drink of the fountain of self-love; and it is not Cynthia. However picked and patterned may be the language of Elizabeth's formal writings, there was no trace of affectation in her private speech or public utterances. Her very oaths identified her with all classes of her people except those who swore by 'yea and nay' or 'indeed la'. In a pious and spirited book which formed half the dowry of Bunyan's wife, Arthur Dent wrote of men who swore less vigorously than his Queen that 'Hell gapeth for them';[12] but fortunately for him his Plain Man's Pathway did not lead him into the Presence. And when she spoke to her people, then, as her great scholar Camden would have wished, she did not follow 'the minion refiners of English'; she spoke not State English, not Court English, not Secretary English, but plain English.[13]

> Though God hath raised me high; yet this I count the glory of my Crown, That I have reigned with your loves. This makes me that I do not so much rejoice, That God hath made me to be a Queen, as, To be a Queen over so thankful a People. . . . There will never Queen sit in my seat, with more zeal to my Country, care for my Subjects; and that sooner with willingness will venture her life for your good and safety, than my self. For it is not my desire to live nor reign longer, than my life and reign shall be for your good.

And though you have had, and may have, many Princes, more mighty and wise, sitting in this State; yet you never had, or shall have, any that will be more careful and loving.[14]

As we read these strong and straightforward sentences we may flatter ourselves that we can read Elizabeth and Shakespeare as good Elizabethans, yet apart altogether from changes in pronunciation the words cannot mean to us what they meant to contemporaries. The words we most value rise from a well of associations fed by a thousand memories, and we cannot rid ourselves of these associations. But we can make an approximation, and in making it the greatest difficulty does not come from obsolete expressions and obscure allusions. When we meet with 'miching mallecho' either we look up a commentary or we pass on. There is a possibility of ignorance here, but not of misunderstanding, unless indeed the commentators mislead us. Nor in some contexts is the danger very great from words which have survived into modern English with very different meanings. Only a very stupid reader would misunderstand when it is said that in the Scotland of Macbeth 'violent sorrow seems A modern ecstasy'. The real danger comes with words to which it is possible to attach the modern meaning and make a sense. But the sense is not Shakespeare's. Sometimes the difference is so slight that the modern meaning does little or no harm. It matters little, to take an example of Henry Bradley's,[15] whether we understand Polonius's 'Still harping on my daughter' to mean 'Now as heretofore harping on my daughter' or, as Shakespeare meant, 'Always harping on my daughter'. It matters more if we forget how the dilatoriness of man has deprived of its urgency such a word as 'presently'.[16] How many a word has lost its vigour by continual usage may be illustrated from a famous passage in *Othello:*

> When you shall these unlucky deeds relate,
> Speak of me as I am; nothing extenuate,
> Nor set down aught in malice: then must you speak
> Of one that loved not wisely but too well;
> Of one not easily jealous, but, being wrought,
> Perplex'd in the extreme.

'These unlucky deeds', 'perplexed in the extreme'. What colourless words, we are tempted to say, and good critics have seen here the irony of understatement. But in Elizabethan English 'unlucky' means or can mean ill-omened, disastrous; and 'perplexed' means or can mean grieved, tortured, the mind on the rack. There is no hyperbole here, but neither is there understatement. In the noble and single magnificence of Othello's speech, the emotion is fully and exactly stated.

Editors have not given us enough help here—Professor Dover Wilson in the later volumes of the New Cambridge Shakespeare is a notable exception—yet since Dr. Onions's *Shakespeare Glossary* of 1911 and the completion of the *Oxford Dictionary* in 1928 much of the evidence has been available. Even with this expert assistance the difficulty of choosing between the many possible meanings of some of the commonest words is often great. It may be important to remember that in addition to bearing its modern meanings the noun 'will' often signifies lust, the carnal passions in control of the reason. It is the last word in the longest speech in which Hamlet rebukes his mother, and it is a climax to the mood of disgust and revulsion which has almost unseated his reason:

> Rebellious hell,
> If thou canst mutine in a matron's bones,
> To flaming youth let virtue be as wax
> And melt in her own fire: proclaim no shame
> When the compulsive ardour gives the charge,
> Since frost itself as actively doth burn,
> And reason pandars will.

And as we should expect, the word is prominent in the plays in which Shakespeare is above all at grips with the sin of lust. 'Redeem thy brother', cries Angelo, 'By yielding up thy body to my will'; of Antony it is said that he 'would make his will Lord of his reason'; and to Troilus eyes and ears are

> Two traded pilots 'twixt the dangerous shores
> Of will and judgement.

So far I have been considering the words apart as if in a dictionary, but let me no longer 'crumble my text into small parts' but draw my observations 'out of the whole text, as it lies entire and unbroken'[17] in Shakespeare himself. For more than a century critics have observed how his line became animated, and his paragraph interanimated, by the rhythms of speech. They have noticed, too, his growing mastery of dramatic prose, and how while never relinquishing its colloquial base it could become upon the lips of Falstaff and Hamlet as quick and forgetive as poetry. And all the time he was slowly working himself free from the over-elaborate use of schemes and tropes inherited by him from his age and by his age from scholastic rhetoric. 'That wonderful poet, who has so much besides rhetoric, is also the greatest poetical rhetorician since Euripides'—these words of Matthew Arnold's[18] remain true of Shakespeare to the end, but there is as much difference between the rhetoric of *Richard III* and *King Lear* as between the verse. An Elizabethan schoolmaster might have set his boys many a speech in Shakespeare's early plays as an exercise in the identification of schemes and tropes, and to name the figures in (say) the soliloquy of Henry VI which begins 'This battle fares like to the morning's war', with its elaborate examples of anaphora with and without climax, would have been well within the capacity of the meanest scholar in Mulcaster's school,[19] although perhaps he would not have observed how the speech is redeemed by the lyricism which cuts across the formalism of the rhetoric. But if the boy had been confronted with *Hamlet* or *King Lear* his task would have been more difficult. There is a development in Shakespeare similar to that which Professor Manly noticed in Chaucer: 'a process of general release from the astonishingly artificial and sophisticated art with which he began and the gradual replacement of formal rhetorical devices by methods of composition based upon close observation of life and the exercise of the creative imagination.'[20] Even in Shakespeare's earliest manner, as in Chaucer's, the natural is ever present with the artificial, but by the turn of the century Shakespeare has forged verse, prose, and rhetoric into the subtlest instrument of dramatic speech the world has known. How this dramatic speech is dependent upon language familiar to all his audience, upon the language of common life, may be illustrated by examining his use of three figures, paronomasia, the image, and the proverb. Paronomasia and the proverb were more valued in his age than in later ages, but command of the image,[21] especially metaphor, has seemed since Aristotle the greatest thing by far for a poet to have.

Johnson recognized that every age has its modes of speech and its cast of thought, but Shakespeare's use of agnomination or paronomasia, or more simply quibbling with words, he could not condone. Camden, too, while quoting Giraldus Cambrensis to the effect that the English and the Welsh 'delighted much in licking the letter, and clapping together of Agnominations', felt that 'this merry playing with words' had been 'too much used by some'.[22] There will be few readers of Shakespeare's comic scenes who do not at times agree. The contrast between Speed's verbal wit and Launce's mother-wit is to be remarked: the one perished almost as soon as it was born, and the other is, in its kind, imperishable. Shakespeare inherited a ripe tradition of clowning —it was Tarleton's legacy to the English stage—and in ripe clowning, in 'merry fooling', there is little to choose between his early work and his late. As his art matures, he may bring everything more and more into a unity—Dogberry and Stephano are essential to the action, while Launce is a music-hall turn—but the humour of Launce's talk with his dog is already ripe, as nothing else in that play is ripe. But if being a good Elizabethan means enjoying word-spinning on the level of Speed, few of us can be good Elizabethans. It is some consolation to have Camden on our side, and Camden's greatest pupil who attacked the 'Stage-practice' of 'mistaking words' in *Bartholomew Fair*. Fortunately Shakespeare grew out of the abuse of the practice, and the fool in *Othello* is the last of his characters of whom it can be said: 'How every fool can play upon the word.'

Ben Jonson was inclined to attack all 'Paranomasie or Agnomination'—it is significant that he puts the words into the mouth of his Poetaster—but like most Elizabethans Shakespeare was never willing to relinquish it altogether. The figure played a chief part in their jests and riddles and in the many word-games of which they were so fond. If we wish to see to what good purpose Shakespeare puts the pun we cannot do better than turn to Beatrice and Falstaff. About the time that Shakespeare was creating them, Jonson's friend John Hoskins was blaming 'the dotage of the time upon this small ornament',[23] but there was no longer any question of Shakespeare doting upon it. While the quibble is Speed's only weapon it is one of many in the crammed arsenal of Beatrice's wit and Falstaff's. Beatrice's 'civil count, civil as an orange, and something of that jealous complexion' is gay and stimulating, one of many touches in Shakespeare's greatest exemplar of a love between man and woman that does not abase but sharpens the wits, so that in both sexes the mind and the senses are fully exercised. Falstaff's puns, too, do not merely spin upon themselves. The quibbles in 'thou camest not of the blood royal, if thou darest not stand for ten shillings' are quibbles with sense and are intimately concerned with the action. In this lively lordship over words he shows the agility of his mind. A contemporary proverb said that he who sought for a fine wit in a fat belly lost his labour. That is only one of the many incongruities that are reconciled in this character. A cony-catcher, he hob-nobs with princes of the realm. A coward, he never shows fear or loses presence of mind in the heat of battle. Surrounded by men who would sacrifice their lives for ambition or honour, he believes only in good fellows, sack, and sugar. An old man, he would persuade himself that he is for ever young. Shaken and diseased by his excesses, he is so exuberant with life that he seems to stand for the indestructibility of matter. No wonder he exacted from Dr. Johnson what is perhaps the only apostrophe in his edition of Shakespeare: 'But Falstaff unimitated, unimitable Falstaff, how shall I describe thee?'

To an Elizabethan the play upon words was not merely an elegance of style and a display of wit; it was also a means of emphasis and an instrument of persuasion. An argument might be conducted from step to step—and in the pamphleteers it often is—by a series of puns. The genius of the language encouraged them. 'So significant are our words,' writes Richard Carew, 'that amongst them sundry single ones serve to express divers things; as by *Bill* are meant a weapon, a scroll, and a bird's beak; by *Grave*, sober, a tomb, and to carve.'[24] And we remember Mercutio's dying jest—which is so much more than a jest—'Ask for me to-morrow, and you shall find me a grave man.' The rich ambiguities of the language were used not merely for fun. Falstaff can jest: 'I would my means were greater, and my waist slenderer'; while in the additions to *The Spanish Tragedy* Hieronimo, in great agony of mind, can implore 'infective night' to 'Grid in my waste of grief with thy large darkness'. So in the famous lines of Lady Macbeth

If he do bleed,
I'll gild the faces of the grooms withal,
For it must seem their guilt

the play upon words is no jest put in to enhance the horror of the scene, nor does it suggest hysteria, for at this point in the play Lady Macbeth is mistress of herself and of the situation. It underlines her determination, it is in Coleridge's words an 'effectual intensive of passion',[25] and it gives to her departure from the stage something of the emphasis and finality of a rhyming couplet.

I have said that the Elizabethans sometimes conducted an argument from step to step by a series of verbal quibbles. In Shakespeare the progression is often indirect and involuntary. This was noticed by Walter Whiter, a friend of Porson's, in his *Specimen of a Commentary on Shakspeare Containing I. Notes on As You Like It. II. An Attempt to Explain and Illustrate Various Passages, on a New Principle of Criticism derived from Mr Locke's Doctrine of the Association of Ideas* (1794), a book which anticipates in a most interesting way much modern work on Shakespeare's imagery. Whiter showed among other things how the images in which Shakespeare's train of thought is clothed may be suggested to his unconscious mind sometimes by similarities of sound, sometimes by words with an equivocal meaning, 'though the signification, in which they are really applied, has never any reference and often no similitude to that which caused their association'.

Whiter's most elaborate researches, in part still unpublished, were made upon the words and images which came to Shakespeare's mind, often involuntarily, from association with the theatre and with masques and pageantry. What is perhaps his most interesting discovery relates to the nexus of images which in varying combinations recurs in play after play to express disgust at false flattery and fawning obsequiousness, a nexus represented by Antony's

> The hearts
> *That spaniel'd me at heels,* to whom I gave
> Their wishes, do *discandy, melt* their *sweets*
> On blossoming Caesar.

But the passage which started Whiter on his inquiries was from the speech in which Apemantus upbraids Timon 'with the contrast between his past and present condition':

> What, think'st
> That the bleak air, thy boisterous *chamberlain,*
> Will put thy *shirt* on *warm*? Will these *moist* trees,
> That have outlived the eagle, page thy heels,
> And skip when thou point'st out?

Hanmer in 1744 had read 'moss'd trees', remembering perhaps the description of the oak in *As You Like It* 'whose boughs were moss'd with age'; and in this reading he has been followed not indeed by the *Oxford Dictionary*[26] but by most, if not all, editors. To make a participial adjective of the past participle 'moss'd', where the metre did not accommodate itself to 'mossy', was not beyond the capacity of any Elizabethan, particularly of Shakespeare, yet there is no evidence that any writer did this before Hanmer did it for the purpose of his emendation. But the seventh canon of criticism for an editor of Shakespeare is, according to Thomas Edwards, that "he may find out obsolete words, or coin new ones; and put them in the place of such as he does not like or does not understand'. By changing 'moist' to 'moss'd' the editors have given the passage a meaning the very opposite to that which Shakespeare intended. The emphasis in *Timon* is not on aged trees. The bleak air, Apemantus means, the trees whose strength is such that they have withstood the harshness of nature longer than the long-lived eagle, the cold brook, the naked creatures of nature, these will not flatter Timon. Whiter did not see that 'moist' in this passage bears the meaning 'full of sap', 'pithy'; but he did see that by an unconscious asssociation of ideas the image of the chamberlain putting his master's shirt on 'warm' or 'aired' impressed the opposite word 'moist' or 'unaired' upon the imagination of the poet, and that while 'moss'd' may be the more elegant epithet, what Shakespeare wrote and intended was 'moist'.[27]

'In the fictions, the thoughts, and the language of the poet,' Whiter writes, 'you may ever mark the deep and unequivocal traces of the age in which he lived, of the employments in which he was engaged, and of the various objects which excited his passions or arrested his attention.' Later and more systematic inquirers have proved, what the researches of Whiter suggest, that the great bulk of Shakespeare's images is taken from everyday things, from the goings-on of familiar life, images as familiar as the chamberlain putting his master's shirt on warm, or that image of heaven peeping 'through the blanket of the dark' which excited Johnson's risibility but does not excite ours.[28] Remoter images there are, for example the simile—to Pope 'an unnatural excursion'—in which Othello likens his determination for revenge to the Pontic sea

> Whose icy current and compulsive course
> Ne'er feels retiring ebb, but keeps due on
> To the Propontic and the Hellespont.

But usually the images are images from sights and sounds and experiences of a kind that came home immediately to the senses of his audience, and even in Othello's simile the emphasis is not on the remote geographical names, as it might have been in Marlowe, but on a natural phenomenon readily grasped by a people that used sea and river as the Elizabethans did. Owing to Shakespeare's instinct for what was permanent and central, his images are perhaps less often obscure than those of some of his contemporaries, but it must sometimes happen that what was obvious to the groundlings of the Globe Theatre because they had seen it with their own eyes or heard it with their own ears becomes apparent to us only after painful research. I take an example from a puzzling passage in *Love's Labour's Lost*. Berowne and the King of Navarre have broken their oaths to renounce love, and when the third perjurer Longaville is unmasked, Berowne observes:

> Thou makest the triumviry, the corner-cap of society,
> The shape of Love's Tyburn that hangs up simplicity.

What image did 'corner-cap' call up in the minds of Shakespeare's audience and by what association of ideas did he proceed from 'corner-cap' to Tyburn? Corner-caps were worn in Shakespeare's time in the universities, in the church, and by the judges of the land, but by an injunction of 1559 these caps were always square, nor do I know of one scrap of evidence that Shakespeare could have seen in England the three-cornered cap which his image so clearly demands. But we may be very sure that a Catholic scholar, Dr. John Story, 'a Romish Canonical Doctor', wore 'a three-cornered cap'. Story was martyred at Tyburn on 1 June 1571, and the execution was recorded in the usual way by ballad, broadside, dying confession, and by pamphlets both official and unofficial. What impressed itself upon the memory of the people was the use in this execution of 'a new pair of Gallows made in triangle manner',[29] and for many a year Tyburn or the gallows was known as 'Dr. Story's corner-cap' or his 'triangle', or simply as his 'cap'. It is not likely that Shakespeare was thinking of Story or of his 'simplicity' or folly; it was sufficient that 'corner-cap' could be associated without difficulty with a triumviry and with Tyburn. Longaville, as the third member of the company or 'society', has made up the triumviry and so recalls the shape of the gallows upon which Love hangs these foolish men who have tried to escape from her in their little academe. To an archaeologist 350 years is a short span, but the historian of manners may find all in doubt after the passage of a generation.

I have mentioned paronomasia, and I have mentioned the image. Let me mention another figure in rhetoric much valued by the Elizabethans. It can best be introduced by quoting a speech made in the Parliament of 1601. After the member for Southwark had begun to speak, had shaken for very fear, stood still a while, and at length sat down, the member for Hereford made this speech on a bill to avoid double payments of debts:

> It is now my chance to speak something, and that without humming or hawing. I think this law is a good law; even reckoning makes long friends; as far goes the penny, as the penny's master. *Vigilantibus non dormientibus jura subveniunt.* Pay the reckoning over night, and you shall not be troubled in the morning. If ready money be *Mensura Publica,* let every man cut his coat according to his cloth. When his old suit is in the wain, let him stay till that his money bring a new suit in the increase. Therefore, I think the law to be good, and I wish it a good passage.[30]

If this were played upon a stage now—those of us who do not read Hansard will say—we could condemn it as an improbable fiction, and indeed Thomas Jones's speech, with its clusters of homely proverbs, is paralleled by many a speech put by the dramatists into the mouths of downright or simple characters; Downright in *Every Man in his Humour,* Basket Hilts in Jonson's only play of rustic humours, *A Tale of a*

Tub, and the goldsmith Touchstone in the citizenly *Eastward Ho* are as full of proverbs as an egg of meat. Shakespeare seldom uses proverbs in this way. He does, however, in two of his earliest plays, use the catch-phrase as a pointer to character or the lack of it, and the Elizabethans made no sharp distinction between catch-phrases and proverbs. Every age has its own catch-phrases, and in every age they are the staple of conversation among those whose wits barely cross the threshold of intelligence. Luce in *The Comedy of Errors* and Jaquenetta in *Love's Labour's Lost* have no conversation outside such pert, ready-made phrases as 'Lord! how wise you are!', 'When? can you tell?', 'With that face?', 'Fair weather after you'. There is a similar dialogue in Lyly's *Mother Bombie* which Shakespeare may be imitating. Lyly calls them 'all the odd blind phrases that help them that know not how to discourse'. Some of them have survived to this day with little change: 'The better for your asking', 'You are such another', 'And therewithal you waked', 'Yea, in my other hose,' and 'quoth you'. Some dramatists exploited the elementary humour which comes from the repetition of a catch-phrase, but in the first quarto of *Hamlet*—the doctrine is Shakespeare's if not the words—the clown is condemned who keeps one suit of jests, like 'You owe me a quarter's wages' or 'Your beer is sour'. The laugh it raised was too easy for Shakespeare, the label it attached to character too superficial, the character to which the label could be attached too shallow. Falstaff has no catch-phrases. His sentiments are a perpetual surprise.

There must still be many a proverb in Shakespeare which his audience recognized as proverbial and which we do not. 'The nature of his work', says Johnson, 'required the use of the common colloquial language, and consequently admitted many phrases allusive, elliptical, and proverbial, such as we speak and hear every hour without observing them; and of which, being now familiar, we do not suspect that they can ever grow uncouth, or that, being now obvious, they can ever seem remote.'[31] When Lovell in *Henry VIII* speaks of 'fool and feather', and the Princess in *Love's Labour's Lost* asks 'What plume of feathers is he that indited this letter?', the collocation was already so well established as to have become proverbial, and for many generations 'he has a feather in his cap' was a periphrasis for a fool. Again, when Falstaff says that if Bardolph were any way given to virtue he would swear by his face and his oath would be 'By this fire, that's God angel', it has been supposed that Shakespeare was borrowing from Chapman in whose *Blind Beggar of Alexandria* a similar expression is to be found. But he was drawing upon the proverbial stock of oaths—the saying is at least as old as the *Misogonus* of about 1570[32]—and his audience received that peculiar delight which comes from the apt application of an old saying to a modern instance, Bardolph's nose.

Sometimes we are left in doubt whether Shakespeare was using a proverb or inventing one. Was Portia's 'a light wife doth make a heavy husband'[33] proverbial or is it Shakespeare's punning variation of 'Light gains make heavy purses'? And when Dekker and Webster use the same sentiment in *Westward Ho*,[34] were they borrowing from Shakespeare or making use of proverbial stock?

Then there are many 'sentences' in Shakespere which are commonplaces of his age yet were never crystallized into a set proverbial form. Hamlet's 'there is nothing either good or bad, but thinking makes it so' is an example. Spenser's 'It is the mind that maketh good or ill' has been cited in evidence, and a closer parallel is found in *Politeuphuia, Wit's Commonwealth*, an anthology of 'sententiae' published in 1597: 'There is nothing grievous if the thought make it not'.[35] Whether Shakespeare kept a commonplace book like Jonson, Bacon, Webster, and most of his contemporaries, is not known. Long before the evidence was discovered by Charles Crawford, J. A. Symonds hinted that Webster kept one.[36] But in Shakespeare there are no ill-fitting joins which betray the borrower. He brings everything into a unity. In the anthology just mentioned we find 'Our good name ought to be more dear unto us than our life',[37] and the sentiment may be as old as civilized man; it is no temporary opinion; but when Iago says to Othello

> Good name in man and woman, dear my lord,
> Is the immediate jewel of their souls

the commonplace takes on a new meaning. The maxim is embedded in the evil in the play: it has become an essential part of a great design.

It is a little difficult to adjust ourselves to the seriousness with which the Elizabethans treated the proverb. Soon after Shakespeare's death it began to lose favour. The decline of the native and homely proverb is suggested by the preference of George Herbert for 'outlandish proverbs', which, in comparison, have 'too much feather and too little point',[38] or by Glanvill's attack on preachers who use 'vulgar Proverbs, and homely similitudes';[39] and before Swift made the graveyard of proverbs and catch-phrases which he called *Polite Conversation* proverbs had almost disappeared from polite literature. This change in taste happened long before Lord Chesterfield called them 'the flowers of the rhetoric of a vulgar man' and said that 'a man of fashion never has recourse to proverbs and vulgar aphorisms'.[40] But to an Elizabethan the proverb was not merely or mainly of use for clouting a hob-nailed discourse; it still retained its place as an important figure in rhetorical training, and the many sixteenth-century collectors and writers who acclimatized foreign proverbs to the English soil were hailed as benefactors who enriched the 'copy' of their native tongue. Proverbs were invaluable for amplifying a discourse, or they added grace and variety to wit-combats. Sometimes they are hardly distinguishable in kind or function from the 'sentence' and the 'example': as Richard Carew said, they prescribed 'under the circuit of a few syllables . . . sundry available caveats'.[41] Preachers, orators, wits, dramatists, found them excellent persuasion. They could strengthen an argument, for they contained in themselves the authority of experience—'it must needs be true what every one says'; they were vivid and epigrammatic so that they stuck in the mind when abstract precepts were forgotten; and the use of a homely proverb might put preacher and congregation, orator or dramatist and audience, upon a friendly and familiar footing, one with each other.

Of the great English poets only Chaucer makes so good use of proverbs as Shakespeare. The contrast between Shakespeare and Jonson is striking. On the title-page of his best and most popular comedy, *The Alchemist,* Jonson put the words:

—Neque, me ut miretur turba, laboro:
Contentus paucis lectoribus.

As he despised the 'green and soggy multitude', so he despised their collective wisdom. Ancient proverbs, he said, might illuminate 'A cooper's wit, or some such busy spark',[42] and they have their place in his comedies, but they could serve no serious function in the work of this robust and independent writer. In *Volpone* one proverb, and only one, stands out by reason of its position and the new turn which Jonson gives it. It is the last line of the scene in which the Fox departs in disguise to gloat over the discomfiture of his victims. 'Sir, you must look for curses', says Mosca, to which Volpone replies in one of Jonson's magnificent exits:

Till they burst;
The Fox fares ever best, when he is curst.

If we turn to *Sejanus* and *Catiline* we shall not be surprised to find a dearth of proverbs or even proverbial phrases.[43] Gnomic passages there are in plenty, and in the first quarto of *Sejanus* the reader's attention is directed to the tragedy's 'fullness and frequency of sentence' by inverted commas. But English proverbs he rigorously excluded from the dignity of tragedy. His practice is of a piece with that fundamental contempt for the people which gives to his art so much of its bent and bias. Of all ancient proverbs, he would most strenuously have repudiated that which maintained that the voice of the people was the voice of God. And when in his tragedies his verses 'break out strong and deep in the mouth',[44] as they often do, they owe little or nothing of their strength to colloquial English idiom.

In Shakespeare proverbs are used as rhetorical ornaments, as moral sententiae, and occasionally as a means of building up character. From Richard's dissimulations in *Henry VI, Part 3,* until he achieves his throne in *Richard III,* old saws like 'I hear, yet say not much, but think the more' come pat to his purpose, especially in sardonic aside. He clothes his 'naked villany' with 'odd old ends'. In Faulconbridge, a character that sees the worst, seems to approve of it, and follows the best, bluntness and good humour are strongly marked in the first scene by the proverbs that pour from his mouth, but as his character is tested and proved by events his speech, while remaining direct and vigorous, becomes less proverbial. Richard seeks popularity for his own ends, Faulconbridge has a native disposition to it, while Coriolanus despises it. To him the 'vulgar wisdoms' of the people are contemptible.

> They said they were an-hungry; sigh'd forth proverbs,
> That hunger broke stone walls, that dogs must eat,
> That meat was made for mouths, that the gods sent not
> Corn for the rich men only: with these shreds
> They vented their complainings.

It is a little ironical that when Aufidius prophesies the doom of Coriolanus he does so with a couple of proverbs: 'One fire drives out one fire; one nail, one nail.'

What the proverb meant to Shakespeare is best shown not by the number and variety which he uses, although those so far identified are indeed many, but by his use of them in the gravest and greatest passages in his plays. Proverbs are mingled with folk-tale and ballad in the snatches, half sense and half nothing, spoken by the mad Ophelia: 'They say the owl was a baker's daughter. Lord, we know what we are, but know not what we may be.' In *King Lear* Shakespeare puts into the mouth of the Fool the silliest catch-phrase—'Cry you mercy, I took you for a joint-stool'—with poignant effect, and the Fool's last speech is a reference to the homely, ironical proverb: 'You would make me go to bed at noon.' Perhaps the most famous proverb in the whole of Shakespeare is that of the cat who would eat fish but would not wet her feet, to which Lady Macbeth refers in pluming up her husband's faltering will; but there are others in this play as striking and powerful in their operation. Keats has said that 'nothing ever becomes real till it is experienced. Even a proverb is no proverb to you till your life has illustrated it.'[45] Macbeth has indeed tested the truth of the line, 'It will have blood: they say, blood will have blood', and with what potency is the proverb charged. As moving is the 'what's done is done' of Lady Macbeth. It is one of the many thoughts and deeds which recurr to her broken mind in the sleep-walking scene —'What's done cannot be undone: to bed, to bed, to bed.' They give to her prose the concentration and associative force of poetry.

I have mentioned Jonson's care to exclude popular proverbs from his tragedies, and the reason lies not only in his conception of tragedy as something 'high and aloof'[46] but also in his strict sense of decorum. Shakespeare interprets the Renaissance doctrine of decorum more liberally. His decorum is dramatic, not historical. His tact in translating the manners of the ancient world to the modern stage is superb. He concentrates on what is permanent in spiritual and human values, and if clocks strike and doublets go unbraced, there is no offence for he never sacrifices the dignity of his theme by introducing the trivialities of the present or the pedantries of the past. He is as far from the revolting anachronisms of Heywood's *Rape of Lucrece, a true Roman Tragedy*, in which a Roman senator sings a ditty

> Shall I woe the lovely Molly,
> She's so fair, so fat, so jolly, . . .

as from Jonson's attempts at exact reconstruction of the manners and sentiments of the old Roman world. As the translators of the Bible did not hesitate, when necessary, to change the remote for the familiar, the unknown for the known—the musical instruments of Israel for the cornets, flutes, harps, and sackbuts of Elizabethan England, or the vanities of the attire of Israelitish women for the mufflers, the bonnets, the mantles, the wimples, the crisping pins of the sixteenth century—so Shakespeare writes of the entry of Coriolanus into Rome in words which are also applicable to the triumphal entry of James into the City of London:

> the kitchen malkin pins
> Her richest lockram 'bout her reechy neck,
> Clambering the walls to eye him: stalls, bulks, windows,
> Are smother'd up, leads fill'd and ridges hors'd
> With variable complexions, all agreeing
> In earnestness to see him.

Unlike Jonson, Shakespeare thinks nothing unclean that can deepen and widen his tragic art. He works not by exclusion but by bringing all aspects of life into a sense of order. Other men of his day, Webster or Middleton, tried to be as all-embracing, but the Shakespearian unity is incomparably more sensitive and more closely articulated. The poet's power reveals itself, says Coleridge, in the balance or reconciliation of opposite or discordant qualities. Only the disinterested artist who has no cause to serve (for the moment) except his art can bring himself to balance or reconcile such discordant and opposite qualities as are revealed, for example, in *Antony and Cleopatra*. In this many-sided play he seems to balance nobility and self-indulgence, renunciation and vanity, the glory and the corruption of the flesh, the greatness and the pettiness of the world. In the scene on Pompey's galley, where if anywhere in Shakespeare we find the diction and conduct of common life, the famous triumvirate, 'These three world-sharers, these competitors', drown their schemings and enmities in drink until Lepidus, the weak member of the axis, is carried drunk away, and the first and second parts of the world sing the refrain 'Cup us, till the world go round'. Is this a play then about a set of fools and rogues struggling for power in a world which does not signify? It is, and it would be less rich if it were not. But we remember how these baser elements are balanced by others, and as the play ends it is all 'fire and air'.

I have tried to suggest a few of the ways in which Shakespeare's drama is continually irrigated by the diction of common life. But it does not remain the diction of common life. It is transmuted, and with what nobility let us remind ourselves from his greatest play. When the tempests in Lear's mind and in nature have spent themselves, when 'the great rage . . . is kill'd in him', there is a simplicity in his speech which persists to the end. It is no mannered simplicity such as we sometimes find in Webster when he is trying to write like Shakespeare; but it is as if the fire of genius had reduced language to its elements. The monosyllabic base which some of his contemporaries thought the misfortune of our language he turns into glory. In these sentences there is no gap between the inspiration and the expression, between the mind and the hand, and without wastage they gather up together all the love, terror, and pity that have gone before:

> Pray, do not mock me:
> I am a very foolish fond old man,
> Fourscore and upward, not an hour more nor less;
> And, to deal plainly,
> I fear I am not in my perfect mind.

Methinks I should know you and know this man;
Yet I am doubtful; for I am mainly ignorant
What place this is, and all the skill I have
Remembers not these garments, nor I know not
Where I did lodge last night. Do not laugh at me;
For, as I am a man, I think this lady
To be my child Cordelia.

These are among the words and rhythms in which Shakespeare expresses his vision of good and evil. It is no system of morality which remains in the mind. The play provides symbols for the experience which it gives us—a wheel of fire, or incense of the gods upon such sacrifices—but there are no words to express our experience, or only Shakespeare's words.

NOTES

Annual Shakespeare Lecture of the British Academy, read April 23, 1941.

[1] *Trolius and Cressida,* I. iii. 7-21: conflux, tortive, protractive, persistive.

[2] T. C., *A Pleasant and Delightful History of Galesus, Cymon, and Iphigenia* (1560?), sig. A6.

[3] Dion Chrysostom, translated by A. O. Prickard (*Longinus on the Sublime,* 1906, pp. 93-4).

[4] *Coleridge's Shakespearean Criticism,* ed. T. M. Raysor (1930), i. 149-50.

[5] *Works* (1910), ii. 3-4.

[6] *Love's Labour's Lost,* III. i. 15, and L. Wager, *Mary Magdalene* (1566), 1. 585.

[7] *Hamlet,* III. i. 59, and Sir R. Barckley, *Of the Felicity of Man* (1598), pp. 147, 275.

[8] *Hamlet,* II. ii. 321, and *O.E.D.,* s.v. sear, *sb.*[1] I b.

[9] Hayward Townshend, *Historical Collections* (1680), p. 80.

[10] *Unpublished Letters of S. T. Coleridge,* ed. E. L. Griggs (1932), i. 163.

[11] *Imaginary Conversations,* 'Samuel Johnson and John Horne Tooke' (*Works,* ed. T. Earle Welby, 1927, v. 5).

[12] *The Plain Man's Pathway to Heaven* (1601), p. 165.

[13] *Remains* (1605), p. 28.

[14] Townshend, p. 263.

[15] *Shakespeare's England,* ii. 559.

[16] 'By and by' and 'anon' could still mean 'at once', and they sometimes bear their older meaning in the Bible of 1611; but in Shakespeare they can be given the modern meaning of 'soon'. In the 'anon, anon, sir' of the drawer the promise seems to bear the older meaning and the performance the modern.

[17] Cf. George Herbert, *A Priest to the Temple,* ch. 7.

[18] *Merope* (1858), p. xlv.

[19] The Elizabethan equivalent of 'every schoolboy knows'. Cf. F. Hering, *A Modest Defence* (1604), p. 27: 'a meane scholler of *Mul-*

casters schoole will easily tell him that . . .'.

[20] 'Chaucer and the Rhetoricians' (*Proceedings of the British Academy,* 1926, p. 97).

[21] See Note A.

[22] *Remains* (1605), p. 27.

[23] *Directions for Speech and Style,* ed. H. H. Hudson (1935), p. 16.

[24] *Elizabethan Critical Essays,* ed. G. Gregory Smith, 1904, ii. 288.

[25] Op. cit. i. 150.

[26] See under 'mossed', *ppl. a.,* and 'moist', *adj.* 2.

[27] Whiter, pp. 70, 73, 81-2, 138-40. See Note B.

[28] *Macbeth,* I. v. 53; *Rambler,* no. 168. It is a judgement on Johnson that in this essay he should give Lady Macbeth's speech to Macbeth.

[29] *A Declaration of the Life and Death of John Story, late a Romish Canonical Doctor by Profession* (1571), sig. C2. See Note C.

[30] Townshend, p. 283.

[31] *Proposals* (1756), p. 5.

[32] III. i. 240: 'By this fier that bournez thats gods aungell'.

[33] *Merchant of Venice,* v. i. 130.

[34] v. iii.

[35] p. 59b.

[36] 'Vittoria Accoramboni' (*Italian Byways,* 1883, p. 179): 'The sentences, which seem at first sight copied from a commonplace book, are found to be appropriate'; C. Crawford, *Collectanea,* First (1906) and Second (1907) Series.

[37] p. 106b.

[38] *Baconiana* (1679), ed. T. Tenison, p. 93: 'the *Jacula Prudentum,* in Mr. *Herbert*; which latter some have been bold to accuse as having too much Feather, and too little Point.' So Fuller may have thought, but not Jeremy Taylor, who adds Italian proverbs to the margins of *Holy Living.*

[39] *An Essay Concerning Preaching* (1678), p. 77.

[40] Letter to his son, 27 September 1749.

[41] Op. cit. ii. 288.

[42] *A Tale of a Tub,* Prologue.

[43] See Note D.

[44] *News from the New World* (1640, ii. 42).

[45] *Letters,* ed. M. Buxton Forman (1935), p. 318.

[46] *The Poetaster,* 'To the Reader', l. 238, and again in the 'Ode to Himself' in *Underwoods.*

Supplementary Notes

A

Image in its rhetorical sense is now understood to include metaphor and simile, and I use it so here; but in the sixteenth century the sense was much narrower. Quintilian (v. xi. 24) in discussing 'similitudo' refers to the kind of comparison called by the Greeks εἰκών, which expresses the appearance of things and persons, and advises a more sparing use of it in oratory than of those comparisons or similes which help to prove a point. Something of this survives by what is no doubt a long and devious route in Richard Sherry's *Treatise of Schemes and Tropes* (*c.* 1550), sig. F6: '*Icon,* called of the latines *Imago,* an Image in Englyshe, is muche lyke to a similitude, and if you declare it is a similitude: as if you saye: As an Asse wyll not be driuen from her meat, no not with a club, vntyl she be full: no more wil a warriour reste from murther vntyll he hath fylled his mynd with it. This is a similitude: but if you saye that a man flewe vpon his enemies like a dragon, or lyke a lyon, it is an Image. Howbeit an Image serueth rather to euidence or grauitie, or iocunditie, then to a profe. There is also a general comparacion, speciallye in the kynde demonstratiue, person wyth person, and one thing with an other, for praise or dispraise.' As in Quintilian the examples of 'similitudo' are usually in the elaborate 'ut . . . ita (sic)' form, so in Sherry and usually in Francis Meres's anthology of similes, *Palladis Tamia* (1598), they are expanded into the 'As . . . so' form. This is perhaps what Sherry means by 'if you declare', i.e. 'set out your comparison in full'. In his *Treatise of Schemes and Tropes* and also in his *Treatise of the Figures of Grammar and Rhetoric* (1555), pp. 53 and verso, Sherry's discussion of the image follows his discussion of the example, which he calls comparison with an act done, and his discussion of the similitude or 'comparacion', which he calls comparison with something that is dumb or lifeless. His treatment and instances of these figures correspond in part to those found in the *Epitome Troporum ac Schematum* of Johannes Susenbrotus. The instances of the rhetorical use of image, resemblance, and icon given above are earlier than those in the *O.E.D.*, where the earliest instance of image is dated 1676 and of icon and resemblance 1589: the rhetorical sense of comparation is not given, although comparison in the sense of simile goes back to Wyclif.

B

As he acknowledged on his title-page, Whiter based his work on the doctrine of association of ideas in Locke's *Essay concerning Human Understanding*, especially the passage quoted on p. 64: 'Ideas, that in themselves are not at all of kin, come to be so united in men's minds, that it is very hard to separate them; they always keep in company, and the one no sooner at any time comes into the understanding, but its associate appears with it; and if they are more than two which are thus united, the whole gang always inseparable shew themselves together.' By this involuntary association of ideas the poet is supplied with words and ideas suggested to the mind by a principle of union unperceived by himself and independent of the subject to which they are applied (p. 68). Whiter saw and illustrated the value of the principle for the establishment of Shakespeare's text, for the interpretation of his meaning, for deciding upon works of disrupted authorship, and for the light it might throw on 'the employments in which he was engaged, and . . . the various objects which excited his passions or arrested his attention' (p. 73). He even hinted at the presence of recurrent imagery: 'There is scarcely a play of our Author, where we do not find some favourite vein of metaphor or allusion by which it is distinguished' (p. 124). The whole tendency of his work, both in the commentary on certain passages in *As You Like It* and in the more general and more important essay which follows, was to support the readings of the original texts against the emendations of the editors. Many of the readings in *As You Like It* which he defended have been restored by modern editors, though seldom for the same reasons. Whiter is not uniformly happy in his arguments. He had in his nature 'much labour and shrewdness, with a considerable share of credulity' (Francis Jeffrey in a review of Whiter's *Etymologicon Magnum* in the *Monthly Review*, June and July, 1802, cited in the *D.N.B.*), and it is unfortunate that he should have chosen to illustrate the importance of his principle in deciding upon works of disputed authorship by attempting to prove that the Rowley poems, apart from some impurities introduced by the transcriber, are the genuine progeny of a medieval poet. 'Is he a sound man?' is the question asked of

Whiter the philologist in *Lavengro* (ch. 24), and the answer is: 'Why, as to that, I scarcely know what to say; he has got queer notions in his head . . . upon the whole, I should not call him altogether a sound man.'

In his *Etymologicon Magnum* (1800, p. 300) Whiter referred to himself *sine nomine* as 'an obscure writer, who in "A Specimen of a Commentary on Shakespeare" has laboured to enlarge the boundaries of Criticism, by applying a metaphysical principle to the elucidation of Poetic imagery, and figurative description'. He was disappointed with the reception of his book. From an extract from his Journal inserted in his interleaved copy of the *Specimen,* now in the Cambridge University Library, it appears that even his friends were indifferent, an indifference which proceeded perhaps more from 'want of thought than want of feeling. But what is *feeling* but thought?' One of them, however, Raine, a lawyer, considered the book 'as able to form an æra in the style of our language, by which the strength of expression and the grace of composition are preserved without the apparent and perpetually occurring artifice of Johnson and Gibbon'. His diffuse style is overpraised here, as his learning is overpraised in W. B. Donne's statement that he was 'equal to Steevens in acuteness, in black-letter learning to Malone, and immeasurably superior to them both in his perception of the meaning and his sensibility to the metre of Shakespeare' (*British and Foreign Review,* 1844, xvii. 231).

Coleridge and the critics of his generation ignored Whiter as they ignored Maurice Morgann, although both writers anticipated the romantic criticism of Shakespeare if only by their insistence upon the importance of the less conscious workings of the mind. Later editors and critics would not have left Whiter so severely alone if his work had been more often quoted in the Boswell-Malone Variorum edition of 1821. Four of his remarks are quoted or referred to in the commentary on *As You Like It,* but his work left no mark upon the text of that edition. We look in vain for any reference to his criticism of Hanmer's 'moss'd trees'; perhaps Malone would have agreed with the reviewer who wrote: 'From such associations good Lord deliver us! . . . We wish Mr. Whiter would learn to separate his ideas, instead of associating them' (*The Critical Review,* 1795, xiii. 100).

So far as I know, R. W. Babcock was the first modern writer to call attention to Whiter's work on Shakespeare (*The Genesis of Shakespeare Idolatry,* 1931), although he hardly does justice to Whiter's genuine merits. The rediscovery of Whiter has taken place at the moment when the main preoccupation of critics is with Shakespeare's language and imagery, as the rediscovery of Morgann took place when criticism was still mainly preoccupied with Shakespeare's characters. J. Isaacs noticed Whiter's interest in the recurrent association of candy and fawning dogs in *A Companion to Shakespeare Studies* (1934), p. 313. For modern discussions of this nexus of images by writers who did not know that Whiter had to some extent anticipated them, see E. E. Kellett, *Suggestions* (1923), pp. 72-3; G. H. W. Rylands, *Words and Poetry* (1928), pp. 176-8; Caroline F. E. Spurgeon, *Shakespeare's Iterative Imagery* (1931), pp. 13-17, and *Shakespeare's Imagery* (1935), pp. 194-9.

C

In the Arden edition of *Love's Labour's Lost* (1906) H. C. Hart called attention to the expression 'Dr. Story's cap' for Tyburn, and asked the question whether three-cornered caps were worn in Elizabethan England. But he did not notice that a special triangular gallows was used for the first time at Tyburn at Story's execution. Some recollection of this was in the mind of Joseph Healey, translator of Hall's *Mundus Alter et Idem,* when to the words 'hee is forthwith condemned to commence at *Doctor Stories* cappe' he adds in the margin: 'Tiborne was built for him, as some say' (*The Discovery of a New World, c.* 1609, p. 225).

The history of the square cap is discussed by N. F. Robinson, 'The *Pileus Quadratus*' in the *Transactions of the St. Paul's Ecclesiological Society,* v (1905), pp. 1-42, and by E. C. Clark, 'College Caps and Doctors' Hats' in the *Archaeological Journal,* lxi (1904), pp. 33-73. Much is heard of the square cap as a relic of Popish apparel, both in the Vestiarian controversy of the early years of Elizabeth's reign and in the Marprelate controversy. Martin Marprelate often writes contemptuously of 'cater-caps'. And to take a later example Edmund Bolton, in a passage very like some speeches of Candido's in Dekker's *Honest Whore,* part 2, I. iii, and derived perhaps from a common source, observes that 'the square capp is retained not onely in the *Vniuersities,* but also abroad among vs, as well by Ecclesiasticall persons in high places, as by Iudges of the land' (*The City's Advocate,* 1629, p. 41). Philip Stubbes refers to the symbolism which was by some attached to the *pileus quadratus* of the Catholic Church in these words: 'The cornered cappe, say these misterious fellows [the Papists], doth signifie, and represent the whole monarchy of the world, East, West, North, and South, the gouernment whereof standeth vpon them, as the cappe doth vppon their heades' (*Anatomy of Abuses,* 1583, part 2, ed. Furnivall, p. 115).

In another place (part I, p. 69) Stubbes compares women's 'Lattice cappes with three hornes, three corners I should say' to 'the forked cappes of Popishe Priestes', and just possibly the reference may be to the Italian three-horned biretta, a post-Reformation variation of the four-horned or four-cornered cap (Robinson, 6, and Clark, 36). The new triangular gallows might well have been named after Story even if he had worn a square cap, but if as a 'Romish Canonical Doctor' he was known to wear a three-cornered cap, the coincidence between the shape of the strange cap and the strange gallows would make the invention of Tyburn's new name irresistible. An expression of a similar kind—'Tyburn tippet' for a hangman's rope—is at least as old as Latimer (1549); the phrase appears in the margin of John Cornet's *Admonition to Doctor Story* (1571), a broadside in verse.

The earliest use I have met with of 'cornered' or 'corner' cap is in Gascoigne's *Supposes* (acted 1566), v. iv. 24: 'we will teache maister Doctor to weare a cornerd cappe of a new fashion', where the jest is the usual one of cuckoldry. Lyly, in his *Pap with an Hatchet* of 1589 (Bond III. 401. 31), provides the earliest example yet found of the association of Tyburn with a corner-cap: 'Theres one with a lame wit, which will not weare a foure cornerd cap, then let him put on Tiburne, that hath but three corners.' I have not met with the expression 'Dr. Story's cap' before 1592 (*Defence of Cony-Catching,* ed. G. B. Harrison, p. 6), but it may well have got into print earlier. A late example is in *The Wandering Jew* (1640), where Tyburn is said to wear 'a Three Cornered Cappe' and the criminal to 'ride Westward, at the Sheriffs charges, on Doctor Stories wooden horse of *Troy*'.

Professor Dover Wilson explains 'the corner-cap of society' as a reference to the 'black cap' of the judge. The difficulties are: (1) A corner-cap was the wear of the learned professions, don, divine, as well as judge, and there is nothing in the context to indicate a reference to the corner-cap of a judge. (2) I know of no passage in which corner-cap is used in the sense of the sentence-cap. (*O.E.D.'s* earliest example of 'black cap' is from *Oliver Twist*; it does not give 'sentence-cap'.) According to Robinson (p. 7), in the sixteenth and seventeenth centuries judges wore their corner-caps in the courts at Westminster and during circuit sat in church in them: the wearing of them was not reserved to the sole occasion of pronouncing the death-sentence. (3) The judge's cap was square, and Shakespeare's image requires a three-cornered cap; there are not 'four woodcocks in a dish' until Dumaine has joined the triumvirate.

D

In the whole of *Sejanus* and *Catiline* I find only three homely, familiar proverbs—'laugh and lie down' (*Catiline,* iii. 697), and in oblique reference 'a woman's reason —because it is so' (*Catiline,* ii. 57-8) and 'Still waters run deep' (*Catiline,* iii. 571-2). The first two are to be found in those scenes of scornful comedy between Fulvia, Galla, and Sempronia which Dryden's Eugenius thought 'admirable of their kind, but of an ill mingle with the rest'. In addition there are two proverbs of a more sententious kind. 'He threatens many, that hath iniur'd one' (*Sejanus,* ii. 476) gets into Apperson's *English Proverbs* from Gabriel Harvey's *Marginalia* (ed. G. C. Moore Smith, 1913, p. 101), where it is found in the form 'He threatenith many, That hurtith any', Harvey took it from the lost *Flowers of Philosophy* (1572) of Sir Hugh Platt, who could have found it in Publilius Syrus. A 'sentence' more often met with is 'Great honors are great burdens' (*Catiline,* iii. 1), of which examples are given in Latin (e.g. *Onus est honos*) and English in Tilley's *Elizabethan Proverb Lore* (1926), no. 346. I suppose that none of the English writers who observed 'watch the watcher' (*Catiline,* iii. 108) or exclaimed 'O age and manners' (*Catiline,* iv. 190) did so without remembering the originals. Of proverbial phrases—to limit these conveniently if mechanically to those mentioned by Apperson or in the *Oxford Book of Proverbs*—I notice only 'to fear no colours' (*Sejanus,* i. 285), 'to have in the wind' (*Sejanus,* ii. 406), and, doubtfully, an oblique reference to 'take counsel of one's pillow' (*Catiline,* ii. 319).

Style and Certitude

Don Cameron Allen

During the early part of the Renaissance in England we come on man universally merry for the last time in the modern world. He dresses like a gamecock and like Chanticleer calls up the sun with his crowing. He struts in the lanes of London, in bower and in hall; and he delights to make grand spectacles at which he is both the observer and the observed. The pen of his major chronicler, Edward Hall, drips color to the five senses and the twentieth century reader is conquered by the passion and the sound. It seems to us that man was, for a moment, putting aside the ancient doubts, that he was becoming more certain of himself, and that a bright new world was seemingly parading before him. His greatest joy was that everything seemed to be fenced about with a perdurability which appeared to have all the blessings of philosophy, politics, and theology. Then suddenly it is all over. There was no noise, no tumult; it was an apocalyptic end. One day they were eating and drinking and listening to the lutanist and the next day they were struck with infinite despair.

No one can say what happened; the age itself was perplexed to know. The transcendental background had collapsed and the disease of reason had set in. With the spread of this infection, the old feeling of personal certitude which depended on the stability of the transcendal norm began to depart. The dikes of philosophy had been cut again, and once more the skeptic's sea rolled westward in Europe. Men now began to talk about life as if it were a dream, something between a sleep and a sleep. Vives compares existence to dreaming that one is rich for a day, and Spenser, as well as his model Du Bellay, perceives in dreams the transitoriness of things. The dreamer of Vives takes dramatic flesh in Shakespeare's *The Taming of the Shrew*, and

John Donne pondering the intricacies of love represents himself as more tormented and more satisfied by what he dreams than by what he knows. The situation of the sensitive European is pathetically summed up by a speaker in Calderon's significantly-named play, *Life is a Dream:*

> What is life? A thing that seems,
> A mirage that falsely gleams
> Phantom joy, delusive rest
> And even dreams themselves are dreams.[1]

Under these circumstances, it is not surprising that Descartes, seeking certainty and attempting to purge his mind of doubts, considered whether or not he was burdened with a dream. At almost the same hour that Descartes was scrutinizing this possibility, Sir Thomas Browne was writing, "it is not a melancholy conceit to think that we are all asleep in this world, and that the conceits of this life are as mere dreams."[2] But Browne was one of the few intellectuals of this age who were able to find a point of rest between reason and faith and so he adds, "to those of the next."

In time, science and the revised theology of the nineteenth century propped up temporarily the sagging backdrop of certainty and so put apart for the while the awful maxim that "we are such stuff as dreams are made on and our little life is rounded with a sleep." But before this progression occurred, much had happened both to the heart and brain of man. The brain was saying dreary things to the heart and the heart was beating faster and more irregularly. The things that men said and the way in which they said them changed, too. The tone and accent of verse and prose alter, for the brain was saying dreary words to the heart and men could hear their hearts pounding in their brains. The phenomenon is of great contemporary interest for it almost convinces one that there is a fixed coincidence between the degree of an artist's positiveness in philosophy and the mode of his expression. The evidences of this spiritual distress and its consequent expression may be observed in the prose of the Jacobeans.

The prose of the joyous period of the early English Renaissance was humanistic prose, the child of a blissful marriage between the Latinity of Cicero, in all of its copiousness and measure, and the native English manner that had been purified by More and his associates of what Ascham called "its augmentations" and "indenture language." Ascham, too, added his stone to the new structure. He might hold for a style that "rose and fell" with the matter and he might praise More for perfecting the historical language of the English; nonetheless, it was his influence that turned many Englishmen to practising as apes of Cicero and that settled the formal prose style of Tudor thinkers, the serious style that culminates in the soaring periods of Hooker. All of this happened in the face of Erasmus' early attack on those who would rather be disciples of Cicero than saints of God. And though we now know that Erasmus was thinking of linguistic purists when he wrote his *Ciceronianus* and of the stylistic procedure only obliquely, we can estimate the shock that this work caused by remembering that the knights of Cicero, as they named themselves, rode at once to the master's aid. On the Continent, Scaliger and Longolius wrote acid replies in long sentences; and in England, Gabriel Harvey attempted to distinguish the true Cicero from the false in his imitation of the polemic of Erasmus. The English opposition to Cicero began, to the contrary, in a sly and cautious manner. Ascham, writing almost in the year of Muretus' declaration of independence, was unaware of the French position; he even tries to moderate between the dead Erasmus and the dead Longolius: "the one seemth to give overmoch, the other over little, to him whom they both loved."[3]

The story of Muretus' and Lipsius' criticism of the style of Cicero and their championing of the rhetorical technique of Tacitus and Seneca has been told in a series of magisterial essays by the late Professor Croll,[4] but the ground for the new direction was more thoroughly prepared in England than we have been inclined to admit. Early in the seventeenth century, the epistles of Seneca and Lipsius were seriously threatening the long reign of Cicero's letters in the public schools. One cannot imagine a schoolmaster like Ascham pausing long over Lipsius' letter to Petrus Villerius in which the Belgian humanist expounds his views with a Judas kiss: "Ciceronem amo. Olim etiam imitatus sum: alius mihi sensus nunc viro."[5] If this sort of heresy could be glossed in the lower forms of the Elizabethan grammar school, orthodoxy must have been breached long before. Such seems to have been the case, for not only are the adjectives with which Muretus and Lipsius hallowed Seneca and Tacitus to be found in English mouths prior to the great vernacular imitation, but a sturdy opposition seems also to have been gathering force.

Thomas Gataker praises the style of Seneca as "eximia, utilia, fortia, sublimia, et arguta, subtiliaque"; and Camden, after calling attention to Tacitus' contracted diction and his "ictus sententiarum," says that there is more to be understood in him than one reads.[6] At an earlier stage of the discussion, Harvey mentions "weightie and speedie Sallust, deep Tacitus, sharp Seneca." The state of affairs is also revealed by the early opposition. Before the close of the sixteenth century, Sergeant Hoskins wrote in his *Directions* that the *sententiae* are better for the bench than the bar.

> Then of all others, why would the writers of these days imprison themselves in the straitness of these maxims? It makes their style like *arena sine calce,* as one saith of such a writer, and doth not he vouchsafe to use them that called them posies for rings? If it be a matter of short direction for life and action, or notes for memory, I intend not to discredit this new trick. But otherwise he that hath a long journey to walk in that pace is like a horse that overreacheth and yet goes slow.[7]

Two years later, Robert Johnson complains about the arrogance of the Neo-stoics which makes them "busie-headed and turbulent," and of the "stranglie brief sentences" of Tacitus.[8]

By the time of James' coronation, this new way of writing had become rooted in English soil. It was the style of the rationalists, the style of the doubters, the style of those who were looking for the causes of things. Here and there, a few meditative writers like Richard Greenham and John Weemes or a few reactionary and well-settled men like David Persons or Thomas Sheafe still clung to the Ciceronian period, but a great Ciceronian is hard to find. Now one must not avoid the seemingly contradictory fact that this rationalistic style crept into the pulpit with Bishop Andrews and was fondled by Dean Donne, Bishop Hall, and others. With the possible exception of Donne, all of these men were certain of their mission and quite capable of sweeping away the doubts that cluster with a dogmatic broom. The momentary preference of some clerics for this style is not too difficult to understand.

There is an elocutionary force in the fragmentation of the Senecan line that is lost in the long sough of the period; or to put the case in the words of Owen Felltham:

> Long and distended clauses, are both tedious to the ear, and difficult for their retaining. A sentence well couched takes both the sense and the understanding. I love not those Cart-rope speeches that are longer than the memory of man can fathom.[9]

But there are other reasons. The attraction of Seneca for the Jacobean divine resided more in his matter than in his form. Seneca was the moralist *par excellence;* his reputation in this respect had carried him triumphantly through the Middle Ages, and Petrarch had introduced him to the Renaissance as the equal of Cicero and the superior of the Greeks in the moral sciences.[10] All of this was further consecrated by the fact that Seneca was a favorite among the Fathers, not only for his almost apostolic doctrine but also for his alleged correspondence with Saint Paul. Tertullian speaks of Seneca with the possessive adjective "noster" and is one of his earliest stylistic disciples. In fact, one can say that much that seems to be Senecan in the pulpit prose of the early seventeenth century is really Tertullian. Bishop Hall, who carried his title of "our English Seneca" with not too much lightness, is obviously partial to Tertullian, whose works he read more completely and quoted more copiously than those of his so-called master. The use of the Senecan manner in the pulpit and in the works of some religious thinkers was motivated by Seneca's reputation as a moral philosopher and by his affiliations with the early Fathers rather than by the adaptability of his nervous, efficient prose to rational speculation. This conclusion may explain in part the echoing of Seneca that we find in secular writers, but it is not the whole explanation.

It has sometimes been said that the Senecan style is the badge of the libertine. There is a certain truth in this observation, but it is not all that may be said. Bacon, who followed the Senecan formularies in his early writings, may have had the instincts of a libertine, but this cannot be said of other secular writers of Senecan English prose. The times made the stoa and, consequently, the manner of the best known stoic attractive. The failure of faith had happened before in the prechristian era, and on one of these occasions, Zeno had established one place of retreat and Epicurus another. Both of these philosophers had founded systems that tried to poultice the bruises of humanity after it had fallen from another height of positive philosophy. Yet, they were both negative cults and, in the course of time, even they borrowed some of the utilitarian aspects of skepticism, the disease that they were intended to cure. Then, too, they were also diametrically opposed in method to eclecticism (the method of Cicero and the early Renaissance), for it faced all problems, whereas they avoided as many as they could. It was this failure of eclecticism, which is indicated by the inability of Pico della Mirandola, Ficino, and others to create satisfactory *summas,* that is probably as responsible as a change of vogue for the discarding of the Ciceronian prose method. The periodic style is the prose manner of those who have struck a balance, who have a system in which they can trust; hence it is the only style in which Hooker could have written, but it would have been organically discordant to the ultimate purposes of Bacon. Since men were in doubt, and searchingly in doubt, Seneca and Epicurus provided the best stylistic crutches to be found in ancient times. We know that at this particular time the reputation of Epicurus was being refurbished on the Continent and that his atomic doctrines were subsequently to play a great part in the seventeenth century rational explanation of the assembly of the universe; but his style, which was only known through the fragments of Diogenes, had, of course, no influence in an age that was confessedly anti-Greek. We must also not forget that Seneca was the author of the *Natural Questions* and a lost geographical treatise, so he had an additional attraction for the scientific writers who wished to inquire into the causes of things.

Bacon regarded the curt Senecan style as the correct form of expression for the rationalist. He used it in the so-called first essays and in the *Novum organum.* The Ciceronians, he tells us, are more interested in "the sweet falling of clauses than after the weight of matter." Their style hinders "the severe inquisition of truth, and the deep progress into philosophy."[11] The same sort of objections may be found in other men of this time; this is a great falling off from the practices of the Elizabethans; but more interesting yet is the emphasis of the Neo-Senecans. On most subjects they stress the stoic position, but like Bacon they are principally interested in working out the practical approaches to problems that are capable of solution. The doctrine of use is strong in them, and with it goes a stern interest in tangible and positive fact. Their interests and temperaments are reflected in their style. The transcendent contentments of faith have gone with the Ciceronian syntax, and a new nervous style which is consonant with doubt, with speculation, and with utility has taken its place. This seventeenth century position is also seen in the careful avoidance of what we should call "idealistic matters" among these men. "Does it work?" they ask. If it does, it is good. Bishop Hall, as a practical clergyman, might decorate his Christian metaphysics with stoic morality, but the secular Neo-stoics discreetly passed over any discussion of the supra-mundane. It was beyond the realm of the knowable. As a consequence, morality rather than religion seems only too often to be the theme of seventeenth century English writers.

But, as Professor Croll noticed, the terse Senecan style was replaced by a looser style, a baroque style, which is familiarly known to the readers of Sir Thomas Browne and Jeremy Taylor. It is also apparent that Bacon eventually abandoned his earlier prose manner for what he called "methods," a persuasive style more capable of converting the average reader. The real alteration in mode can be detected in men writing towards the middle of the seventeenth century. Lord North, who once prided himself on his "strong and clear" style tells us that he is now placing a line "of easy strain" among his other "tough and pithy" sentences. Lord Chandos can write a long essay on Tacitus without being stained by his dark manner, and Thomas Culpepper can even complain that Tacitus "has trussed up" history.[12] It is perhaps a mistake to call this new variation "the loose Senecan style," for it is rather an outgrowth of the awakened interest in the Church Fathers of the fourth and fifth centuries. When Sir Richard Baker published his *Meditations* in 1636, Sir Henry Wotton named this style in a commendatory epistle.

> I must needs observe and much admire the very Character of your Stile, which seemeth unto mee to have not a little of the African Idea of St. Augustines age, full of sweet Rapture, and of researched Conceipts; nothing borrowed; nothing vulgar; and yet all flowing from you (I know not how) with a certaine equall facility. So as I see, your worldly troubles have been but Pressing-yrons to your Heavenly cogitations.[13]

The name, then, that we might give to the style of Browne, of Taylor, and of their fellows is the "African style," a style of which Milton, that forthright and rigid Ciceronian, complained when he wrote about "the knotty Africanisms, the pampered metaphors, the intricate and involved sentences of the fathers."[14] It is the style of those seventeenth century men who had solved their metaphysical problems by clinging to or returning to the traditions of faith, of those who thought that they had erected a bridge between faith and reason, of those who were no longer perplexed by rational doubts.

There is certainly an esthetic of unbelief and it may be observed in the seventeenth century in the equation that seems to exist between the prose style of some men and their sense of certainty. The curt, terse, nervous manner is, in many respects, the characteristic of those seculars who "are troubled with a perplexed doubt" and who have limited themselves to rational speculations about sensible matters. The looser, lax style belongs to men who think that they have solved their difficulties and understand their world. It is the difference between Bacon and Browne. The latter, we remember, loved to lose himself in a "O altitudo," whereas the former remarked that "in divinity many things must be left abrupt and concluded with an 'O altitudo.'" Bacon with his scientific projects and his *Sylva sylvarum* seems not unlike Browne with his natural experiments and his *Vulgar errors;* but Bacon observed all things by the dry light of reason, by the *lumen naturale* whereas Browne, to use Coleridge's phrase, "read the book of nature by the faery light around his head."

NOTES

[1] Trans. by Denis MacCarthy, 2. 2182-7.

[2] Religio medici, *Works* (Ed. Keynes, London, 1928), I, 92.

[3] *The scholemaster* (Ed. Arber, London, 1927), p. 124.

[4] "Attic prose in the seventeenth century," *SP,* XVIII (1921), 79-128; "Juste Lipse et le mouvement anti-Ciceronien," *Revue du Seizieme Siecle,* II (1914), 200-42.

[5] Epistolae, *Opera omnia* (Antverpiae, 1637), II, 75.

[6] Thomas Blount, *Censura celebriorum authorum* (Genevae, 1694), pp. 98, 139.

[7] *Op. cit.* (Ed. Hudson, Princeton, 1935), p. 40.

[8] *Essaies or rather imperfect offers* (London, 1601), sig. D3.

[9] *Resolves* (London, 1677), p. 36.

[10] Epistolae ad viros quosdam, *Opera* (Basel, 1554), pp. 782-3.

[11] Advancement of learning, *Works* (Ed. Ellis, Spedding, Heath, Boston, 1861), VI, 119-20.

[12] *Moral discourses* (London, 1655), p. 46.

[13] Sig. A4r-v.

[14] Of reformation, *Works* (Ed. Ayres, New York, 1931), III, 34.

Symbolism in Medieval Literature

Morton W. Bloomfield

> Unde in nulla scientia, humana industria inventa, proprie loquendo, potest inveniri nisi litteralis sensus; sed solum in ista Scriptura, cujus Spiritus sanctus est auctor, homo vero instrumentum.—THOMAS AQUINAS, *Quaestiones quodlibetales* vii, a.16.

It is exceedingly fashionable today in the general intellectual flight from history to interpret literature symbolically or, as it is often called, "allegorically." The particularity of fact and event is passed over for the general, the cyclic, and the mythical, which is presumably more universal and more meaningful. Unless the significance of a literary work can be subsumed in a system of interpretation—usually Christian, although not always—it is assumed to have no real meaning.[1] Parallel to this revolt against history is a revolt against psychology, which is another facet of the same disregard for the unique. Those works which may easily be interpreted symbolically, such as Melville's *Moby Dick*, have leaped into new favor, and the great classics of English and American literature are everywhere, as far as is possible, being reinterpreted along symbolic, usually Christian, lines.

Needless to say, this movement has not left medieval literature untouched, for in the Middle Ages there is at hand a fully worked-out, even if contradictory, theoretical symbolical system, especially in the works of the early Fathers. The general awareness in medieval studies outside theology and the history of theology, at least in English-speaking countries, of the so-called four or three levels of meaning theory which goes back chiefly to Origen[2] and Philo and the Alexandrine

School[3] and ultimately to the Stoics, dates from the publication of Harry Caplan's article "The Four Senses of Scripture" in *Speculum* in 1929 and of Dr. H. Flanders Dunbar's *Symbolism in Medieval Thought and Its Consummation in the Divine Comedy* in 1929.[4] Since that time, medieval scholars and literary students have increasingly concentrated on interpreting medieval literature in terms of the exegetical method used in medieval biblical criticism, at least in the earlier Middle Ages.[5]

It seems to me that this method, while not totally wrong, is essentially erroneous as a method of understanding most medieval literary works historically, and it is the purpose of this article to discuss briefly the implications and limits of this method in the study of medieval secular literature, especially of the later Middle Ages.

First of all, it must be admitted that meaning is at least partially symbolic. A literary work of any sort and of any period always has some symbolic meaning. Beyond the fact that language itself is a system of sound and written symbols, which is of little significance to my main point, the substance and figures of literature must stand for more than themselves if they are to be fully meaningful. The unique has a meaning of a special sort. If Hamlet is only Hamlet, he is a primary datum; but if he stands for man in a dilemma, or a truth-seeker, or a ditherer, he has another dimension. Although its attention may be captured by it, the human mind comprehends the singular in a special way and not completely intellectually—a limitation, incidentally, of human creatureliness to medieval scholasticism. Meaning in literature comes through the unique but is not equivalent to it.

In this sense, all literature has a *nucleus* and a *cortex* and conveys *sententia*.[6] This is no peculiarity of medieval literature and thought. Historically, of course, medieval man tended to think in Christian categories, and most frequently the *sententia* he put into or discovered in literature was a Christian one. Indeed, no proper understanding of medieval literature is possible without a good knowledge of the Christian categories of thought and beliefs. Yet medieval man was also the heir of late classical antiquity and of barbarian cultures, and their categories of thought, their literary genres, their points of view, were also part of his heritage. He was well aware of a secular tradition which had not been completely transformed by Christianity.

Christianity gave meaning to existence for medieval man, was the framework of his thought generally, and was backed by the state and society with a strength and vigor no longer displayed today. The very form of the universe, with its hierarchy of being, as reflected in nature, in society, in the church, and in the next world, supported a view of a providential and ordered universe. What could be more natural—indeed, inevitable—than to see a Christian *sententia* in secular literature if that literature were to have any deep and important meaning at all. The Bible was, of course, in a class by itself, as the composition of God through various gifted and graced men to reveal his Truth to all men.

What also could be more natural than that students should be taught the letter and the *sensus* and the *sententia*[7] of a text. Although we do not use the terms, we still do so today if the instruction is more than memory work. However, then as now, I suspect, the *sensus* and *sententia* got less emphasis in practice than in theory. A glance at medieval commentaries, especially of the earlier period, on secular works and even occasionally on the Bible shows for the most part an overwhelming interest in the purely grammatical and rhetorical.

The first objection, then, to the symbolic approach is not that it finds a Christian *sententia* in medieval literature but that it assumes that this symbolic method is unique to the period and that there is no essential difference between literary works and theological or pastoral works. It misunderstands the nature of meaning and of literature. It neglects the concrete for the universal and assumes that the concrete exists only for the universal in a work of art,[8] which is not true even of the Bible. It is as if one were to love a woman because she represented eternal beauty or eternal good. Her particularity—her figure, face, skin, and personality—is submerged in her "meaning." She is what Professor Wimsatt would call a "sign," not an icon. There is no "concrete universal" in the world of the symbolists, only the universal.

The second objection is that the emphasis on the symbolic as opposed to the literal[9] approach to the Bible is not characteristic of the later Middle Ages, except perhaps in sermons, which are very conservative and must, of necessity, stress the moral. Although there are warnings earlier against neglect of the literal or historical sense of Scripture,[10] beginning in the twelfth century the symbolic method as applied to biblical exegesis underwent strong attacks, and in the later Middle Ages, except for certain standard interpretations dealing mainly with the prediction of Jesus in the Old Testament and the normal interpretation of any tale or event, the literal sense was the one which received the major attention.[11] In other words, at the time of the rise of the great vernacular literatures, we find a corresponding decline in the emphasis put on the symbolic method in biblical interpretation. In fact, both movements may be viewed as manifestations of a change of attitude in Western man, a new interest in the world of the senses and experience, which is seen in much else and which culminated in the Renaissance and the modern period.

Third, even in the period of its greatest use the symbolic method with its three- or fourfold levels was never mechanically or completely applied to Scripture. These levels should rather be viewed as possible ways of interpreting the manifold meanings in the Bible. All meaning at any time is multiple. The cross, for instance, can stand today for Jesus' sufferings, for Christianity, for the church, for the truth, for good as opposed to evil, and so forth. To attempt to systematize various possible meanings, without understanding what is involved, can lead only to a debased and mechanical interpretation of the highest mysteries. Such attempts reveal a profound misunderstanding of all historical study and, even though the Middle Ages loved system theoretically, medieval history in particular. Besides, in effect, no one can consistently apply the fourfold criterion except to a few hackneyed terms like Jerusalem.

One has only to look at the *Distinctiones*,[12] those symbolic dictionaries chiefly of the twelfth century, to see that there was no science of symbolism. The commonest objects and animals embrace a wide variety of meanings, often contradictory.[13] The meaning could be interpreted only in context, if at all, and even then multiple interpretations would frequently be possible.[14]

It was also at all times recognized that the Bible could be taken symbolically only partially. Much in the Old Testament is literally binding on Christians, and parts of the New Testament must be metaphorically interpreted.[15] Although some parts and elements of the Old Testament were usually interpreted symbolically, there is no evidence whatsoever for a consistent application of any level of meaning interpretation in Scripture. One of the basic arguments for the truth of Jesus' claims is that he fulfils certain Old Testament prophecies and, in general, gives a profound (christological) sense to that collection of divine books. Typology, as it is called, is found in the New Testament itself where Old Testament prophecies and figures are applied to the fulfillment in Christ.[16] Certain other parts of the Bible tend to be morally interpreted. Babylon and Egypt, for example, are always the supreme types of evil. This interpretation is obvious and does not require any special insight or method beyond a normal intelligent reading of the text.

Fourth, the polysemantic school makes no difference between the Bible which was dictated by God in the form of the Holy Ghost and literary works written purely by sinful and erring man. There is very little evidence that the latter were written to be interpreted consistently in a symbolic manner, beyond the normal demands of literary figurative expression.[17] To suppose that medieval man would presume to put himself on the level of God in the writing of literature of whatever sort is surely most astounding. To think that he would write literature, which to him was both for *sentence* and *solace,* merely to convey profound religious truths clothed in many-colored "allegory" seems to me to involve a great misunderstanding of that literature and that man. I do not deny an occasional symbolic reference based on standard biblical interpretations, but to imagine a consistent and elaborate systematic application of a multilayered web of symbolism is unthinkable.

It is also true that certain classical works especially venerated by the Middle Ages, the *Aeneid,* the *Metamorphoses,* for example, were also occasionally interpreted by the symbolic method. Even these special cases, however, did not pass without protest.[18] No medieval writer would ever think of himself on a level with these masters, and the method was chiefly used to Christianize pagan writers. And no one ever maintained that Ovid or Virgil had put the symbolism there himself.

It must be remembered that the advocates of secular literature in the Middle Ages were on the defensive. The pagan worldiness of much of it clashed with Christian otherworldliness, and those who loved the ancient poets were hard put to defend their poetry. The only way out, as the accessus and glosses to many a classical and pagan work show, was to argue strongly for the *utilitas* of such literature, and *utilitas* meant finding a moral meaning.

The medieval scholastics following Aristotle gave, in general, a very low position in the soul to imagination and a very low rank to poetry in the hierarchy of the "sciences."[19] To most, poetry was a branch of logic, but the lowest and weakest branch. This created difficulties, as Thomas' remarks show:

> The science of poetry pertains to those things which because of their lack of truth cannot be grasped by reason; therefore it is necessary that reason be almost beguiled by such similitudes. Theology, however, pertains to those things which are above reason, and so the symbolic method is common to both as neither is proportioned to reason [*In sent.* i. prol. a. 5. 3].

Yet, having quickly removed the problem of certain similarities between poetry and theology, Thomas gives no more thought to this useless art. Those on the defensive were the men who, like Boccaccio, felt that they must defend the claims of poetry and could do so only by arguing that it contained a "sentence." Yet this argument was obviously never taken very seriously by the real thinkers of the Middle Ages, who were content to ignore the so-called claims of poetry as beneath reason and the concern of rational men who did not need *ficta* to see the truth. Reason, authority, and divine revelation were the ways to truth. We have little evidence that the supporters of poetry did in fact interpret their poetry as symbolic, in spite of the theories of some of them.

Then common sense must step in. In a poem like *Piers Plowman*, as in many medieval literary works, the obvious technique is personification, not symbolism. Personification is making what is abstract concrete. It cannot normally have more meanings than what it says. If Mercy kisses Peace, what else does that mean than that peace and mercy embrace?[20] Symbolism is used but not in any wide and consistent pattern.

St. Eucher of Lyons is apparently the only patristic author who admitted that secular works could have levels of meaning.[21] All the other Fathers or theologians I have been able to examine, when they do not tacity assume its applicability only to Scripture, reserve the method exclusively for biblical exegesis.

If the purpose of scholarship is to determine the historical circumstances surrounding a work of art and the probable intention of the author in terms of his background and the evidence of the text itself, then the burden of proof lies with those who would claim a religious symbolic multileveled meaning for medieval literature. If this is not the aim of scholarship, then, of course, there is no objection to finding any meaning or meanings one wants in the literary relics of the past. The really serious reason for opposing this procedure is the historical exactitude which is claimed or implied. One can, if one chooses, interpret a work of literature in any way whatsoever, provided that one does not claim to be thereby revealing the conscious intention of the author.

In view of the fact that the historical trend was moving away from the heavy symbolic interpretation of Scripture and that a secular tradition of entertainment and literature was very much alive in the Middle Ages, it seems to me that to believe that the medieval author would presume to write as God wrote through his chosen servants in Holy Scripture is the height of folly. This, of course, is not to deny that in certain literary works—possibly the *Divine Comedy*, in the case of which there is some evidence for the assumption, although not totally above question—the multiple method may have been used. It is, however, the task of the historical scholar who makes such a claim to substantiate it in each case. The *Divine Comedy,* if it is an exception, is almost the exception which proves the rule. It is significant, as Auerbach points out,[22] that Dante arrogates to himself, against all precedence, polysemy—a special mission in keeping with his high view of himself as poet and prophet. Even in the *Divine Comedy,* however, it is impossible to work out a consistent fourfold scheme of meaning.[23] The basic and important meaning of the *Divine Comedy* except in the case of a few obvious symbols is its literal meaning. Individual symbols are often used therein in multiple senses, but this fact is not equivalent to discovering a consistent four- or threefold level of meaning. And, as we have already admitted, all meaning is, at least to some extent, symbolic. In every sin there is something of the sin of Adam; in every goal there is something of the Promised Land.

Nor do I mean to deny that in many medieval works a Christian meaning is not aimed at or assumed, but this need not imply the acceptance of a multileveled system of symbolism, which in any case for the most part did not exist. The Christian meaning of medieval literature is usually very clearly underlined by the normal meaning of the words, as in Chaucer's *Troilus and Criseyde* or the *Divine Comedy,* where we are expressly told by the authors what the poems mean in Christian moral, dogmatic, or mystical terms.

The multileveled interpretation cannot be consistently applied to any work, including the Bible, without involving contradictions, omissions, and denials. The long history of biblical exegesis proves this to the hilt. To assume that a medieval author would be so proud and unperceptive as to take a system which is largely the creation of modern systematizing scholars and the mere repetition of patristic formulas and apply it to the composition of secular literature is most unwise.[24]

Literature has ends of its own, and even if in a Christian society these are fundamentally Christian, they are not exclusively so. If the work is felt as literature, it would belong to one or more genres which had traditions of their own generally going back to classical antiquity. A work of literature cannot have been written fundamentally to expound in Bible-wise the truths of Christianity. These would be assumed by the writers, or if Christian themes were to be the main point of a work, as in, say, *Piers Plowman,* these are openly discussed or at least in a normal rhetorical manner.[25]

Fifth, above all, the multileveled system of symbolism provides no criterion of corrigibility except, as in the case of biblical exegesis, tradition. There is no way, seeing the wide variety of symbolic interpretations of the same thing, to correct any particular interpretation. At the most, one might say a certain interpretation is not right, but of many alternate explanations there is no way of deciding which one is correct, for supporting texts from the wide variety of medieval and patristic theology can be found for each one. Consistency to some extent could, it is true, be used as a criterion of truth; but, as the history of Dante scholarship abundantly shows, it is easy enough to work out a variety of consistent interpretations of at least cantos of a poem, and, in most cases, there is no way of deciding between them. It was this strong subjective element in medieval symbolism, which was so patently misused for various selfish interests in the later Middle Ages, that, along with other factors, led to the strong attacks on and even repudiation of the method from the thirteenth century on, and by the Reformers. In the fourteenth and fifteenth centuries, the gloss on a biblical text was frequently treated as a joke.[26]

Mere assertion and the quotation of a theological or pastoral text are not satisfactory proofs. One cannot perhaps adequately prove any interpretation of literature, but if the words of the text are taken as of primary importance, there is always a court of appeal. With sixteen meanings for the peacock, who is to decide between them?

Finally, the assumption of the organized use of the symbolic method in medieval literature is essentially simplistic. It imposes a non-historical order and system on what was in fact disordered and unsystematic. The theologians of the high Middle Ages were saddled with a theory of levels of meanings from early Christianity and had to give lip service to the principle, but actually there was never any consistent application of that theory anywhere at any time, except for particular biblical passages, in Christian medieval exegesis and, above all, in literary composition.

I would like to conclude with the words of Roger Bacon:

> In sensu litterali jacet tota philosophiæ potestas, in naturis et proprietatibus rerum naturalium, artificialium et moralium; ut per convenientes adaptationes et similitudines eliciantur sensus spirituales. Ut sic simul sciatur [sociatur?] philosophia cum theologia. . . .[27]

NOTES

[1] Unless the system implied by them really gives meaning to the world and man, the general, the cyclic, and the mythical are no more meaningful than the particular, the unique, and the fact. This axiom is

not always kept in mind by the "symbolists." The mere cycles of nature, for instance, are as meaningless as any unique fact unless one is satisfied by a purely biological vision of the world.

I am indebted to Professor Phillip W. Damon for several suggestions which I have used in this paper.

[2] For a recent treatment and defense of Origen's exegetical method see Henri de Lubac, *Histoire et esprit: l'intelligence de l'Écriture d'après Origène* ("Théologie: études publiées sous la direction de la Faculté de Théologie S.J. de Lyon-Fourvière" [Paris, 1950]); see, however, P. Th. Camelot, "La Théologie de l'image de Dieu," *Revue des sciences philosophiques et théologiques,* XL (1956), 453, n. 20, and 455, where the literalness of Origen's biblical exegesis is emphasized.

[3] The Antiochene school, which emphasized the literal more than the spiritual sense (to use inexact but common terms for the sake of convenience), was, however, always opposed to Alexandrine flights of fancy. Its influence, chiefly expressed through Theodore of Mopsuestia (although Ambrosiaster, John Chrysostom, and Junilius must not be neglected), never completely died in the Middle Ages and in the early period is to be found in Ireland and elsewhere, notably England and northern France. See M. L. W. Laistner, "Antiochene Exegesis in Western Europe during the Middle Ages," *HTR,* XL (1947), 19-31; Alberto Vaccari, "La Teoria esegetica della scuola antiochena," *Scritti di erudizione e di filologia,* I (Rome, 1952), 101-42 (reprinted from *Biblica,* 1920 and 1934); and the important article by Bernard Bischoff, "Wendepunkte in der Geschichte der lateinische Exegese im Frühmittelalter," *Sacris erudiri,* V (1954), 189-281. The latter protests against the facile setting of Alexandria against Antioch in the early Middle Ages. He points out that even Bede, who did much to push the Alexandrine method, was essentially historical in his exegesis. In fact, the whole subject seems to be hopelessly confused. One thing is certain that, except for typology (the veiled prediction of Christ in the Old Testament), at no time did any biblical exegete repudiate the importance and often the primacy of the biblical letter. There are, however, degrees of emphasis.

Even Augustine's *De doctrina Christiana,* which is supposed to have established the fourfold method for the Middle Ages, contains no reference at all to it. In fact, the whole point of that work as regards the Bible is that what is taught is clearly taught, and, if it is occasionally obscure, it is elsewhere in the Bible made very plain. Augustine does refer, it is true, to a four-fold method of interpreting the Bible in *De utilitate credendi* 3 (*PL,* XLII, 68 ff.) and *De genesi ad litteram* 2 (*PL,* XXXIV, 222), but the four meanings are history (the letter), etiology (normal explanation of difficult biblical passages to a Christian), analogy (typology or agreement of the two Testaments), and allegory (figurative meaning, usually typology). The recognition of the figurative meaning of parts of the Old Testament is either typology as found in the New Testament itself or the normal application of a criterion of meaning to a written text. In practice, however, Augustine frequently does indulge in symbolic biblical exegesis. Gregory the Great by his practice did perhaps more to make the early Middle Ages pass over the literal for the figurative (usually moral) meaning of the Bible than anyone else. He had great influence on Bede and Rabanus Maurus, the most important of the early medieval biblical commentators. For some recent discussions of

Augustine's exegetical methods see Maurice Pontet, *L'Exégèse de S. Augustin prédicateur* ("Théologie: études publiées sous la direction de la Faculté de Théologie S.J. de Lyon-Fourvière [Paris, 1944?]), and Allen A. Gilmore, "Augustine and the Critical Method," *HTR*, XXXIX (1946), 141-63. Neither Augustine, Gregory, nor Bede thought of a consistent and continuous multileveled interpretation of Scripture but that the nature of the particular text determined the "level" desired. Bede, for example, gives as an example of tropology I John 3:18, which he says must be taken literally, and of anagogy Matt. 5:8, which also must be taken literally (see his *De tabernacula* i [*PL*, XCI, 410B-411B]).

[4] There are, of course, earlier treatments of the subject in English; e.g., Frederic W. Farrar, *History of Interpretation: Eight Lectures Preached before the University of Oxford* . . . (London, 1886), and H. Preserved Smith, *Essays in Biblical Interpretation* (Boston, 1921).

[5] For a good summary of early Christian exegesis and a review of recent literature on the subject see Walter J. Burchardt, "On Early Christian Exegesis," *Theological Studies*, XI (1950), 78-116. The literature on patristic and medieval exegesis is too vast to be suitably summarized here. My comments in this paper should not, of course, be interpreted to mean that I do not believe that traditional biblical exegesis is not of great value in interpreting biblical allusions and symbols when used by medieval authors.

[6] On the history of *sententia*, see G. Paré, A. Brunet, and P. Tremblay, *La Renaissance du XIIe siècle, les écoles et l'enseignement* ("Publications de l'Institut d'Études Médiévales d'Ottawa." Vol. III [Paris and Ottawa, 1933]), pp. 267 ff. Isidore of Seville interprets it to be an impersonal general dictum from which its general, but not only, medieval meaning of "meaning" or "truth" probably derives.

[7] As at least John of Salisbury and Hugh of St. Victor put it (see Paré, Brunet, and Tremblay, p. 116).

[8] ". . . All the senses are founded on one—the literal—from which alone can any argument be drawn" (Thomas Aquinas, *ST* i, q.1, a.10). "He [Aristotle] has to do this [criticize the obvious sense of Plato's words] because Plato's method of teaching was faulty; he constantly used figures of speech, teaching by symbols and giving his words a meaning quite other than their literal sense" (Aquinas, *Commentary on De anima* i. 3, lectio 8, trans. K. Foster and S. Humphries [London, 1951], p. 107). Cf. Wyclif (*De benedicta incarnacione* iii, ed. Edward Harris [London: Wyclif Society, 1886], pp. 37 ff., esp. p. 40), who argues for the importance of the literal meaning of Scripture. This attitude can be found everywhere in later Middle Ages (see below, pp. 200-201).

[9] In the earlier period the word "literal" had a much narrower meaning than it does in the later Middle Ages or today. We include the sense of the "plain meaning of the text" in the term; to the early Middle Ages "literal" tended to be limited to the form of the words. "Most of the Fathers considered the meaning behind a metaphor not a literal but a secondary sense" (R. E. Brown, *The "Sensus plenior" of Sacred Scripture: A Dissertation . . . of St. Mary's University, Baltimore* . . . [Baltimore, 1955], p. 6). This shift in meaning explains some of the confusions in our understanding of what the Fathers mean by their comments on and practice of biblical exegesis. Yet Thomas writes: "Quamvis spiritualia sub figuris rerum corporalium proponantur, non tamen ea quae circa

spiritualia intenduntur per figuras sensibiles, ad mysticum pertinent sensum, sed litteralem; quia sensus litteralis est qui primo per verba intenditur sive proprie dicta, sive figurate" (*In Job* [Parma ed.], XVIII, 6).

[10] See Henri de Lubac, "Sur un vieux distique, La doctrine du 'quadruple sens,'" *Mélanges offerts au A. P. Ferdinand Cavallera . . . à l'occasion de la quarantième année de son professorat à l'Institut catholique* (Toulouse, 1948), p. 352 n.

[11] Our recent awareness of this trend is largely due to the important work of Miss Smalley, *The Study of the Bible in the Middle Ages* (2d ed. rev. and enl.; Oxford, 1952). The author has emphasized the importance of the exegesis of Andrew of St. Victor in the development of later medieval biblical study. Bonaventure writes: "Qui litteram sacrae Scripturae spernit ad spirituales eius intelligentias numquam assurget" (*Breviloquium* Prologue 6).

[12] See M. D. Chenu, "Théologie symbolique et exégèse scolastique aux XIIe–XIIIe siècles," *Mélanges Joseph de Ghellinck* (Gembloux, 1951), II, 509-26; and Smalley, pp. 246 ff.

[13] Augustine (*De doctrina Christiana* iii. 25) recognizes that one and the same thing (his examples are the lion, serpent, and bread) may have different and even opposing meanings; see also G. G. Coulton, *Art and the Reformation* (2d ed.; Cambridge, England, 1953), Appendix 18, p. 554, who refers to the sixteen meanings for the peacock; and D. W. Robertson, Jr., and Bernard F. Huppé, *Piers Plowman and Scriptural Tradition* (Princeton, 1951), pp. 5-6, who point to the seven meanings of *dormitio*.

[14] Dante in *De monarchia* III, iv, 6, recognizes how easy it is to misinterpret the "sensum misticum."

[15] See Jean Daniélou, *Essai sur le mystère de l'histoire* (Paris, 1953). p. 211.

"Si vero aperte fidem predicat vel bonos mores astruit, sive hoc sit ita quod vetat flagitium vel facinus, sive sit ita quod utilitatem vel beneficentiam iubet, sive sit ita quod radicem omnium malorum exstirpat . . . non est ad aliud refferendum quasi figurative dictum, quia per hoc vigor eorum eneruaretur" (Ulrich of Strassburg, *Liber de summo bono* i, tr. 2, cap. 11, ed. J. Daguillon [Paris, 1930], pp. 59-60).

"We must discover first of all, whether the [biblical] expression which we are trying to understand is literal or figurative" (Augustine *De doctrina* iii. 24, trans. John J. Gavigan, *The Fathers of the Church: A New Translation* [New York, 1947]). Gerald of Bologna in his *Summa* Q. XI, a.1, written in 1317, makes this same point (that the Old Testament is not always to be taken allegorically) (see Paul de Vooght, *Les Sources de la doctrine chrétienne . . .* [Bruges, 1954], pp. 425-26).

[16] For a study of the use of typology by the New Testament writers and its general background, see Leonhard Goppelt, *Typos: Die typologische Deutung des Alten Testaments im Neuen* ("Beiträge zur Förderung Christlicher Theologie," ed. Schlatter and Althaus, Vol. II, No. 43 [Gütersloh, 1939]).

St. Thomas Aquinas says that the literal is what the author intends, the spiritual what God intends. In the eyes of God the whole Bible is, however, clear and literal: "Quia vero sensus litteralis est quem auctor intendit, auctor sacrae Scripturae Deus est, qui omnia simul suo intellectu comprehendit: non est inconveniens . . . si etiam secundum litteralem sensum, in una littera

Scripturae, plures sint sensus" (*ST* i, q.1, a.10, in c). This statement implies that only God composes polysemously. See below, next paragraph.

[17] "Auctor sacrae Scripturae est Deus in cujus potestate est ut non solum voces ad significandum accommodet (quod etiam homo facere potest), sed etiam res ipsas" (Aquinas *ST* i, q.1, a.10). Thomas specifically denies a spiritual sense in writings other than the Bible in *Quodl.* vii, a. 16, quoting Gregory the Great, *Moralia* 22. The whole point of the creed is that it is literally true on the authority of faith as interpreted by the church, unlike art, which is only metaphorically true. In one sense the Bible is not symbolic at all but completely literal, i.e., true. Cf. "In caeteris igitur scripturis solae voces significantur, in scriptura divina non solum voces, sed etiam res significativae sunt quamvis non in omnibus" (Conrad of Hirsau, *Dialogus super auctores sive Didascalon*, ed. G. Schepss [Würzburg, 1889], p. 75) and "sciendum est etiam quod in divino eloquio non tantum verba, sed etiam res significare habent" (Hugo of St. Victor, *PL*, CLXXVI, 790).

"In liberalibus disciplinis ubi non res sed dumtaxat verba significant, quisquis primo sensu litterae contentus non est, aberrare videtur mihi" (John of Salisbury, *Polycraticus*, ed. Webb, vii. 12, p. 144). I owe this last reference to Jean Misrahi's excellent review in *Romance Philology*, IV (1951), 350.

[18] See Paré, Brunet, and Tremblay, pp. 119-21. It was Macrobius who probably first suggested for the Middle Ages that the great classical poets consciously used "allegory" (see, on the allegorizing of Virgil, Pierre Courcelle, "Les Pères de l'église devant les enfers virgiliens," *Archives d'histoire doctrinale et littéraire du moyen âge*, XXII [1955], 5-74). Much earlier, of course, the Stoics and Alexandrines had "allegorized" Homer to their taste and no doubt set a pattern.

[19] See Ernst Robert Curtius, *European Literature and the Latin Middle Ages*, trans. W. R. Trask (London, 1953), p. 224.

[20] See Robert Worth Frank, Jr., "The Art of Reading Medieval Personification Allegory," *ELH*, XX (1953), 237-50, for an excellent discussion of this point as well as other related ones.

[21] See André Pézard, *Dante sous la pluie de feu* (*Enfer, Chant XV*) ("Études de philosophie médiévale," Vol. XL [Paris, 1950]), pp. 382-84.

[22] See his "Figurative Texts Illustrating Certain Passages of Dante's Commedia," *Speculum*, XXI (1946), 475, n. 5. Cf. "To claim to use the allegory of the theologians (as Dante did in his letter to Can Grande) is to remove *The Divine Comedy* from the category of poetry as his contemporaries understood it" (Joseph A. Mazzeo, "Dante's Conception of Poetic Expression," *Romantic Review*, XLVII [1956], 241; see also his "Dante and the Pauline Modes of Vision," *HTR*, L [1957], 275-306). Dante thought of himself as prophet rather than poet, and perhaps on a level with Paul and Moses (see also Curtius, pp. 221 ff. and 377: ". . . Dante believed that he had an apocalyptic mission").

[23] A recent attempt is by Dorothy L. Sayers in *Introductory Papers on Dante* (London, 1954), who presumes at last to tell the simple truth. She finds most astoundingly that the allegorical (in its narrow meaning of a level) sense has to mean the historical or political level of meaning (pp. 104-5) and gives us only a few generalized clues to this quad-

ruple meaning that she claims to have found in the poem. A number of great Dante scholars have denied that there are systematic levels of meaning in the poem at all. I have never seen this fourfold meaning completely worked out in the case of any literary work, including Dante's.

[24] An easily available fourteenth-century discussion of the problem of multiple meanings (of Scripture) may be found in the second article (pp. 43 ff., esp. pp. 46 ff.) of the recently published *Quaestio de Sacra Scriptura et de veritatibus catholicis* of Henry Totting of Oyta (d. 1397), edited by Albert Lang ("Opuscula et textus, series scholastica," ed. J. Koch and Fr. Pelster [Münster i.W., 1953, editio altera]). Totting was much influenced by English thought of the period—in particular by Scotus, Woodham, and Fitzralph. His discussion of the question is surprisingly modern: he is well aware of the difficulties. He struggles to preserve the validity of the symbolic approach to the Bible. This whole *Quaestio* reveals interestingly some of the doubts raised in Totting's time about scriptural accuracy.

[25] See above, p. 202.

[26] Cf. The words of the greedy friar in Chaucer's "Summoner's Tale,"

"Glosynge is a glorious thyng, certeyn."
For lettre sleeth, so as we clerkes seyn."

—*Canterbury Tales*, ed. F. N. Robinson (2d ed., III, 1793-94).

[27] *Opus tertium*, 24, ed. Brewer, p. 81. Cf. "Freedom of thought was not repressed in the Middle Ages. It was fostered by the allegorical method of interpretation, whereby the philosopher could connect his private theory with established truth" (E. K. Rand, "Medieval Gloom and Medieval Uniformity," *Speculum*, I [1926], 267). Cf. also Erasmus' attacks on the method in his *Praise of Folly*.

Method and Scope of *American Renaissance*

F. O. Matthiessen

The starting point for this book was my realization of how great a number of our past masterpieces were produced in one extraordinarily concentrated moment of expression. It may not seem precisely accurate to refer to our mid-nineteenth century as a *re-birth;* but that was how the writers themselves judged it. Not as a re-birth of values that had existed previously in America, but as America's way of producing a renaissance, by coming to its first maturity and affirming its rightful heritage in the whole expanse of art and culture.

The half-decade of 1850-55 saw the appearance of *Representative Men* (1850), *The Scarlet Letter* (1850), *The House of the Seven Gables* (1851), *Moby-Dick* (1851), *Pierre* (1852), *Walden* (1854), and *Leaves of Grass* (1855). You might search all the rest of American literature without being able to collect a group of books equal to these in imaginative vitality. That interesting fact could make the subject for several different kinds of investigation. You might be concerned with *how* this flowering came, with the descriptive narrative of literary history. Or you might dig into its sources in our life, and examine the economic, social, and religious causes *why* this flowering came in just these years. Or you might be primarily concerned with *what* these books were as works of art, with evaluating their fusions of form and content.

By choosing the last of these alternatives my main subject has become the conceptions held by five of our major writers concerning the function and nature of literature, and the degree to which their practice bore out their theories. That may make their process sound too deliberate, but Emerson, Thoreau, and Whitman all commented very explicitly on language as well as expression, and the creative intentions of Hawthorne and Melville can be readily discerned through scrutiny of their chief works. It has seemed to me that the literary accomplishment of those years could be judged most adequately if approached both in the light of its authors' purposes and in that of our own developing conceptions of literature. The double aim, therefore, has been to place these works both in their age and in ours.

In avowing that aim, I am aware of the important books I have not written. One way of understanding the concentrated abundance of our mid-nineteenth century would be through its intellectual history, particularly through a study of the breakdown of Puritan orthodoxy into Unitarianism, and of the quickening of the cool Unitarian strain into the spiritual and emotional fervor of Transcendentalism. The first of those two developments has been best sketched by Joseph Haroutunian, *Piety versus Moralism: The Passing of New England Theology* (1932). The whole movement will be genetically traced in Perry Miller's monumental study of *The New England Mind,* the first volume of which (1939), dealing with the seventeenth century, has already extended the horizons of our cultural past. Another notable book could concentrate on how discerning an interpretation our great authors gave of the economic and social forces of the time. The orientation of such a book would not be with the religious and philosophical ramifications of the transcendental movement so much as with its voicing of fresh aspirations for the rise of the common man. Its method could be the one that Granville Hicks has inherited from Taine, and has already applied in *The Great Tradition* (1933) to our literature since the Civil War. An example of that method for the earlier period is Newton Arvin's detailed examination (1938) of Whitman's emergent socialism.

The two books envisaged in the last paragraph might well be called *The Age of Swedenborg* and *The Age of Fourier*. Emerson said in 1854, 'The age is Swedenborg's,' by which he meant that it had embraced the subjective philosophy that 'the soul makes its own world.' That extreme development of idealism was what Emerson had found adumbrated in Channing's 'one sublime idea': the potential divinity of man. That religious assumption could also be social when it claimed the inalienable worth of the individual and his right to participate in whatever the community might produce. Thus the transition from transcendentalism to Fourierism was made by many at the time, as by Henry James, Sr., and George Ripley and his loyal followers at Brook Farm. *The Age of Fourier* could by license be extended to take up a wider subject than Utopian socialism; it could treat all the radical movements of the period; it would stress the fact that 1852 witnessed not only the appearance of *Pierre* but of *Uncle Tom's Cabin;* it would stress also what had been largely ignored until recently, the anticipation by Orestes Brownson of some of the Marxist analysis of the class controls of action.[1]

But the age was also that of Emerson and Melville. The one common denominator of my five writers, uniting even Hawthorne and Whitman, was their devotion to the possibilities of democracy. In dealing with their work I hope that I have not ignored the implications of such facts as that the farmer rather than the businessman was still the average American, and that the terminus to the agricultural era in our history falls somewhere between 1850 and 1865, since the railroad, the iron ship, the factory, and the national labor union all began to be dominant forces within those years, and forecast a new epoch. The forties probably gave rise to more movements of reform than any other decade in our history; they marked the last struggle of the liberal spirit of the eighteenth century in conflict with the rising forces of exploitation. The triumph of the new age was foreshadowed in the gold rush, in the full emergence of the acquisitive spirit.[2]

The old liberalism was the background from which my writers

emerged. But I have concentrated entirely on the foreground, on the writing itself. I have not written formal literary history—a fact that should be of some relief to the reader, since if it required a volume of this length for five years of that record, the consequences of any extension of such a method would be appalling. Parrington stated in his *Main Currents of American Thought* (1927): 'With aesthetic judgments I have not been greatly concerned. I have not wished to evaluate reputations or weigh literary merits, but rather to understand what our fathers thought . . .' My concern has been opposite. Although I greatly admire Parrington's elucidation of our liberal tradition, I think the understanding of our literature has been retarded by the tendency of some of his followers to regard all criticism as 'belletristic trifling.' I am even more suspicious of the results of such historians as have declared that they were not discussing art, but 'simply using art, in a purpose of research.' Both our historical writing and our criticism have been greatly enriched during the past twenty years by the breaking down of arbitrary divisions between them, by the critic's realization of the necessity to master what he could of historical discipline, by the historian's desire to extend his domain from politics to general culture. But you cannot 'use' a work of art unless you have comprehended its meaning. And it is well to remember that although literature reflects an age, it also illuminates it. Whatever the case may be for the historian, the quality of that illumination is the main concern for the common reader. He does not live by trends alone; he reads books, whether of the present or past, because they have an immediate life of their own.

What constitutes the secret of that life is the subject of this volume. It may be held that my choice of authors is arbitrary. These years were also those of Whittier's *Songs of Labor* (1850), of Longfellow's *Hiawatha* (1855), of work by Lowell and Holmes and Simms, of Baldwin's *Flush Times in Alabama and Mississippi,* of T. S. Arthur's *Ten Nights in a Barroom.* Nor were any of my authors best sellers. The five hundred copies of Emerson's first book, *Nature* (1836), had been disposed of so slowly that a second edition was not called for until 1849; and though his lecturing had made him well known by then, the sales of none of his books ran far into the thousands. Thoreau recorded in his journal that four years after the appearance of his *Week on the Concord and Merrimack* (1849) only 219 copies had been sold; so he had the publisher ship the remainder back to him and said: 'I have now a library of nearly nine hundred volumes, over seven hundred of which I wrote myself. Is it not well that the author should behold the fruits of his labor?' After that *Walden* was considered a great risk, but it managed to go through an edition of two thousand. Whitman set up and printed *Leaves of Grass* for himself, and probably gave away more copies than were bought, whereas Longfellow could soon report (1857) that the total sales of his books had run to over three hundred thousand, and *Fern Leaves from Fanny's Portfolio* (1853), by the sister of N. P. Willis, sold a hundred thousand in its first year. Although *Typee* (1846) was more popular than Melville's subsequent work, it never came within miles of such figures. Hawthorne reported that six or seven hundred copies of *Twice-Told Tales* (1837) had been disposed of before the panic of that year descended. To reach a wider audience he had to wait until *The Scarlet Letter,* and reflecting on the triumphant vogue of Susan Warner's *The Wide, Wide World* (1850), Maria Cummins' *The Lamplighter* (1854), the ceaseless flux of Mrs. E. D. E. N. Southworth's sixty novels, he wrote to Ticknor in 1855: 'America is now wholly given over to a damned mob of scribbling women, and I should have no chance of success while the public taste is occupied with their trash—and should be ashamed of myself if I did succeed. What is the mystery of these innumerable editions of *The Lamplighter,* and other books neither better nor worse?—worse they could not be, and better they need not be, when they sell by the hundred thousand.'

Such material still offers a fertile field for the sociologist and for the historian of our taste. But I agree with Thoreau: 'Read the best books first, or you may not have a chance to read them at all.' And during the century that has ensued, the successive generations of common readers, who make the decisions, would seem finally to have agreed that the authors of the pre-Civil War era who bulk largest in stature are the five who are my subject. That being the case, a book about their value might seem particularly unnecessary. But 'the history of an art,' as Ezra Pound has affirmed, 'is the history of masterwork, not of failures or mediocrity.' And owing to our fondness for free generalization, even the masterworks of these authors have been largely taken for granted. The critic knows that any understanding of the subtle principle of life inherent in a work of art can be gained only by direct experience of it, again and again. The interpretation of what he has found demands close analysis, and plentiful instances from the works themselves. With a few notable exceptions, most of the criticism of our past masters has been perfunctorily tacked onto biographies. I have not yet seen in print an adequately detailed scrutiny even of 'When lilacs last in the dooryard bloom'd,' or of *Moby-Dick.* And such good criticism as has been written has ordinarily dealt with single writers; it has not examined many of the interrelations among the various works of the group.

My aim has been to follow these books through their implications, to observe them as the culmination of their authors' talents, to assess them in relation to one another and to the drift of our literature since, and, so far as possible, to evaluate them in accordance with the enduring requirements for great art. That last aim will seem to many only a pious phrase, but it describes the critic's chief responsibility. His obligation is to examine an author's resources of language and of genres, in a word, to be preoccupied with form. This means nothing rarefied, as Croce's description of De Sanctis' great *History of Italian Literature* can testify: form for De Sanctis 'was not the "form" pathologically felt by aesthetes and decadents: it was nothing else than the entire resolution of the intellectual, sentimental, and emotional material into the concrete reality of the poetic image and word, which alone has aesthetic value.'

The phases of my somewhat complex method of elucidating that concrete reality can be briefly described. The great attraction of my subject was its compactness:[3] for though I made no attempt to confine my study of these authors to the strait jacket of a five-year segment of their careers, the fact remained that Emerson's theory of expression was that on which Thoreau built, to which Whitman gave extension, and to which Hawthorne and Melville were indebted by being forced to react against its philosophical assumptions. The nature of Emerson's achievement has caused me to range more widely in my treatment of him than in that of the others. *Representative Men* has no more right to be called his masterpiece than *Nature* (1836) or *The Conduct of Life* (1860). He wrote no masterpiece, but his service to the development of our literature was enormous in that he made the first full examination of its potentialities. To apply to him his own words about Goethe: he was the cow from which the rest drew their milk. My discussion of his theory has always in view his practice of it, and its creative use by the others. My prime intention is not Sainte-Beuve's: to be 'a naturalist of minds,' to relate the authors' works to their lives. I have not drawn upon the circumstances of biography unless they seemed essential to place a given piece of writing;[4] and whenever necessary, especially in the case of Melville, I have tried to expose the modern fallacy that has come from the vulgarization of Sainte-Beuve's subtle method—the direct reading of an author's personal life into his works.

The types of interrelation that have seemed most productive to understanding the literature itself were first of all the obvious debts, of Thoreau to Emerson, or Melville to Hawthorne. In the next place there were certain patterns of taste and aspiration: the intimate kinship to the seventeenth-century metaphysical strain that was felt by Emerson, Thoreau, and Melville; the desire for a functional style wherein Thoreau and Whitman especially were forerunners of our modern interest. That last fact again suggests one of my chief convictions: that works of art can be best perceived if we do not approach them only through the influences that shaped them, but if we also make use of what we inevitably bring from our own lives. That is an unorthodox postulate for literary history. But if we can see *Moby-Dick* and *Pierre* much more accurately by uncovering Melville's extraordinary debt to Shakespeare, and come closer to Hawthorne's intentions by observing that his psychological assumptions were still fundamentally the same as Milton's, it seems equally clear that Henry James and Eliot can cast light back on Hawthorne, and that one way of judging *Leaves of Grass* is by juxtaposing it with the deliberate counterstatement made by Whitman's polar opposite, Hopkins. I have, therefore, utilized whatever interrelations of this type have seemed to grow organically from my subject. I do not expect the reader to be willing at this point to grant any relevance to the juxtaposition of Whitman with the painters Millet and Eakins, or to that of Thoreau with the theories of the forgotton sculptor Horatio Greenough. It will be my responsibility to demonstrate those relevances.

The phase of my subject in which I am most interested is its challenge to pass beyond such interrelations to basic formulations about the nature of literature. In the chapter, 'Allegory and Symbolism,' Hawthorne and Melville have been its center, but I have attempted, so far as I was able, to write also an account of these two fundamental modes of apprehending reality. In the concluding chapter, 'Man in the Open Air,' the concern was to bring all five writers together through their subject matter, through their varied responses to the myth of the common man. But these serious responses can be better defined if set into contrast with the comic myth of the frontier, especially in its richest expression by George Washington Harris' *Sut Lovingood.* And the function of myth in literature can be clarified by the rediscovery of its necessity by the age of Joyce and Mann. As a final descriptive instance of my method, I have conceived of the two central books on Hawthorne and Melville as composing a single unit in which the chief value would be the aspects of tragedy that could be discerned through its representative practice by these two writers. I have made no pretence of abstracting a general theory of tragedy, but have crystallized out certain indispensable attributes that are common also to the practice of both Shakespeare and Milton.

After this description of my method, it is obvious that the division into four books is merely to indicate the central emphasis of each. This division, with the index, should make it easy for a reader particularly concerned with a single writer to concentrate on his work alone. Since volumes of criticism are now conventionally supposed to be short, I might have concealed the length of mine by printing it as four separate books, spaced, say, a year apart. But that would have defeated one of my main purposes: to make each writer cast as much light as possible on all the others. Moreover, our chief critical need would seem to be that of full-length estimates. I saw no use in adding further partial portraits to those of Parrington and Van Wyck Brooks, but wanted to deal in both analysis and synthesis. That required extensive quotation, since a critic, to be of any use, must back up his definitions with some of the evidence through which he has reached them. Only thus can the reader share in the process of testing the critic's judgments, and thereby reach his own. I trust that the further division into sixty-odd short essays will help the reader to skip wherever he wants. However, when dealing with the work of one writer, I have made as many transitions as practicable to that of the others.

It may be of some help to the reader to know from the start that the structure of the volume is based on recurrent themes. In addition to the types of interrelation I have mentioned, the most dominant of these themes are: the adequacy of the different writers' conceptions of the relation of the individual to society, and of the nature of good and evil—these two themes rising to their fullest development in the treatment of tragedy; the stimulus that lay in the transcendental conviction that the word must become one with the thing; the effect produced by the fact that when these writers began their careers, the one branch of literature in which America had a developed tradition was oratory; the effect of the nineteenth century's stress on seeing, of its identification of the poet with the prophet or seer; the connection, real if somewhat intangible, between this emphasis on vision and that put on light by the advancing arts of photography and open-air painting; the inevitability of the symbol as a means of expression for an age that was determined to make a fusion between appearance and what lay behind it; the major desire on the part of all five writers that there should be no split between art and the other functions of the community, that there should be an organic union between labor and culture.

The avenue of approach to all these themes is the same, through attention to the writers' use of their own tools, their diction and rhetoric, and to what they could make with them. An artist's use of language is the most sensitive index to cultural history, since a man can articulate only what he is, and what he has been made by the society of which he is a willing or an unwilling part. Emerson, Hawthorne, Thoreau, Whitman, and Melville all wrote literature for democracy in a double sense. They felt that it was incumbent upon their generation to give fulfilment to the potentialities freed by the Revolution, to provide a culture commensurate with America's political opportunity. Their tones were sometimes optimistic, sometimes blatantly, even dangerously expansive, sometimes disillusioned, even despairing, but what emerges from the total pattern of their achievement—if we will make the effort to repossess it[5]—is literature for our democracy. In reading the lyric, heroic, and tragic expression of our first great age, we can feel the challenge of our still undiminished resources. In my own writing about that age, I have kept in mind the demands made on the scholar by Louis Sullivan, who found a great stimulus for his architecture in the functionalism of Whitman. 'If, as I hold,' Sullivan wrote, 'true scholarship is of the highest usefulness because it implies the possession and application of the highest type of thought, imagination, and sympathy, his works must so reflect his scholarship as to prove that it has drawn him toward his people, not away from them; that his scholarship has been used as a means toward attaining their end, hence his. That his scholarship has been applied for the good and the enlightenment of all the people, not for the pampering of a class. His works must prove, in short (and the burden of proof is on him), that he is a citizen, not a lackey, a true exponent of democracy, not a tool of the most insidious form of anarchy . . . In a democracy there can be but one fundamental test of citizenship, namely: Are you using such gifts as you possess for or against the people?' These standards are the inevitable and right extension of Emerson's demands in *The American Scholar*. The ensuing volume has value only to the extent that it comes anywhere near measuring up to them.

NOTES

[1] See A. M. Schlesinger, Jr., *Orestes A. Brownson* (1939), and Helen S. Mims, 'Early American Democratic Theory and Orestes Brownson'

(*Science and Society,* Spring 1939).

[2] See Norman Ware, *The Industrial Worker,* 1840-1860 (1924), and E. C. Kirkland, *A History of American Economic Life* (1936).

[3] I have avoided, therefore, the temptation to include a full length treatment of Poe. The reason is more fundamental than that his work fell mainly in the decade of 1835-45; for it relates at very few points to the main assumptions about literature that were held by any of my group. Poe was bitterly hostile to democracy, and in that respect could serve as a revelatory contrast. But the chief interest in treating his work would be to examine the effect of his narrow but intense theories of poetry and the short story, and the account of the first of these alone could be the subject for another book: the development from Poe to Baudelaire, through the French symbolists, to modern American and English poetry. My reluctance at not dealing with Poe here is tempered by the fact that his value, even more than Emerson's, is now seen to consist in his influence rather than in the body of his own work. No group of his poems seems as enduring as *Drum-Taps;* and his stories, less harrowing upon the nerves than they were, seem relatively factitious when contrasted with the moral depth of Hawthorne or Melville.

[4] I have provided a Chronology of the principal events in the five authors' lives on pages 657-61 [of *American Renaissance*].

[5] Santayana has said that the American mind does not oppose tradition, it forgets it. The kind of repossession that is essential has been described by André Malraux in an essay on 'The Cultural Heritage' (1936): 'Every civilization is like the Renaissance, and creates its own heritage out of everything in the past that helps it to surpass itself. *A heritage is not transmitted; it must be conquered;* and moreover it is conquered slowly and unpredictably. We do not demand a civilization made to order any more than we demand masterpieces made to order. But let us demand of ourselves a full consciousness that the choice made by each of us out of the past—out of the boundless hopes of the men who came before us—is measured by our thirst for greatness and by our wills.'

George Moore and the Nineties

Graham Hough

I am not one who oft or much delights in contemplating the division of literary history into periods: at best it is a barren exercise. Nevertheless it has a certain importance; largely a negative importance. No doubt all history is a seamless web, and everything is continuous with everything else, and our subdivisions are imposed and arbitrary schemes. No doubt these schemes have no substantial existence, and we have no real criterion for deciding that one is right and another wrong; the most we can say is that some are appropriate and useful and others less so. The best-laid scheme cannot give us much positive assistance; but regarded simply as a heuristic mechanism an inappropriate scheme can do a good deal to deform our picture of literary history. It has seemed to me for a long time that the concept of "the Victorian age" has had just this effect. The Victorian age presumably extends from somewhere about the accession of that respectable monarch in 1837 to her death in 1901. But the life of the spirit does not coincide very accurately with the vicissitudes of the temporal power, and as a division of literary history this slice of time makes very little sense. It has presented us with the picture of an age of patient moral and social fervor on the one hand, of the slow decline of the romantic impulse on the other, both fading into a sort of penumbra after the Victorian heyday. This is succeeded by a short space of total eclipse, until the darkness is dispelled by the sudden emergence of the light of Eliot and Pound. What we have here is plainly not a very complete or accurate account of what went on, so we have been persuaded to intercalate a short period called the nineties, just to signalize our recognition of the fact that various changes were taking place. As an alternative I should like to propose for consideration a period extending from about 1880 to 1914, a period distinct in spirit from what we usually think of as Victorianism, a period in which all the foundations of modern literature were being laid, but recognizably distinct from modern literature too. I am not quite sure about 1880; a case might be made for putting the beginning of our period back into the 1870s, perhaps to the publication of Pater's *Renaissance* in 1873; but on balance 1880 is probably about right. It is not until the late seventies that the influence of Pater on style and feeling becomes decisive, or that the influence of French realism begins to make itself felt in the novel. And as for 1914—perhaps it ought to be 1910; but 1914 is such a landmark in cultural as well as political history that it seems the most appropriate point to choose.

A paper on the nineties ideally should not begin by abolishing the nineties, or by merging them in a larger unit; and one may well concede that it is in the nineties that the tendencies of the period find their fullest expression. It is the decade of the one serious poetical *cénacle,* the Rhymers' Club; of the two most characteristic literary magazines, *The Yellow Book* and *The Savoy;* of what is probably the best of the English realist novels, Moore's *Esther Waters;* and of the great social-literary scandal, the Oscar Wilde trial. But a decade is an embarrassing unit in literary history; in general it is far too short to be useful, and there is not a writer of any weight in the nineties whose significant work does not extend outside them. One has only to cite the names of James, Hardy, Conrad, Moore, Gissing, and Yeats. It is sometimes said that the nineties were not an attitude but a state of mind—a state whose peculiar color has been variously described as mauve and greenery-yallery. This is a good enough starting period for period nostalgia, a vision of the poppies and the lilies, the green nightgowns, the blue china, the gas lamps reflected in a Whistlerian Thames, the Sickert music halls, and Sherlock Holmes's Inverness cape. One may become an addict to these historic stimulants, but they do not really tell us very much. And the trouble about the actual achievements of the nineties in their most characteristic forms is that they are so minuscule. The poetry of Dowson and Lionel Johnson, Crackanthorpe's stories and Henry Harland's, will not bear very much weight. Yeats's ninetyish phase is largely proleptic—it looks forward to a much greater achievement of a different kind later on. And Wilde, except as a personality and a portent, seems to me a greatly overrated figure. So if we insist on looking at the nineties by themselves we are presented with a decade where many forces are stirring but not to any very complete purpose.

Having proposed a longer period as the appropriate unit, I should like just to suggest its general characteristics; but only in a very summary fashion, since the bare existence of these twenty-five years as a literary concept has not yet been generally recognized, still less examined. I see three principal developments. First, a greatly increased range and a new freedom in the choice of subjects from actual life; all that we ordinarily call realism. I shall not make any distinction between realism and naturalism, for though in French literary history they are always carefully distinguished, this has no particular relevance to English, and in the controversy of the 1880s the word realism is the one that seems always to have been used. Leaving aside the shocked indignation, of which there was much, we can get an idea of the cautious welcome extended to realism, and the recognition of both its novelty and its foreign origin, from Henry James's remarks on Zola:

> A novelist with a system, a passionate conviction, a great plan—incontestable attributes of M. Zola—is not now easily to be found in England or the United States, where the story-teller's art is almost exclusively feminine, is mainly in the hands of timid (even

> when very accomplished) women, whose acquaintance with life is severely restricted, and who are not conspicuous for general views. The novel, moreover, among ourselves, is almost always addressed to young unmarried ladies, or at least always assumes them to be a large part of the novelist's public.
>
> This fact, to a French story-teller, appears, of course, a damnable restriction. . . . Half of life is a sealed book to young unmarried ladies, and how can a novel be worth anything that deals with only half of life? These objections are perfectly valid, and it may be said that our English system is a good thing for virgins and boys, and a bad thing for the novel itself, when the novel is regarded as something more than a simple *jeu d'esprit,* and considered as a composition that treats of life at large and helps us to *know.*

I take this quotation from an advertisement for the series of translations of Zola published by Vizetelly from 1884 onwards. Vizetelly was, of course, the publisher who was most closely associated with the realist movement; he was prosecuted for his publications and eventually imprisoned, in 1888. In subsequent comment on the affair he is generally represented as a sort of martyr for culture, but a further perusal of the advertisement pages I am speaking of leads one to take this with just a small pinch of salt. It may be that Vizetelly was filled only with a pure desire to serve modern letters and to show contemporary society the realities on which it was based, but it is also fairly evident that Vizetelly's Realistic Novels are advertised with half an eye towards a possibly scandalous success; and I mention this because the suggestion that "This is not for young ladies" (or the alternative suggestion that "This will certainly be read by young ladies but their parents ought not to know"), made seriously, or defiantly, or with a behind-the-hand snigger, is a very recognizable element in the literature of this time, quite as recognizable as the high Victorian attitude of Tennyson –

> The prudent partner of his blood
> Lean'd on him, faithful, gentle, good,
> Wearing the rose of womanhood–

and so forth. The advertisement of George Moore's *A Mummer's Wife,* for example, begins with the announcement: "This book has been placed in the Index Expurgatorius of the Select Circulating Libraries of Messrs. Mudie and W. H. Smith and Son."

The second development is a confused set of tendencies that cluster round the notion of art for art's sake. These never amount to a formal doctrine in England, and they hold together in a loose synthesis a number of different ideas, mostly derived from France. Parnassians, symbolists, decadents—these school labels have a tolerably plain meaning in French literary history, but English literary ideas are much less clearly analyzed. Art for art's sake, for what the phrase is worth, goes back to Gautier, and Gautier had been an influence on Swinburne in the 1860s. Transposed into a moral rather than a literary code, it reappears in the preface to Pater's *Renaissance;* and the cult of exquisite sensations, expressed in the languid Paterian rhythms, haunts the production of the nineties and extends some considerable distance into this century. But the strictly literary ideals to which it gave rise remain shifting and uncertain. On the one hand we are constantly hearing echoes of "L'Art," the last poem in *Émaux et Camées,* with its praise of a hard-chiseled perfection of form:

> Lutte avec le carrare,
> Avec le paros dur
>   Et rare,
> Gardiens du contour pur;
>
> Peintre, fuis l'aquarelle,
> Et fixe la couleur
>   Trop frêle
> Au four de l'émailleur.

On the other hand, the quite contrary doctrine of Verlaine's "Art Poètique":

> Il faut aussi que tu n'ailles point
> Choisir tes mots sans quelque méprise:
> Rien de plus cher que la chanson grise
> Ou l'Indécis au Précis se joint.
>
> Car nous voulons la Nuance encore,
> Pas la Couleur, rien que la Nuance!

So that we are left uncertain whether the prevalent ideal is an intaglio cut in the hardest stone or a misty Whistler nocturne. But what these ideals have in common is an insistence on the claims as the artist as artificer against those of the artist as interpreter of life. "The Yellow Dwarf," the pseudonymous book reviewer of *The Yellow Book* (his name, by the way, is borrowed from *Le Nain Jaune,* a Parnassian periodical of the 1860s), makes a great point of the purely aesthetic nature of his criticism, and he is greatly disturbed when he suspects that a work of fiction might have a moral or be intended as a tract for the times. And, as in France, this lightweight aestheticism passes over into symbolism. Whether there is anything in English letters that can be called a symbolist movement I am not sure; but the word seems inevitable, and is not without its uses. Symbolism can be said to occur when the cult of the exquisite, particular sensation, embodied in the perfect form, begins to acquire transcendental overtones, begins to be seen as a means of access to a more authentic world underlying the world of appearances. As a half-sentimental literary idea we see this floating around in a good many places. As a serious conviction, involving the whole moral and literary personality, we see it in the early essays of Yeats.

Now these two tendencies, the realist and the symbolist-aesthetic, are inveterately opposed in France. But in England they show a curious tendency to fuse together. This is because moral ideas in England are commonly clearer and more strongly held than literary ones; a literary controversy tends to shift itself to the moral plane. And morally the two different schools are in fact moving in the same direction. Both place the demands of art outside and above the moral exigencies, and the need for a moral emancipation is so much more pressing in England that it obscures other differences. The movement may be towards fantasy and dream, or it may be towards the recognition of the most sordid social actualities; but these do not feel themselves to be vitally opposed, for they are both expressions of the same need. Moral and psychological adventurousness and the pursuit of an exquisite and refined form go hand in hand in England, and even tend to be seen as much the same thing. George Eliot, we may notice, comes in for equally heavy knocks on both counts—for lumbering bluntness of style and form, and for the ever-present moral superintendence under which her work is seen to labor.

The third very marked feature of the time is a conscious reaction against the English literary tradition. This is something relatively new, at any rate since neo-classical times. It formed no part of the romantic upheaval, though I suppose a foretaste of it may be found in Matthew Arnold's exhortations against English provincialism and complacency. But the reaction I am speaking of has a new flavor, and it continues into the most formative literature of the next decades. It is the beginning of that chronic Francophilia that affects many of the Anglo-American intelligentsia even to our own day. The manifestations that first leap to the mind are the slightly absurd ones—Pater murmuring that Poe was so coarse, he could only read him in Baudelaire's translation; Wilde writing *Salomé* in not very good French; the scraps of French idiom that interlard the pages of Henry James—down to the still current illusions that French coffee is good and the architecture of Paris beautiful. Of course the influence of France was necessary; it was the only one possible. It was an example of that perpetual process of fruitful interchange of which the history of European letters is composed. But there was in this particular wave of French influence an element of affectation. Yeats's use of Mallarmé—whom he cannot possibly have understood—as a name to conjure with provides us with one instance. There went with it a slightly perverse determination to throw overboard some of the most characteristic achievements of the English genius—Moore's dismissal of Shakespeare and the traditional English novel, for example. Without the slightest leaning to that absurdest of attitudes, a literary nationalism, it remains true that the actual achieved body of work in a given language is an inescapable condition for future work. The nineties show signs of wishing to make an escape; and, though this is another subject, and complicated by Anglo-American literary relations, the tendency persisted into the *avant garde* of the twentieth century.

In a period where may of the representative writings are on a very small scale it is difficult to find a typical figure to stand for the central movement of the time. I have a candidate to propose for this office; it is George Moore. There is no particular virtue in being typical; but even if it is the portrait of an age that we are trying to draw there are advantages in examining an individual man, an actual writer, rather than tendencies exhibited in fragments. George Moore has some qualifications that are particularly useful to us in this respect. In the first place, he exists. He is discernible with the naked eye, which can hardly be said for Crackanthorpe or Dowson. Never quite in the center of the picture, he nevertheless played a real part in the literary history of the *fin de siècle,* and in his vivid, outrageous autobiography he has played a considerable part in chronicling it. He has a large body of work to his credit, uneven it is true, but some of it of undeniable excellence, and much of it of peculiar interest. And although his career extends far into this century, he remained remarkably faithful to the intuitions of his earlier years. Even his defects are for our present purpose a recommendation. Moore was not Prince Hamlet, nor was meant to be; almost at times the fool. He was incapable of what in any ordinary acceptation of the term would be called thought. He picks up ideas from everywhere, never understands them quite thoroughly or thinks them out, mixes them up to make a miscellaneous stew, and often pretends to knowledge that he does not really possess.

As an informant on matters of fact he is unreliable in the extreme. To anyone attempting a critical examination of Moore, particularly to anyone who is sensible of his merits, these are highly embarassing qualities. But if we want to feel the form and pressure of the time they are extremely useful ones. He wrote of himself:

> My soul, so far as I understand it, has very kindly taken colour and form from the many various modes of life that self-will and an impetuous temperament have forced me to indulge in. Therefore I may say that I am free from original qualities, defects, tastes, etc. . . . I came into the world apparently with a nature like a smooth sheet of wax, bearing no impress but capable of receiving any; of being moulded into all shapes.

And it is so with his literary development too; he picks up like a magpie all the notions and influences at large in the world around him, spills them out with an air of proud discovery—in fact, as Oscar Wilde said to him, conducts his education in public. If we want to find out what the literary scene looked like to a young man of advanced tastes in the eighties and nineties we can hardly do better than look at his early works. Greater literary personalities will tell us less. The tireless spiritual energy of Yeats, the quick-witted positiveness of Shaw, are too idiosyncratic to tell us much except about their possessors.

The document I wish to look at is the *Confessions of a Young Man.* It was written in 1886; it refers to a period between 1873, when Moore first went to Paris, and 1883, when his first novel appeared; and as we now have it, it was annotated by its author at two later dates. I remember abominating it when I first read it, years ago; and it does indeed give the picture of an intolerable young coxcomb. But I entirely failed to see its significance. It is an account of Moore's literary education, and pretty well the complete account, since he was almost illiterate when he first went to France. It is an education picked up in cafés and studios, the editorial offices of magazines, and the Gaiety bar. We need not stickle for the factual accuracy of the story. The apartment with the red drawing-room, the Buddha, the python, and the Turkish couches is unlikely to have been as Moore describes it in the mid-1870s. It seems to owe far too much to Huysmans's *A Rebours.* And *A Rebours* did not come out till 1884. What we are contemplating in fact is a panoramic view of the formation of a taste and an attitude, of all the varied aesthetic and social influences that went to make it, from the standpoint of 1886. It is a view that still seemed valid to Moore in 1904, and even beyond the limits of our period, in 1916.

The inevitable first reaction to the book is to find it an appalling muddle. Enthusiasms and recantations seem to follow each other in no sort of order. Every opinion is contradicted by its opposite a few pages farther on. There are no dates, and no possibility of making the story into an intelligible chronological sequence. Then one realizes that Moore is perfectly well aware of this and has even made his capriciousness into a sort of principle. "Never could I interest myself in a book," he writes, "if it were not the exact diet my mind required at the time, or in the very immediate future." And later, in excusing himself for lack of sensibility to Shakespeare, "There are affinities in literature corresponding to, and very analogous to, sexual affinities—the same unreasoned attractions, the same pleasures, the same lassitudes. Those we have loved most we are most indifferent to. Shelley, Gautier, Zola, Flaubert, Goncourt! how I have loved you all; and now I could not, would not, read you again." But there are other ways of revealing a sensibility and an attitude than the ordered chronological *Bildungsroman*. This pell-mell jumble of passions and revulsions spreads out, as it were, the contents of Moore's imagination for our inspection; and we can see that the objects displayed, apparently a mere chance assortment, actually fall into two groups. One group is composed of fantasies and dreams, often slightly perverse fantasies and dreams, unchecked by bourgeois ethics or ordinary social reality. The other group consists of equally passionate aspirations after the actualities of life, the tangible realities of contemporary experience and modern urban living. These two enthusiasms sometimes clash violently. Each at times tries to deny the existence of the other, yet both continue to exist—and even in the end come to a kind of reconciliation. They are united, not only as the most staring opposites may be, by the accident of inhering in the same personality, but by a real common factor. The common element is the purely literary one, the need that each passion has to find its fullest and justest verbal expression. Starting with a notable ignorance of both English grammar and the English vocabulary, Moore ultimately finds the ruling passion of his life in the desire to write well.

Fantasy and dream came first, and came even at first in a verbal embodiment. His first literary passion was for the mere name of a novel he heard his parents discussing—*Lady Audley's Secret*. This was followed by the revelation of Shelley, also turned to initially for the same reason. "Lady Audley! What a beautiful name! . . . Shelley! That crystal name, and his poetry also crystalline." Most of the English lyric poets were read soon after. But from Shelley the young Moore had learnt atheism, and he followed this up by a course of the rationalist classics, Lecky and Buckle. It is noticeable that George Eliot comes in with these. She appears as the great agnostic, not as an artist; and the only one of the classic English novelists that Moore mentions with any enthusiasm is Dickens. Then to France, to study painting; not that he had any talent, but France and art became the objects of a romantic devotion, like the names of Lady Audley and Shelley. There were some flirtations with Hugo and Musset; but the first real revelation came from Gautier, from reading *Mademoiselle de Maupin.* It would be hard to exaggerate the influence of this work on the sensibility of the *fin de siècle* in England. It is constantly cited and referred to; and still more often its situations and its spirit are echoed without open acknowledgement. Both his own panegyrics and later scholarship have shown how decisive was the influence of Gautier on Swinburne; and Moore was sufficiently acute to notice it himself. "The 'Hymn to Proserpine' and 'Dolores' are wonderful lyrical versions of Mlle de Maupin," he writes. The frank sensuality, the delight in visible and tangible beauty, combined with the unquiet romantic *Sehnsucht,* the longing for an ideal satisfaction, was a combination of ingredients that the more decorous English romanticism had never supplied. Above all there was the hint of perversity brought in by the epicene nature of the hero-heroine; a double delight, for it was at once a new source of erotic stimulation and a new means to *épater le bourgeois.* Moore expresses the spirit in which it was accepted with uncommon clarity:

> I read "Mlle de Maupin" at a moment when I was weary of spiritual passion, and this great exaltation of the visible above the invisible at once conquered and led me captive. This plain scorn of a world exemplified in lacerated saints and a crucified Redeemer opened up a prospect of new beliefs and new joys in things and new revolts against all that had come to form part and parcel of the commonalty of mankind. Shelley's teaching had been, while accepting the body, to dream of the soul as a star, and so preserve our ideal; but now I saw suddenly, with delightful clearness and intoxicating conviction that by looking with shame and accepting with love the flesh, I might raise it to as high a place within as divine a light as ever the soul had been set in.

It was above all the tone of *Mademoiselle de Maupin* that Moore picked up, and it is a tone that is to echo through much of the literature of the nineties and to give it much of its peculiar flavor. It is a young man's tone, and that of a young man whom our elders would certainly have called a cad. It is rather lightheartedly erotic, and quite openly predatory. It is haunted by sexuality and makes a great deal of its "paganism," yet it does not for a moment suggest the antique world; rather a setting of *deuxsième empire* frou-frou, tea-roses, Parma violets, the minor pleasures of an elegant nineteenth-century Bohemianism. Yet beneath this wordly assurance the note of romantic idealism is never quite absent; the young social and sexual buccaneer is haunted by the ghost of a sad Pierrot sighing after an impossible love. Let us look at a few examples.

> Why should I undertake to keep a woman by me for the entire space of her life, watching her grow fat, grey, wrinkled and foolish? Think of the annoyance of perpetually looking after any one, especially a woman! Besides, marriage is antagonistic to my ideal.
>
> (Moore, *Confessions*)

> If I were to be the lover of one of these ladies like a pale narcissus, moist with a tepid dew of tears, and bending with willowy languor over the new marble tomb of a spouse, happily and recently defunct, I should be as wretched as the dear departed was in his lifetime.
>
> (Gautier, *Maupin*)

> He can read through the slim woman whose black hair, a-glitter with diamonds, contrasts with her white satin; an old man is talking to her, she dances with him, and she refused a young man a moment before. This is a bad sign, our Lovelace knows it; there is a stout woman of thirty-five, who is looking at him, red satin bodice, doubtful taste. He looks away; a little blonde woman fixes her eyes on him, she looks as innocent as a child; instinctively our Lovelace turns to his host. "Who is that little blonde women over there, the right-hand corner?" he asks. "Ah, that is Lady——." "Will you introduce me?" "Certainly." Lovelace has made up his mind.
>
> (Moore, *Confessions*)

> All this does not prevent me from positively wanting a mistress. I do not know who she will be, but among the women of my acquaintance I see nobody who could suitably fill this dignified position. Those who may be regarded as young enough are wanting in beauty or intellectual charm; those who are beautiful and young are basely and forbiddingly virtuous, or lack the necessary freedom; and then there is always some husband, some brother, a mother or

an aunt, somebody or other, with prying eyes and large ears, who must either be cajoled or given short shrift.

(Gautier, *Maupin*)

I was absorbed in the life of woman—the mystery of petticoats, so different from the staidness of trousers! the rolls of hair entwined with so much art, and suggesting so much colour and perfume, so different from the bare crop; the unnaturalness of the waist in stays! plentitude and slenderness of silk. . . . A world of calm colour with phantoms moving, floating past and changing in dim light —an averted face with abundant hair, the gleam of a perfect bust or the poise of a neck turning slowly round, the gaze of deep translucid eyes. I loved women too much to give myself wholly to one.

(Moore, *Confessions*)

It makes me have a low opinion of women when I see how infatuated they often are with blackguards who despise and deceive them, instead of taking a lover—some staunch and sincere young man who would consider himself very lucky, and would simply worship them; I myself, for example, am such a one. It is true that men of the former kind abound in the drawing-rooms, where they preen themselves for all to behold, and are always lounging on the back of some settee, while I remain at home, my forehead pressed against the window-pane, watching the river shroud itself in haze and the mists rising, while silently setting up in my heart the scented shrine, the peerless temple, in which I am to install the future idol of my soul.

(Gautier, *Maupin*)

I have two points to make in setting these extracts side by side. One is how extraordinarily closely Moore echoes Gautier's tone, and how easy it is to recognize that tone as particularly characteristic of the nineties. We find it again and again in Wilde, in *The Yellow Book* and *The Savoy*, and even, though decorously veiled and entirely without the connivance of the author, in some of the characters of Henry James. The second point is that the attitudes implied here are entirely social and sexual. But *Mademoiselle de Maupin* had a preface—the famous preface which was the manifesto of the art-for-art's-sake movement. Moore does not mention it, but we can hardly suppose that he did not read it. And we later find, by a curious linkage, that he associates *Mademoiselle de Maupin* with Pater's *Marius the Epicurean.* There seems to be little in common between the aesthetic sensuality of Gautier and the spiritualized hedonism of Pater. It may of course be that the one is simply the Oxford version of the other, and Moore partly makes the association on those grounds—with a certain rude psychological insight and a good deal of injustice to what Pater supposed himself to be saying.

Mr. Pater can join hands with Gautier in saying

> je trouve la terre aussi belle que le ciel, et je pense que la correction de la forme est la vertu.

"I think that correctness of form is virtue"; that is the real link that Moore makes between Gautier and Pater. The social and sexual antinomianism is only the correlative of a general pursuit of formal beauty, which can manifest itself as much in the sphere of verbal arrangement as in the sphere of conduct.

> But "Marius the Epicurean" was more to me than a mere emotional influence, precious and rare though that may be, for this book was the first in English prose I had come across that procured for me any genuine pleasure in the language itself, in the combination of words for silver or gold chime, and unconventional cadence, and for all those lurking half-meanings, and that evanescent suggestion, like the odour of dead roses, that words retain to the last of other times and elder usage. . . . "Marius" was the stepping-stone that carried me across the channel into the genius of my own tongue.

I said before that psychological adventurousness and the search for perfection of form go hand in hand. Here we see the process in action. Gautier suggests a style of life; Pater extends it; and at the same time he suggests a style of writing. The cultivation of a mannered exquisitness of sensation leads directly into the cultivation of prose as a deliberate aesthetic instrument.

After the reading of *Maupin* Moore plunged deep into the waters of aestheticism. Other tales of Gautier followed, and the delicately chiseled nostalgias of *Émaux et Camées*. The inevitable next step was Baudelaire.

> No longer is it the grand barbaric face of Gautier; now it is the clean-shaven face of the mock priest, the slow, cold eye, and the sharp, cunning sneer of the cynical libertine who will be tempted that he may better know the worthlessness of temptation. "Les Fleurs du Mal," beautiful flowers, beautiful in sublime decay. What a great record is yours, and were Hell a reality how many souls would we find wreathed with your poisonous blossoms.

(There is no need to suppose that Moore in 1886 wrote these lines without a tinge of irony.) Bertrand's *Gaspard de la Nuit;* Villiers de l'Isle Adam, whom Moore used to meet at the Nouvelle Athènes; Verlaine; Gustave Kahn's experiments in *verse libre* and faint evocative vocabulary; Ghil's theory of colored vowels, a development of the doctrine of Rimbaud's sonnet, which gave rise to an often quoted passage in *Muslin;* Mallarmé, whose conversation Moore enjoyed, while confessing that he was quite unable to understand either the poetry or the Symbolist theory. Excited by this heady brew, it is not surprising that Moore was unable to appreciate the contemporary experiments in the poetry of common life. When he came to read Coppée he was able to enjoy only his early Parnassian poems.

> But the exquisite perceptivity of Coppèe showed in his modern poems, the certainty with which he raised the commonest subject, investing it with sufficient dignity for his purpose, escaped me wholly, and I could not but turn with horror from such poems as "La Nourrice" and "Le Petit Epicier." I could not understand how anybody could bring himself to acknowledge the vulgar details of our vulgar age.

But a new force was piling up behind the aesthetic screen, and it was soon to burst out. Moore was busy trying to write short stories apparently in the manner of Villiers' *Contes Cruels,* and poems, "Roses of Midnight," in what he believed to be the manner of Baudelaire. One day by chance he read in a magazine an article by Zola (presumably *Le Roman Experimental*). The words *naturalisme, la verité, la science* affronted his eyes. He learnt that one should write with as little imagination as possible, that contrived plot in a novel or a play was illiterate and puerile. It all struck him as a revelation, and he realized the sterile eccentricity of his own aestheticism. He had read a few chapters of *L'Assommoir* when it had appeared in serial form, but like others of his tastes had dismissed it as an absurdity. Now he began to buy up the back numbers of the *Voltaire,* the weekly in which Zola was making propaganda for the naturalist cause.

> The idea of a new art based on science, in opposition to the art of the old world that was based on the imagination, an art that should explain all things and embrace modern life in its entirety, in its endless ramifications, be, as it were, a new creed in a new civilisation, filled me with wonder, and I stood dumb before the vastness of the conception, and the towering height of the ambition.

This mood of enraptured stupefaction did not last; at the time of writing the *Confessions,* in 1886, he is able to look back at the Zola articles and say "Only the simple crude statements of a man of powerful mind, but singulary narrow vision." And a few pages farther on from the account of the naturalist revelation is a thoroughgoing attack on Zola's limitations, an attack whose consequences are amusingly described in the essay "A Visit to Médan." But it is not my purpose to write the history of Moore's literary opinions in detail. The point is that from now on the idea of a distinctively modern art, grounding itself on the realities of the contemporary world, lies side by side with aesthetic fantasy in Moore's mind. It is surprising how easily they came to lie side by side. On a later page of the *Confessions, Mademoiselle de Maupin* and *L'Assommoir* are cited together as the two books above all from which the respectable circulating-library young lady must turn away; they are mentioned almost as though they were the twin pillars of modern letters, in spite of the fact that *Maupin* had appeared in 1836, and that the two works had nothing whatever in common, except that neither is exactly the thing *à mettre entre les mains de toute jeune fille*. And the fact is that naturalism did not drive out aestheticism, it substituted a new aestheticism of an extended kind. The immediate effect of the Zola discovery was to send Moore back to Coppée's modern poems, and to persuade him to modernize his "Roses of Midnight." But this soon proved to be a hopeless enterprise, and he turns to reflect, not at all on the social and descriptive implications of naturalism, but on its purely literary qualities. He rereads *L'Assommoir* and is impressed by its "strength, height and decorative grandeur," by the "immense harmonic development of the idea, and the fugal treatment of the different scenes," by "the lordly, riverlike roll of the narrative." In short, it was "the idea of the new aestheticism—the new art corresponding to modern, an ancient art corresponded to ancient life" that captivated him and was to compel his imagination for many years to come.

The later history of Zola's reputation has borne out Moore's intuition. Towards the end of the *Confessions* he writes:

> One thing that cannot be denied to the realists: a constant and intense desire to write well, to write artistically. When I think of what they have done in the matter of the use of words, of the myriad verbal effects they have discovered, of the thousand forms of composition they have created, how they have remodelled and refashioned the language in their untiring striving for intensity of expression, for the very osmazome of art, I am lost in ultimate wonder and admiration. What Hugo did for French verse, Flaubert, Goncourt, Zola, and Huysmans have done for French prose.

It would once have seemed eccentric to talk of Zola in this way, perhaps did even when Moore was writing. But in later years nobody has been very interested in Zola the reporter and sociologist; and complaints about the supposed coarseness and crudity of his style have given way, and justly, to admiration for his impressionist painting and the organization of his large set pieces. The massive symbolism in his writing has not passed unnoticed, and the flat opposition between naturalist and symbolist has been much played down. By now, when the professed "scientific" pretensions of *Le Roman Experimental* can no longer be taken seriously, the real nature of Zola's achievement can be seen more clearly, and it is seen much as Moore saw it. In making the transition from Zola's untenable naturalist theory to his far more interesting and comprehensive practice Moore is taking the line that both criticism and fiction itself were to take in the years to come.

But Moore's discipleship to Zola was brief. He soon saw something nearer to his real aim in Flaubert, where the demands of a scrupulous realism are united with an equal scrupulosity of rhythm and phrasing. However great the difference between their achievements, Flaubert's strict attachment to the truth, to be sought only through formal perfection, probably came nearest to embodying Moore's artistic ideal. *A Mummer's Wife* is his only Zolaesque novel; he was annoyed if one did not recognize that *Esther Waters* was in inspiration "pure Flaubert." But strangely, even Flaubert was not the object of Moore's lasting devotion. Talking of his own literary infidelities he says "even a light of love is constant, if not faithful, to her *amant de coeur*"; and the most enduring of his literary passions was for Balzac. "Upon that rock I built my church, and his great and valid talent saved me from the shoaling waters of new aestheticisms, the putrid mud of naturalism, and the faint and sickly surf of the symbolists." It is only in Balzac that he can find an unrestricted romantic imagination united with a complete engagement in the involved turmoil of contemporary life. Essentially a spectator on the sidelines, Moore is fascinated by that colossal vitality; and if for Alisander he is more than a little o'erparted, we can at least recognize in the totality of his work something of his master's passion for the diversity of human experience.

Disorderly and capricious as Moore's expression of his enthusiasms is, it can still tell us something, and something that is of importance beyond his own career. He was more completely involved in French literature than any other writer of the nineties—more even than Symons; and we can see in him a complete microcosm of the French influences that were then reshaping English literature. His experience tells us of the opening of a new chapter in the history of English fiction. Three steady preoccupations can be discerned among his shifting allegiances: one is with telling the truth about experience instead of merely devising an agreeable story; the second is with imaginative freedom in spite of the circulating libraries and the young ladies; the third is with formal justness and beauty in expression and organization, instead of the labored or slapdash approximations to which the English novel in all but its highest moments had been prone. Together they make a break with many of the traditions of English fiction—with the traditions of picaresque adventure, indiscriminate humor, genial satire, and reforming zeal. A severer artistic ideal takes their place. And this break is not merely a matter of Moore's own work. We are not considering his intrinsic quality at the moment, though my own conviction is that it is far higher than has been generally recognized; we are using him simply as a convenient periscope to survey the literary scene of his time. And the lessons he was learning were also being learnt, wholly or in part, by Hardy, Conrad, and Henry James.

James is a far greater, Hardy and Conrad more central writers than Moore. It is relatively easy to fit them into a "great tradition" of English fiction. Moore has always his own marked idiosyncrasy, and the criticism of our time, in its preoccupation with prevalent trends and successful revolutions rather than with individual quality, has been inclined to see it as a dead end. This is not, I think, true; and if it is necessary to justify Moore to the trend-mongers one may do so by showing that he was leading, if not up the main road, into an area where the greatest prose experiment of our time has its beginning. We have seen Moore oscillating between aesthetic reverie and realism, and if we were to follow the development of his art we should find him in the end arriving at a style that was to harmonize the two. He manages in his best work to present in all their uncompromising contingency the actualities of common experience, and yet to preserve the inevitability of impression, the delicate rightness of diction and rhythm that he had learned from the high priests of a scrupulous art. At the end of our period, when Moore was past the threshold of old age, another Irish writer brought out his youthful confessions; and in it he defined the function of the poet, the literary artist, as it appeared to his eyes. It is to be "the mediator between the world of reality and the world of dreams." No writer in any age has carried farther than James Joyce the dual allegiance to an exhaustive naturalism on the one hand and a complex aesthetic symbolism on the other; and I think it is likely that neither the title nor the content of Joyce's *Portrait of the Artist as a*

Young Man would have been quite the same in 1916 if it had not been for the prior existence of Moore's *Confessions of a Young Man* in 1886. And there are other resemblances more strongly marked. Critics have often spoken about the absolute originality of Joyce's *Dubliners;* and that is a curious instance of how far George Moore's achievements have dropped out of sight—itself perhaps a curious instance of the general failure to recognize the importance of the *fin de siècle* as a formative power in modern literature. For *Dubliners* has an obvious ancestor in Moore's stories in *The Untilled Field.* Joyce's stories have an urban instead of a rural setting, and make far more use of the romantic-ironical contrast. But it is surprising that the closeness of his manner to Moore's has not been observed. Part of it no doubt is a matter of a common discipleship. Moore's debt to Pater's prose has always been achknowledged; and Joyce's use of the same master is obvious, especially in *Portrait of the Artist.* It would be too long to illustrate in detail, but the echoed cadences sometimes reveal themselves in a sentence.

> From without as from within the waters had flowed over his barriers: their tides once more began to jostle fiercely above the crumbled mole.
>
> (Joyce, *Portrait of the Artist*)

> I could see that he believed the story, and for the moment I, too, believed in an outcast Venus becoming the evil spirit of a village that would not accept her as divine.
>
> (Moore, *The Untilled Field*)

Neither of these dying falls would be quite as they are if they had not echoed so often already through Pater's prose. In feeling and treatment too we can see common obligations. "The Window" in *The Untilled Field* and "Clay" in *Dubliners* are both stories about humble old women; and I doubt whether either of them would exist if Flaubert had not written "Un Coeur Simple." But the similarities between the two volumes are so marked and pervasive that I am persuaded the debt is more direct. Moore said later that he began *The Untilled Field* "with the hope of furnishing the young Irish of the future with models"; and reading *Dubliners* beside the earlier book we can hardly doubt that for Joyce he achieved just that. He also said that, as the work progressed, "the first stories begot a desire to paint the portrait of my country"; almost the words in which Joyce described to his publisher the purpose of *Dubliners:* "to write a chapter of the moral history of my country." One could go on to speak of the last story in

Dubliners, "The Dead," and of how extraordinarily close it is in feeling to, say, "The Exile" and "Home Sickness" in Moore's collection. But to do justice to the charity, the gentleness, the centrality of feeling that these two lonely antinomian writers achieve in these beautiful tales would be to desert periods and influences, and would demand quite other tools and another manner. I end on this note just to give a small illustration of what is still often forgotten—how intimate the connection is between the writing of the late nineteenth century and what is most new and living in the twentieth.

The Importance of Shaftesbury

Ernest Tuveson

1

It has generally been acknowledged that the third Earl of Shaftesbury exercised an immense influence on the eighteenth century.[1] His collected works, the *Characteristics,* went through eleven editions between 1711 and 1790; and the list of authors who demonstrated the influence of Shaftesbury would include a majority of those published in the eighteenth century. Yet there is a puzzle about Shaftesbury's effect on his own and later times. It was long assumed that this influence consisted in his originality, the newness of his theory of the "moral sense" in particular, as well as his "preromantic" and supposedly original glorification of external nature. The notable growth in altruism in eighteenth century literature, says Professor C. A. Moore, "is to be traced largely, I think, to the *Characteristics* . . . of Lord Shaftesbury," and he adds, "It has long since been established that his system of philosophy constitutes a turning point in the history of pure speculation, especially in ethics."[2] In more recent years, however, this view has been challenged. Professor R. S. Crane has shown that the essentials of the "moral sense" theory were being preached by "Latitudinarian" divines even before Shaftesbury was born. He writes:

> If we wish to understand the origins and the widespread diffusion in the eighteenth century of the ideas which issued in the cult of sensibility, we must look, I believe, to a period considerably earlier than that in which Shaftesbury wrote and take into account the

> propaganda of a group of persons whose opportunities for moulding the thoughts of ordinary Englishmen were much greater than those of even the most aristocratic of deists.[3]

It can be shown as well that the exaltation and adoration of external nature was anticipated by and reflected a complex of ideas that the new science in combination with religion had already prepared.[4]

Must we, then, give up Shaftesbury as "original"? And if we do, how are we to account for the astonishing influence which he exerted? The answers to these questions, I believe, lie along other lines than have usually been suggested. In the world of thought, the whole is greater than the sum of the parts; and if the age that followed Shaftesbury was to a considerable extent *Characteristical,* it was not because his ideas separately were new or startling, but because he constructed of many elements a complete and artistically consistent whole, in a setting which had not previously existed.

As to the "moral sense" theory. There was as Professor Crane indicates, a cloud of divines who to some extent advanced the propositions that virtue is centered in a natural impulse towards humanitarian feeling for and sympathy with one's fellows, and that the exercise of this virtue is accompanied by an inward feeling of satisfaction and joy, while the spectacle of distress produces sympathetic pain. Yet, however striking these statements may be in themselves, we must remember that they were embedded in a context which did much to reduce their revolutionary effect.

Let us consider as examples two influential members of what is loosely called the "Cambridge Platonist" group. John Norris's *The Theory and Regulation of Love* (1694) postulates a "moral Gravity" of the soul, impressed on it by God Himself. This gravity

> will be its *Connaturality* to all Good, or Good in general, that is to God as its primary adequate Object, and to particular Goods only so far as they have something of the common Nature of Good, something of God in them.[5]

The image borrowed from the new philosophy, which makes goodness seem as inevitable in men as the operation of natural law in the cosmos, is striking and apparently radical enough; yet the theory is not what it seems to be. For Norris still sees good as merely participation in a transcendental God. The "moral gravity," it appears, is the result of a spiritual ascent. "From the Original Pravity and Degeneracy of our Nature, among *all* these particular Goods, that which we most eagerly propend to, is *sensual* Good."[6] The "Animal" impressions are formed first, "Sensuality comes to be *Adult* and *Mature*, when our discourses are but *young* and *imperfect*." When we arrive at an age for reflection we have, therefore, to "unravel the Prejudices of our Youth, and *unlive* our former Life . . .," and we are assured that it is not an easy job. This curious theory, with its mixture of new science, psychology, and old theology, represents in sum a partly scientific, partly Neoplatonic version of the doctrine of original sin. At no time did Norris, despite his seemingly radical phrase "moral gravity," really absorb morality into nature, or identify the end of existence with conduct in this world. Against this view Norris's friend Henry More advanced another account of moral action, also seemingly radical in its imagery.

> For, as the eye, . . . if it be vitiated in it self, cannot rightly discern the Condition of the visible Object it fixes its Sight upon; so the Mind of Man, let him set himself never so diligently to contemplate any *Moral* or *Intelligible* Object, if she be made dim by Moral Corruptions and Impurities, will not be able or free to close with what is best in the Circumstances that lye before her, being held captive by the Vices the Party has not yet purified himself from . . . our being redeemed into an Ability or freedom of chusing what is best, is not from *mere attention* to the Object, but from Purification, *Illumination*, and *real Regeneration* into the *Divine Image*.[7]

Here are two liberal clergymen who speak indeed of "goodness" as "natural," as natural as gravity in the physical world, or as seeing in the animal; yet the images certainly are not to be taken by themselves. Platonized Christianity, though modified by Cartesianism and early Newtonianism, nevertheless did not lose sight of "*Purification, Illumination,* and *real Regeneration*" as essential before the "divine Image" can be complete.

Other preachers, of a later generation, do in fact carry the naturalizing tendency further; but we see, if we read the works of these divines, that the basic Christian pattern is always to be discerned in the background. Isaac Barrow, one of the most extreme of them all, can exclaim:

> In fine, the wisest observers of man's nature have pronounced him to be a creature gentle and sociable, inclinable to and fit for conversation, apt to keep good order, to observe rules of justice, to embrace any sort of vertue, if well managed; if instructed by good discipline, if guided by good example, if living under the influence of wise laws and virtuous governours. Fierceness, rudeness, craft, malice, all perverse and intractable, all mischievous and vitious disposi-

> tions do grow among men (like weeds in any, even the best soil) and overspread the earth from neglect of good education; from ill conduct, ill custome, ill example; ('tis the comparison of Saint *Chrysostome,* and of Plutarch.)[8]

The combination of a Father and a pagan philosopher as authorities should remind us that such ideas go back very far and derive from the amalgamation of classical philosophy with Christianity which early began to take place. That man has some—perhaps a fairly large—capacity for goodness was part of orthodox Christian theology. But we must always view such statements against the whole background. Barrow, for instance, frequently points out that the soul must undergo a spiritual awakening before its goodness can be released:

> If also being, through divine grace awakened out of that drowsie state (which naturally in great measure hath seised upon all men) he discovereth his moral or spiritual wants, and imperfections; he is then apt to breathe and endeavour a nearer similitude to God. . . .[9]

The sacrifice of the Cross is essential to that "rousing." We must seek divine illumination "to enflame us with ardent love unto thee, and to direct our steps in obedience to thy Laws through the gloomy shades of this world, into that region of eternal light and bliss, where thou reignest in perfect Glory and Majesty, . . ."[10] In the famous sermon "The Nature, Properties and Acts of Charity," which has been considered a very close approach to the theory of natural benevolence, we find him telling his hearers that we cannot disregard any man as "contemptible," for the reason that "Every man is of a divine extraction, and allied to heaven by nature and by grace, as the Son of God, and Brother of God Incarnate."[11] Such a theory of altruism, a version of the great tradition of Christian charity and brotherhood, is still some distance from a consistently naturalistic one. On other occasions he shows his remoteness from the "social" doctrine of Shaftesbury and the eighteenth century when he praises the virtues of solitude quite in the old tradition, implying that in it is to be found the climax of religion; man is "social" by nature because of his potentialities as a son of God, but he manifests the true glory of his nature in his solitary immediate relation to God.

It would be a fatal mistake to assume that the Christian and other worldly elements in the thinking of these preachers were mere vestigial remains, so to speak, hanging on to a new, secular, optimistic opinion about human nature. However great their "latitude"—and of course to such conservatives as Swift it seemed dangerously wide—they were never really out of touch with the great traditional belief that men are destined to recover, by supernatural aid, from a disastrous cosmic fall into a transcendental state. Thus it would be easy, on the basis of isolated passages alone, to place Samuel Parker among the most completely naturalistic benevolists. In attempting to defend the existence of a divinely ordained law of nature against the attacks of skepticism, he cites such facts as strength of parental feeling, and that "as for the Generality of Men their hearts are so tender and their natural affections so humane, that they cannot but pity and commiserate the afflicted with a kind of fatal and mechanical sympathy."[12] Before we conclude that such a remark anticipates the man of feeling, however, we should recall that elsewhere he very emphatically asserts that the instincts are insufficient guides.

> God may possibly have put some secret Notices into the Minds of Men for the greater security of Justice and Honesty in the world; but then, beside that there is no way to prove the Certainty or demonstrate the Obligation of any such inward Record, this plainly resolves the Authority of the Law of Nature into uncertain and unaccountable Principles, or such as may be pretended and, when they are, ought to be admitted without any Proof or Evidence of Reason. . . .[13]

Many other examples might be cited.[14] But in sum they would, I think, show that, while the Latitudinarian preaching certainly had much to do with bringing about a new emphasis on altruism, it did not present a really new concept of human nature.

The Anglican apologists were on the *qui vive* against opinions of many kinds which they regarded as erroneous. They strongly emphasized free will and the possibility of the general access to grace, in opposition to the extreme of "total depravity." They were aware of the fact that for some time there had been a tendency to depreciate "right reason" as a reliable governor of personal conduct. Montaigne could remark that reason, like wax, takes any form imposed on it. Such skeptical idealists as Rochester were led into an attitude resembling romantic irony, seeing in reason a faculty which serves only to make men worse than the animals whose impulses they share; as Mackenzie, much later, puts the view:

> Men must have passions; paint them, if you can;
> Where less the brute enjoys, and more the man.
> To combat passion when our reasons rise,
> Reasons are better passions in disguise. . . .
> The world's dull reason, sober, cool, and pure,
> The world's dull reason is a knave demure.[15]

To combat this attitude, destructive alike of belief in the divine possibilities of the soul and of the concept of the "dignity of man," it was necessary to show that the universe as a whole is "rational" and that human behavior, even though man stands in need of assistance from beyond himself, is not truly anarchic.

The school of Hobbes, of course, powerfully reinforced the tradition of doubt, and it was said that every aspiring bachelor of divinity broke a spear against the steel cap of the sage of Malmesbury. He represented what was thought of as the "naturalistic" school, and the culmination of the skepticism about reason. But he was more easily condemned than answered. The powerful realism or apparent realism, of his demonstration that crass self-interest, however dressed up, is the true motive of all actions, could not be answered except by descending into the deep subrational drives of human nature. To answer Hobbes involved showing that this subrational part of our nature has more than one drive, that it can be good and "social" instead of warring and chaotic.

In answering these and other attacks, the Anglican divines were polemicists, it must be remembered, and the polemicist is notoriously prone to exaggerate in making whatever point he immediately has in hand. Defending religion did for many reasons involve defending the relative natural goodness of human beings; but while this fact certainly is important, it should not obscure our recognition that the polemical treatises and sermons are not representative of the whole views of both preachers and congregations. A most important result of the complex of thought in this time was a largely unconscious drift among these preachers towards a kind of Pelagianism: the proposition that the potentialities of human nature remain, and that corruption has entered from a long accumulation of pejorative changes in customs, educations, etc. Yet theological Pelagianism, although a heresy, remains within religion, and implies need for grace and redemption; and one can say no more than that it hovered in the air, and was hardly more than a vague omen of what was to come.[16] It is undoubtedly true, however, that a vague Christian Pelagianism could easily prepare the way for the powerful secular development of Pelagianism which is dominant in our own time. Contributing to the drift was the great mass of new information about other cultures that had been reaching Western Europe since the time of Henry the Navigator, which was making people realize more and more the real importance of environment and training on personality; this was the age of Locke, and the old faith in innate ideas went out with astounding rapidity.

Before a new sensibility could arise, however, a kind of catalytic agent was necessary to precipitate these undefined and unintegrated elements. That agent was supplied, in considerable part, by Shaftesbury. He did it by combining the spiritual idealism of the divines with the "naturalistic" view of the psychologists, and by applying consistently the full implications of the new world-view in science to the problems of ethics. It is usually said that he defends the "natural goodness" of man. In a general way this is true, but only if we remember that "goodness" has for him a new kind of meaning. It would be more accurate to say that Shaftesbury represents the human being as naturally adapted, with a kind of psychological ethical fitness, to live in his surroundings. The new philosophy depicted a universe of a myriad of parts, harmoniously operating according to immutable laws; it is not a universe in need of transformation or salvation, but one perfect and complete. The sum of these operations represent the *raison d' être* of the whole: the *process* is the final cause, not eternal principles rising above the flux.

It is logical to assume, therefore, that the human being, as an operating part of the great Whole, must be so constructed that in all his action he will, if he behaves "naturally," do those things which will promote his happiness and the happiness of the universe. With Shaftesbury we take the difficult step that this conclusion involves: with Shaftesbury we begin to see conduct in terms of what we should now call "normal" instead of in terms of obedience to divine or natural law; and with Shaftesbury we begin to think of departures from desirable behavior as the "abnormal" and "maladjustment" rather than "sin." The villains become environment and training, rather than the hereditary "degenerate nature of man," as Swift puts it.

Yet Shaftesbury was intensely aware of the fact that, to the human view at least, society in his time was far from being the ideal harmonious system it should be. Mandeville did Shaftesbury a great injustice by caricaturing him as a retiring patrician, favored by a gentle education, viewing through rose-colored glasses a world which he did not understand. The truth is that the noble philosopher remarkably anticipated Rousseau's passionate indictment of the social order, as we see in such passages as this:

> Tho however we may, in passing by, observe, that whilst we see in all other Creatures around us so great a proportionableness, constancy and regularity in all their passions and affections; so great a harmony, and such an adherence to Nature; no failure in the care of the Offspring, or of the Society (if living in Society). . . . Man in

> the mean time, vicious and unconsonant man, lives out of all rule and proportion, contradicts his Principles, breaks the Order and Oeconomy of all his Passions, and lives at odds with his whole Species, and with Nature: so that it is next to a Prodigy to see a Man in the World who lives NATURALLY, and as A MAN.[17]

The last clause, of course, has the stinger, for in it Shaftesbury uncompromisingly asserts that it is coming back to nature, not rising above her, that will solve the ethical problem.

Why, then, is there an air of hope about the whole work of Shaftesbury, an air of "enthusiasm" which was to infect future generations? Here the real purpose of the moralist has been misusderstood. It seems that he was not writing a mere complacent defense of the universe, or seeking to rehabilitate the aesthetic side of life as against "mechanism." His real goal was much larger. Shaftesbury, the heir to the great Whig tradition of his grandfather, thought of himself as carrying on, in the field of morals, the work of the reformer. In *The Moralists* (1709) he speaks of the

> Grace or Beauty in that original Native Liberty, which sets us free from so many inborn Tyrannys, gives us the Privilege of Ourselves, and makes us our own, and Independent. . . . A sort of Property, which, methinks, is as material to us to the full, as that which secures us our Lands, or Revenues.[18]

Now that security of estate and freedom of thought have been established after the Glorious Revolution, and the way is clear to remove fanaticism from religion, a great prospect for the betterment of life is opening up; the way is open to free men from the perversions engendered by religious dogmas and zeal, from false, derogatory ideas of human nature, and from artificial customs which separate man from nature, God from nature, and all three from the unity in which they should exist. Above all, if men are to be "natural" and therefore happy, they must stop connecting morality with meretricious ideas of the future life, which remove the emphasis from nature and its harmony. But argument and attack were not Shaftesbury's method; rather, he envisioned something like therapy, the treatment of an urbane and insinuating style, the application of raillery rather than the the traditional satire, the artistic presentation of external nature and encouragement of the communion of the mind with landscape untouched by man.

In an age intoxicated by the wonders of mechanism, it was necessary to show how this adaptation of the moral nature to environment could work. If man is to be represented as merely "natural" how can the presence of the impulse to good within the mind be explained without resorting to some such hypothesis as that reason is the "candle of the Lord"? And if good behavior is "natural," how can it be reconciled with so abstruse a faculty as advanced logical thought?

I have suggested that Shaftesbury combined a tradition of spiritual idealism with naturalistic psychology. The first he inherited from the Cambridge Platonists, at least in large part. We have seen how Henry More reduced the moral action to a kind of process, thus showing the influence of the new philosophy. In the *Enchiridion Ethicum,* he describes virtue as "rather a Power than a Habit."[19] This "power" is manifested in a "boniform Faculty," which More calls, borrowing but changing in connotation an Aristotelian phrase, the "very Eye of the Soul." This boniform faculty is the manifestation in action of "right reason," but—most importantly—it does not consist of innate propositions, or reasoning therefrom. Indeed, these things are at best crutches for the numerous race in whom the boniform faculty is regrettably weak. The highest kind of moral judgment consists in a kind of super-intuition, but one which is emphatically not a purely natural endowment. It has affinities with the "mens" or "intellectus angelicus" of Ficino's Christian Neoplatonism, and More once defines it as a divine power "by which we are lifted up and cleave unto God," which produces a "ravishing" and supra-worldly pleasure in those lofty spirits who have it. Those who belong to this group can perceive a "symmetry of the passions" as immediately as the average man perceives a parallelism of lines. It appears that More describes a kind of "moral sense"; his emphasis on a "power" rather than a reasoning faculty is part of his movement away from the "clear and distinct ideas" of Descartes, that philosopher who came to seem to him an *ignis fatuus,* and this movement More shared with his age. The idea, nevertheless, remains firmly embedded in a concept of the universe both other worldly and aspirational. The process of moral intuition is the result of an extensive purification of the soul from its corruption by matter.

Shaftesbury's innovation was the naturalization of this moral faculty. The moral intuition, in the successful developed personality, is the original, not final state of man. In other words, the ancient picture is turned upside down: the task of the human being is to retain a natural and original moral sense, instead of to attain it by a long course of redemption. Exactly how could such a natural moral sense be shown to exist? Fortunately, there was available a means of implementing the idea in terms of the master of the new psychology himself.

The older idea that Locke was a complete empiricist has been challenged in recent years.[20] In saying that the soul at birth is like a blank sheet of paper, he meant only that ideas are not somehow mysteriously present in us before we have any contact with the outside world. He did not, however, mean to imply that our ideas are formed by a purely passive action, through the automatic effect of sense impressions. In fact the mind plays the decisive part in cognition. It is autonomous, the ever alert observer, combining, separating, creating order out of the chaos of sensations which constantly are borne in upon it. First it is an *observer:* all mental action, to Locke, is ultimately a matter of "perceiving." He reduces the whole of thought to three kinds of "perception":

> 1. The perception of ideas in our minds. 2. The perception of signification of signs. 3. The perception of the connexion or repugnance, agreement or disagreement, that there is between any of our ideas.[21]

Certainly the independent power of the mind in the second and third kinds of thinking cannot be denied, and it is possible that it has some creative function even with regard to the first; and when sensations associate themselves arbitrarily, without the mind's ordering control, we have "association of ideas," the manifestation of irrationality and even insanity. By identifying "perception" and "understanding," therefore, Locke placed the pivot of intellectual action in the imagination, and not without reason did Berkeley object to Locke's attempt to show that abstractions can be made, independent of any one image. The image, indeed, is the very center of the mental process. A constant procession of images pass before the mind, even when it is not experiencing directly, and even in sleep.[22]

If Locke had presented a convincing epistemology, he had, it was feared, set forth a wholly inadequate system of ethics—or, some thought, none in fact at all. Practical morality, according to him, depends on the fear of eternal punishment threatened by the Supreme Being for those who disobey His revealed will.[23] Shaftesbury, the disciple of the Cambridge Platonists, objected to the proposition that good and evil are not absolutes but rather mere arbitrary commandments of God, which to be known, must be revealed. Certainly it seemed, further, if good and evil are absolutes, they must have their representative faculty in man's mind; he surely is not left helpless to drift without a moral rudder. Much of Shaftesbury's aversion to his teacher Locke arises from his horror of Locke's calloused attitude towards the moral problem. Yet the calm confidence which earlier philosophers, such as Lord Herbert of Cherbury, had displayed in innate ideas, was no more. How, without invoking a supernatural and mystical power, could the absolute standard of right and wrong be brought into relation to human life?

The solution lay at hand in the adaptation of Locke's own system to moral idealism of the kind Henry More had displayed. If the mind perceives the connection, repugnance, etc., of ideas derived from sensation, why should not this process apply to morality as well? Why should not the mind perceive the harmony or repugnance of images of action and passions, just as it perceives the difference between a triangle and a circle? And so Shaftesbury, in the *Inquiry concerning Virtue,* combines the two:

> In a Creature capable of forming general Notions of things, not only the sensible things that offer themselves to the sense, are the objects of the Affections; but the very *actions* themselves, and the affections of Pity, Charity, Kindness, Justice, and so their contraries, being brought into the Mind by reflection, become Objects; . . .[24]

The imagination, as in Locke, makes possible the action; the similarity to Locke's "perception" is evident.

> And thus the several Motions, Inclinations, Passions, Dispositions and consequent Carriage and Behavior of Creatures in the various Parts of Life, being in several scenes represented to the Mind, which readily discerns the good and the ill towards the species or Public; it proves afterwards a new work for the affection, either virtuously and soundly to incline to, and affect what is just and right; and disaffect what is contrary; or, vitiously and corruptly to affect what is ill, and disregard or hate what is worthy and good.

The actual "moral sense" is not in itself an emotion. It is an action of the mind in viewing the "several scenes" of behavior, etc.; the affections follow, and should be properly related as effect to cause. Shaftesbury implies that the actual recognition of good and evil is in itself sound. The process goes wrong when the affections get out of kilter with the perceptions, and the wrong passion, or the right passion to excess becomes attached to an intuition. But a powerful natural impulse should produce the normal kind of reaction: the reflex action must be distorted by long habit before it goes wrong. The affection in turn is a drive to action. Here of course something like instrumental reason has its place. The affection may produce the right intention but, because of poor judgment, inappropriate action may be taken. It is important, nevertheless, to recognize that "reason" here is a means of implementation rather than the judicial governor of basic decisions.

Shaftesbury's conception of the affections also clearly shows the influence of Locke. The latter reduced emotion to pleasure and pain, which he identified with good and evil for the individual.[25] Things, whether experienced in the present or only as images in reflection, produce thoughts of pain and pleasure, and "our ideas of love and hatred are but the dispositions of the mind, in respect of pleasure and pain in general, however caused in us." The various emotions—love, joy, sorrow, etc.,—are states of mind, "easiness" or "uneasiness." These conscious states of pleasure or pain enable us, among other things, to be sure that we exist separately from the objects which we perceive. Locke even hints at a kind of moral sense: shame, he says, "is an uneasiness of the mind upon the thought of having done something which is indecent, or will lessen the valued esteem which others have for us," and a father delighting in the well-being of his children need only call up that idea into reflection to have pleasure.

Locke, however, had separated knowledge from moral decisions. Morality, he did admit, may be theoretically as certain as knowledge—but only when moral propositions are abstractions.

> And hence it follows that moral knowledge is as capable of real certainty as mathematics. For certainty being but the perception of the agreement or disagreement of our ideas, and demonstration nothing but the perception of such agreement, by the intervention of other ideas or mediums; our moral ideas, as well as mathematical, being archetypes themselves, and so adequate and complete ideas; all the agreement or disagreement which we shall find in them will produce real knowledge, as well as in mathematical figures.[26]

But of course Locke is speaking only of "archetypes," abstracted from concrete events. The kind of adaptation of archetype to experience which Kant was to make lay far in the future, but Shaftesbury as well as other philosophers groped for something of the kind. They thought they had found what they wanted in the seeming fact that men have a capacity for observing the "harmony" among images of passions and actions as certain as their capacity for knowing the existence and differences between things of the outside world. Such a belief fitted in perfectly with the rising conviction that the universe is a great system in which each smallest part operates in perfect mathematical harmony with all the other parts. It is not surprising that Shaftesbury thought there could be an "arithmetic" of the moral sense.

The later versions of the *Inquiry* and other works, however, contain a very important modification of the "moral sense." At first Shaftesbury seemed to identify it with Locke's third, "complex" form of understanding. Later he suggested that moral ideas are more like Locke's first class of perception, so immediate and direct are the impressions they make on the mind.

> Is there then, said he, a natural Beauty of *Figures*, and is there not as natural a one of ACTIONS? No sooner the Eye opens upon *Figures*, the Ear to *Sounds*, than straight the *Beautiful* results, and *Grace* and *Harmony* are known and acknowledged. No sooner are ACTIONS view'd no sooner the *human Affections* and *Passions* discern'd (and they are most of 'em as soon discern'd as felt) than straight *an inward* EYE distinguishes and sees the *Fair* and *Shapely*, the *amiable* and *Admirable*, apart from the Deform'd *the Foul, the Odious*, or *the Despicable*. . . .[27]

The addition of the analogy with aesthetic experience makes it even clearer that the "moral sense" is a naturalized "spiritual eye" of the kind More and others had described. The point is even more emphatic in the later editions of the *Inquiry*, which have three added paragraphs, beginning as follows:

> The Case is the same in the *mental* or *moral* subjects, as in the ordinary *Bodys*, or common Subjects of *Sense*. The Shapes, Motions, Colours, and Proportions of these latter being presented to our Eye; there naturally results a Beauty or Deformity, according to the different Measure, Arrrangement, and Disposition of their several Parts. . . .[28]

In the next of these added paragraphs, Shaftesbury tells us that the mind is continually observing other minds; in the third, that as the forms and images of things continually move before our senses, "even when we sleep" (a statement obviously suggested by Locke) so the forms and images of the "moral and intellectual kind" continually move before the mind, even when the objects themselves are absent.

The extremely "aesthetic" form of the moral sense theory, then, was an afterthought in Shaftesbury, but it is the form in which his theory is best known. He was not the first to suggest such an analogy.[29] There may be several reasons for the desire to reduce the moral sense to a reflex so immediate. For one thing, the age increasingly was impressed by the essential importance of the direct sense impression.

The fashion for study of epistemology itself betrays this preoccupation, as well as the central place given images in thinking. Again, in this time the standards of taste, at least on the level of forms, seemed absolutely decisive; More, to take one example, often appeals to aesthetic comparisons to make more nebulous matters seem clear-cut. Finally, the desire to take the moral intuition out of the field of "ratiocination" altogether, to remove it from any possible contamination by innate ideas, would tend to make the analogy with immediate sensation tempting.

Many questions remained unanswered. There was, most difficult of all, still the problem of relativism. Granted that there is some kind of innate potentiality for sensing good and bad, are its contents really absolute and immutable, even where development of the personality has been "natural"? These issues, as we shall see, were to prove more than troublesome. But Shaftesbury had made his contribution by combining in a system the deepest desires and beliefs of his age. He had effectually severed morality from righteousness; the supernatural had been absorbed into the natural. He had furthered the process by which, as Panofsky has said, the dualism between Christian and classical "ceased to be real, . . . because the very principle of reality was shifted to the subjective human consciousness."[30]

2

Consequences of the first importance follow from the new *kind* of thinking about man and society and the universe which I have sketched, and in no field more than in literature. In this section I shall try to outline very generally a few of the results of the position Shaftesbury represents (though not necessarily Shaftesbury's direct influence), as we see them in some eighteenth century writing. The full consequences of great changes in thought do not become evident until some time after they have taken place, and the examples cited not unnaturally come several decades after Shaftesbury's death.

Attention has been so completely concentrated on Shaftesbury's "natural goodness" theory that few realize how much of his work is devoted to the study of the "ill" in human nature (the very term is significant in that he does not use "evil" or "sin"). A reading of the *Inquiry*, however, reveals a catalogue of something like case studies in abnormal psychology, presented with an acuteness of insight and a sympathetic power which deserve recognition. Perhaps it was in this field that Shaftesbury was most "original." His two main contributions may be, first, the conception of undesirable behavior as "maladjustment"—to use a modern term; and second, the call for study of states of mind in themselves, impartially and so to speak from within.

The cause of "unsocial" behavior, as we have seen, is described as the disharmony of the moral perception with the drives to action. Shaftesbury's immediate purpose was to show, by imaginative presentation of states of mind, that these dislocations of the personality produce an "uneasiness" such as Locke describes. Thus Shaftesbury departed from the tradition of morality handbooks, with their listings of virtues and vices considered with relation to a given natural or divine law. He did preserve the names of the virtues and vices, but they are only specialized forms of two great basic impulses. In a broader sense Shaftesbury attempted to study the personality to find what causes produce such results—logically enough if the villain is not the will but the external factors which have warped the growth of the mind. Thus he stands in the tradition of objective study of nature—which from Bacon's time on included as a desideratum the natural history of man. The reform of an ill society would require first of all clearing away the false notions about man which have caused infinite mischief. The principal source of "ill" states of mind is the undue strengthening of man's natural and in its place wholly desirable impulse of self-interest. Shaftesbury, describing the basic impulses as self-love and the social sense, combined the two great views of ethics in the Restoration period: the Hobbesian and the Latitudinarian. His style is adapted to the gradations of this self-interest: as he proceeds through the forms which its excess may take, ranging from the slight to the pathological, there is an increasing emotional tension; and at the last, with the "unnatural" emotions, we experience unrelieved horror, which arises from participation with the experiencing mind itself. No one can read these descriptions and feel that the author is the complacent aristocrat of fable.

The progress is from something like "neuroses" to the "psychopathic." Locke pointed out, as he discussed association of ideas, that we all have vagaries in our thinking; the difference between our everyday eccentricities and madness is one of degree. Much the same kind of distinction applies to Shaftesbury's division of the "ill" emotions into those which merely represent over-action of self-interest and those in which the drives to action have become twisted into something tragically self-defeating.

> Now if these SELFISH PASSIONS, besides what other ill they are the occasion of, are withal the certain means of losing us our *natural Affections*; then 'tis evident, That they must be the certain means of losing us the chief Enjoyment of Life, and raising in us those horrid

and unnatural Passions, and that Savageness of Temper, which makes the Greatest of Miseries, and the most wretched State of Life.[31]

Shaftesbury's isolation of sadism as a psychopathological condition and his serious interest in it, which anticipates later developments in literature, is an example of his method:

> To see the Sufferance of an Enemy with Cruel Delight may proceed from the height of Anger, Revenge, Fear, and other extended Self-Passions: But to delight in the Torture and pain of other Creatures indifferently, Natives or Foreigners, of our own or of another Species, Kindred or no Kindred, known or unknown; to feed, as it were, on Death, and be entertain'd with dying agonys. . . .[32]

He asks whether the unnatural passions may not carry with them a sort of pleasure, barbarous as it is—nevertheless a real kind of satisfaction, from tyranny, sadism, and the like. He grants that this is the fact, but going in subtlety far beyond the crude analysis of Hobbes, finds it is the very perversion of the mind that produces the pleasure:

> For as the cruellest bodily Pains do by Intervals of Assuagement, produce (as has been shewn) the highest bodily Pleasure; so the fiercest and most raging Torments of the Mind, do, by certain Moments of Relief, afford the greatest of mental Enjoyments, to those who know little of the truer kind.[33]

Such a theory is susceptible of other interpretations, however, and this fact perhaps as much as anything illustrates the real weakness in an ethics grounded on the subjective consciousness. The pleasures of perversity were to provide material for the "Satanist" school of writers. The parallel of physical and mental pleasure and pain, and the obvious implication that the most intense pleasure can derive from the extreme pathological, could have startling results. How can we distinguish "true" from "false" pleasure if the test is the quantity of sensation: how can one be "falser" than the other? Shaftesbury's own "arithmetic" of the moral sense would betray him here. Not without reason did Archibald Campbell ridicule the pretensions of those "refined spirits" who affect to follow only a "disinterested moral sense," for, as Campbell says, the self-approval which follows a generous action provides a pleasure and is the real motive of action, however loftily disguised.[34]

Shaftesbury's rhetoric in his character sketches often anticipates later developments in literature. His subsequent shortening and smoothing of the following passage from the 1699 edition of the *Inquiry*, for example, obscure its kinship of mood and language and imagery with descriptions of heroic villains we find in later romantic fiction:

> How thorow and deep must that Melancholy be, where there is nothing softning or pleasing from the side of Friendship to allay or divert it when once risen: no flattering view or imagination of kindness, or affection from any part; but where every thing around is gastly and horrid, every thing in appearance hostile, and, as it were, *bent* against a privat and single being, who is divided from, and at war with the rest of Nature, in a disagreement and irreconciliation with every thing, and with the Order and Government of the Universe? 'Tis thus at last that a Mind becomes a Wilderness where all is laid waste, everything fair and goodly remov'd, and nothing extant but what is dismal and horrid. Now if any thing that but looks desert, or that feels like banishment or expulsion from human Commerce, be so heavy to bear; what must it be to be thus estranged from Mankind, and to be after this manner in a Desert, and in the horridest of Solitudes, even when in the midst of Society; and to live with Mankind as with a foren Species and as with those Creatures that are most remote from Man, and such as he has the most cause to fear?[35]

But there is a deep contradiction in the very use of "unnatural" to describe pathological states of mind. How, in a universe perfectly planned and operating, can there be anything not ultimately harmonious? Shaftesbury was one of the philosopers who encouraged that intoxication with the Whole which was to lead to Voltaire's bitter protest in the letter on the Lisbon earthquake. There must be a "*Resignation*, . . . a Sacrifice and mutual yielding of Natures one to another," and all "Inferiour Natures" must be subjected to the "Superiour Nature of the World." "The Central Powers, which hold the lasting Orbs in their just Poize and Movement, must not be controul'd to save a fleeting Form, and rescue from the Precipice a puny Animal. . . ."[36] Some such scheme, it appears operates in the human as well as all other systems, and the intersection of the majestic, impersonal forces can produce there, too, what seem to finite eyes disasters. He does suggest, with a sly trace of raillery, that even those who see nature as imperfect may have their use. " 'Twas not its [nature's] Intention to leave us without some Pattern of Imperfection; such as we perceive in Minds like these, perplex'd with froward thought."[37]

The theory has, however, a very important potentiality. The study of the "ill" in all its varieties is a means of determining, by contrast, what is "natural." Literary theory soon reflected the concept. But the theory, like others of Shaftesbury's, could be carried to lengths of which the moralist never dreamed. It is one thing to rise to the level of the great over-all Plan and ask with Pope

> If plagues or earthquakes break not Heav'n's design,
> Why then a Borgia, or a Catiline?

It is quite another to look at the matter from the viewpoint of the Borgia or the Catiline, as we do in this passage from the Marquis de Sade:

> C'étaient des monstres, m'objectent les sots. Oui, selon nos moeurs et nôtre façon de penser; mais relativement aux grandes vue de la nature sur nous, ils m'étaient que les instruments de ses desseins; c'était pour accomplir ses lois qu'elle les avait doués de ses caractères féroces et sanguinaires.[38]

Is not the "monster," in being a monster, living according to his nature, and is he not therefore among the new enlightened who seek the "natural"?

The necessity for sympathetic, imaginative representations of the mind and experience is a vital part of Shaftesbury's philosophy. Of the early philosophical writings which Horace mentions in the *Ars Poetica*, he says:

> 'Twas not enough that these Pieces treated fundamentally of *Morals,* and in consequence pointed out *real Characters* and *Manners:* They exhibited 'em *alive,* and set the Countenances and Complexions of Men plainly in view. And by this means they not only taught us to know *Others;* but, what was principal and of highest virtue in 'em, they taught us to know Our-selves.[39]

The best poet, Shaftesbury tells an author to whom he addresses "Advice,"

> describes no Qualitys or Virtues; censures no Manners: makes no Encomium, nor gives Characters himself; but brings his actors still in view. 'Tis they who shew themselves. For the poet is a second Maker: a just PROMETHEUS, under Jove.[40]

He is a maker, because, like the Deity, he is a "moral Artist," and it is a fundamental principle in Shaftesbury that the world is to be considered as a work of art. The creation of the poet presents through the imagination a series of scenes, appealing through artful arrangement to the moral sense; the business of the poet is to present the scenes so effectively that the sense will operate of itself, and he should not tell in so many words and abstractions what the "moral" is. Distinguishing the "unnatural" from the "natural" therefore is a matter of arousing response and not giving formal instruction. Aesthetic form is inseparable from truth as images are from thought. One of Shaftesbury's principal differences from his old tutor Locke is the fact that the one was by nature aesthetic in response, the other not; but it was, as we have seen, Locke's own epistemology, with its basis of "perception," that did a vital service in promoting the cult of the imagination. Shaftesbury here as elsewhere began to draw out the consequences of this epistemology.

These forms of art supplement and extend our primary source of knowledge about man—ourselves. Even that "rectification" of society which so much concerned Shaftesbury is found to depend in considerable part on introspection.

> But the knowledg of our Passions in their very Seeds, the measuring well the Growth and Progress of Enthusiasm, and the judging rightly of its natural Force . . . may teach us to oppose more successfully those Delusions which . . . come arm'd with the specious Pretext of moral certainty. . . .[41]

Thus Shaftesbury cast his *Advice to an Author* as a "solioquy," a form to which he gives the highest praise. He expands the Socratic tradition of "Know thyself." Not meditations or essays written with one eye on the audience, he says—but true soliloquy, self-examination to the very depths of the soul, is what is needed. One thinks involuntarily of Rousseau's *Confessions.* He praises *Hamlet* in a significant but neglected piece of criticism as "one continu'd *Moral:* a Series of deep Reflections, drawn from *one* Mouth, upon the Subject of *one* single Accident and Calamity naturally fitted to move Horrour and Compassion."[42] Here, it may be, is the beginning of the change in the tradition of *Hamlet* criticism, wherein the play moves from a tragedy of action to that of an inward and subjective revelation, the "*one*" absorbing everything.

In this tradition is the critic William Richardson, who came much later in the century and was influenced by such followers of Shaftesbury as Lord Kames and Reid (although he refers to Shaftesbury directly, too). In the Introduction to the *Lectures on Shakespeare's Dramatic Characters,* he dilates upon the points made briefly in Shaftesbury. Our "internal feelings" are the beginning of our understanding of human nature. But they are far from sufficient to give us the insight we need.

> We judge of mankind by referring their actions to the passions and principles that influence our own behaviour. We have no other guide, since the nature of the passions and faculties of the mind are [*sic*] not discernible by the senses.[43]

Shaftesbury had lightly assumed that we continually observe other minds, recreating their experience as our inner sense observes the "scenes" representing their characteristics and qualities. But this simple idea, like so many derived from Locke, had all manner of complexities lurking in it. Shaftesbury himself suggested that we need the second maker under Jove to extend our knowledge. Richardson explains that there are many barriers between our minds and those of others. We ourselves are seldom "indifferent" while we observe others; we are biassed, and we can seldom see all that is going on from external actions and signs; our memories are fallible; and the emotions which are weak in us are strong in others, and *vice versa,* so that we unconsciously distort our picture of others' characters.

> If we measure the minds of others precisely by our own, . . . our theories must necessarily be inadequate. But, by considering the copy and portrait of minds different from our own, and by reflecting on these latent and unexerted principles, augmented and promoted by imagination, we may discover many new tints, and uncommon features. Now, that class of poetical writers that excel by imitating the passions, might contribute in this respect to rectify and enlarge the sentiments of the philosopher; and if so, they would have the additional merit of conducting us to the temple of truth, by an easier and more agreeable path, than mere metaphysics.[44]

Thus carrying observers, so to speak, into the very minds of other personalities—as wide a range of personalities as possible—becomes a primary function of art. This vicarious introspection sets, moreover, a new task for literature, one which powerfully encourages a "psychological" approach.

It was inevitable that Shakespeare should become the ideal poet of this new ideal kind. His principal characters come to be seen as types of the relations between the social passions, self-interest, and society; his method is praised as the pattern of that sympathetic imagination which was essential to the poet. A new school of criticism came into being: "An exercise no less adapted to improve the heart, than to inform the understanding," Richardson boasts of his essays. The kind of effect the poet is to produce is indicated in a famous passage from another pioneer critic of this group:

> The reader will perceive that I distinguish between *mental impressions* and the *understanding*. . . . There are none of us unconscious of certain feelings or sensations of mind, which do not seem to have passed through the understanding; the effects, I suppose, of some secret influences from without, acting upon a certain mental sense,

> and producing feelings and passions in just correspondence to the force and variety of those influences on the one hand, and to the quickness of our sensibility on the other.[45]

The conception that poetry may produce "certain feelings or sensations of mind, which do not seem to have passed through the understanding" owes much, I think it is clear, to the kind of thinking Shaftesbury did so much to inaugurate.

The new critical method may be seen at work in relation to a peculiar problem which arose from the new secularized Pelagianism. If the fall is really the fall of society, what becomes of those rare spirits who seemingly cannot do anything other than live according to nature—what becomes of them in a world where the great majority live "out of all rule and proportion"? That there is an aesthetic value in this situation Shaftesbury himself hinted.

> The very Disturbances which belong to natural Affection, though they may be wholly contrary to Pleasure, yield still a Contentment and Satisfaction greater than the Pleasures of indulg'd Sense. . . . We continue pleas'd even with this melancholy Aspect or Sense of Virtue. Her Beauty supports it-self under a Cloud, and in the midst of surrounding Calamitys.[46]

The problem is twofold. There is the conflict of the natural man with an unnatural world, and there is the difficulty of ascertaining a desirable balance between sensibility and self-interest. Shaftesbury unmistakably implies that in some cases unbalance of the moral sense and the emotions is due to temperament; there may be need for patterns of imperfection, and he suggests, again, that the moral sense may be too tender. May there be need, also, for patterns of perfection?

Hamlet soon became the image of this dilemma. Mackenzie, who probably led the way in the "sentimental" interpretation of this hero, explains that

> Naturally of the most virtuous and most amiable disposition, the circumstances in which he was placed unhinged those principles of action which, in another situation, would have delighted mankind, and made himself happy. Finding such a character in real life, of a person endowed with feelings so delicate as to border on weakness, with sensibility too exquisite to allow of determined action, he has placed it where it could be best exhibited, in scenes of wonder, of terror, and of indignation, where its varying emotions might be most strongly marked amidst the workings of imagination, and the war of the passions.[47]

Hamlet is, indeed, as Mackenzie says, a new kind of tragedy if we accept this interpretation. The plot and the other characters are reduced to mere contrasting "scenes" against which the sensibility of the hero is exhibited.

In *Mirror* No. 39 Mackenzie goes so far as to suggest that the fall of society is responsible for many of the most affecting tragedies. Unfortunately, "honest ambition" for recognition is accompanied by "delicacy of taste and sentiment" out of place in the present world. In earlier times, when mankind was uncorrupted by excessive luxury and refinement, there could be confidence that recognition would be given where it was due; but now a man of true worth, seeing himself set aside in favor of the worthless and contemptible, gives way to despair, and is "in danger of changing . . . into a morose and surly misanthrope." Mackenzie implies that reason is a power of the mind, one of many potentialities which can be "brought into action as chance or circumstances direct." In the imperfect state of society in which we find ourselves, it is the part of prudence to adjust ourselves with cheerfulness and good humor (the Shaftesburian tone is obvious in the emphasis on these qualities) and "firmly rise above injustice, and refuse to retreat into the passive virtues."

Perhaps it is the absence of the revolutionary or even reforming spirit that is the keynote to Mackenzie's puzzling combination of idealistic sensibility and hard-headed prudence. He condemns at once the unnatural society and the fine spirit who is too "natural" for it. The story of Emilia (*Mirror* No. 101), a girl whose "delicacy and fineness of feeling" lead her to an irreconcilable conflict with Mrs. Grundy, produces no more than an effect of hysterical emotion; the difficulty arises from the ambivalence of the author's attitude, which is at once passionately sympathetic with the sensitive heroine and condemnatory of her perfect sensibility. We miss the single effect of melancholy beauty which unfallen goodness in a fallen society could produce. The Man of Feeling himself represents the dilemma. He has had, significantly, a sheltered life, his remarkable moral sense has unfolded without obstacle, and from his conflict with a selfish and cruel society Mackenzie tries to extract the essence of tragedy. The situation is presented during the stagecoach conversation of chapter 33. The stranger enthusiastically maintains that the "poetical inclination" has at least one advantage—"the causes of human depravity vanish before the romantic enthusiasm [the poet] professes, and many who are not able to reach the Parnassian heights, may yet approach so near as to be bettered by the air of the climate." To which the now disillusioned Harley replies: "I have always thought so; but this is an argument of the prudent against it; they urge the danger of unfitness for the world." The suggestion that the poet, although hopelessly ineffectual in the world as it is, may yet have his function as a "pattern of perfection" both etherealizes the nature of poetry and emphasizes its evocative rather than its communicative aspect.

Richardson's essay on the character of Hamlet shows the relation of his view to the Shaftesbury school:

> On reviewing the analysis now given, a sense of virtue, if I may use the language of an eminent philosopher, without professing myself of his sect, seems to be the ruling principle in the character of Hamlet. In other men, it may appear with the ensigns of high authority: in Hamlet, it possesses absolute power.[48]

So delicate is this sense of virtue that it governs his every action, his every personal relation:

> It even sharpens his penetration; and, if unexpectedly he discerns turpitude or impropriety in any character, it inclines him to think more deeply of their transgression, than if his sentiments were less refined. . . . As it excites uncommon pain and abhorrence on the appearance of perfidious and inhuman actions, it provokes and stimulates his resentment; yet, attentive to justice, and concerned in the interests of human nature, it governs the impetuosity of that unruly passion.

Hamlet's sufferings caused by this acute sensibility occupy an essay devoted to the paradox of the pathological "amiable." The whole play takes on a new character, and to go from Johnson's criticism, with its concern about plot, characterization and outcome, to that of Richardson is to go from one age to another. In Richardson's analysis is the germ of the melancholy of Werther, and there is the anticipation of his death: one can hardly escape the suspicion that Richardson and Mackenzie secretly feel that suicide would have been a really appropriate ending to the play. Strange dilemma! That the most "natural," the most harmonious and sensitive to moral beauty, should so fail, so come to cross purposes with the order of the world! "We love, we almost revere the character of Hamlet; and grieve for his sufferings. But we must at the same time confess, that his weaknesses, are the cause of his disappointments and early death."

That a strong sensibility produces "weakness" in action became a commonplace. In Thomas Whately's *Remarks on Some of the Characters of Shakespeare* it even transforms Macbeth. This critic, significantly, tells us that the emphasis on "fable" in criticism is erroneous, and that "character" is the real center of a play.[49] In line with this principle, he studies *Macbeth* and *Richard III*. The former hero he finds to be a "man of sensibility" led astray by what Shaftesbury would have called the "zeal" introduced by the weird sisters' suggestions. He shows indecision and fear everywhere, as is to be expected from a man of "gentle and amiable qualities." Richard, on the other hand, shows firmness and courage, for he "is totally destitute of every softer feeling."[50] Irresolute, showing the "symptoms of a feeble mind," Macbeth is yet, in an absolute sense, by far the more admirable, for he has a strong sense of virtue, whereas Richard has none. It is not merely the conflict within himself that weakens Macbeth, moreover; it would be easy to turn him the other way and see a Hamlet in him. The conclusion is that the noblest of men are by a strange paradox the weakest of men, and that a strong moral sense means an inevitably tragic life.

More celebrated theories of Hamlet carry on these themes. The sense of the fatal conflict of highly developed sensibility with real facts underlies Goethe's account of the hero, in *Wilhelm Meister*. "The feeling for the good and graceful," we learn, "had unfolded in him together with his consciousness of his high birth." The natural development is strongly emphasized; he was "polished by nature, courteous from the heart." But such a soul, so perfect in itself, comes into inevitable conflict with the necessity for action, for he "is endowed more properly with sentiment than with a character." Hamlet is, when we consider the setting of the discussion in the novel, plainly the image of that conflict which Mackenzie's stranger in the stagecoach suggests.

Coleridge's view is more purely psychological, and more straightforwardly analyzes Hamlet in terms going back to Shaftesbury's modification of the Locke epistemology. There must, in the healthy mind, be a balance between "the impressions of outward objects and the inward operations of the intellect: if there be an overbalance in the contemplative faculty, man becomes the creature of meditation, and loses the power of action."[51] The *Notes on the Tragedies of Shakespeare* makes the process more explicit. "In Hamlet this balance does not exist—his thoughts, images and fancy being far more vivid than his perceptions, and his very perceptions instantly passing thro' the medium of his contemplations, and acquiring as they pass a form and color not naturally their own."[52] It is logical that the stream of images passing before the inner sense could be too vivid and be transformed too much in the process of imaginative working.

The function of Shakespeare thus appeared in a new light. Coleridge sees Shakespeare as providing those "patterns of imperfection" which the new philosophy of man called for: "conceiving characters out of his own intellectual and moral faculties, by conceiving any one intellectual or moral faculty in morbid excess and then placing himself, thus mutilated and diseased, under given circumstances." Among the important results of this new criticism were lifting characters out of plays and making them, as it were, living beings—represented by the tendency to write separate studies of Shakespeare's *dramatis personae;* and the increasing decline of emphasis on dramatic action as such, implicit in Shaftesbury's remark about *Hamlet's* being a long soliloquy and culminating in the romantic aversion to seeing Shakespeare's plays performed. The distant descendant of the theory of the function of the poet is, perhaps, to be seen in T.S. Eliot's theory of the "objective correlative," in his remark that

> If you examine any of Shakespeare's more successful tragedies, you will find this exact equivalence; you will find that the state of mind of Lady Macbeth walking in her sleep has been communicated to you by a skilful accumulation of imagined sensory impressions; the words of Macbeth on hearing of his wife's death strike us as if, given the sequence of events, these words were automatically released by the last event in the series.

Communication of a state of mind by "imagined sensory impressions" is indeed in keeping with Shaftesbury's vision of the poet as a "second maker under Jove"; vicarious experience is the purpose of poetry.

If Hamlet was the supreme symbol of the tragedy of the natural in a degenerate world, there was another figure who as a kind of foil was to loom especially large in romantic literature. William Richardson adumbrates the type in describing Jaques as the frustrated benevolist, but one whose mental history has been different from that of Hamlet. Even the prince, in whom the conflict of his sense of virtue with society is the ruling principle, eventually is led into violence; but his hesitations are "amiable." In Jaques, on the other hand, the result of frustration of a keen sense of benevolence has been less amiable. Richardson starts from the doctrine of the "ruling passion." What if the dominating impulse in a person is the "social and beneficent Affections," and what if those affections are so strong as to be irresistible—and then, as they come into conflict with an uncongenial, selfish world, are twisted into evil ways? The result of this thwarting of the "natural" will be misanthropy. The social affections lead men to society, and society being what it is, to dissipations and regrets. Jaques accordingly turned into a "dissipated and sensual libertine," and, like la Rochefoucauld's old roué (but for different reasons) into a gloomy moralist as well. This "white" melancholy (as distinguished from the "black" melancholy of the true villain) is, then, really a good impulse perverted by its contact with a world to which it should be suited, but, because of the evil of society, is not.[53]

The Byronic hero, I might suggest, often shows this kind of thwarting of the exceptional moral sense.

> With more capacity for love than earth
> Bestows on most of mortal mould and birth,
> His early dreams of good outstripp'd the truth,
> And troubled manhood follow'd baffled youth;
> With thought of years in phantom chase misspent,
> And wasted powers for better purpose lent; . . .
> Too high for common selfishness, he could
> At times resign his own for others' good,
> But not in pity, not because he ought,
> But in some strange perversity of thought,
> That sway'd him onward with a secret pride,
> To do what few or none would do beside. . . .[54]

The few examples sketched above give some idea of the changes which the complex of thought which Shaftesbury pioneered could produce. All of them assume the continued existence of the system of society as it exists. Obviously, however, another road was open. Could it be that a "root and branch" reformation of the social order is necessary to release the supposed normal state of mankind? It would be outside the limits of this paper to show that there is little in Rousseau that is not in Shaftesbury also, but that the French moralist carries things much farther than does the English one. Both were optimists in a deeper sense; it is not that all *is* well, but that all *can* be well in society. They both declare the eternal possibility of living "NATURALLY, and as a MAN." The enchanting prospect they offer is that nature is always before and within men, divinely harmonious, beautiful and serene, and that every generation, if it will only awaken from the nightmare dreams of the past, can find happiness and freedom in this life and on this earth.

NOTES

[1] Two recent books deal with Shaftesbury and his influence: A. O. Aldridge, *Shaftesbury and the Deist Manifesto* (Transactions of the American Philosophical Society, 1951); and R. L. Brett, *The Third Earl of Shaftesbury* (London, 1951). Since these studies, as well as the still essential book of Fowler, *Shaftesbury and Hutcheson,* give detailed accounts of this author's life and writings, I am not repeating this material. I am trying only to suggest a new interpretation of Shaftesbury's relationship to his own time, especially to the Cambridge Platonists and to Locke, and to suggest some new lines which study of his influence may take. In suggesting these lines I am not trying to define direct and exact "sources," but rather significant changes which the *kind* of thinking Shaftesbury pioneered helped to produce. It is to be remembered, however, that we can assume nearly every educated man of the eighteenth century had some acquaintance with the *Characteristics* of Lord Shaftesbury, just as nearly every educated person today has some acquaintance with the writings of, say, John Dewey.

[2] "Shaftesbury and the Ethical Poets in England, 1700-1760," *PMLA*, 31 (1916), 264 ff.; and see also W. E. Alderman, "Shaftesbury and the Doctrine of Moral Sense in the Eighteenth Century," *PMLA*, 46 (1931), 1087 ff.

[3] "Suggestions toward a Genealogy of the 'Man of Feeling,'" *ELH*, 1 (1934), 207.

[4] See F. E. L. Priestley, "Newton and the Romantic Concept of Nature," *UTQ*, 17 (1948), 323 ff.; Miss Marjorie Nicolson's books, especially *The Breaking of the Circle* (Evanston, 1950); and an article of the writer, "Space, Diety, and the 'Natural Sublime,'" in *MLQ,* March 1951.

[5] Pages 9-10.

[6] P. 55.

[7] *Ibid.*, pp. 156-8.

[8] *Works of Isaac Barrow,* ed. Tillotson (London, 1696), II: 107-8.

[9] *Ibid.*, 105.

[10] *Ibid.*, I: 11-12.

[11] *Ibid.*, I: 356.

[12] *A Demonstration of the Divine Authority of the Law of Nature, and of the Christian Religion* (London, 1681), 55.

[13] *Ibid.*, 5.

[14] Archbishop Tenison, for example, contrasts the "generous Spirit of Charity," a soul that animates society and makes it possible, with the self-love which is becoming all too prevalent; but this state of affairs is to be expected since St. Paul predicted that "the nigher [men] are to the Last Judgment, the more Criminal they grow." *A Sermon against Self-Love* (London, 1689), 12. It is Christian charity, not benevolence, of which he speaks, and it cannot be equated with the social feeling of Shaftesbury or Rousseau. The idea that the growth of self-interest argues the approach of the Judgment, furthermore, is a very old one among theologians. Again, we find one of the most "liberal" of the Latitudinarians, Archbishop Tillotson, describing how God in His mercy has provided, by the "abundance and *Grace* of the Gospel, so powerful a *Remedy* for this hereditary Disease of our corrupt and de-

generate Nature." *Six Sermons,* 2d ed. (London, 1694), 51. It is "common humanity," to be sure, that makes us concerned for the welfare of our families, etc., but this fact does not argue innate goodness of men.

[15] *The Pursuits of Happiness* (London, 1771).

[16] It is interesting to note that Tillotson carefully guards himself against the imputation of this heresy by emphasizing that the "disease of the depravity of human nature" is transmitted by traduction, from parent to child, and not by imitation. His student Thomas Burnet was one of the first to go the whole way in saying that the fall was a gradual affair, really consisting in the corruption of society.

[17] *Inquiry concerning Virtue,* p. 99. This first, "imperfect" edition, now extremely rare, published though it was without Shaftesbury's knowledge, often gives us more immediately and more impressively the very spirit of its author than does the later, "polished" *Inquiry concerning Virtue, or Merit* as published in the *Characteristics.*

[18] *Characteristics* (London, 1737), II. 252.

[19] *An Account of Virtue: Or, Dr. Henry More's Abridgment of Morals, Put into English,* tr. Edward Southwell (London, 1690), 11.

[20] This assumption may be the most serious fault in Mr. Brett's recent book on Shaftesbury—which otherwise has many acute insights. To oppose Shaftesbury as the champion of the belief that perception involves a "creative process" over against Locke as the philosopher of "passive association" seems to me misleading. The close connection of Shaftesbury's theory with Locke's epistemology has not, so far as I know, been pointed out. Locke in fact is the fountain head of the two great schools of thought about the mental life; on one side, he leads to the romantic psychology and ethics inaugurated by Shaftesbury—on the other, to the Hartley associationist school, depending on which element in his thought is stressed at the expense of the other.

[21] *An Essay concerning Human Understanding,* ed. A. C. Fraser (Oxford, 1914), II: xxi: 5.

[22] The implications for literature of this yoking of the image to thought are of course incalculable. Shaftesbury and Addison immediately show the results. Philocles, in Shaftesbury's *The Moralists,* says that he must have a "kind of material Object," an "Image" in mind before he can love a person or an abstraction; he has been in love, for example, with the "People of old Rome" under the form of a beautiful youth "call'd *the* GENIUS *of the People.*" *Characteristics,* II: 242 ff. This should be the lower rung of the Platonic ladder of beauty, which should ascend to the immaterial pure Idea, but the ladder is never completed. Later, when Shaftesbury presents his very important idea of the organic unity of the universe, he cites as an authority Locke's *Essay,* IV: vi: 11, where it is shown that we cannot understand the essence of any object unless we perceive its intricate physical integration into the workings of the universal machine; we perceive a collection of related images. See *The Moralists,* in *ed. cit.,* II: 285 ff. And in one of the most significant passages of all Shaftesbury's works, in the late *Miscellaneous Reflections,* he sets forth his version of the "scale or catalogue of beauty" (the equivalence of the terms is interesting for a Platonist) in the form of greater and greater combinations of

images into patterns, in both the animate and inanimate worlds. *Ed. Cit.*, III: 182-3, footnote. The spirit, the enthusiasm, the language, are Neoplatonic, but the substance has much of Locke in it.

[23] On the objections to Locke's ethics, see my article "The Origins of the 'Moral Sense,'" in *HLQ*, XI (1948), 241-59.

[24] P. 27.

[25] *Essay*, II: xx.

[26] *Essay*, IV: iv: 7.

[27] *The Moralists*, in *Characteristics*, II: 414 f.

[28] *Characteristics*, II: 28 ff.

[29] Thomas Burnet, in three pamphlets directed against Locke (first in 1697, the second and third in 1699), appears to have originated the comparison. He wrote in 1697: "This I am sure of, that the Distinction, suppose of Gratitude and Ingratitude, Fidelity, and Infidelity, . . . and such others, is as sudden without any Ratiocination, and as sensible and piercing, as the difference I feel from the Scent of a Rose, and of Assa-foetida. . . ." For an account of these pamphlets and of Locke's reaction thereto—a reaction which may be assumed in large part to Shaftesbury also—see my article, cited above.

[30] *Studies in Iconology* (New York, 1939), 229. It may be well to say a little about the question of Shaftesbury's attitude towards religion, a problem which has rather unnecessarily vexed his critics and biographers from his own century onwards. Of his dislike for and fear of any strong religious belief involving any form of "mystery" or supernatural faith there can be no doubt. It is true that in the preface to Whichcote's Sermons, and in some letters he speaks of the Anglican state church in respectful and even affectionate terms; but careful reading of these passages will show, I think, that it is the absence of "zeal" and the generally good therapeutic effect which belief in providence may have that he means. Of his certainty that the universe is God's creation, in which He is imminent, there is no doubt, either. But no one who takes revealed religion seriously can look on Shaftesbury as a confrere. The really governing fact is that, as I have tried to point out, his basic assumptions about the nature of man rule out original sin and the belief in a supernatural destiny as the true goal of life. And as Swift says, "So I affirm original sin, and that men are now liable to be damned for Adam's sin, to be the foundation of the whole Christian religion." It must be added that Shaftesbury was not argumentative. To attack religion dogmatically would be a manifestation of that very "zeal" which he felt had produced so much damage. Better is the convincing presentation, in imaginative form, of the truth about men, accompanied by a raillery against superstition. Shaftesbury's artistic achievement in the latter form has never been studied satisfactorily.

[31] *Characteristics*, II: 163.

[32] *Ibid.*, II: 164.

[33] *Ibid.*, II: 169.

[34] *An Enquiry into the Original of Moral Virtue* (Edinburgh, 1733), 324 ff.

[35] Pp. 193-4. The psychological state, the warfare of the mind with itself, is the essence of the horror in this passage, rather than pride, a sense of disobedience to God, or remorse, as in Milton's Satan, or Marlowe's Faustus.

[36] *Characteristics*, II: 214-15.

[37] *Ibid.*, II: 283.

[38] Quoted by Mario Praz, *The Romantic Agony*, tr. Angus Davidson (London, 1951), 98. Diderot, as is well known, expressed similar ideas.

[39] *Ibid.*, I: 194. And so Shaftesbury casts his own work in artistic forms, such as dialogues and "soliloquies," a fact which accounts at once for its suggestiveness and its vagueness. One must always remember that Shaftesbury was, by choice, no systematizer, and that, not isolated statements, but as in creative works, the effect of the whole is what counts.

[40] *Ibid.*, I: 207. The applicability of this statement to Shaftesbury's own work, even the *Inquiry,* is worth noting. He is not a judicial moralist.

[41] *Ibid.*, I: 43. Professor R. D. Havens has pointed out that as early as 1725 Henry Baker wrote a "natural History of myself, truly pointing out the Turn and Disposition of my Soul at the Time it gave them [the poems he was publishing] birth." The shift to introspection, as Professor Havens indicates, is noteworthy. It comes fourteen years after the publication of the *Characteristics,* when the reading of Shaftesbury was ubiquitous. "Unusual Opinions in 1725 and 1726," *PQ,* 30 (1951), 447. In line with this change in presentation of character, attention may be called to Professor Edward Hooker's article "Humour in the Age of Pope," *HLQ,* 11 (1948), 361 ff. The attitude changes from one of condemnation according to an objective standard, to sympathetic depiction of diversity. This change is entirely in accord with Shaftesbury's principle.

[42] *Ibid.*, I: 275-6.

[43] (Sixth edition, London, 1812). For an account of this book and its evolution, see R. W. Babcock, "William Richardson's Criticism of Shakespeare" *JEGP,* 29 (1929), 117 ff.

[44] *Ibid.*, pp. 19-20. On the history of the sympathetic imagination see W. J. Bate, "The Sympathetic Imagination in Eighteenth Century English Criticism," *ELH,* 12 (1945), 144 ff.

[45] Maurice Morgann, *An Essay on the Dramatic Character of Sir John Falstaff* (London, 1825), 6-7.

[46] *Op. cit.*, II: 106.

[47] *Mirror,* No. 99.

[48] *Op. cit.*, 117.

[49] (London, 1785), Introduction.

[50] *Ibid.*, 15.

[51] Bristol Lecture III, in *Coleridge's Shakespearean Criticism,* ed. Raysor (London, 1930), II: 272.

[52] *Ibid.*, I: 37.

[53] Richardson, *op. cit.*, 168 ff.

[54] *Lara,* I: xvii. The last four lines recall Richardson's analysis of that supreme example of misanthropy, Timon at Athens, whose morbid condition is supposed to result from a combination of a ruling passion—desire for eminence—with a strong sense of benevolence. The new casuistry could indeed adopt many forms!

'Dissociation of Sensibility': Modern Symbolist Readings of Literary History

Frank Kermode

> The primary pigment of poetry is the IMAGE.
>
> BLAST
>
> The poetic myths are dead; and the poetic image, which is the myth of the individual, reigns in their stead.
>
> C. DAY LEWIS

When the accounts come to be rendered, it may well appear to future historians that the greatest service done by early twentieth-century criticism to contemporary poetry has been this: it has shown poets a specially appropriate way of nourishing themselves from the past. It has shown them that their isolation, and their necessary preoccupation with the Image, do not cut them off from all their predecessors, and that there are ways of looking at the past which provide valuable insights into essentially modern possibilities and predispositions. The need was to bring literary history—and this involved other kinds of history too—to the support of the Image; to rewrite the history of poetry in Symbolist terms. The whole effort crystallised, in 1921, in Mr. Eliot's famous announcement of the doctrine of the dissociation of sensibility, and although this was by no means so original an idea as it has been called, it will necessarily be at the centre of what I have to say about this extremely important phase of my subject.

The doctrine has lately been wilting under well-directed criticism, though there is no doubt that it will continue, whether under the same name or not, whether fallacious or not, to exert a powerful influence for a long time yet. My business here is merely to establish that it has a strong connexion with the development, in the present century, of the theory of the Image, and to ask why it has had such success.

What I say about its value as a key to literary history is really incidental to this.

Mr. Eliot first used the expression 'dissociation of sensibility' in an essay on 'The Metaphysical Poets' (1921), and his last recorded comment upon the theory is in his British Academy lecture on Milton (1947). The first passage, as printed in *Selected Essays*, runs like this: Mr. Eliot has been saying that the dramatic verse of the late Elizabethans and early Jacobeans "expresses a degree of development of sensibility which is not found in any of the prose. . . . In Chapman especially there is a direct sensuous apprehension of thought, or a recreation of thought into feeling, which is exactly what we find in Donne." He then compares a passage of Chapman's and one by Lord Herbert of Cherbury with bits of Tennyson and Browning, and comments:

> The difference is not a simple difference of degree between poets. It is something which had happened to the mind of England between the time of Donne or Lord Herbert of Cherbury and the time of Tennyson and Browning; it is the difference between the intellectual poet and the reflective poet. Tennyson and Browning are poets, and they think; but they do not feel their thought as immediately as the odour of a rose. A thought to Donne was an experience; it modified his sensibility. When a poet's mind is perfectly equipped for its work, it is constantly amalgamating disparate experience; the ordinary man's experience is chaotic, irregular, fragmentary. The latter falls in love, or reads Spinoza, and these two experiences have nothing to do with each other, or with the noise of the typewriter or the smell of cooking; in the mind of the poet these experiences are always forming new wholes.
>
> We may express the difference by the following theory: The poets of the seventeenth century, the successors of the dramatists of the sixteenth, possessed a mechanism of sensibility which could devour any kind of experience. They are simple, artificial, difficult, or fantastic, as their predecessors were; no less nor more than Dante, Guido Cavalcanti, Guinicelli, or Cino. In the seventeenth century a dissociation of sensibility set in, from which we have never recovered; and this dissociation, as is natural, was aggravated by the influence of the most powerful poets of the century, Milton and Dryden.

Observe that there are certain qualifications for poetry described as operative *now*, though possessed by the poets of the seventeenth century and none since (until now?). There are other places in Mr. Eliot's earlier criticism which amplify this statement, but we will content ourselves with his last pronouncement on the subject:

> I believe that the general affirmation represented by the phrase 'dissociation of sensibility' . . . retains some validity; but . . . to lay the burden on the shoulders of Milton and Dryden was a mistake. If such a dissociation did take place, I suspect that the causes are too complex and profound to justify our accounting for the change in terms of literary criticism. All we can say is, that something like this did happen; that it had something to do with the Civil War; that it would be unwise to say it was caused by the Civil War, but that it is a consequence of the same cause which brought about the Civil War; that we must seek the causes in Europe, not in England alone; and for what these causes were, we may dig and dig until we get to a depth at which words and concepts fail us.

In this passage Mr. Eliot seems to be recommending, as a desideratum, what had in fact already been done; for by 1947 supplementary enquiries into the dissociation had long ceased to be conducted entirely in terms of literary criticism. Almost every conceivable aspect of seventeenth-century life had been examined by scholars anxious to validate the concept, though it is true that the investigators were usually historians of literature by profession. In very general terms it might be said that the notion of a pregnant historical crisis, of great importance in every sphere of human activity, was attractive because it gave design and simplicity to history; and because it explained in a subtly agreeable way the torment and division of modern life. Feeling and thinking by turns, aware of the modern preference for intellect over imagination, a double-minded period measured itself by a serenely single-minded one. Poets tried again to be concrete, to charge their thinking with passion, to restore to poetry a truth independent of the presumptuous intellect. They looked admiringly to those early years of the seventeenth century when this was normal, and the scholars attended them with explanations of why it was so, and why it ceased to be so. There was, I think, an implicit parallel with the Fall. Man's soul, since about 1650, had been divided against itself, and it would never be the same again—though correct education could achieve something.

It is a measure of Mr. Eliot's extraordinary persuasiveness that thinkers in this tradition have for so long accepted the seventeenth century as the time of the disaster. As we see from his second pronouncement, he has himself stuck to this position, although he advises us to look back into earlier history for fuller explanations. Nor is his attitude difficult to understand; it is animated by a rich nostalgia for the great period of Anglican divinity, the period when the Church of England, beset on all sides by determined recusancy, confidently proposed itself as truly Catholic and apostolic—looking back, itself, to a vague past when the folly and arrogance of intellect had not yet begun the process of dissociating Christianity. This period ended with the Civil War, and the end of the first Anglo-Catholicism coincided with the end of an admired poetry and a great drama, both affected, to some extent, by ecclesiastically-determined attitudes, the drama remembering (but how faintly?) its devout origins, 'metaphysical poetry' the *concetto predicabile.* What happens is that the Civil War becomes a kind of allegory, with the Puritans as Pride of Intellect, and the King as Spiritual Unity.

The truth is that, if we look to Europe and not to England alone, we see that there was never much chance that the Church of England would be universally recognised as Catholic, and that 'something' had presumably 'happened' long before to predispose people against such recognition. And this is a characteristic situation. It is not merely a matter of wrong dates; however far back one goes one seems to find the symptoms of dissociation. This suggests that there is little historical propriety in treating it as a seventeenth-century event, even when the historian is serious and respectable enough not to assume that it really was an occurrence like, say, Pride's Purge, after which feeling disappeared from certain mental transactions, leaving a Rump of intellect with which we are still conducting our business. With more thoughtful chroniclers there is usually much emphasis on the dissociative force of science, and on the un-dissociated condition of pre-Baconian and pre-Cartesian philosophy and theology. But it is easy enough to show that scientists were already under Elizabeth incurring odium and the suspicion of atheism for a variety of reasons, all coming in the end to the charge that they were setting nature against God. Bacon's position with respect to religious laws that were apparently contrary to reason is very similar to that of many philosophers, especially those affected by Averroes and the great Aristotelian tradition of Padua, from the thirteenth century onward, to Pomponazzi in the early sixteenth and to Cremonini, an influential teacher who was, incidentally, a friend of that very Lord Herbert of Cherbury who was used as an example of the un-dissociated poet. Obviously the rediscovery of Aristotle involved in some sense a dissociation of Christian thought, tending ultimately to some such escape-device as the 'double-truth' of Averroism, first condemned, by a Church anxious to save rational theology, in the

1270s. And if we were to pursue the dissociation back into the past, we should find ourselves in Athens. Elizabethan 'atheism' was far more than a scientific issue; there was genuine anxiety, a real 'naturalist' movement widely affecting ethical and political conduct. Similarly, the condemnations of the 1270s referred not only to Averroism but to the book on love by Andreas Capellanus, and M. Gilson has spoken of "a sort of polymorphic naturalism stressing the rights of pagan nature" as characteristic of the period as a whole. It would be quite as reasonable to locate the great dissociation in the sixteenth or the thirteenth century as in the seventeenth; nor would it be difficult to construct arguments for other periods. The truth may be that we shall never find a state of culture worth bothering about (from the literary point of view, that is) in which language is so primitive as to admit no thinking that is not numinous; in which there is no possibility of a naturalist assault on the society's beliefs. The Christian 'West' has never wanted to be as primitive even as the Song of Solomon, and its whole immense allegorical tradition is the result of applying intellectual instruments to the dissection of writings in which thought and feeling are, if they are anywhere, inseparable.

But it seems to me much less important that there was not, in the sense in which Mr. Eliot's supporters have thought, a particular and far-reaching catastrophe in the seventeenth century, than that there was, in the twentieth, an urgent need to establish the historicity of such a disaster. And the attempt to answer the question why there should have been takes us back to the Image. The theory of the dissociation of sensibility is, in fact, the most successful version of a Symbolist attempt to explain why the modern world resists works of art that testify to the poet's special, anti-intellectual way of knowing truth. And this attempt obviously involves the hypothesis of an age which was different, an age in which the Image was more readily accessible and acceptable.

When, in fact, the poets and aestheticians of the Image turn their attention to history, it is in search of some golden age when the prevalent mode of knowing was not positivist and anti-imaginative; when the Image, the intuited, creative reality, was habitually respected; when art was not permanently on the defensive against mechanical and systematic modes of enquiry. Since the order of reality postulated as the proper study of the poet tends, in one way or another, to be granted supernatural attributes, the ideal epoch is usually a religious one. Hence the medievalism of Byzantinism of Hulme and the Decadents, of Yeats and Henry Adams. Hulme, in particular—as we have seen—exposes the whole process; he has to go back, using Worringer as a guide, to a moment of crisis (using one that already existed for historians, but using it in a new way) and achieve the required antithesis between his two ages (undissociated and dissociated) by treating all thought between the Renaissance and his own time as of a piece. It was partly because this obviously would not do that the date of the crisis was moved on to 1650. But everybody in the tradition was agreed that there must have been such a crisis; it was necessary to their aesthetic, and the only point of dispute was its date.

There is a passage, to which I have already referred, in Pound's *Make It New,* that illuminates this aspect of the problem.

> When the late T. E. Hulme was trying to be a philosopher . . . and fussing about Sorel and Bergson . . . I spoke to him one day of the difference between Guido's precise interpretative metaphor, and the Petrarchian fustian and ornament, pointing out that Guido thought in accurate terms; that the phrases correspond to definite sensations undergone . . . Hulme took some time over it in silence, and then finally said: "That is more interesting than anything anyone ever said to me. It is more interesting than anything I ever read in a book".

The only aspects of this odd interchange that I want to discuss are those which are relevant to what I am trying to say about the historiography of modern Symbolist aesthetics. One is that Pound is describing Cavalcanti as a poet of the integral image, and contrasting him with Petrarch, a poet of the ornamental image, the image appended to discourse, the flower stuck in sand. In the one there is 'a unification of thought and feeling'; in the other, a dissociation of them. Another is Hulme's reaction to what Pound said. The general idea could not have been unfamiliar to him; after all, it was the reason why he was fussing about Bergson. But a man is never more impressed by an argument than when it provides unexpected support for opinions he already holds, and Hulme could not have been less than charmed to discover that Petrarch, of all people—the First Man of that Renaissance he blamed so strenuously—already exhibited the symptoms of error that characterised the period, whereas Cavalcanti, an older contemporary of Dante, habituated to the hallowed concept of discontinuity, brought up on Original Sin, had precisely those Imagist qualities, that reluctance to glide away into abstraction, which for Hulme was the index of true poetry. Somewhere between Cavalcanti and Petrarch a dissociation of sensibility, it would seem, had set in; and from it, Hulme was willing to add, we have never recovered.

But we have now to remind ourselves that Mr. Eliot claimed for the poets of the seventeenth century the very qualities of Dante, Cavalcanti, and Cino, and believed that the dissociation came after these later poets. It is not in the nature of the concept of dissociation that it should occur at random intervals, any more than it is of the Fall; only on some such theory as Yeats's can it occur more than once. What are we to conclude from this confusion?

The fact is that Mr. Eliot's argument for a general dissociation that can be detected in art is meant to satisfy much the same need as Hulme's, and Yeats's. For Hulme, as we have seen, the Renaissance is the critical moment; men began to ignore the human limitations suggested by the doctrine of Original Sin, and nothing has been right since. Romanticism is just the new disease at the stage of mania. For Yeats the great moment in the present historical phase is 1550; for about a century before that there was a tense perfection, celebrated in some of his most splendid prose; but after that everything changed, art faced in the wrong direction, the artist became more and more an exile. In fact Yeats's history is written in terms of this doctrine, written in a world that offended him socially and imaginatively, a world of 'shopkeeping logicians', the very existence of which he had to explain by exhaustive glosses on every conceivable aspect of the idea of dissociation. My own belief is that Yeats's expression of the whole aesthetic-historical complex is by far the most satisfactory and, in terms of poetry, the most fruitful. But the immediate point is that all these writers search history for this critical moment, and because they share much the same poetic heritage, they are all looking for much the same kinds of rightness and wrongness in historical periods. They seek, in short, a historical period possessing the qualities they postulate for the Image: unity, indissociability; qualities which, though passionately desired, are, they say, uniquely hard to come by in the modern world. That poets and critics so diverse in personality as Pound, Hulme, Yeats and Eliot, should all have made such similar incursions into Symbolist historiography is testimony to the great pressure the idea of the Image has exerted in the formative phase of modern poetic. Mr. Eliot's attempt, distinguished from the others by the accident of his personal concerns in theology, is not essentially different from them. It has only been more successful, partly because of his prestige and persuasive force, partly perhaps because of the growing scholarly tendency to medievalise the Renaissance, so that a later date for the split became more acceptable.

The fact remains that Mr. Eliot's is the version that has had wide currency. Like the others, it is, as I have been trying to show, quite useless historically. It will not do to say that it is partly true, or true in a way, as some people now claim. A once-for-all event cannot happen every few years; there cannot be, if the term is to retain the significance it has acquired, dissociations between the archaic Greeks and Phidias, between Catullus and Virgil, between Guido and Petrarch, between Donne and Milton. As a way of speaking about *periods* the expression is much less useful than even 'baroque'. At its worst, it is merely a way of saying which poets one likes, and draping history over them. At its best it is an interesting primitivism, looking for an unmodern virtue, not as the noble savage was sought in the impossibly remote past or in Tahiti, but in Christian Europe right up to some moment in, or shortly after, what is vaguely called the Renaissance. The most deplorable consequence of the doctrine is that the periods and poets chosen to illustrate it are bound to receive perverse treatment; you must misrepresent them if you propose to make them justify a false theory. If the theory helps to produce good poetry (as it did) this is not worth complaining about, provided that it dies when this work is accomplished. But this theory shows every sign of surviving, and it is therefore a matter of importance to show how it has distorted Donne and Milton, the two poets most affected by it. Once again, the astonishing degree of distortion imposed here is a measure of the power generated by the Image in modern poetic.

Milton and Donne have been involved in an unhappy relationship (existing only in the fantasies of historians) which has seemed to mean that one of them has to be occulted to enable the other to be lit. Milton was to be put out—though it may be noted that Mr. Eliot's change of opinion about Donne was followed by an upward revision of his estimate of Milton. At the time when Donne was being admired for thinking passionately, Milton was being despised for writing monuments to dead ideas in a dead language. Milton, self-conscious postlapsarian that he was, obstinately thought and discoursed *about* feeling, divorcing the body and soul, the form and matter, of the image. Donne, writing before the same Fall, had his intellect at the tip of his senses.

Superficially this argument was attractive because it gave major status to an obscure poet whose diction was inartificial, even colloquial, and who lived in times supposed to be very like modern times, in that the established order was already being threatened by those 'naturalist' forces which eventually dissociated sensibility. There is, of course, a contradiction here: Donne is admired because he was deeply troubled by the new philosophy, and also because he was lucky enough to live just before it became really troublesome. There is also an error of fact: Donne alludes frequently enough to the 'new philosophy,' but nobody who has examined these allusions in their context can seriously believe he was much put out by it, and considering his religious views it would indeed be surprising if he had been. It might have been useful to the dissociationist argument if somebody had been prepared to capitalise this point, by way of emphasising Donne's pre-dissociation status; but there seems to have been a heavy commitment to the view that Donne was important to modern poets because of the ways in which his world resembled theirs, as well as because it was completely different from theirs. As usual, the history is feeble. But pure criticism has had very similar difficulties: Miss Tuve's now famous demonstration that Donne's images have a logical, or at any rate a pseudo-logical function, was a direct affront to the basis of the theory that he was a poet of the modern Image; but it can scarcely have surprised anybody who had read Donne open-eyed and seen how much he depends on dialectical conjuring of various kinds, arriving at the point of wit by subtle syllogistic misdirections, inviting admiration by slight but totally destructive perversities of analogue, which re-route every argument to paradox. Some of this Mr. Eliot perhaps felt when he prematurely prophesied the demise of Donne during the tercentenary celebrations of 1931, and showed how far he had gone towards excluding Donne from the category of unified sensibility, saying outright that in him "there is a manifest fissure of thought and sensibility." Donne is, to say the least, of doubtful value to the Symbolist theory—less use than the poetic and critical experiments of some of his European contemporaries might have been. At first glance, one might be excused for wondering how Donne ever got mixed up with the thoery of dissociation; the explanation of course lies in nineteenth-century thought.

Mr. F. W. Bateson, in a very important critique of the theory, has noticed in passing how little separates Mr. Eliot's formula from the conventional nineteenth-century view, which he exemplifies by Stopford Brooke's opinion that the Restoration saw the end "of a poetry in which emotion always accompanied thought." And something like this view can in fact be found in Coleridge. But after Grosart's edition of 1872 some people were already noticing that Donne wrote poems in which the note of passion, the true voice of feeling, was audible despite the fact that they were love poems unpromisingly couched in terms of alchemy, astronomy and law. It was this discovery of the true voice of feeling in such surroundings that led to what was in effect a late Romantic glorification of Donne. This was contemporary with the Blake revival, the teaching of Pater, and finally with the assimilation of the parallel but more important phenomenon of French Symbolism —in short, with the emergence of the modern Image as it was understood by Symons (a great champion of Donne and the Jacobean drama), and those who came under his influence: Yeats, and later Pound and Eliot. One can watch the older thought-and-feeling formula developing from a Romantic into a characteristically Symbolist hypothesis. George Eliot, who knew Donne by the time she wrote *Middlemarch,* assumes like her master Wordsworth that the true voice comes from artists of higher organic sensibility than other men, but can write in that novel—doubtless unconscious of her role as critical pioneer—that the poet is "quick to discern", but also "quick to feel" because he possesses "a soul in which knowledge passes instantaneously into feeling, and feeling flashes back as a new organ of knowledge".

This period of transition is greatly illuminated in a paper recently published by Mr. J. E. Duncan in the *Journal of English and Germanic Philology.* Anyone who has used the Victorian editions upon which much of our reading in seventeenth-century poetry still depends must have occasionally felt that there was some hallucinatory resemblance between certain observations made by the enthusiastic clerical editors and those of Mr. Eliot. Mr. Duncan has collected a great deal of evidence to show, not only that Donne was well and truly revived long before Eliot's essays, and indeed Grierson's edition, but that even 70 years ago people were talking about the poet in what we recognise as the modern way. By 1911, Courthope, in his *History,* was already complaining that it had probably gone too far. Grierson's great edition of the following year was accepted as merely setting the seal on Donne's reputation. But what is more interesting than this mere setting back of the starting post is the terminology in which the Victorian critics, pleased with their rediscovery of the conceit and of hard-thinking poetry, devised in order to praise the Metaphysical poets. They speak of its intellectual cunning *and* its power of 'sensibility' and then, quite early, we find ourselves approaching, with a sort of unconscious inevitability, the modern formula which combines these two qualities as two sides of a coin. Grosart says that Crashaw's thinking "was so emotional as almost always to tremble into feeling"; Crowley's thought is "made to pulsate with feeling". Symons finds that Donne's "senses speak with unparallelled directness"; Schelling that Donne's contribution to the English lyric was "intellectualised emotion". Poets began to find Donne-like qualities in their own work; in so doing,

Francis Thompson spoke of his own "sensoriness instinct with mind", and the parallel was supported by Symons and by Mrs. Meynell. The familiar comparison between the seventeenth and twentieth centuries began as early as 1900; after that it was easy to play the game of parallel poets, and both Brooke and Bridges were credited with resemblances to Donne. Gosse and Grierson alike saw the similarity between Donne and Baudelaire, and briefly hinted at the parallel between English-Jacobean and French-Symbolist which was later to prove so fertile. Arthur Symons in fact developed the parallel to a considerable extent; he is the link between nineteenth- and twentieth-century orthodoxies of the Image, and of Donne and the seventeenth century.

Long before the great edition of Grierson, which made Donne relatively easy to read, and long before Mr. Eliot's phrase had its remarkable success in the world, powerful aesthetic interests were being satisfied by the conversion of a little-known poet into an English Laforgue; and the same interests demanded a catastrophic start to the modern world shortly after the death of Donne, and before *Paradise Lost,* that great dissociated poem which you must, said Mr. Eliot, read once for the meaning and once for the verse, and which is therefore of no use either to that illiterate audience he desiderates for his unified Symbolist poetry, or for the next best thing, a highly cultivated audience that also likes its art undissociated. The strangest irony in all this—and it is all I have to say about the second of these perverted poets—is that Milton, rather exceptionally, actually believed in and argued for the unity of the soul (a continuum of mind and sense), allowed his insistence on the inseparability of form and matter to lead him into heresy; and believed that poetry took precedence over other activities of the soul because it was simple (undissociated by intellect) sensuous and passionate. But this did not matter; there were overriding reasons why Milton had to be bent or broken. He was the main sufferer in the great experiment of projecting on to an historical scale a developed Romantic-Symbolist theory of the Image. And although, as Mr. Bateson has shown, Mr. Eliot borrowed the phrase 'dissociation of sensibility' from Gourmont's peculiar account of the processes of poetry in the mind of an individual (specifically Laforgue) and applied it to the history of a nation's poetry, it is obvious that behind the theory there is the whole pressure of the tradition I have been discussing. The historical effort of Symbolism has been to identify a period happily ignorant of the war between Image and discourse, an un-dissociated age. In the end, it is not of high importance that any age selected for this role is likely to be found wanting, except of course for the tendency to exclude particular poets and periods from the canon. Hulme could never have justified his selection; Pound was driven to Chinese, and a dubious theory of ideograms; Yeats believed his own theory only in a specially qualified way, admitting that its importance lay in the present and not in the past. This is true of Mr. Eliot also. The essays in which he proposed his theory represent a most fruitful and effective refinement of the Symbolist doctrine, yielding far more than Symons's, for instance, similar though they are in essentials. To attack his position has usually seemed to mean an assault on what most people are content to regard as the main tradition of modern verse.

One such attack, that of Mr. Yvor Winters, seems to me both extremely intelligent and extremely revealing; and it carries me on to the last phase of this essay, a cursory glance at the contemporary relation between Image and discourse. Mr. Winters looks for inconsistencies in Mr. Eliot's criticism, so that he can defend his own position, which is notoriously not a fashionable one. He insists that art is a statement of an understood experience, which it morally evaluates; and that poetry has, in consequence, the same *kind* of meaning as cruder statements of the same sort, so that one would expect it to be paraphrasable. This position is, of course, frankly opposed to a cherished Symbolist doctrine, and Mr. Winters is therefore very hostile to some of Eliot's opinions. For example, the famous sigh for an illiterate audience (analogous, by the way, to Yeats's desire for illiterate actors, and really a hopeless wish for an audience incapable of discourse and so cut off from intellection's universe of death) simply fans Winters' indignation, as does the cognate doctrine that meaning is only the burglar's bait for the housedog of intellect. So, when Eliot writes, in the beautiful essay on Dante, that "clear visual images are given much more intensity by having a meaning—we do not need to know what the meaning is, but in our awareness of the image we must be aware that the meaning is there too," and when Mr. Winters bullies him about this, we have a clear picture of the fundamental opposition between a Romantic-Symbolist criticism and a criticism conscientiously in reaction against it. Mr. Eliot says that a poem can be understood before its 'meaning' is taken, though the 'meaning' is not without importance. Winters replies: "If the meaning is important in the creation of the poem, at any rate, it is foolish to suppose that one can dispense with it in the reading of the poem or that the poet did not take his meaning seriously. Only the frailest barrier exists between the idea of this passage and Poe's theory that the poet should lay claim to a meaning when he is aware of none".

It is no use saying that Mr. Winters has simply misunderstood; he knows very well what Eliot means, as he shows when he traces Eliot's theory of necessary disorder in modern art to Romantic doctrines of organic form, and speaks of *The Waste Land* and *The Cantos* as belonging to the art of revery. He understands the roots of these poems, and even goes so far as to call Pound "a sensibility without a mind", which is, if nothing else, a very just punishment upon abusers of the word 'sensibility'. Mr. Winters, as we should expect, is eccentric in his choice of major modern poets, but he is nevertheless the only critic of any fame who can take for granted the history of the kind of poetry and criticism he is opposed to. In the essay on Eliot he bases a very important argument upon a revealing sentence which is hidden away in the introduction to the *Anabasis* of St. Jean Perse: "There is a logic of the imagination as well as a logic of concepts". (We, I hope, understand what this means, and can see how sharply such a belief separates the modern from the 'Metaphysical' poet.) It is hard to resist Winters' argument that here "the word *logic* is used figuratively", that it indicates nothing but "qualitative progression", "graduated progression of feeling". Yet for all that the argument is false. It indicates no *progression* of any sort. Time and space are exorcised; the emblem of this 'logic' is the Dancer. This misunderstanding, slight as it seems, shows that the difference between these two critics is extremely wide. If you want to mean something, says Mr. Winters, you must mean it in the usual way; in other words, form is not significant. But to Mr. Eliot, and to many others, this is an admission that the speaker has no real notion at all of what art is. "People who do not appreciate poetry," says Mr. Eliot, "always find it difficult to distinguish between order and chaos in the arrangement of images." But Mr. Winters does appreciate poetry. The truth is that he is an anti-Symbolist critic, and this necessarily puts him in opposition to most of his contemporaries. For him, poetry is the impassioned expression on the countenance of *all* science and, as George Eliot called it, an aesthetic teacher. Since he does not believe that it deals in a different order of truth he has not the same difficulties about language, communication and paraphrase as the critics who oppose him.

I draw attention in this sketchy way to Mr. Winters, because he leads us to an understanding of what is one of the main issues of modern poetic. This is the unformulated quarrel between the orthodoxy of

Symbolism and the surviving elements of an empirical-utilitarian tradition which, we are assured, is characteristically English. Yeats had a foot in both camps, the one stubbornly holding to the commonalty of the means of discourse and seeking to define those differences of degree which distinguish poetry, the other talking about images (sometimes indeed forgetting about words and their temporal behaviour altogether, or treating them as physical things like bits of string) and taking poetry to be a different kind of thing, a different mode of cognition, involving, at least as a working hypothesis, a different order of reality from any available to ordinary intellection. The difficulty of the first party is to find some way of talking about poetry and its propositions that does not disqualify it from the serious attention of *honnêtes gens;* for example, Richards's 'pseudo-statement' is asking for trouble, Wellek's theory of genre is too technical. On the other side, nobody can any longer (in the present state of semantics) be so offhand about the linguistic problems of the Image as the French Symbolists were. Indeed a good deal of the best modern criticism is interesting as evidence of the oscillations and tensions in the minds of critics between the claims of the Image and the claims of ordinary discourse.

These tensions are visible also in poetry, and it is possible that in the controlling of them the immediate future of our poetry lies, as well as our criticism and ways of looking at the past. At the moment, perhaps, the movement of the 'thirties away from aesthetic monism, the new insistence on the right to discourse, even to say such things as "We must love one another or die" (as Auden does in an exquisite poem) has ceased. There are good poets who cultivate a quasi-philosophical tone of meditation, but they are careful to have no design upon us, to place their meditation within the confines of reverie; there are others who prefer the ironies of stringently mechanical forms; but no Auden, nobody who wants, apparently, to go that way; and this is a pity. Recently Wallace Stevens has come to be more widely read in this country, and he is a poet who provides a unique, perhaps un-repeatable, solution to the image-and-discourse problem, by making the problem itself the subject of poems:

> Is the poem both peculiar and general?
> There's a meditation there, in which there seems
>
> To be an evasion, a thing not apprehended or
> Not apprehended well. Does the poet
> Evade us, as in a senseless element?

Evade us, this hot, dependent orator,
The spokesman at our bluntest barriers,
Exponent by a form of speech, the speaker

Of a speech only a little of the tongue?

One thing Stevens insists upon, and no poet is now likely to forget it: it is a lesson that Romantic aesthetic has taught once and for all. The poem is

Part of the *res* and not itself about it.
The poet speaks the poem as it is,
Not as it was.

Only by knowing this can the poet be "the necessary angel of the earth." The sentiment is Blake's, but it has become everybody's; yet Stevens's answer to the problem—it is the problem of dissociation—though very complete, and achieving in the late poem called 'The Rock' a most moving comprehensiveness, is not available to all poets, and they must seek their own.

Stevens's problems are the problems also of modern criticism (in its way and of necessity almost as obscure as the poetry). The unique power of the poet, however one describes it, is to make images or symbols, however one understands these,—as somehow visual, or, in the tradition of the new semantics, as the neologisms created by shifting contexts. How are these products related to discourse? Is there any way to talk of poetry without breaking up the monad and speaking of thought and image?

The one thing nearly everybody seems to be agreed upon is that the work of art has to be considered as a whole and that considerations of 'thought' must be subordinated to a critical effort to see the whole as one image; the total work is not *about* anything—"a poem should not mean but *be*"—which is simply a vernacular way of saying what modern critics mean when they speak of it as 'autotelic' (they even speculate as to whether criticism is not also autotelic—the critic as artist once more). Put as simply as this, the position is not much changed since Mallarmé: "nul vestige d'une philosophie, l'éthique ou la métaphysique, ne transparaîtra; j'ajoute qu'il faut incluse et latente . . . le chant jaillit de source innée, antérieure à un concept". And many of the practical difficulties encountered by the holism of French Symbolism recur in modern critics. Take, for example, the problem which must sometimes arise, of what is the whole work of art. Is it the 'Voyage à Cythère' or is it the whole of *Les fleurs du Mal?* Is it 'They that have power to hurt' or the whole collection of Shakespeare's Sonnets? Professor Lehmann considers the first of these problems in his *Symbolist Aesthetic,* and seems to decide that the proper course is to take one poem at a time, since we know that *Les Fleurs du Mal* is not "really a poem with a decisive organization overall" but "poems loosely strung on a string of pre-dominating attitude". But how, it might be asked, can we be sure of this without trying the experiment of reading the whole book as a poem? Where do we get this important bit of information, which determines the whole question in advance? Certainly, on the purist view, from some illicit source—a knowledge of Baudelaire's intention. This may seem very extreme; but on the contrary it turns up with the regularity of an orthodoxy. We are told to read the whole of Shakespeare as one work. Mr. Wilson Knight reads all the Sonnets as one poem; he won his spurs by pioneering the Symbolist criticism of the plays, and is the most thoroughgoing of the holist Symbolist critics, unless we dare to say that Mr. Eliot, in his most famous essay, invites us to treat the whole of literature as one work.

There is a problem here, inherent in the Symbolist approach to poetry, which deserves more serious treatment than it gets, since it concerns the definition of what critics are talking about. In practice, of course, they cut the knot in silence, and assume the discontinuity of the poem they happen to be talking about, and even, for the purposes of exposition, talk about parts of poems as if they were wholes (just as they slyly paraphrase). Occasionally they even justify this practice. Mr. W. K. Wimsatt has several good things to say about the problem in his book *The Verbal Icon,* for instance this:

> Extreme holism is obviously contrary to our experience of literature. (We do not wait until the end of the play or novel to know whether the first scene or chapter is brilliant or dull—no long work in fact would ever be witnessed or read if this were so.) A poem, said Coleridge, the father of holism in English criticism, is a composition which proposes "to itself such delight from the *whole,* as is compatible with a distinct gratification from each component part". The value of a whole poem, while undoubtedly reflecting something back to the parts, has to grow out of parts which are themselves valuable. *The Rape of the Lock* would not come off were not the couplets witty. We may add that good poems may have dull parts; bad poems, bright parts. How minutely this principle could be urged without arriving at a theory of Longinian "sudden flashes", of "cathartically charged images", of Arnoldian touch-

> stones, of poetic diction, or of irrelevant local texture, I do not know. Nor what the minimal dimension of wit or local brilliance of structure may be; nor to what extent a loosely constructed whole may be redeemed by the energy of individual chapters or scenes. Yet the validity of partial value as a general principle in tension with holism seems obvious.

Something might be said against this defence of *littérature,* for the 'spatial' view of works of art, and it is worth considering that there are modern works (*Ulysses* is an obvious example) which are deliberately, and for long stretches, extremely tedious, and without any brilliance of local texture. Yet what Mr. Wimsatt says is satisfactory to common sense, and in fact modern holist criticism is closely related, so far as poetry is concerned, to that other Symbolist article which sets up the lyric poem as the norm, so that for the most part only short poems get the full treatment.

Even so, the question of how to treat partial aspects continues to rise and trouble practical critics, and occasionally provides new insights. Mr. Empson, for example, has developed a habit of referring regularly to the whole work in the discussions of its parts; Mr. Ransom has raised a whole theory upon the assertion that the value of 'texture' resides precisely in its irrelevance to the structural concern of the poem, and he is further heretical in allowing no poem to be without some embodied 'prose discourse', providing the logical relevance denied to the 'texture'. Mr. Winters is right, I think, when he calls this an embarrassing doctrine, holding that Ransom "does not know what to do with the rational content, how to account for it or evaluate it." (Mr. Winters of course does know this.) To put the matter so baldly is, of course, to do wrong to Mr. Ransom's intense though urbane efforts to solve an important problem; but my object here is merely to insist that the problem arises quite naturally out of the attempt (which must be made in any modern poetic) to find a place for discourse in a Symbolist poetry. Ransom accepts most of the Symbolist position,—he calls the poetry of the Image 'physical' and the poetry of discourse 'Platonic'—right down to the psychological theory of the artist as isolated or inhibited from action (the check on action he calls 'sensibility') and without a radical reorientation there is simply no room for discourse in the work of art so conceived. The problem comes up again in the associated criticism of Allen Tate. He also believes that art "has no useful relation to ordinary forms of action," and accepts a distinction similar to that of Ransom, finding the virtue of poetry in the *tension* between idea and image, or between abstraction and concretion, or between discourse and the symbol which can have no logical relation to it.

Such formulations, however fruitful they may be in the exegesis which stems from them (and it is arguable that they are not fruitful in this way at all) have the disadvantages, as well as the benefits, of their Romantic-Symbolist heritage. Mr. R. W. Stallman, in his useful account of these critics, asks us to distinguish between their "formalism" and "the aestheticism of the nineties"; but the differences are by no means as decisive as he suggests, and if one were able to construct a normal modern poetic it would be unlikely to contain much, apart from its semantic content, to surprise Arthur Symons. It is true that a new school of critics, the Chicago 'neo-Aristotelians,' are directing us back to the *Poetics* and away from that preoccupation with metaphor (the rhetorical vehicle of the Image) which is an essential component of modern poetic, but one can truly say, without comment on the quality of this criticism, that, from the standpoint of modern orthodoxy, it is clearly tainted with heresy, the heresy of abstraction. What still prevails is the Symbolist conception of the work of art as aesthetic monad, as the product of a mode of cognition superior to, and different from, that of the sciences. Any alternative is likely to be treated as heretical—dubbed, for instance, 'ornamentalist', as degrading the status of the Image, and dealing to another 'dissociation', another over-valuation of ideas in poetry similar to that effected by Hobbes. One result of this orthodoxy is that the practical business of criticism becomes enormously strenuous, despite the technical facilities provided by Richards and Empson; and that there is a good deal of what must be called cheating, for example in the matter of paraphrase. Good modern criticism is much more eclectic in method than most theoretical pronouncements suggest; it must not seem to believe in paraphrase (or, sometimes, in any form of historical approach to the work in question) yet these and similar forbidden techniques are in fact frequently employed. It may be said that the strenuousness, as well as the obscurity, of such modern criticism, is a direct consequence of its Symbolist inheritance.

The effects of this inheritance may be traced also, so far as I know them, in the philosopher-aestheticians whom critics tend to take notice of (it would not be easy to say why they take notice of some and not of others). There are naturally many variations; but, to take two recent books, the 'concrete universal' as proposed by Mr. Wimsatt is the same thing as the Symbol of Mrs. Langer under a slightly different aspect. Mrs. Langer's is comfortably traditional in design, if not in execution. It starts from music, where the definition of symbol as "articulate but non-discursive form" does not raise the same problems of 'content' and 'ideas' as it does in literature; so far she shares the 'aestheticism' of the 'nineties'. (It is interesting, by the way, to find her quoting with approval a passage from Arthur Michel about the dance which would have pleased Mallarmé and Symons and Yeats—the dancer is conceived as oscillating "between two external poles of tension, thus transplanting the dancing body from the sensually existing atmosphere of materialism and real space into the symbolic supersphere of tension space"; and he speaks of "the dissolution of the dancer into swaying tension".) When she arrives at the problem of the discursive content of poems, Mrs. Langer's answer is that "the poet uses discourse to create an illusion, a pure appearance, which is a non-discursive symbolic form". She distinguishes between this position and that of 'pure poetry' as formulated by Moore and Bremond, accurately calling the latter's a magical solution; it is magical in so far as it is Symbolist, and so, perhaps, in its different way, is hers. But hers is distinguished further by arduous and delightful discriminations. She gives modified approval to Mr. Pottle's view that "Poetry should be no purer than the purpose demands", but calls it a philosophical makeshift; exposes the mass of unphilosophical thinking that vitiates most attempts to distinguish between poetry and non-poetry; and argues that to maintain its interest in life poetry has to traffic with "serious thought". But "the framework of subject-matter" becomes part of the symbolic whole; something has to be *done* to it, it must, in the Croce-Collingwood sense, be 'expressed,' and it will then be part of the work of art which is "a single indivisible symbol, although a highly articulated one".

Mrs. Langer has undoubtedly found a place for 'discourse' in her 'symbol'—so necessary, when the art is one which uses words—and the success of her books is probably an advance towards the dissociation of Romantic-Symbolist aesthetic from the anti-intellectualism with which it has been so persistently and inevitably associated from the beginning, and so potently since Rimbaud. An age of criticism, for so we tend to think of our epoch, is comforted by the assurance that reason can somehow get at poems, and that criticism itself should not be the autotelic act that Wilde as well as some later critics argued it must be (and as it indeed must, if art is the symbol by definition inexplicable). "The situation," says Mr. Wimsatt, "is something like this: In each poem there is something (an individual intuition—or a concept) which can never be expressed in other terms. It is like the square root of two or like pi, which cannot be expressed by rational numbers, but only as their *limit*. Criticism of poetry is like 1.414. . . or 3.1416. . . , not all it would be, yet all that can be had and very useful."

And this is all the critic can expect. He cannot give up the autonomy of the symbolic work of art, a concept of form which has been near the heart of criticism since Coleridge. And so he cannot expect ever to achieve finality in his own work; he is doomed to be limited, even if he remembers the symbolic origin of the discourse he is extracting for discussion. Not that a good critic would wish it otherwise; he is so accustomed to *defending* poetry on these very grounds, his way of thinking about poetry is, in fact, inclined to be defensive, and even when he is asserting poetry's unique powers there is likely to be a cautious anti-positivism in his tone. Reviewing Mr. Philip Wheelright's recent book *The Burning Fountain*, Mr. M. H. Abrams points out that this excellent writer is "a prisoner of the theory he opposes" because he accepts the opposition between scientific and expressive language. And Mr. Abrams goes on to suggest, in a most sympathetic way, that we ought now to go over to the offensive. "An adequate theory of poetry must be constructed, not by a strategy of defense and limited counter-attack on ground chosen by a different discipline, but by a positive strategy specifically adapted to disclose the special ends and structures and values, not only of poetry as such, but of the rich diversity of individual poems. What is needed is not merely a "metagrammar" and a "paralogic." What is needed, and what the present yeasty ferment in criticism may well portend, is simply, a poetic."

If such a poetic emerges it will still, of course, be Symbolist; but it will have a different place for discourse from any found for it during the nineteenth-century struggle with the positivists. It will owe much to modern semantics, but it will not call the discourse of poetry "pseudo-statement." Nor will its differences from scientific statement be reduced to differences of degree; it will not become statement transfigured by impassioned expression. The new poetic would be remote from the radicalism of Blake, have little to do with the forlorn hopes of Mallarmé, and less with the disastrous *derèglement* of Rimbaud. We have perhaps learnt to respect order, and felt on our bodies the effect of irrationalism, at any rate when the sphere of action is invaded by certain elements of the Romantic *rêve*. It will be a waking poetic, respecting order. 'Shape' has no chance of interfering with 'form', to use Coleridge's distinction; but among good poets it never had. But 'reason' will return to poetics, and perhaps Mrs. Langer has shown how to find it a *modus vivendi* with the symbol. One notes also that Mr. Wimsatt, as his title suggests, is willing to allow both meanings of 'symbol' to the words of poetry, I mean those of the semasiologist and of the Romantic critic.

But in the end, of course, these matters are solved by poets and not by critics. That is why, I think, Yeats is so important in what I have been saying. He had a matured poet's concern for the relation of symbol to discourse. He understood that one pole of Symbolist theory is sacramentalism, whether Catholic or theurgic:

> Did God in portioning wine and bread
> Give man His thought, or his mere body?

and was willing to see in the discourse, whether of language or gesture, of the dedicated, symbolic values. He, as we have seen, most fully worked out the problems of the Image and of the nature of the poet's isolation; he understood the importance of magic to Symbolist aesthetic; and he also found his solution to that most urgent problem of discourse, assuming that such a statement as "The best lack all conviction", in contact with the vast image out of *Spiritus Mundi,* puts on the knowledge with the power of that image. So the slaves of time, the non-poets, will find a validity in his symbolic poems that is, for them, absent from the pure poetry of the dream. They share with the poet not only the Great Memory, but also the ordinary syntax of the daily life of action. Yeats's sun may be full of angels hymning Jehovah, but it is also a disc shaped somewhat like a guinea. This is not the dissociation of image that is complained of; it is an admission that art was always made *for* men who habitually move in space and time, whose language is propelled onward by verbs, who cannot always be asked to respect the new enclosure laws of poetry, or such forbidding notices as "No road through to action". Somehow, and probably soon, the age of dissociation—which is to say, the age that invented and developed the concept of dissociation—must end.

The Houyhnhnms, the Yahoos, and the History of Ideas

R. S. Crane

I shall be concerned in this essay with two ways of using the history of ideas—or, in the case of one of them, as I shall argue, misusing it—in literary interpretation. The particular issue I have in mind is forced on one in an unusually clear-cut manner, I think, by what has been said of the 'Voyage to the Country of the Houyhnhnms' in the criticism of the past few decades; and for this reason, and also because I wish to add a theory of my own about Swift's intentions in that work to the theories now current, I shall base the discussion that follows almost exclusively on it.

I

With a very few exceptions (the latest being George Sherburn),[1] since the 1920s, and especially since the later 1930s, writers on the fourth Voyage have been mainly dominated by a single preoccupation.[2] They have sought to correct the misunderstanding of Swift's satiric purpose in the Voyage which had vitiated, in their opinion, most earlier criticism of it and, in particular, to defend Swift from the charge of all-out misanthropy that had been levelled against him so often in the past—by Thackeray, for example, but many others also—on the strength of Gulliver's wholesale identification of men with the Yahoos and his unqualified worship of the Houyhnhnms.

It is easy to see what this task would require them to do. It would require them to show that what Gulliver is made to say about human nature in the Voyage, which is certainly misanthropic enough, and what Swift wanted his readers to believe about human nature are, in certain crucial respects at any rate, two different and incompatible things. It would require them, that is, to draw a clear line between what is both Swift and Gulliver and what is only Gulliver in a text in which Gulliver alone is allowed to speak to us.

The resulting new interpretations have differed considerably in emphasis and detail from critic to critic, but they have been generally in accord on the following propositions: The attitudes of Swift and his hero do indeed coincide up to a certain point, it being true for Swift no less than for Gulliver that men in the mass are terrifyingly close to the Yahoos in disposition and behaviour, and true for both of them also that the Houyhnhnms are in some of their qualities—their abhorrence of falsehood, for instance—proper models for human emulation. That, however, is about as far as the agreement goes: it is to Gulliver alone and not to Swift that we must impute the radical pessimism of the final chapters—it is he and not Swift who reduces men literally to Yahoos; it is he and not Swift who despairs of men because they cannot or will not lead the wholly rational life of the Houyhnhnms. Gulliver, in other words, is only in part a reliable spokesman of his creator's satire; he is also, and decisively at the end, one of the targets of that satire—a character designed to convince us, through his obviously infatuated actions, of the absurdity both of any view of man's nature that denies the capacity of at least some men for rational and virtuous conduct, however limited this capacity may be, and of any view of the best existence for man that makes it consist in taking 'reason alone' as a guide. What, in short, Swift offers us, as the ultimate moral of the Voyage, is a compromise between these extremist opinions of Gulliver: human nature, he is saying, is bad enough, but it is not altogether hopeless; reason is a good thing, but a life of pure reason is no desirable end for man.

Now it is evident that however appealing this interpretation may be to those who want to think well of Swift and to rescue him from his nineteenth-century maligners, it is not a merely obvious exegesis of the 'Voyage to the Houyhnhnms,' or one that most common readers, past or present, have spontaneously arrived at. It is not an exegesis, either, that goes at all comfortably with that famous letter of Swift's in 1725 in which he told Pope that his chief aim was 'to vex the world rather than divert it' and that he never would have peace of mind until 'all honest men' were of his opinion. For there is nothing particularly vexing in the at least partly reassuring moral now being attributed to the Voyage or anything which 'honest men' in 1726 would have had much hesitation in accepting. And again, though we must surely agree that there is a significant difference between Gulliver and Swift, why must we suppose that the difference has to be one of basic doctrine? Why could it not be simply the difference between a person who just discovered a deeply disturbing truth about man and is consequently, like Socrates' prisoner in the myth of the cave, more than a little upset and one who, like Socrates himself, has known this truth all along and can therefore write of his hero's discovery of it calmly and with humour?

I introduce these points here not as decisive objections to the new interpretation but rather as signs that it is not the kind of interpretation which (in Johnson's phrase), upon its first production, must be acknowledged to be just. Confirmatory arguments are plainly needed; and a consideration of the arguments that have in fact been offered in support of it will bring us rather quickly to the special problem I wish to discuss.

A good deal has been made, to begin with, of what are thought to be clear indications in the Voyage itself that Swift wanted his readers to take a much more critical view than Gulliver does of 'the virtues and ideas of those exalted Houyhnhnms' and a much less negative view of human possibilities. If he had designed the Houyhnhmns to be for us what they are for Gulliver, namely the 'perfection of nature' and hence an acceptable standard for judging of man, he would surely, it is argued, have endowed them with more humanly engaging qualities than they have; he would surely not have created them as the 'remote, unsympathetic, and in the end profoundly unsatisfying' creatures so many of his readers nowadays find them to be. We must therefore see in Gulliver's worship of the rational horses a plain evidence of the extremist error into which he has fallen. And similarly, if Swift had expected us to go the whole way with Gulliver in his identification of men with the Yahoos, he would hardly have depicted the human characters in his story—especially the admirable Portuguese captain, Don Pedro de Mendez, and his crew—in the conspicuously favourable light in which they appear to us. They are bound to strike us as notable exceptions to the despairing estimate of 'human kind' to which Gulliver has been led by his Houyhnhnm master; and we can only conclude that Gulliver's failure to look upon them as other than Yahoos, whom at best he can only 'tolerate,' is meant as still another sign to us of the false extremism of his attitude.

All this looks at first sight rather convincing—until, that is, we begin to think of other possible intentions that Swift might have had in the Voyage with which these signs would be equally compatible. Suppose that his primary purpose was indeed to 'vex the world' by administering as severe a shock as he could to the cherished belief that man is par excellence a 'rational creature,' and suppose that he chose to do this, in part at least, by forcing his readers to dwell on the unbridgeable gap between what is involved in being a truly 'rational creature' and what not only the worse but also the better sort of men actually are. It is plain what he would have had to do in working out such a design. He would have had to give to his wholly rational beings precisely those 'unhuman' characteristics that have been noted, to their disadvantage, in the Houyhnhnms; to have made them creatures such as we would normally like or sympathize with would have been to destroy their value as a transcendent standard of comparison. And it would have been no less essential to introduce characters, like Don Pedro, who, in terms of ordinary human judgments, would impress us as unmistakably good; otherwise he would have exempted too many of his readers from the shock to their pride in being men which, on this hypothesis, he was trying to produce. He would have had to do, in short, all those things in the Voyage that have been taken as indications of a purpose very different from the one I am now supposing, and much less misanthropic. Clearly, then, some other kind of proof is needed than these ambiguous internal signs before the current view of Swift's meaning can be thought of as more than one possibility among other competing ones.

A good many defenders of this view, especially during the past decade, have attempted to supply such proof by relating the Voyage to its presumed background in the intellectual and religious concerns of Swift and his age; and it is their manner of doing this—of using hypotheses based on the history of ideas in the determination of their author's meaning—that I want to examine in what immediately follows.

They have been fairly well agreed on these three points: in the first place, that Swift's main design in the Voyage was to uphold what they describe as the traditional and orthodox conception of human nature, classical and Christian alike, that 'recognizes in man an inseparable complex of good and evil,' reason and passion, spiritual soul and animal body; secondly, that he conceived the Houyhnhnms and the Yahoos, primarily at least, as allegorical embodiments of these two parts of man's constitution taken in abstraction the one from the other;

and thirdly, that he developed his defence of the orthodox view by directing his satire against those contemporary doctrines, on the one hand, that tended to exalt the Houyhnhnm side of man in forgetfulness of how Yahoo-like man really is, and those doctrines, on the other hand, that tended to see man only as a Yahoo in forgetfulness of his Houyhnhnm possibilities, limited though these are. All this has been more or less common doctrine among critics of the Voyage since Ernest Bernbaum in 1920; there has been rather less agreement on the identity of the contemporary movements of ideas which Swift had in view as objects of attack. It was usual in the earlier phases of the discussion to say simply, as Bernbaum does, that he was thinking, at the one extreme, of the 'sentimental optimism' of writers like Shaftesbury and, at the other, of the pessimism or cynicism of writers like Hobbes and Mandeville. Since then, though, other identifications have been added to the list, as relevant especially to his conception of the Houyhnhnms; we have been told, thus, that he 'obviously' intended to embody in the principles and mode of life of these creatures, along with certain admittedly admirable qualities, the rationalistic errors of the neo-stoics, the Cartesians and the Deists—some or all of these, depending on the critic.

Now if we could feel sure that what was in Swift's mind when he conceived the fourth Voyage is even approximately represented by these statements, we should have little reason for not going along with the interpretation of his design they have been used to support. For if he was indeed engaged in vindicating the 'Christian humanist' view of human nature against those contemporary extremists who made either too much or too little of man's capacity for reason and virtue, then the current view of Gulliver as partly a vehicle and partly an object of the satire is surely correct. Everything depends, therefore, on how much relevance to what he was trying to do in the Voyage this particular historical hypothesis can be shown to have.

Its proponents have offered it as relevant beyond reasonable doubt; which suggests to me that some special assumptions about the application of intellectual history to the exegesis of literary works must be involved here. For they would find it difficult, I think, to justify their confidence in terms merely of the ordinary canons of proof in this as well as other historical fields.

They can indeed show that the hypothesis is a possible one, in the sense that it is consistent with some of the things we know about Swift apart from the Voyage. We know thus that he was a humanistically educated Anglican divine, with traditionalist inclinations in many matters; that he looked upon man's nature as deeply corrupted by the Fall but thought that self-love and the passions could be made, with the help of religion, to yield a positive though limited kind of virtue; that he held reason in high esteem as a God-given possession of man but distrusted any exclusive reliance on it in practice or belief, and ridiculed the Stoics and Cartesians and made war on the Deists; and that he tended, especially in his political writings, to find the useful truth in a medium between extremes. A man of whom these things can be said might very well have conceived the 'Voyage to the Houyhnhnms' in the terms in which, on the present theory, Swift is supposed to have conceived it. And beyond this, it is possible to point to various characteristics in the Voyage itself which *if* the hypothesis is correct, can be interpreted as likely consequences of it. *If* Swift had in fact intended to symbolize, in the sustained opposition of Houyhnhnms and Yahoos, the deep division and conflict within man between his rational and his animal natures, he would undoubtedly have depicted these two sets of creatures, in essentials at least much as they are depicted in the text (though this would hardly account for his choice of horses as symbols of rationality). So too with the supposition that we were meant to see in the Houyhnhnms, among other things, a powerful reminder of how inadequate and dangerous, for weak and sinful human nature, is any such one-sided exaltation of reason as was being inculcated at the time by the Deists, the neo-Stoics, and the Cartesians: it would not be surprising, if that were actually Swift's intention, to find Gulliver saying of 'those exalted quadrupeds,' as he does, that they consider 'reason alone sufficient to govern a rational creature,' that they neither affirm nor deny anything of which they are not certain, and that they keep their passions under firm control, practise 'universal friendship and benevolence,' and remain indifferent to human fear of death and human grief for the death of others.

Now all this is to the good, to the extent at least that without such considerations as these about both Swift and the fourth Voyage there would be no reason for entertaining the hypothesis at all. But can we say anything more than this—so long, that is, as we judge the question by the ordinary standards of historical criticism? In other words, do the considerations I have just summarized tend in any decisive way to establish the hypothesis as fact? The answer must surely be that they do not, and for the simple reason that they are all merely positive and favouring considerations, such as can almost always be adduced in support of almost any hypothesis in scholarship or common life, however irrelevant or false it may turn out to be. It is a basic maxim of scholarly criticism, therefore, that the probability of a given hypothesis is proportionate not to our ability to substantiate it by confirmatory evidence (though there obviously must be confirmatory evidence) but to our inability—after serious trial—to rule it out in favour of some other hypothesis that would explain more completely and simply the particulars it is concerned with. We have to start, in short, with the assumption that our hypothesis may very well be false and then permit ourselves to look upon it as fact only when, having impartially considered all the counter-possibilities we can think of, we find disbelief in it more difficult to maintain than belief. This is a rule which few of us consistently live up to (otherwise we would not publish as much as we do); but there are varying degrees of departure from it; and I can see few signs that its requirements are even approximated to in the current historical discussions of the fourth Voyage. It would be a different matter if these critics had been able to show statements by Swift himself about *Gulliver's Travels* that defy reasonable interpretation except as references to the particular issues and doctrines which the hypothesis supposes were in his mind when he wrote the Voyage. But they have not succeeded in doing this; and they have given no attention at all to the possibility that there were other traditions of thought about human nature in Swift's time (I can think of one such, as will appear later) which he can be shown to have been familiar with and which they ought to have considered and then, if possible, excluded as irrelevant before their hypothesis can be said—again on ordinary scholarly grounds—to be confirmed.

What are, then, the special assumptions about interpretative method in the history of ideas on which, in view of all this, their confidence must be presumed to rest? Their problem has naturally led them, as it would any historian, to make propositions about Swift's thought apart from *Gulliver* and about the thought of Swift's age: what is distinctive is the character of these propositions and the use they are put to in the interpretation of the Voyage. In the eyes of the ordinary historian of ideas inquiring into the intellectual antecedents and causes of this work, the thought of Swift as expressed in his other writings is simply an aggregate of particular statements and arguments, some of which may well turn out to be relevant to an understanding of its meaning; for any of them, however, this is merely a possibility to be tested, not a presumption to be argued from. It is the same, too, with the thought of Swift's age: this, again, in the eyes of the ordinary historian, is nothing more determinate than the sum of things that were being written in the later seventeenth and early eighteenth centuries, from varying points of view and in varying traditions of analysis, on the general theme of human nature; some of these, once more, may well be relevant to the argument developed in the Voyage, but the historian can know what they are only after an unprejudiced inquiry that presupposes no prior limitation on the ideas Swift might have been influenced by or have felt impelled to attack in constructing it. For the ordinary historian, in short, the fact that the 'Voyage to the Houyhnhnms' was written by Swift at a particular moment in the general history of thought about man has only this methodological significance: that it defines the region in which he may most hopefully look for the intellectual stimuli and materials that helped to shape the Voyage; it gives him, so to speak, his working reading-list; it can never tell him—only an independent analysis of the Voyage can do that—how to use the list.

That the critics we are concerned with have taken a different view of the matter from this is suggested by the title of the book in which the current historical theory of Swift's intentions in the Voyage is argued most fully and ingeniously—Kathleen Williams's *Jonathan Swift and the Age of Compromise.* For to think of a period in intellectual history in this way—as the age *of* something or other, where the something or other is designated by an abstract term like 'compromise'—is obviously no longer to consider it as an indefinite aggregate of happenings; it is to consider it rather as a definite system of happenings; something like the plot of a novel in which a great many diverse characters and episodes are unified, more or less completely, by a principal action or theme. It is to assume, moreover, not only that the historian can determine what was the central problem, the basic conflict or tension, the dominant world-view of a century or generation, either in general or in some particular department of thought, but that he can legitimately use his formula for this as a confirmatory premise in arguing the meanings and causes of individual works produced in that age. It is to suppose that there is a kind of probative force in his preferred formula for the period which can confer, a priori, if not a unique at least a privileged relevance on one particular hypothesis about a given work of that period as against other hypotheses that are less easily brought under the terms of the formula, so that little more is required by way of further proof than a demonstration, which is never hard to give, that the work makes sense when it is 'read' as the hypothesis dictates.

These are, I think, the basic assumptions which underlie most of the recent historical discussions of the fourth Voyage and which go far toward explaining the confidence their authors have felt in the correctness of their conclusions. It would be hard, otherwise, to understand why they should think it important to introduce propositions about what was central and unifying in the moral thought of Swift's age; the reason must be that they have hoped, by so doing, to establish some kind of antecedent limitation on the intentions he could be expected to have had in writing the Voyage. And that, indeed, is the almost unavoidable effect of the argument for any reader who closes his mind, momentarily, to the nature of the presuppositions on which it rests. For suppose we agree with these critics that the dominant and most significant issue in the moral speculation of the later seventeenth and early eighteenth centuries was a conflict between the three fundamentally different views of man's nature represented by the orthodox 'classical-Christian' dualism in the middle and, at opposite extremes to this, by the newer doctrines of the rationalists and benevolists on the one side and of the materialists and cynics on the other. Since this is presented as an exhaustive scheme of classification, it will be easy for us to believe that the view of man asserted in the Voyage must have been one of these three. And then suppose we agree to think of Swift as a character in this three-cornered plot, who was predisposed by his humanist education and his convictions as an Anglican divine to adhere to the traditional and compromising view as against either of the modern extremisms. It will be difficult for us now to avoid believing that the 'Voyage to the Houyhnhnms' was therefore more probably than not an assertion of this middle view against its contemporary enemies, and it will be harder than it would be without such an argument from the age to the author to the work, to resist any interpretations of its details that may be necessary to make them accord with that theory of Swift's intentions.

This is likely to be our reaction, at any rate, until we reflect on the peculiar character of the argument we have been persuaded to go along with. There are many arguments like it in the writings of modern critics and historians of ideas in other fields (those who have interpreted Shakespeare in the light of 'the Elizabethan world-picture,' for instance); but they all betray, I think, a fundamental confusion in method. The objection is not that they rest on a false conception of historical periods. There is nothing intrinsically illegitimate in the mode of historical writing that organizes the intellectual happenings of different ages in terms of their controlling 'climates of opinion,' dominant tendencies, or ruling oppositions of attitude or belief; and the results of such synthesizing efforts are sometimes—as in A. O. Lovejoy, for example—illuminating in a very high degree. The objection is rather to the further assumption, clearly implicit in these arguments, that the unifying principles of histories of this type have something like the force of empirically established universal laws, and can therefore be used as guarantees of the probable correctness of any interpretations of individual writings that bring the writings into harmony with their requirements. That this is sheer illusion can be easily seen if we consider what these principles really amount to. Some of them amount simply to assertions that there was a tendency among the writers of a particular time to concentrate on such and such problems and to solve them in such and such ways; there is no implication here that this trend affected all writers or any individual writer at all times; whether a given work of the age did or did not conform to the trend remains therefore an open question, to be answered only by independent inquiry unbiased by the merely statistical probabilities affirmed in the historian's generalization. But there are also principles of a rather different sort, among which we much include, I think, the formula of Swift's critics for the dominant conflict about human nature in his time. These are best described as dialectical constructs, since they organize the doctrinal facts they refer to by imposing on them abstract schemes of logical relationships among ideas which may or may not be identical with any of the various classifications of doctrines influential at the time. Thus the characterization of Swift's age and of Swift himself as a part of that age in our critics derives its apparent exhaustiveness from a pattern of general terms—the concept of 'Christian humanism' and the two contraries of this—which these critics clearly owe to the ethical and historical speculations of Irving Babbitt and his school. Now it may be that this scheme represents accurately enough the distinctions Swift had in mind when he conceived the fourth Voyage; but that would be something of a coincidence, and it is just as reasonable to suppose that he may have been thinking quite outside the particular framework of notions which this retrospective scheme provides. We must conclude, then, that this whole way of using the history of ideas in literary interpretation is a snare and a delusion. From the generalizations and schematisms of the synthesizing historians we can very often get suggestions for new working hypotheses with which to approach the exegesis of individual works. What we cannot get from them is any assurance whatever that any of these hypotheses are more likely to be correct than any others that we have hit upon without their aid.

I should now like to invite the reader's criticism, in the light of what I have been saying, on another view of the intellectual background and import of the fourth Voyage (or a considerable part of it at least) which I have attempted to argue on the basis merely of ordinary historical evidence, independently of any general postulates about Swift or his age.

II

Whatever else may be true of the Voyage, it will doubtless be agreed that one question is kept uppermost in it from the beginning, for both Gulliver and the reader. This is the question of what sort of animal man, as a species, really is; and the point of departure in the argument is the answer to this question which Gulliver brings with him into Houyhnhnmland and which is also, we are reminded more than once, the answer which men in general tend, complacently, to give to it. Neither he nor they have any doubt that only man, among 'sensitive' creatures, can be properly called 'rational'; all the rest—whether wild or tame, detestable or, like that 'most comely and generous' animal, the horse, the reverse of that—being merely 'brutes,' not 'endued with reason.' The central issue, in other words, is primarily one of definition: is man, or is he not, correctly defined as a 'rational creature'? It is significant that Gulliver's misanthropy at the end is not the result of any increase in his knowledge of human beings in the concrete over what he has had before; it is he after all who expounds to his Houyhnhnm master all those melancholy facts about men's 'actions and passions' that play so large a part in their conversations; he has known these facts all along, and has still been able to call himself a 'lover of mankind.' The thing that changes his love into antipathy is the recognition that is now forced upon him that these facts are wholly incompatible with the formula for man's nature which he has hitherto taken for granted—are compatible, indeed, only with a formula, infinitely more humiliating to human pride, which pushes man nearly if not quite over to the opposite pole of the animal world.

What brings about the recognition is, in the first place, the deeply disturbing spectacle of the Houyhnhnms and the Yahoos. I can find nothing in the text that forces us to look on these two sets of strange creatures in any other light than that in which Gulliver sees them—not, that is, as personified abstractions, but simply as two concrete species of animals: existent species for Gulliver, hypothetical species for us. The contrast he draws between them involves the same pair of antithetical terms (the one positive, the other privative) that he has been accustomed to use in contrasting men and the other animals. The essential character of the Houyhnhnms, he tells us, is that they are creatures 'wholly governed by reason'; the essential character of the Yahoos is that 'they are the most unteachable of brutes,' without 'the least tincture of reason.' The world of animals in Houyhnhnmland, in other words, is divided by the same basic differences as the world of animals in Europe. Only, of course—and it is the shock of this that prepares Gulliver for his ultimate abandonment of the definition of man he had started with—it is a world in which the normal distribution of species between 'rational creatures' and irrational 'brutes' is sharply inverted, with horses, whom he can't help admiring, in the natural place of men, and man-like creatures, whom he can't help abhorring, in the natural place of horses.

This is enough in itself to cause Gulliver to view his original formula for his own species, as he says, 'in a very different light.' But he is pushed much farther in the same misanthropic direction by the questions and comments of his Houyhnhnm master, acting as a kind of Socrates. What thus develops is partly a reduction to absurdity of man's 'pretensions to the character of a rational creature' and partly a demonstration of the complete parity in essential nature between men and the Houyhnhnmland Yahoos. There is of course one striking difference—unlike the Yahoos, men are after all possessed of at least a 'small proportion,' a 'small pittance' of reason, some in greater degree than others. But I can see no clear signs in the text that this qualification is intended to set men apart as a third, or intermediate, species for either Gulliver or the reader. For what is basic in the new definition of man as a merely more 'civilized' variety of Yahoo is the fundamentally irrational 'disposition' which motivates his habitual behaviour; and in relation to that his 'capacity for reason' is only an acquired attribute which he is always in danger of losing and of which, as Gulliver says, he makes no other use, generally speaking, than 'to improve and multiply those vices' whereof his 'brethren [in Houyhnhnmland] had only the share that nature allotted them.'

It is clear what a satisfactory historical explanation of this line of argument in the Voyage would have to do. It would have to account for Swift's very patent assumption that there would be a high degree of satirical force, for readers in 1726, in a fable which began with the notion that man is pre-eminently a 'rational creature' and then proceeded to turn this notion violently upside down, and which, in doing so, based itself on a division of animal species into the extremes of 'rational creatures' and irrational 'brutes' and on the paradoxical identification of the former with horses and of the latter with beings closely resembling men. Was there perhaps a body of teaching, not so far brought into the discussion of the Voyage but widely familiar at the time, that could have supplied Swift with the particular scheme of ideas he was exploiting here? I suggest that there was, and also that there is nothing strange in the fact that it has been hitherto overlooked by Swift's critics. For one principal medium through which these ideas could have come to Swift and his readers—the only one, in fact, I know of that could have given him all of them—was a body of writings, mainly in Latin, which students of literature in our day quite naturally shy away from reading: namely, the old-fashioned textbooks in logic that still dominated the teaching of that subject in British universities during the later seventeenth and early eighteenth centuries.[3]

It is impossible not to be impressed, in the first place, by the prominence in these textbooks of the particular definition of man which the Voyage sought to discredit. *Homo est animal rationale:* no one could study elementary logic anywhere in the British Isles in the generation before *Gulliver* without encountering this formula or variations of it (e.g., *Nullus homo est irrationalis*) in his manuals and the lectures he heard. It appears as the standard example of essential definition in the great majority of logics in use during these years at Oxford, Cambridge, and Dublin; and in most of those in which it occurs, it is given without comment or explanation as the obviously correct formula for man's distinctive nature, as if no one would ever question that man is, uniquely and above all, a rational creature. It is frequently brought in many times over, in various contexts, in individual textbooks: I have counted a dozen or so occurrences of it in Milton's *Art of Logic*, and many times that number in the *Institutionum logicarum . . . libri duo* of Franco Burgersdijck (or Burgersdicius), which was one of the most widely used, and also one of the longest lived, of all these writings—it appeared in 1626 and was still prescribed at Dublin when Edmund Burke went there as a Junior Freshman in 1744.[4] I shall have some more to say of Burgersdicius, or 'Burgy' as Burke called him, presently; but it is worth noting that he provides us, in one passage, with the very question on which much of the fourth Voyage was to turn, with the answer Swift was *not* to give to it: 'Quærenti enim, Quale animal est homo? apposite respondetur, Rationale.'

Not only, however, was the definition omnipresent in these books, but there is some evidence that it was thought of, in Swift's time, as the special property of the academic logicians. Locke, for instance, calls it in his *Essay* 'the ordinary Definition of the Schools,' the 'sacred Definition of *Animal Rationale*' of 'the learned Divine and Lawyer'; it goes, he implies, with 'this whole *Mystery* of *Genera* and *Species*, which make such a noise in the Schools, and are, with Justice, so little regarded out of them' (III.iii.10; vi.26; iii.9). And there are other later testimonies to the same effect; among them these opening lines of an anonymous poem of the period after *Gulliver*, once ascribed to Swift—'The Logicians Refuted':

Logicians have but ill defin'd
As rational, the human kind;
Reason, they say, belongs to man,
But let them prove it if they can.
Wise Aristotle and Smiglesius,
By ratiocinations specious,
Have strove to prove with great precision,
With definition and division,
Homo est ratione preditum;
But for my soul I cannot credit 'em.[5]

But the logicians had more to offer Swift than the great authority which they undoubtedly conferred on the definition 'rational animal.' They could have suggested to him also the basic principle on which the inverted animal world of Houyhnhnmland was constructed, and consequently the disjunction that operated as major premise in his argument about man. Whoever it was, among the Greeks, that first divided the genus 'animal' by the differentiae 'rational' and 'irrational,' there is much evidence that this antithesis had become a commonplace in the Greco-Roman schools long before it was taken up by the writer who did more than any one else to determine the context in which the definition *animal rationale* was chiefly familiar to Englishmen of Swift's time. This writer was the Neoplatonist Porphyry of the third century A.D., whose little treatise, the *Isagoge*, or introduction to the categories of Aristotle, became, as is well known, one of the great sources of logical theorizing and teaching from the time of Boethius until well beyond the end of the seventeenth century. There is no point in going into the details of Porphyry's doctrine: what is important for our purpose here is the new sanction he gave to the older division of animal species through his incorporation of it into the general scheme of differentiae for the category of substance which was later known as the *arbor porphyriana* or Porphyry's tree, especially in the diagrams of it that became a regular feature of the more elementary textbooks. Here it is, set forth discursively, in the crabbed prose of Burgersdicius (I quote the English version of 1697, but the Latin is no better). In seeking the definition of man, he writes, we must first observe that

> Man is a Substance; but because an Angel is also a Substance; *That it may appear how Man differs from an Angel,* Substance ought to be divided into Corporeal and Incorporeal. A Man is a *Body,* an Angel *without a Body:* But a Stone also is a *Body:* That therefore a Man may be distinguished from a Stone divide Bodily or Corporeal Substance into Animate and Inanimate, that is, *with or without a Soul.* Man is a Corporeal Substance Animate, Stone Inanimate. But Plants are also *Animate:* Let us divide therefore again Corporeal Substance Animate into *Feeling and void of Feeling.* Man feels, a Plant not: But a Horse *also feels,* and likewise other Beasts. Divide we therefore Animate Corporeal Feeling Substance into Rational and Irrational. Here therefore *are we to stand,* since it appears that every, and only Man *is Rational.*[6]

And there was, finally, one other thing in these logics that could have helped to shape Swift's invention in the fourth Voyage. In opposing man as the only species of 'rational animal' to the brutes, Porphyry obviously needed a specific instance, parallel to man, of an 'irrational' creature; and the instance he chose—there were earlier precedents for the choice[7]—was the horse. The proportion 'rational' is to 'irrational' as man is to horse occurs more than once in the *Isagoge;* and the juxtaposition, in the same context, of *homo* and *equus* was a frequently recurring cliché in his seventeenth-century followers, as in the passage in Burgersdicius just quoted: other species of brutes were occasionally mentioned, but none of them nearly so often. And any one who studied these books could hardly fail to remember a further point —that the distinguishing 'property' of this favourite brute was invariably given as whinnying *(facultas hinniendi)*; *equus,* it was said again and again, *est animal hinnibile.*

To most Englishmen of Swift's time who had read logic in their youth—and this would include nearly all generally educated men— these commonplaces of Porphyry's tree, as I may call them for short, were as familiar as the Freudian commonplaces are to generally educated people today, and they were accepted, for the most part, in an even less questioning spirit, so that it might well have occurred to a clever satirist then that he could produce a fine shock to his readers' complacency as human beings by inventing a world in which horses appeared where the logicians had put men and men where they had put horses, and by elaborating, through this, an argument designed to shift the position of man as a species from the *animal rationale* branch of the tree, where he had always been proudly placed, as far as possible over toward the *animal irrationale* branch, with its enormously less flattering connotations. But have we any warrant for thinking that this, or something like it, was what Swift actually had in mind? It is clearly possible to describe the Voyage as, in considerable part at least, an anti-Porphyrian satire in the genre of the poem I quoted from earlier, 'The Logicians Refuted.' But is there any evidence that Swift planned it as such?

That the Porphyrian commonplaces had been known to him in their full extent from his days at Trinity College in the early 1680s we can hardly doubt in view of the kind of education in logic he was exposed to there. Among the books which all Junior Freshmen at Dublin in those years were required to study or hear lectures on, we know of three in which the Porphyrian apparatus and examples had a prominent place: the *Isagoge* itself (which was prescribed by the statutes of the College to be read twice over during the year), the older logic of Burgersdicius, and the newer *Institutio logicae* of Narcissus Marsh. It is true that Swift, according to his own later statement, detested this part of the curriculum, and it is true that on one examination in his last year his mark in Philosophy was *Male* (he had a *Bene* in Greek and Latin). But this was an examination in the more advanced branches of the Aristotelian system, and it is likely that he had fared better in the earlier examination in logic, since he had evidently been allowed to proceed with his class. It is possible, moreover, to infer from his occasional use of logical terms in his later writings that, abhorrent as the subject was to him, the time he had been compelled to spend on it as a Junior Freshman was not a total loss. He at least remembered enough of it to allude familiarly in different places to such things as a 'long sorites,' 'the first proposition of a hypothetical syllogism,' and the fallacy of two middle terms in a single syllogism;[8] and if this was possible, there is good reason to suppose that he had not forgotten the much simpler Porphyrian points about genera, species, and definition, 'rational' versus 'irrational' animals, men and horses which he had been introduced to at the same time.

The crucial question, however, is whether he had these notions of the logicians at all actively in mind when, in the 1720s, he conceived and wrote the 'Voyage to the Houyhnhnms.' And here it will be well to take a fresh look at the two much-quoted letters about *Gulliver's Travels* which he sent to Pope in 1725, just after that work was completed. In the first of these, that of September 29, after having told Pope that his chief aim is 'to vex the world rather than divert it' and that he hates and detests 'that animal called man,' he goes on to remark: 'I have got materials towards a treatise proving the falsity of that definition *animal rationale,* and to show it should be only *rationis capax.* Upon this great foundation of misanthropy, though not in Timon's manner, the whole building of my Travels is erected; and I never will have peace of mind till all honest men are of my opinion.' In the second letter, that of November 26, he desires that Pope and 'all my friends' will 'take a special care that my disaffection to the world may not be imputed to my age, for I have credible witnesses . . . that it has never varied from the twenty-first to the f——ty-eighth year of my life.' He then adds a passage which has been read as a retraction of the judgment on humanity expressed in the first letter, though the final sentence makes clear, I think, that it was not so intended: 'I tell you after all, that I do not hate mankind; it is *vous autres* [i.e., Pope and Bolingbroke] who hate them, because you would have them reasonable animals, and are angry for being disappointed. I have always rejected that definition, and made another of my own. I am no more angry with ——than I am with the kite that last week flew away with one of my chickens; and yet I was glad when one of my servants shot him two days after.'

The casual references in both letters to 'that definition'—'*animal rationale*' and 'reasonable animals'—which Swift tells Pope he has 'always rejected' have usually been interpreted by modern critics as allusions to such contemporary philosophical or theological heresies (from Swift's point of view) as the 'optimism' of Shaftesbury or the 'rationalism' of Descartes and the Deists. It is surely, however, a much less far-fetched conjecture, especially in view of the familiar textbook Latin of the first letter, to see in 'that definition' nothing other or more than the 'sacred definition' of the logicians which he had had inflicted on him, by thoroughly orthodox tutors, in his undergraduate days at Dublin.

I find this explanation, at any rate, much harder to disbelieve than any other that has been proposed; and all the more so because of another passage in the first letter which is almost certainly reminiscent of the Trinity logic course in the early 1680s. It is the famous sentence —just before the allusion to 'that definition *animal rationale*' and leading on to it—in which Swift says: 'But principally I hate and detest that animal called man, although I heartily love John, Peter, Thomas, and so forth.' Now to any one at all widely read in the logic textbooks of Swift's time two things about this sentence are immediately evident: first, that the distinction it turns on is the distinction to be found in nearly all these books between a species of animals and individual members of that species; and second, that the names 'John, Peter, Thomas, and so forth' are wholly in line with one of the two main traditions of names for individuals of the species man that had persisted side by side in innumerable manuals of logic since the Middle Ages: not, of course, the older tradition of classical names—Socrates, Plato, Alexander, Caesar—but the newer tradition (which I have noted first in Occam, though it doubtless antedates him) that drew upon the list of apostles—Peter, John, Paul, James, Thomas, in roughly that descending order of preference. (Other non-classical names, like Stephen, Catharine, Charles, Richard, also appear, but much less frequently.)

We can go farther than this, however. For although all three of Swift's names occur separately in divers texts (Thomas least often), the combination 'John, Peter, Thomas, and so forth' was an extremely unusual one. I have met with it, in fact, in only one book before 1725; and I have examined nearly all the logics, both Latin and English, down to that date for which I can find any evidence that they had even a minor circulation in Great Britain. The exception, however, is a book which Swift could hardly have escaped knowing as an undergraduate, since it was composed expressly for the use of Trinity College students by the then Provost and had just recently come 'on the course' when he entered the College in 1682—namely, the *Institutio logicae*, already referred to, of Narcissus Marsh (Dublin, 1679: reissued Dublin, 1681). Early in the book Marsh gives a full-page diagram of Porphyry's tree, with its inevitable opposition of *animal-rationale-homo* and *animal-irrationale-brutum;* and here, as *individua* under *homo,* we find 'Joannes, Petrus, Thomas, &c.' And a little later in the book the same names are repeated in the same order as individual specimens of *homo* in Marsh's analytical table for the category *substantia.*

Was this combination of names, then, Marsh's invention? There is one further circumstance which suggests that it may well have been. We know from his own testimony,[9] as well as from internal evidence, that the source on which he based the greater part of his Dublin logic of 1679 was his own revision, published at Oxford in 1678, of the *Manuductio ad logicam* of the early seventeenth-century Jesuit logician Philippe Du Trieu. Now of the two passages in the Dublin book that contain Swift's three names, the first—the diagram of Porphyry's tree—has no counterpart in the Oxford book of 1678, though it has in

Du Trieu's original text, where the names are 'Petrus' and 'Joannes.' It would seem likely, then, that Marsh first thought of the combination 'John, Peter, Thomas, and so forth' when he revised his earlier revision of Du Trieu for his Trinity students in 1679; and this is borne out by what he did at the same time with the other passage—the table of substance. This he retained almost exactly as it had been in Du Trieu except for the names under *homo:* here, where in 1678 he had reprinted Du Trieu's 'Stephanus, Johannes, Catharine, &c.,' he now wrote 'Johannes, Petrus, Thomas, &c.' Which would seem to imply a certain sense of private property in these particular names in this particular combination.

It is somewhat hard, then, not to conclude that Swift was remembering Marsh's logic as he composed the sentence, in his letter to Pope, about 'John, Peter, Thomas, and so forth.' But if that is true, can there be much doubt, in view of the Porphyrian context in which these names appear in Marsh, as to what tradition of ideas was in his mind when he went on to remark, immediately afterwards, that 'the great foundation of misanthropy' on which 'the whole building' of his *Travels* rested was his proof—against Marsh and the other logicians he had been made to study at Trinity—of 'the falsity of that definition *animal rationale*'?[10]

NOTES

This paper was read, in somewhat different form, at Wadham College, Oxford, in April, 1959, before the Annual Conference of Nonprofessorial University Teachers of English of the British Isles.

[1] See his 'Errors Concerning the Houyhnhnms,' *MP,* LVI (1958), 92-97.

[2] The list of writings that reflect this preoccupation is now a fairly long one; in the present essay I have had in view chiefly the following: Ernest Bernbaum, 'The Significance of "Gulliver's Travels,"' in his edition of that work (New York, 1920); T. O. Wedel, 'On the Philosophical Background of *Gulliver's Travels,*' *SP,* XXIII (1926), 434-50; John F. Ross, 'The Final Comedy of Lemuel Gulliver,' in *Studies in the Comic* ('University of California Publications in English,' Vol. VIII, No. 2, 1941), pp. 175-96; Robert B. Heilman, Introduction to his edition of *Gulliver's Travels* (New York, 1950), especially pp. xii-xxii; Ernest Tuveson, 'Swift: the Dean as Satirist,' *University of Toronto Quarterly,* XXII (1953), 368-75; Roland M. Frye, 'Swift's Yahoo and the Christian Symbols for Sin,' *JHI,* XV (1954), 201-15; W. A. Murray's supplementary note to Frye, *ibid.,* pp. 596-601; Samuel H. Monk, 'The Pride of Lemuel Gulliver,' *Sewanee*

Review, LXIII (1955), 48-71; Irvin Ehrenpreis, 'The Origins of *Gulliver's Travels*,' *PMLA*, LXXII (1957), 880-99 (reprinted with some revisions in his *The Personality of Jonathan Swift* [London, 1958]); Kathleen Williams, *Jonathan Swift and the Age of Compromise* (Lawrence, Kansas, 1958); Calhoun Winton, 'Conversion on the Road to Houyhnhnmland,' *Sewanee Review*, LXVIII (1960), 20-33; Martin Kallich, 'Three Ways of Looking at a Horse: Jonathan Swift's "Voyage to the Houyhnhnms" Again,' *Criticism*, II (1960), 107-24.

[3] There are useful descriptions of many, though by no means all, of these in Wilbur Samuel Howell, *Logic and Rhetoric in England, 1500–1700* (Princeton, 1956).

[4] *The Correspondence of Edmund Burke*, ed. by Thomas W. Copeland, I (Cambridge and Chicago, 1958), 4, 7-9, 21, 28.

[5] *The Busy Body*, No. 5, October 18, 1759. Both the ascription to Swift, which occurs in a note prefixed to this first known printing of the poem, and the later ascription to Goldsmith seem to me highly dubious.

[6] *Monitio Logica: or, An Abstract and Translation of Burgersdicius his Logick* (London, 1697), pp. 13-14 (second pagination).

[7] E.g., Quintilian, *Institutio oratoria*, VII.iii.3, 24. For the contrast of man and horse in Porphyry see especially Migne, *PL*, LXIV, col. 128 (Boethius' translation): 'Differentia est quod est aptum natum dividere ea quæ sub eodem genere sunt: rationale enim et irrationale, hominem et equum quæ sub eodem genere sunt animali dividunt.'

[8] See John M. Bullitt, *Jonathan Swift and the Anatomy of Satire* (Cambridge, Mass., 1953), p. 73. Cf. also Swift, 'A Preface to the B——p of S——m's Introduction,' in *Works*, ed. by Temple Scott, III, 150.

[9] See his preface 'Ad lectorem' in the 1681 issue (it is missing from some copies but can be found in the Cambridge University Library copy and in that belonging to Archbishop Marsh's Library, Dublin); also the entry for December 20, 1690, in his manuscript diary. I owe this latter reference to Miss Mary Pollard, of Archbishop Marsh's Library. For the rather complicated bibliographical history of Marsh's *Institutio logicae* (the title was altered to *Institutiones logicae* in the reissue of 1681), see her article, 'The Printing of the Provost's Logic and the Supply of Text-books in the late Seventeenth Century,' in *Friends of the Library of Trinity College, Dublin: Annual Bulletin*, 1959-61.

[10] Since this essay went to press I have discussed some further aspects of the subject in a brief article, 'The Rationale of the Fourth Voyage,' in *Gulliver's Travels: An Annotated Text with Critical Essays*, ed. by Robert A. Greenberg (New York, 1961), pp. 300-7, and in a review of two recent papers on Swift and the Deists, in *PQ*, XL (1961), 427-30.

A Greek Theater of Ideas

William Arrowsmith

Several years ago I made a plea that scholars and critics should recover a feeling for what I called turbulence in Greek tragedy.[1] By turbulence I meant both "the actual disorder of experience as that experience gets into Greek drama" and "the impact of ideas under dramatic test." What I want to do here is to take up the turbulence of ideas, as I see those ideas expressed by Euripidean drama, with the purpose of showing that the Greeks possessed a theater which we should have no difficulty in recognizing as a genuine theater of ideas. By theater of ideas I do not mean, of course, a theater of intellectual *sententiae* or Shavian "talk" or even the theater of the sophist-poet; I mean a theater of dramatists whose medium of thought was the stage, who used the whole machinery of the theater as a way of *thinking*, critically and constructively, about their world.

In such a theater I assume that the emphasis will be upon ideas rather than character and that a thesis or problem will normally take precedence over development of character or heroism; that aesthetic or formal pleasure will be secondary to intellectual rigor and thought; and that the complexity of ideas presented may require severe formal dislocations or intricate blurrings of emotional modes and genres once kept artistically distinct. It is also likely that the moral texture of an action will be "difficult," and that moral satisfaction will not come easily or even at all; that problems may be left unresolved; that is, that the effect of a play may very well be discomfort or even pain, and that the purpose of this discomfort will be to influence the social rather than the individual behavior of the spectator. Beyond this I would expect such a theater to be commonly concerned with the diagnosis and dramatization of cultural crisis, and hence that the universe in which the dramatic action takes place would tend to be either irrational or incomprehensible. All of these characteristics are, of course, abstracted at random from the historical theater of ideas from Hebbel to the present, but in their ensemble they serve to give at least a general sense of the kind of theater of ideas I have in mind.

That such a theater—so specifically modern and anti-traditional a theater—existed among the Greeks is not, I believe, exactly an article of faith among scholars and critics. To be sure, the Greek theater, like any other great theater, made abundant use of ideas, and the Athenians regarded the theater, not as entertainment, but as the supreme instrument of cultural instruction, a democratic *paideia* complete in itself. Aeschylus, for instance, uses ideas with stunning boldness, showing in play after play how the great post-Hesiodic world-order could be compellingly and comprehensively adapted to Athenian history and society; and his theater not only provides a great, and new, theodicy, but dramatically creates the evolving idea of Athens as the supreme achievement of the mind of Zeus and the suffering of mankind. As for Sophocles, I am not of those who believe that he, like Henry James, possessed a mind so fine that no idea could violate it. In Oedipus, for instance, we have Sophocles' image of heroic man, shorn of his old Aeschylean confidence in himself and his world, and relentlessly pursuing the terrible new truth of his, and human, destiny. Oedipus looks into the abyss that yawns beneath him—the frightful knowledge of his nature which fifth-century man had learned from the war, the plague and the atrocities, the sophistic revolution, and the collapse of the old world-order—and dashes out his eyes at the unbrookable sight. Similarly in Sophocles' Ajax I think we are meant to see a somewhat earlier symbol of the old aristocratic ethos; caught in new and anti-heroic circumstances which degrade him and make him ludicrous, Ajax consistently prefers suicide to a life of absurdity in an alien time.[2] But all this is merely to say that Sophocles, like Aeschylus, uses the perceptions of cultural crisis as framing dramatic ideas or symbolically, not that his theater is in any meaningful sense a theater of ideas. Clearly it is to Euripides—the innovator and experimentalist, the anti-traditional "immoralist" and "stage-sophist"—that we must look for any valid fifth-century theater of ideas.

That the second half of the fifth century B.C. was a period of immense cultural crisis and political convulsion is, fortunately for my purpose here, beyond any real doubt. The evidence itself needs only the barest rehearsal, but it should at least be *there,* the real though sketchy weather of my argument. Let me therefore brush it in.

There is, first of all, the breakdown of the old community, the overwhelming destruction of that mythical and coherent world-order which Werner Jaeger has described so fully in *Paideia*. Political convulsion—stasis and revolution—broke out everywhere. If civil war was nothing new among the Greek city-states, civil war on the fifth-century scale was absolutely unprecedented in its savagery: city against city, man against man, father against son. Under such conditions the whole kinship structure on which the polis was theoretically and constitutionally founded was irretrievably weakened. In culture the sophistic revolution ushered in something like a transvaluation of morals. In society there was the rise of a new bourgeoisie provided with new sanctions and new theories of human nature, as well as a politically conscious proletariat. In the arts restless innovation was the rule, and throughout the Hellenic world—in literature, thought, and politics—there took place a vast debate whose very terms vividly report the schism in the culture, especially in the great argument between *physis* (nature) and *nomos* (custom, tradition, and law). Men begin to wonder now whether the laws of the state and the state itself, once thought divinely established, are any longer related to *physis* at large or to human *physis* in particular. Thus the great experience of the late fifth century is what can be called "the loss of innocence." Sophocles, Euripides, Aristophanes, and Thucydides are all, each in his different way, haunted by the disappearance of the old integrated culture and the heroic image of man that had incarnated that culture. There is a new spirit of divisiveness abroad in the Hellenic world; appearance and reality, nature and tradition, move steadily apart under the destructive pressure of war and its attendant miseries. Subjected to harsh necessity, human nature now shows itself in a new nakedness, but also in a startling new range of behavior, chaotic and uncontrollable.

How wrenching that convulsion was, how extreme and catastrophic, is told us by no less an authority than Thucydides himself:

> So bloody was the march of the revolution [in Corcyra], and the impression which it made was the greater as it was one of the first to occur. Later on, one may say, the whole Hellenic world was convulsed. . . . The sufferings which revolution entailed upon the cities were many and terrible, such as have occurred and always will occur, as long as the nature of mankind remains the same; though in a severer or milder form, and varying in their symptoms, according to the variety of the particular cases. In peace and prosperity states and individuals have better sentiments, because they do not find themselves suddenly confronted with imperious necessities; but war takes away the easy supply of daily wants, and so proves a

rough master that brings most men's characters to a level with their fortunes. Revolution thus ran its course from city to city, and the places which it arrived at last, from having heard what had been done before, carried to a still greater excess the refinement of their inventions, as manifested in the cunning of their enterprises and the atrocity of their reprisals. Words had to change their ordinary meaning and to take that which was now given them. Reckless audacity came to be considered the courage of a loyal ally; prudent hesitation, specious cowardice; moderation was held to be a cloak for unmanliness; ability to see all sides of a question, inaptness to act on any. Frantic violence became the attribute of manliness; cautious plotting, a justifiable means of self-defence. The advocate of extreme measures was always trustworthy; his opponent a man to be suspected. . . . Even blood became a weaker tie than party, from the superior readiness of those united by the latter to dare everything without reserve; for such associations had not in view the blessings derivable from established institutions but were formed by ambition for their overthrow; and the confidence of their members in each other rested less on any religious sanction than upon complicity in crime. . . .

The cause of all these evils was the hunger for power arising from greed and ambition; and from these passions proceeded the violence of parties once engaged in contention. The leaders in the cities, each provided with the fairest professions, on the one side with the cry of political equality for the people, on the other of a moderate aristocracy, sought prizes for themselves in those public interests which they pretended to cherish, and, recoiling from no means in their struggles for ascendancy, engaged in the direct excesses; in their acts of vengeance they went to even greater lengths, not stopping at what justice or the good of the state demanded, but making the party caprice of the moment their only standard, and invoking with equal readiness the condemnation of an unjust verdict or the authority of the strong arm to glut the animosities of the hour. Thus religion was in honor with neither party, but the use of fair phrases to arrive at guilty ends was in high reputation. Meanwhile the moderate part of the citizenry perished between the two, either for not joining in the quarrel or because envy would not suffer them to escape.

Thus every form of evil took root in the Hellenic countries by reason of the troubles. The ancient simplicity into which honor so largely entered was laughed down and disappeared; and society became divided into camps in which no man trusted his fellow. To put an end to this, there was neither promise to be depended upon, nor oath that could command respect; but all parties dwelling rather in their calculation upon the hopelessness of a permanent state of affairs, were more intent upon self-defence than capable of confidence. In this contest the blunter wits were most successful. Apprehensive of their own deficiencies and of the cleverness of their antagonists, they feared to be worsted in debate and to be surprised by the combinations of their more versatile opponents, and so at once boldly had recourse to action; while their adversaries, arrogantly thinking that they should know in time, and that it was unneccessary to secure by action what policy afforded, often fell victims to their want of precaution.

Meanwhile Corcyra gave the first example of most of the crimes alluded to; of the reprisals exacted by the governed who had never experienced equitable treatment or indeed anything except outrage from their rulers—when their hour came; of the iniquitous resolves of those who desired to get rid of their accustomed poverty, and ardently coveted their neighbors' possessions; and lastly, of the savage and pitiless excesses into which men who had begun the struggle, not in a class but a party spirit, were hurried by their ungovernable passions. In the confusion into which life was now thrown in the cities, human nature, always rebelling against the law and now its master, gladly showed itself uncontrolled in passion, above respect for justice, and the enemy of all superiority; since revenge would not have been set above religion, and gain above justice, had it not been for the fatal power of envy. Indeed men too often take upon themselves in the prosecution of their revenge to set the example of doing away with those general laws to which all alike can look for salvation in their day of adversity, instead of allowing them to exist against the day of danger when their aid may be required. (III, 82 ff. Trans. Crawley)

Every sentence of that account deserves to be read, slowly and meditatively, with due weight given to every phrase, every word, lest we underread, as we so often do with the classics, and translate the greatest cultural crisis of the Hellenic world into a parochial and ephemeral time of troubles. If Thucydides is to be trusted, the culture of his time had been shaken to the roots, and he feared for its survival.

How did this convulsion of a whole culture affect the idea of a theater as we find that idea expressed by Euripides?

The immediate, salient fact of Euripides' theater is the assumption of a universe devoid of rational order or of an order incomprehensible to men. And the influence of Aristotle is nowhere more obvious than in the fact that this aspect of Euripides' theater is the one least often recognized or acted upon by critics. Yet it is stated both explicitly and implicitly from play to play throughout Euripides' lifetime. "The care of god for us is a great thing," says the chorus of Hippolytus, "if a man believe it. . . . So I have a secret hope of someone, a god who is wise and plans; / but my hopes grow dim when I see / the actions of men and their destinies. / For fortune always veers and the currents of life are shifting, / shifting, forever changing course." "O Zeus, what can I say?" cries Talthybius in *Hecuba.* "That you look on men and care? Or do we, holding that the gods exist, / deceive ourselves with unsubstantial dreams / and lies, while random careless chance and change / alone control the world?" Usually desperate, feeble, and skeptical in the first place, it is the fate of these hopes to be destroyed in action. In *Heracles* the fatal chaos of the moral universe is shown formally; a savage reversal which expresses the flaw in the moral universe splits the entire play into two contrasting actions connected only by sequence. Thus the *propter hoc* structure required by Aristotelian drama is in Euripides everywhere annulled by *created* disorder and formal violence. What we get is *dissonance, diparity, rift, peripeteia;* in Euripides a note of firm tonality is almost always the sign of traditional parody; of the false, the unreal, or lost innocence remembered in anguish. What this assumption of disorder means is: first, that form is not organic; second, that character is not destiny, or at best that only a part of it is; and third, that Aristotelian notions of responsibility, tragic flaw, and heroism are not pertinent.

The central dissonance assumes a variety of forms. But the commonest is a carefully construed clash between myth (or received reality) on the one hand, and fact (or experienced reality) on the other. Λόγῳ μέν . . . ἔργῳ δέ as the Greeks put it, contrasting theory (*logos*) and fact (*ergon*), appearance (or pretence) and reality, legend and truth. In *Alcestis,* for instance, Euripides juxtaposes the traditional, magnanimous Admetus with the shabby egotist who results when a "heroic" character is translated into realistic fifth-century terms. By making Alcestis take Admetus at his own estimate, Euripides delays the impact of his central idea—the exposure of Admetus' *logos* by his *ergon*—until the appearance of Pheres, whose savage "realistic" denunciation of his son totally exposes the "heroic" Admetus. By a similar translation, Euripides' Odysseus becomes a demagogue of *realpolitik*, Agamemnon a pompous and ineffectual field marshal, and Jason a vulgar adventurer. It was, of course, this technique of realism, this systematic exposure and deflation of traditional heroism, which earned Euripides his reputation for debasing the dignity of the tragic stage. And in some sense the charge is irrefutable. Euripides' whole bent is clearly anti-traditional and realistic; his sense of rebelliousness is expressed beyond doubt by the consistency with which he rejects religious tradition, by his restless experiments with new forms and new music, and by his obvious and innocent delight in his own virtuosity—his superior psychology and his naturalistic stagecraft. With justifiable pride he might have seen himself as a dramatic pioneer, breaking new ground, and courageously refusing to write the higher parody of his predecessors which his world—and ours—have demanded of him. There must be, I imagine, very few theaters in the world where the man who writes of "people as they are" is automatically judged inferior to the man who writes of "people as they should be."

But it would be wrong to assume that realism was the whole story or that Euripides was drawn to realism because he knew it would offend the worthies of his day. For it was life, not Euripides, which had abandoned the traditional forms and the traditional heroism. What Euripides reported, with great clarity and honesty, was the widening gulf between reality and tradition; between the operative and the professed values of his culture; between fact and myth; between *nomos* and *physis;* between life and art. That gulf was the greatest and most evident reality of the last half of the fifth century, *the* dramatic subject par excellence, and it is my belief that the theater of Euripides, like Thucydides' history, is a radical and revolutionary attempt to record, analyze and assess that reality in relation to the new view of human nature which crisis revealed. To both Thucydides and Euripides, the crisis in culture meant that the old world-order with its sense of a great humanity and its assumption of an integrated human soul was irrecoverably gone. The true dimensions of the human psyche, newly exposed in the chaos of culture, forbade any return to the old innocence or heroism. Any theater founded on the old psyche or the old idea of fate was to that extent a lie. The task imposed upon the new theater was not merely that of being truthful, of reporting the true dimensions and causes of the crisis, but of coping imaginatively and intellectually with a change in man's very condition.

It is for this reason that Euripides' theater almost always begins with a severe critique of tradition, which necessarily means a critique of his predecessors. Such programmatic criticism is what we expect from any new theater, and in the case of Greek theater, where the dramatist is official *didaskalos,* charged with the *paideia* of his people, it was especially appropriate. Aeschylus and Sophocles were not merely great theatrical predecessors; they were the moral tutors of Athens and their versions of the myths embodied, as nothing else did, the values of tradition and the old *paideia.* Given such authority and power, polemic and criticism were only to be expected, the only possible response; indeed, were it not for the fact that Euripides' criticism has generally been construed as cultural *lèse-majesté*, the point would hardly be worth making. When Shakespeare or Ibsen or Shaw or Brecht criticizes the theater of his immediate predecessors, we applaud; this is what we expect, the aggressive courage a new theater requires. When Euripides does it, it becomes somehow sacrilege, a crime against the classics. We respond, if at all, with outraged traditionalism, automatically invoking that double standard which we seem to reserve for the classics, that apparent homage which turns out to be nothing but respect for our own prejudices.

In Euripides' case, the prejudice is usually justified by the argument that Euripides' criticism of his predecessors is destructive and negative; that his attack on the old order is finally nothing but the niggling rage for exposure, devoid of constructive order. If this argument were sound, it would be impressive; but it is not enough to offer on Euripides' behalf the reply which Morris Cohen is said to have made to a student who accused him of destroying his religious beliefs: "Young man, it is recorded of Heracles that he was required only to *clean* the Augean stables." Not, that is, if we are serious in maintaining that Euripides was a great dramatist. Negative criticism of dead tradition and inert values is often of positive therapeutic effect, but no really great dramatist, it seems to me, can escape the responsibility for imaginative order. Actually the charge that Euripides is negative is based upon misreading of the plays. For one thing Euripides did not always expose myth and tradition; this is his bias, to be sure, but there are exceptions in which the received myth and its values are used to criticize contemporary reality and public policy. The obvious example is the *Trojan Women*. A more revealing instance is the *Iphigenia in Tauris*, in which the cult of Artemis of Brauron is reestablished by Athena at the close of the play in order to lay bare the immense human "blood sacrifice" of the Peloponnesian War.

The point here, I believe, is both important and neglected. Let me try to restate it. Euripides' favorite technique for demonstrating the new dissonance in Athenian culture, the disparity between putative values and real values is simply realism of the pattern λόγῳ μέν . . . ἔργῳ δέ. But it is balanced at times by the converse technique—allowing the myth to criticize the everyday reality—ἔργῳ μέν . . . λόγῳ δέ. And these exceptions are important, since they show us that Euripides' realism is not a matter of simple anti-traditionalism, but consistent dramatic technique. What is basic is the mutual criticism, the mutual exposure that occurs when the incongruities of a given culture—its actual behavior and its myth—are juxtaposed in their fullness. That this is everywhere the purpose of Euripidean drama is clear in the very complaints critics bring against the plays: their tendency to fall into inconsistent or opposed parts (*Heracles, Andromache*); their apparent multidimensionality (*Alcestis, Heracles*), the frequency of the *deus ex machina.* This last device is commonly explained by a hostile criticism as Euripides' penchant for archaism and aetiology, or as his way of salvaging botched plays. Actually it is *always* functional, a part of the very pattern of juxtaposed incongruities which I have been describing. Thus the appearance of any god in a Euripidean play is invariably the sign of *logos* making its epiphany, counterpointing *ergon.* Most Euripidean gods appear only in order to incriminate themselves (or a fellow god), though some—like Athena in the *Iphigenia in Tauris*—criticize the action and the reality which the action mirrors. But it is a variable, not a fixed, pattern, whose purpose is the critical counterpointing of the elements which Euripides saw everywhere sharply and significantly opposed in his own culture: myth confronted by behavior, tradition exposed by, or exposing, reality; custom and law in conflict with nature. What chiefly interested him was less the indictment of tradition, though that was clearly essential, than the *confrontation,* the *dramatic juxtaposition,* of the split in his culture. This was his basic theatrical perception, *his* reality, a perception which makes him utterly different from Aeschylus and Sophocles, just as it completely alters the nature of his theater.

Is that theater merely analytical then, a dramatic description of a divided culture? I think not. Consider this statement: "As our knowledge becomes increasingly divorced from real life, our culture no longer contains ourselves (or only contains an insignificant part of ourselves) and forms a social context in which we are not 'integrated.' The problem thus becomes that of again reconciling our culture with our life, by making our culture a living culture once more. . . ." That happens to be Ionesco on Artaud, but it could just as well be Euripides' description of the nature and purpose of his own theater. The reconciliation of life and culture is, of course, more than any theater, let alone a single dramatist, can accomplish; and it is perhaps enough that the art of a divided culture should be diagnostic, should describe the new situation in its complexity. Only by so doing can it redefine man's altered fate. It is my own conviction that Euripidean theater is critical and diagnostic, and that, beyond this, it accepts the old artistic burden of constructive order, does not restrict itself to analysis alone.

But what concerns me at the moment is the way in which his basic theatrical perceptions altered his theater.

First and most significant after the destruction of *propter hoc* structure is the disappearance of the hero. With the sole exception of *Heracles*—Euripides' one attempt to define a new heroism—there is no play which is dominated by the single hero, as is Sophocles' *Oedipus* or *Ajax.*

Corresponding to the disappearance of the hero is Euripides' "Fragmentation" of the major characters. What we get is typically an agon or contest divided between two paired characters (sometimes there are three): Admetus and Alcestis; Jason and Medea; Hippolytus and Phaedra; Andromache and Hermione; Pentheus and Dionysus, etc. In such a theater, the Aristotelian search for a tragic hero is, of course, meaningless. But the significance of the fragmentation is not easy to assess; it is not enough to say merely that Euripides was temperamentally drawn to such conflict because they afforded him opportunities for psychological analysis. What is striking about the consistently paired antagonists one finds in Euripides is, I think, their obsessional nature. They function like obsessional fragments of a whole human soul: Hippolytus as chastity, Phaedra as sexuality. The wholeness of the old hero is now represented divisively, diffused over several characters; the paired antagonists of the Euripidean stage thus represent both the warring modes of a divided culture and the new incompleteness of the human psyche. Alternatively, as in the *Bacchae,* they embody the principles of conflicting ideas: Pentheus as *nomos,* Dionysus as *physis.*

This fragmentation is also the sign of a new psychological interest. That the convulsion of the late fifth century had revealed new dimensions in the human psyche is sharply expressed by Thucydides, and just as sharply by Euripides. Indeed, Euripides' interest in abnormality and mental derangement is so marked that critics have usually seen it as the very motive of his drama. This, I think, is a mistake. The interest in psychology is strong, but it is always secondary; the real interest lies in the analysis of culture and the relationship between culture and the individual. If I am correct in assuming that Euripides' crucial dramatic device is the juxtaposition and contrast of *logos* and *ergon,* then it follows that the characters of his plays must bear the burden of the cultural disparity involved. I mean: if a myth is bodily transplanted from its native culture to a different one, then the characters of the myth must bear the burden of the transplantation, and that burden is psychological strain. Consider, for example, Euripides' Orestes, a man who murders his mother in an Argos where civil justice already exists; or the heroic Jason translated into the context of a fifth-century Corinth; or an Odysseus or Hermione or Electra cut off from the culture in which their actions were once meaningful or moral, and set in an alien time which *immoralizes* or *distorts* them. The very strain that Euripides succeeds in imposing upon his characters is the mark of their modernity, their involvement in a culture under similar strain. And it is the previously unsuspected range of the human psyche, the discovery of its powers, its vulnerability to circumstance, its incompleteness, and its violence, that interest Euripides, not the psychological process itself. The soliloquy in which Medea meditates the murder of her children is much admired; but Euripides' dramatic interest is in the collapse or derangement of culture—the gap between *eros* and *sophia*—that makes the murder both possible and necessary.

Side by side with cultural strain is the striking loneliness of the Euripidean theater. Loneliness is, of course, a feature of traditional tragedy, but the difference between Euripides and his predecessors in this respect is marked. In Aeschylus the loneliness of human fate is effectively annulled by the reconciliation which closes trilogies and creates a new community in which god and man become joint partners in civilization. In Sophocles the sense of loneliness is extremely strong, but it is always the distinguishing mark of the hero, the sign of the fate which makes him an outcast, exiled from the world to the world's advantage and his own anguish. But in Euripides loneliness is the common fate. Insofar as the characters are fragmented and obsessional, their loneliness is required. The one thing they normally cannot do is communicate, and typically, even such communications as occur (for instance, Heracles' moving reunion with his children) are liable to almost certain destruction by the malevolence of fate. Again and again Euripides gives us those exquisite, painterly groupings which stress the impassable gulf which separates the old from the young, man from god, woman from man, and even hero from hero. The climax of the *Heracles* comes when Heracles, touched by Theseus' *philia,* makes his great decision to live; but the understanding is then immediately and deliberately clouded as Theseus fails to understand the enormous range of his friend's new heroism. The touch is typically and revealingly Euripidean. The gulf seems to close only to widen out again.

From the point of view of traditional tragedy nothing is more strikingly novel than the Euripidean fusion and contrast of comic and tragic effects. Thus at any point in a tragedy the comic, or more accurately, the pathetic or ludicrous, can erupt with poignant effect, intensifying the tragic or toughening it with parody. Nor is this a device restricted to Euripides' so-called "romantic" plays or his tragicomedies; it occurs even in the most powerful and serious tragedies. Tiresias and Cadmus in the *Bacchae,* for instance, are seen simultaneously as tragic and comic, that is, directly pathetic and incongruous: two old mummers of ecstasy; they try to dance for Dionysus as the god requires, but their bodies, like their minds, are incapable of expressing devotion except as a ludicrous mimicry. Aegeus, in *Medea,* has puzzled traditional interpretation from Aristotle on, precisely because he is Euripides' pathetic and ironic embodiment of Athens—that Athens which the chorus hails later as the place

> where Cypris sailed,
> and mild sweet breezes breathed along her path,
> and on her hair were flung the sweet-smelling garlands
> of flowers of roses by the Lovers, the companions
> of Wisdom, her escort, the helpers of men
> in every kind of *arete.*

The irony is not, of course, the cutting irony of exposure, but the gentler irony that comes when *logos* and *ergon* of things not too far apart are juxtaposed: we feel it as a light dissonance. Which is merely another way of saying that the new element of the comic in Euripidean tragedy is just one more instance of the dramatist's insistence upon preserving the multiplicity of possible realities in the texture of his action. In the traditional drama, such dissonance is rightly avoided as an offence against seriousness and tragic dignity; Euripides significantly sees both tragedy and comedy as equally valid, equally necessary. A drama of truth will contrive to contain them both; the complex truth requires it.

It is for this same reason that Euripides accentuates what might be called the multiple moral dimension of his characters. Every one of them is in some sense an exhibit of the sophistic perception that human character is altered by suffering or exemption from suffering; that every human disposition contains the possibilities of the species for good or evil. Aristotle objects, for instance, that Euripides' Iphigenia changes character without explanation. And so, in fact, she does, and so does Alcmene in *Heraclidae.* They change in this way because their function is not that of rounded characters or "heroes" but specifications of the shaping ideas of the play. Besides, if Heraclitus was right, and character is destiny, then the complex or even contradictory destiny which Euripidean drama assumes and describes must mean complex and contradictory characters. But the one kind of character which Euripides' theater cannot afford is that splendid integrated self-knowledge represented by the "old fantastical Duke of dark corners" in *Measure for Measure;* Euripides' theater is all Angelos, Lucios, and Claudios—average, maimed, irresolute, incomplete human nature. The case of Heracles himself, the most integrated hero Euripides ever created, is darkened by Euripides' insistence that we observe, without passing judgment, that even the culture-hero has murder in his heart. This fact does not, of course, compose a tragic flaw, but rather what Nietzsche called "the indispensable dark spring" of action. Moral judgment is, as Euripides tried to show, no less precarious and difficult than the comprehensive description of reality. How could it be otherwise?

This does not mean that Euripides avoids judgment or that his plays are attempts to put the problematic in the place of dramatic resolution. It means merely that his theater everywhere insists upon scrupulous and detailed recreation of the complexity of reality and the difficulty of moral judgment. The truth is concealed, but not impenetrably concealed. There can be little doubt, for instance, that Euripides meant his *Medea* to end in a way which must have shocked his contemporaries and which still shocks today. His purpose was, of course, not merely to shock, but to force the audience to the recognition that Medea, mortally hurt in her *eros,* her defining and enabling human passion, must act as she does, and that her action has behind it, like the sun, the power of sacred *physis.* There is no more savage moral oxymoron in Greek drama. But if Euripides here speaks up for *physis* against a corrupt *nomos,* he is capable elsewhere of defending *nomos* and insisting that those who prostrate themselves before *physis,* like the Old Nurse in *Hippolytus,* are the enemies of humanity. Necessity requires submission, but any necessity that requires a man to sacrifice the morality that makes him human, must be resisted to the end, even if it cost him—as it will—his life. Better death than the mutilation of his specifically human skill, that *sophia* which in Euripides is mankind's claim to be superior to the gods and necessity. Only man in this theater makes morality; it is this conviction, the bedrock classical conviction, that provides the one unmistakable and fixed reference-point in Euripides' dramatic world. Above that point all truths are purposely played off against one another in endless and detailed exactness of observation.

Within this new context of changed reality, Euripides' whole theater of ideas is set.

Several examples.

The *Iphigenia in Tauris* is a play commonly classified as romantic or escapist melodrama, and seems at first, or even second, sight extremely remote from the theater of ideas. Aristotle, for instance, particularly admired its elegant finish and its tightness of structure—especially its famous recognition scene—and he talks about it with the enthusiasm a nineteenth-century critic might have shown for a good "well-made" play. Smooth, urbane, and exciting, the play appears to be pure entertainment, lively and sophisticated but without a thought in its head. Clearly not tragic, its plot is as improbable as it is skillful; situation clearly counts for a great deal, characterization for very little. None of the leading characters, for instance, is given more than deft, generalizing traits, and the very slightness of the characterization draws attention to the virtuosity of the plot and the remarkable facility of execution.

But the romantic atmosphere is by no means absolute; again and again Euripides intrudes into this artificial world the jarring dissonance of a harsh contemporary reality. Quite deliberately, and with odd effect, he evokes and remembers the real war: the vision of the dead and the doomed; the illusion of ambition and the deceptive hope of empire; the exile's yearning for home; the bitter image of a Hellas at peace, remembered with longing from the impossible distance of the present. *Logos* set against *ergon;* form in partial conflict with subject; romantic myth undercut by, and therefore intensifying in turn, the actual world, as though the story of Cinderella were suddenly revealed as set on the outskirts of Auschwitz. If his play is melodrama, it is melodrama subtly but sensibly tilted toward the experience of national tragedy and exploiting that experience symbolically.

Symbolically how? It is perhaps easy for moderns to misunderstand or overread. But I wonder what Athenian, even the most insensitive, could have failed to grasp or respond to the image which this play sets before him, especially in the light of that experience of war which the play so powerfully exploits. *A sister dedicates her brother to death by the sword.* It seems perhaps melodramatic to moderns, but, unless I am badly mistaken, that symbolism is directly addressed to the experience—and the conscience—of a people who, for nearly twenty years, had suffered all the horrors of fratricidal war. The symbolism is available and familiar, and it culminates naturally in the great recognition scene, when Iphigenia, on the point of butchering her brother Orestes, suddenly discovers his true identity. For this scene the whole play was built, and its quite remarkable power is ultimately based, I think, upon the explosive liberation of love which reunites a family or a people grown hostile, estranged, and unfamiliar. Behind the recognition of brother and sister in the play lies a people's recognition, a recognition of *kind.* For Argos, read Hellas; for the history of the house of Atreus, the history of Hellas. What is war but blood sacrifice? Why, the play asks, should Greeks kill Greeks? And to give his argument further point, Euripides introduces Athena to establish in Attica the cult of the civilized Artemis who will put an end to human sacrifice and, by implication, the needless butchery which is war. The symbolism is, of course, the more effective for being unobtrusive, but once felt, it drastically alters the experience of the play. What seems at first romantic escape becomes confrontation and recognition, a true tragicomedy in which the tragic shapes the comic or romantic and the romantic gives poignancy to the tragic. In short, the kind of play we might have expected from the dramatist of the *Alcestis* and the humanist of the *Trojan Women.* Admittedly a fresh political interpretation of its major symbolism does not transform the *Iphigenia in Tauris* into a true drama of ideas; but the existence of a deeply serious and critical intent in a play universally regarded as Euripides' most frivolous "entertainment," is indicative of the dramatist's bent in the "darker" plays.

In the *Orestes,* for instance. Here, if anywhere in Euripides' work, the contrast between *logos* and *ergon* is structural and crucial. The play falls abruptly into two distinct parts. *Ergon* is represented by the body of the play proper, a freely invented account of the events which followed Orestes' matricide; *logos,* by the concluding epiphany of Apollo, an archaizing *deus ex machina,* in which the god foretells the known mythical futures of the characters. These two parts are enjambed with jarring dissonance, since the characters as developed in the play and their mythical futures as announced by Apollo are incompatible. Through this device the play becomes problematic: the spectator is literally compelled, it seems, to choose between his own experience of the play and Apollo's closing words, between *ergon* and *logos,* behavior and myth. Moreover, the choice is a hard one; for, if the experience of the play proper is of almost unbearable bitterness and pessimism, Apollo's arrangements are foolish and traditional to the point of unacceptability. In short, impasse, or so at first sight it might seem. But here, as so often in Euripides, a crux or problem or impasse is the dramatist's way of *confronting* his audience with the necessity of choosing between apparently antithetical realities or positions (Hippolytus or Phaedra? Pentheus or Dionysus? *Physis* or *nomos?* Cold expedience or passionate *eros*? Barbarian or Greek? Victim or oppressor? *Logos* or *ergon*?).[3] Almost without exception, these seemingly necessary choices are finally illusory alternatives, the dramatist's device for stimulating his audience and forcing it on to the critical perception which underlies and comprehends the alternatives, unifying them in a single, complex, synthetic judgment—the judgment which holds each play together and for which the plays were written in the first place. That Euripides' critics have so seldom managed to arrive at this final judgment would seem to indicate that his theatrical strategies were ineffective; on the other hand, Euripides' critics have usually assumed that his consistency of technique necessarily meant a consistent failure to write correct traditional tragedy in the (imagined) manner of Sophocles.

Certainly the impasse between *logos* and *ergon* in the *Orestes* is apparent only. What resolves it is a common purpose in both parts—an ascending curve of exposure, first of the "heroic" Orestes who killed his mother and tried to kill Helen, and then of the traditionally "wise" Apollo who drove Orestes to matricide. The exposures are, in fact, mutual and cumulative, compelling us to see that if Orestes, by any human standard of morality, is mad, Apollo is utterly insane (for madness or incompetence in a god, and a god of radiant reason at that, is a fortiori more dangerous than in a mortal). *Logos* and *ergon*, apparently contradictory, are in fact complementary: depraved and immoral human action in the play proper is mirrored and sanctioned by the callous folly of heaven and the brutality of the myth; Orestes and Apollo mutually create, mutually deserve, each other: murderers both. Man and god project each other; myth influences behavior, and behavior in turn shapes the myth in a vicious circle of moral deterioration. If from this perspective we ask why Euripides freely invents the story of Orestes instead of recreating the traditional matricide, the answer is immediately clear: because he wants to demonstrate through the abortive attempt to kill Helen—a crime in which Apollo significantly plays no part—that Orestes is a murderer born, a man who kills not from necessity but in *freedom*, out of his sickness and hatred. Having demonstrated this, Euripides can proceed to the complementary exposure of Apollo, a god made in the image of Orestes.

Produced just half a century after Aeschylus' *Oresteia*, Euripides' *Orestes* is not only an indictment of the Aeschylean myth, its values and its hero, but a savage critique of Hellenic society in the last decade of the fifth century. If the impasse between *logos* and *ergon* is, as I claim, resolved by a continuous mutual exposure, the purpose of that exposure is a complex and profoundly bitter cultural statement. Euripides seems to be saying something like this: A society whose sacred legend is embodied in a god like Apollo and a man like Orestes runs the risk that its citizens may emulate the myth, revive it, in their own political behavior. That is, Athens and Greek society generally are in danger of realizing their own myths, of at last reconciling *logos* and *ergon*, myth and conduct, in a new synthesis of murderous brutality and insanity—the worst myth fused now with the worst behavior. In earlier plays Euripides critically contrasted myth and behavior with the aim of letting the better expose the worse; here, in the bitterest play of all, he shows how bad behavior and bad myth interact for the defeat of culture and communal life.

That this bleak conclusion is the purpose of the play is supported by the systematic desolation which Euripides visits upon every aspect of moral and political behavior. Thus there is not a character in the play who is not defined either by inhuman devotion to sound principle, by patient treachery, or by nightmare loyalty of complicity or stupidity. Every moral word is consistently inverted or emptied of its meaning, as the action proceeds from madness to "honorable" murder on a wave of sickening heroic rhetoric. As for justice, if Orestes creates none, he gets none either; for human justice here is merely power politics or mob passion, and Apollo rules in heaven. Between health and sickness, heroism and depravity, morality and immorality, every distinction is removed. Politics is either brutal power or demagoguery; the only honorable motives are self-interest and revenge. In short, the world of the *Orestes* is indistinguishable from the culture in convulsion described by Thucydides; point for point, Euripides and Thucydides confirm each other. And, presumptuous or not, I am tempted to see in this frightening play Euripides' apocalyptic vision of the final destruction of Athens and Hellas, or of that Hellas to which a civilized mind could still give its full commitment. In the house of Atreus we have the house of Hellas: the great old aristocratic house, cursed by a long history of fratricidal blood and war, brought down in ruin by its degenerate heirs.

Finally, consider the *Medea*. Traditionally classified as psychological tragedy, it is better interpreted as a genuine drama of ideas. Superficially it is a critique of relations between men and women, Greeks and barbarians, and of an *ethos* of hard, prudential self-interest as against passionate love. At a profounder level it is a comprehensive critique of the quality and state of contemporary culture. Like the *Bacchae*, Euripides' other great critique of culture, the *Medea* is based upon a central key term, *sophia.* Inadequately translated "wisdom," *sophia* is an extremely complex term, including Jason's cool self-interest, the magical and erotic skills of the sorceress Medea, and that ideal Athenian fusion of moral and artistic skills which, fostered by *eros,* creates the distinctive *arete* of the civilized polis. This third sense of *sophia*—nearly synonymous with "civilization" and specifically including the compassion[4] for the suppliant and the oppressed for which Athens was famous and which Aegeus significantly shows to Medea—is the standard by which the actions of Jason and Medea are to be judged. Thus the vivid harmony of *eros* and *sophia* which Athens represents is precisely what Jason and Medea are not. Jason's calculating, practical *sophia* is, lacking *eros,* selfish and destructive; Medea's consuming *eros* and psychological *sophia* (an emotional cunning which makes her a supreme artist of revenge) is, without compassion, maimed and destructive. They are both destroyers, destroyers of themselves, of others, of *sophia,* and the polis.[5] And it is this *destructiveness* above all else which Euripides wants his audience to observe: the spirit of brutal self-interest and passionate revenge which threatens both life and culture, and which is purposely set in sharp contrast to life-enhancing Athens where the arts flourish, where *eros* collaborates with *sophia,* and where creative *physis* is gentled by just *nomoi.* Behind Jason and Medea we are clearly meant to see that spreading spirit of expedience and revenge which, unchecked by culture or religion, finally brought about the Peloponnesian War and its attendant atrocities. For it cannot be mere coincidence that a play like this was performed in the first year of the war.

What of Medea herself? Upon our understanding of her depends the final interpretation of the play. Thus those who find in Medea a barbarian woman whose lack of self-control, hunger for revenge, and male courage set her in firm contrast to the Corinthian women of the chorus, with their Greek praise of *sophrosunē* and their fear of excess, usually see the play as a psychological tragedy of revenge. Against this interpretation there are decisive arguments. For one thing, Euripides takes pains to show that Medea is not at all pure barbarian femininity, but rather a barbarian woman who has been partially and imperfectly Hellenized. Thus Medea's first appearance is an intentionally striking one, domniated by her attempt to pass for Greek, to say the right thing; she talks, in fact, the stock language of Greek women, *hēsuchia* and *sophrosunē.* Now this may be a pose, but it may just as well be genuine cultural imitation, the sort of thing a barbarian woman in Corinth might be expected to do. But the point is important for, if I am right, this play records the loss of the civilized skills through the conflict of passion; and for this reason Euripides first shows us his Medea making use of those civilized virtues which, in the throes of passion, she promptly loses, reverting to barbarism. Euripides' point is not that Medea *qua* barbarian is different in nature from Greek women, but that her inhibitions are weaker and her passions correspondingly nearer the surface. Thus she can very quickly be reduced to her essential *physis,* and it is this nakedness of *physis,* shorn of all cultural overlay, that Euripides wants displayed. Unimpeded *eros* (or unimpeded hatred) can be shown in Medea with a concentration and naturalness impossible in a Greek woman, not because Greek women were less passionate, but because their culture required them to repress their passions. If culture is truly effective, the control of passion eventually becomes true self-mastery (*sophrosunē*); where culture is less effective or out of joint (as in the Corinth of this play), *physis* is checked only by fear, and reveals itself in resentment of the punishing authorities and ready sympathy with those who rebel against them. Hence the profound resentment which the chorus in this play feels against male domination. This—and not mere theatrical convention or necessity—is why Medea can so easily convince the chorus to become her accomplices in her "crusade" against Jason and male society. Their control over their passions, while greater than Medea's perhaps, is still inadequate and precarious (as their bitter resentment of men makes clear); and Medea's revenge arouses their fullest sympathy, just as war evokes the barbarian in an imperfectly civilized man. And this is Euripides' point, that "one touch of nature" makes kin of Hellene and barbarian. In Medea's barbarism we have a concentrated image of human *physis* and a symbol of the terrible closeness of all human nature to barbarism. In her inadequate *sophrosunē* and her imperfect *sophia* is represented the norm of Hellenic, and most human, society. Thus when Jason cries out, "No Greek woman would have dared this crime," we are meant, not to agree, but to wonder and doubt, and finally to disbelieve him.

The validity of that doubt and disbelief is immediately confirmed by the appearance of the golden chariot of the Sun in which Medea makes her escape to Athens. In this chariot Euripides does two related things: he first restates, vividly and unmistakably, the triumph of Medea over Jason, and secondly he provides the whole action with a symbolic and cosmological framework which forces the private *agon* of Jason and Medea to assume a larger public significance. And by showing Medea, murderess and infanticide, as rescued by the Sun himself—

traditionally regarded as the epitome of purity, the unstained god who will not look upon pollution—he drives home his meaning with the shock of near sacrilege. As for the chariot of the Sun, it is the visible cosmic force which blazes through Medea's motives and which her whole *pathos* expresses: the blinding force of life itself, stripped of any mediating morality or humanizing screen; naked, unimpeded, elemental *eros;* intense, chaotic, and cruel; the primitive, premoral, precultural condition of man and the world. If that force vindicates Medea as against Jason, her ardor as against his icy self-interest, it is only because her *eros* is elemental and therefore invincible. But she is vindicated only vis-à-vis Jason; and she is not *justified* at all. Of justification there can be no question here, not only because *eros* is, like any elemental necessity, amoral and therefore unjustifiable, but also because Euripides clearly believes the loss of *sophia* to be a tragic defeat for man and human culture.

In the *agon* of Jason and Medea, passion, vengeance, and self-interest expel *sophia.* That *agon,* as we have seen, stands for the Peloponnesian War—the war which Euripides, like Thucydides, feared would expel *sophia* from civilized cities, thereby barbarizing and brutalizing human behavior. At any time, in both individuals and cities, *sophia* is a delicate and precarious virtue; if anywhere in the Hellenic world, *sophia* flourished in Athens, but even there is bloomed precariously (how precariously the plague which overtook the city in the following year proved). And with the coming of Medea to Athens, Euripides seems to imply, comes the spirit of vengeance and passion, endangering *sophia,* that *sophia* whose creation and growth made Athens, in Thucydides' phrase, "the education of Hellas." For Hellas and humanity a new and terrible day dawns at the close of the *Medea.*

In sum, the Greeks possessed a recognizable and developed form of what we should not scruple to call a classical theater of ideas. And there, in substance, my argument rests. Whatever its critical shortcomings may be, its historical basis is, I think, sufficiently secure. If, historically, the theater of ideas tends to occur in times of severe cultural crisis, then we may properly expect it in late-fifth-century Athens, for of all the cultural crises of Hellenism, the late-fifth-century crisis was by far the most profound. Among its casualties are classical tragedy and comedy; the old mythical cosmology and the culture which it mirrored and sanctioned; the gods of the polis; the sense of community on which the polis was based, and therefore in a sense the polis itself. In short, the whole cloth of culture, fabric and design together.

In the fourth century Plato's attempt to repiece the old culture—to reconcile *physis* and *nomos,* myth and behavior, to reweave the moral community of the polis—was heroic but finally unsuccessful. Plato was a great conservative and a great revolutionary, but the Hellas he preserved was only preserved by being radically changed, in fact revolutionized. The old Greek culture—the culture to which the Western world most owes its being and to which it returns for life and freshness when Platonic Hellenism threatens to swamp it—died in the fifth century B.C., and it is this culture in its crisis of disintegration that Euripides records. If Euripides could no longer hold out the old heroic image of man, it is because he preferred to base his theater upon what he actually saw as the prime reality of his time: the new emerging human psyche, tested and defined by crisis, and the apparently uncontrollable chaos of human behavior and therefore the turbulence which any viable culture must know how to contain, but without repressing.

Put it this way. The complex knowledge and experience about politics and culture so evident in *Hecuba* or the *Bacchae* look forward to Plato and also explain Plato's response to the same crisis. Both men share the conviction that war and greed for power have corrupted culture or deranged it; both are convinced that chaotic human nature, as revealed by crisis, cannot be controlled within the framework of existing culture. But Euripides' liberating perception has become Plato's restrictive premise. For Euripides any new cultural order must somehow contain what is uncontrollable in behavior; the failure to allow for turbulence, the failure to democratize its ethics, was what had made the old culture so susceptible to crisis. The Athenian democracy after Pericles could no more make do on aristocratic *sophrosunē* than industrial England could run on knightly chivalry. The solution, however, was not to reorganize society to operate on *sophrosunē* and the old aristocratic ethos but to revise *sophia* and *sophrosunē* in terms of a more democratic view of human nature. It is for this reason that in the *Bacchae* Pentheus' inability to control his inward turmoil is matched by his incompetence to control the public situation. He is an emblem of his age, attempting out of his ignorance of himself and his culture to cope with chaos by means of an inadequate or corrupted aristocratic *sophrosunē*. For whatever the solution to Dionysiac chaos may be, it is not repression, but perhaps a more responsibly Dionysiac (that is to say, liberated and liberating) society. The new polis may not be quite "polymorphously perverse," but it will at least be free, disciplined by experience of inward and outward chaos to a larger self-mastery.

For Plato the ideal polis can only be based upon a coercion that looks like consent. And it is therefore subject to the fate of Euripides' Pentheus, the terrible revenge which *physis* takes upon a *nomos* that cannot enlarge itself to a true human order. In short, the culture envisaged by Plato rests ultimately upon suppression of the natural, and is to that degree profoundly pessimistic and anti-Hellenic. Euripides' specifications for culture rest upon an extremely realistic judgment of human nature and its potentialities for disorder; but because what is chaotic is seen as the thrust of life itself, as something *below* (or *beyond*) good or evil, morally neutral, culture is always a project for hope, for free order, for the creation of new institutions in which man's society will not be in conflict with his nature. The Athens which Euripides had so triumphantly hailed in the great choral ode of the *Medea* may have betrayed what it stood for, but the creative fusion between the passions (*erotes*) and the civilized and artistic skills (the large sense of *sophia,* nearly synonymous with "culture") which produced *arete—here,* however transient, was a paradigm of ideal social order, the polis which made man's fulfillment possible.

That Euripides is an innovator is, of course, not an altogether new idea; Werner Jaeger's word for him is, flatly, revolutionary. But those who regard Euripides as an innovator or a revolutionary rarely see in him much more than a theatrical sophist or the inventor of a realistic and psychological tragedy. So far as I know, nobody has seriously proposed what I am proposing here: that Euripides' theater is no less revolutionary than his ideas, and that these ideas are implicitly expressed in the assumptions of his theater and his dramatic hypotheses. In short, that his theater *is* his ideas; that his radical critique of crisis in culture is not just Sophoclean tragedy turned topical and sophistic, but a wholly new theater, uneasily based upon the forms and conventions of the old. That is, not tragedy at all, but a critical drama related to Aeschylus and Sophocles in much the same way that Hebbel's theater was, at least in theory, related to Schiller's.[6] And for this very reason, I suppose, the argument will be discounted: Why, it will be objected, has a point like this been somehow missed for twenty-five hundred years?

To this question it is possible to make a great many answers. For one thing, the identification of the theater of ideas is of very recent date, even among critics of the theater. For another, classicists have traditionally been—as they remain—hostile or indifferent to literary criticism. For this reason they have very rarely asked the kind of question which might have led them to a literary answer. Instead of giving the dramatist the customary benefit of the doubt, they have assumed that a hostile tradition was generally sound and that Euripides was an interesting aberration but finally too realistic, irreverent and vulgar to fill the bill as a bona fide classic. With deplorable regularity scholars have insisted that it was Euripides' fate to be an imitator or higher parodist of his predecessors, and then, just as regularly, have condemned him for bungling the job. I doubt, in fact, that the history of literature can show a more pathological chapter. Surely no great dramatist of the world has ever received less benefit of the critical doubt or been more consistently patronized; a fourth-rate Broadway hack will normally demand, and get, more courtesy from critics than Euripides has received from six centuries of scholarship. Even when he is praised by comparison with other dramatists, the comparison is inevitably patronizing. We do not honor our greatest classics by asserting their modernity; if classicists and critics compare Euripides to Ibsen, this is more to Ibsen's credit than to Euripides'—though this is *not* the assumption. We pay no honor to Shakespeare when we compliment him on his modernity: we merely reveal the true proportions of our contempt for the classics. Having said that, I can now say without being misunderstood: the theater of Brecht and of Sartre, and even the Theater of the Absurd, are in many ways remarkably like the theater of Euripides.

In any traditional perspective, Euripidean theater is complex and uncomfortably strange, almost exasperating to a taste founded on Aeschylus and Sophocles. Its premises, as we have seen, are unlike, and almost the inversion of those of the traditional Greek theater. Typically it likes to conceal the truth beneath strata of irony because this is the look of truth: layered and elusive. For the same reason it presents its typical actions as problems and thereby involves the audience in a new relation, not as worshippers but as jurors who must resolve the problem by decision. But because the problem is usually incapable of outright resolution, is in fact tragic, the audience is compelled to forfeit the only luxury of making a decision—the luxury of *knowing* that one has decided wisely. Something—innocence, comfort, complacency—is always forfeited, or meant to be forfeited, by the audience of jurors. This suggests that the essential anagnorisis of Euripidean theater is not between one actor and another but between the audience and its own experience, as that experience is figured in the plays. Anagnorisis here is knowing moral choice, exercised on a problem which aims at mimicking the quandary of a culture. As such, it is a pattern of the way in which the psyche is made whole again, and the hope of a culture.

It is thus a difficult theater, and difficulty in literature, as opposed to textual difficulty or a doubtful manuscript reading, has never quickened the pulses of classical scholars. Indeed, the commonest scholarly response to the suggestion of a complex critical reading is that no classical writer could ever have been so unclear as not to be immediately transparent. If he was unclear or unusually complex or at all contorted, he was clearly unclassical; to such a degree has Winckelmann's criterion of "noble simplicity" seized the imagination of classical scholars. To those who believe that Euripides could not possibly have meant more than the little they are willing to understand, there is no adequate reply. But if it is true that critics who interpret great dramatists often seek to involve themselves in the dramatist's greatness, those who deny the dramatist any ideas but their own clearly involve the dramatist in their own dullness. John Finley's words to those who charge that more is read into Thucydides' speeches than the average Athenian citizen could have understood, are appropriate:

> It might be replied that the mass of the people could not have followed speeches of so general a character, but to make such an objection is to misunderstand the mind of the fifth century, indeed of any great period. The plays of Shakespeare and the sermons of early Protestantism give proof enough of the capacity assumed in an ordinary audience or congregation. It could be argued that any era which offers the ordinary man vast horizons of opportunity demands and receives from him a fresh comprehension proportionate to his fresh self-respect. Attic tragedy, even the philosophical and political subjects treated by Aristophanes, cannot be explained on any other assumption.[7]

As for Euripides, if I am right in assuming that his subject was nothing less than the life of Greek and Athenian culture, respect for the intelligence and good faith of the ordinary audience *must* be forthcoming, since it is the premise of culture itself. If Euripides for the most part failed to win the understanding of his audience, as I think he did, the fact does not disprove the intent. It is, I think, not sufficiently recognized that the very scholars who object that literary criticism means importing modern prejudices into an ancient text are themselves usually the worst offenders. Utterly unconsciously they take for granted all the cramping prejudices which a culture like ours can confer upon an uncritical man, and confer them in turn upon antiquity. "The classicist's attitude toward the ancient world," wrote Nietzsche, "is either apologetic or derives from the notion that what our age values highly can also be found in antiquity. The right starting point is the opposite, i.e., to start from the perception of modern absurdity and to look backward from that viewpoint—and many things regarded as offensive in the ancient world will appear as profound necessities. We must make it clear to ourselves that we are acting absurdly when we justify or beautify antiquity: who are *we?*"

Among literary men and critics of literature, as opposed to scholars, it might be assumed that a Greek theater of ideas would find favor, if only as a sanction and precedent for the new intellectual theater. But I suspect that this is not the case, precisely because contemporary critics are so stubbornly and unreasonably convinced that the entire Greek theater from Aeschylus to Euripides is firmly ritualistic. In saying this, I am thinking of the fact that the modern poetic theater, in searching for anti-naturalistic models, turned significantly to Greek drama. What interested contemporaries in Greek drama was, of course, the belief that they would find in it those features—ritual, stylization, gesture, a sacramental sense of life and community—which promised release from the restrictions of the naturalistic theater. They were confirmed in this by the literary vogue of anthropology, and the apparent success of the so-called Cambridge school, especially Francis Cornford and Jane Harrison. But the strongest argument for the ritual view of Greek drama came, I think, from the inability of the classicists themselves to give any substantial meaning to Greek drama. Thus literary men, always a little nervous when confronted with a Greek text and seldom inclined to quarrel with scholarship, eagerly accepted a scholarly view of the Greek plays that at least had the merit of making them mean *something* and which also suited their own theatrical programs. Ritual for them was a "find." For Greek drama it was, as I have tried to show elsewhere, an unqualified disaster.

But because its basis is "need," ritual interpretation is particularly insidious. My own objections to it are threefold; first, the belief that developed tragedy still bears the visible structural and esthetic effects of its origin is a clear case of the genetic fallacy; second, there is so little evidence for it in extant tragedy that its own originator, Gilbert Murray, recanted it; and third, it is really Cornford's argument for comedy—a far sounder argument in view of comedy's late nationalization—that gives it cogency. My critical objection to the ritual approach is that it tends to diminish rather than enhance the literary value of the plays; in short, it tends to make priests of tragedians and worshipers of audiences. This is not, of course, to deny the religious importance of the Greek tragedian or his religious concern. But it is to deny that his subject was prescribed, his treatment wholly conventional or stylized, and his thought unimportant or unadventurous. Whatever value the ritual approach may have for Aeschylus or Sophocles (and I think the value is small) its application has obscured even further the nature and originality of the Euripidean theater of ideas, since it is precisely discursive, *critical* thought, the complex dialectic of Euripidean drama, that ritualist interpretation regularly suppresses. Thus the only result of the ritual criticism of Greek drama has been, in my opinion, a further falsification.

But the essential, the crucial reason for our misunderstanding of Greek drama in general, and Euripidean theater in particular, is one which classicists and literary men alike share with the whole modern world. And this is our special cultural need of the classics, our own crucial myth of classical culture. A tradition is, after all, like love; we "crystallize" it, endow it with the perfections it must have in order to justify our need and our love. And classical Greek culture has for some time stood in relation to modern culture as a measure of our own chaos—a cultural Eden by which we measure our fall from grace and innocence. Thus we view the Greeks with the same envious and needful wonder that Nietzsche and Thomas Mann reserved for Goethe—that integrated soul—and which Euripides' age felt for the age of Aeschylus. To our modern dissonance, the Greeks play the role of old tonality, the abiding image of a great humanity. They are our lost power; lost wholeness; the pure *presence* and certainty of reality our culture has lost.

Against a need like this and a myth like this, argument may be futile. But we should not, I think, be allowed to mythologize unawares. If we first deprive classical culture of its true turbulence in order to make ourselves a myth of what we have lost, and then hedge that myth with false ritual, we are depriving ourselves of that community of interest and danger that makes the twentieth century true kin to the Greeks. We deprive ourselves, in short, of access to what the past can teach us in order to take only what we want. And that is a cultural loss of the first magnitude.

NOTES

[1] See "The Criticism of Greek Tragedy," in *The Tulane Drama Review*, III, No. 3 (Spring, 1959), 31 ff.

[2] Compare Ajax' situation with Thucydides' statement in the Corcyraean excursus: "The ancient simplicity into which honor so largely

entered was laughed down and disappeared."

[3] A dramatic adaptation, I believe, of Protagoras' *antilogoi* (the rhetorical technique of first attacking and then defending a thesis, or of antithetical theses). Thucydides' method of contrasting set speeches (the Mytilenean debate, for instance) is an historian's adaptation of the *antilogoi* and a way of indicating, between the lines, by what is omitted and shared by both speakers, the crucial spoken and unspoken assumptions of politics and ethics. So too in the case of Euripides.

[4] Cf. Euripides' *Electra,* 294–96, where Orestes says: "Compassion is found in men who are *sophoi,* never in brutal and ignorant men. And to have a truly compassionate mind is not without disadvantage to the *sophoi.*"

[5] Just as Medea and Jason between them destroy Creon and his daughter Glauke, so Medea, once she is domiciled in Athens, will attempt to murder Theseus, the son whom Aegeus so passionately desires—a fact which Athenians could be expected to know and hold against Medea, especially in view of Aegeus' generosity to her. Wherever Medea goes, the polis, as represented by the ruling family, is threatened.

[6] A comparison I owe to Eric Bentley's *The Playwright as Thinker* (New York, 1955), p. 27. Hebbel described his new theater in this way: "At its every step there throngs around it a world of views and relations, which point both backwards and forwards, and all of which must be carried along; the life-forces cross and destroy one another, the thread of thought snaps in two before it is spun out, the emotion shifts, the very words gain their independence and reveal hidden meaning, annulling the ordinary one, for each is a die marked on more than one face. Here the chaff of little sentences, adding bit to bit and fiber to fiber, would serve the purpose ill. It is a question of presenting conditions in their organic totality. . . . Unevenness of rhythm, complication and confusion of periods, contradiction in the figures are elevated to effective and indispensable rhetorical means."

[7] John H. Finley, Jr., *Thucydides* (Cambridge, Mass., 1947), pp. 64–65.

Control of Distance in Jane Austen's *Emma*

Wayne C. Booth

Sympathy and Judgment in Emma

Henry James once described Jane Austen as an instinctive novelist whose effects, some of which are admittedly fine, can best be explained as "part of her unconsciousness." It is as if she "fell-a-musing" over her work-basket, he said, lapsed into "wool-gathering," and afterward picked up "her dropped stitches" as "little masterstrokes of imagination."[1] The amiable accusation has been repeated in various forms, most recently as a claim that Jane Austen creates characters toward whom we cannot react as she consciously intends.[2]

Although we cannot hope to decide whether Jane Austen was entirely conscious of her own artistry, a careful look at the technique of any of her novels reveals a rather different picture from that of the unconscious spinster with her knitting needles. In *Emma* especially, where the chances for technical failure are great indeed, we find at work one of the unquestionable masters of the rhetoric of narration.

At the beginning of *Emma,* the young heroine has every requirement for deserved happiness but one. She had intelligence, wit, beauty, wealth, and position, and she has the love of those around her. Indeed, she thinks herself completely happy. The only threat to her happiness, a threat of which she is unaware, is herself: charming as she is, she can neither see her own excessive pride honestly nor resist imposing herself on the lives of others. She is deficient both in generosity and in self-knowledge. She discovers and corrects her faults only after she has almost ruined herself and her closest friends. But with the reform in her character, she is ready for marriage with the man she loves, the man who throughout the book has stood in the reader's mind for what she lacks.

It is clear that with a general plot of this kind Jane Austen gave herself difficulties of a high order. Though Emma's faults are comic, they constantly threaten to produce serious harm. Yet she must remain sympathetic or the reader will not wish for and delight sufficiently in her reform.

Obviously, the problem with a plot like this is to find some way to allow the reader to laugh at the mistakes committed by the heroine and at her punishment, without reducing the desire to see her reform and thus earn happiness. In *Tom Jones* this double attitude is achieved, as we have seen, partly through the invention of episodes producing sympathy and relieving any serious anxiety we might have, and partly through the direct and sympathetic commentary. In *Emma,* since most of the episodes must illustrate the heroine's faults and thus increase either our emotional distance or our anxiety, a different method is required. If we fail to see Emma's faults as revealed in the ironic texture from line to line, we cannot savor to the full the comedy as it is prepared for us. On the other hand, if we fail to love her, as Jane Austen herself predicted we would[3]—if we fail to love her more and more as the book progresses—we can neither hope for the conclusion, a happy and deserved marriage with Knightley following upon her reform, nor accept it as an honest one when it comes.[4] Any attempt to solve the problem by reducing either the love or the clear view of her faults would have been fatal.

Sympathy Through Control of Inside Views

The solution to the problem of maintaining sympathy despite almost crippling faults was primarily to use the heroine herself as a kind of narrator, though in third person, reporting on her own experience. So far as we know, Jane Austen never formulated any theory to cover her own practice; she invented no term like James's "central intelligence" or "lucid reflector" to describe her method of viewing the world of the book primarily through Emma's own eyes. We can thus never know for sure to what extent James's accusation of "unconsciousness" was right. But whether she was inclined to speculate about her method scarcely matters; her solution was clearly a brilliant one. By showing most of the story through Emma's eyes, the author insures that we shall travel with Emma rather than stand against her. It is not simply that Emma provides, in the unimpeachable evidence of her own conscience, proof that she has many redeeming qualities that do not appear on the surface; such evidence could be given with authorial commentary, though perhaps not with such force and conviction. Much more important, the sustained inside view leads the reader to hope for good fortune for the character with whom he travels, quite independently of the qualities revealed.

Seen from the outside, Emma would be an unpleasant person, unless, like Mr. Woodhouse and Knightley, we knew her well enough to infer her true worth. Though we might easily be led to laugh at her, we could never be made to laugh sympathetically. While the final unmasking of her faults and her humiliation would make artistic sense to an unsympathetic reader, her marriage with Knightley would become irrelevant if not meaningless. Unless we desire Emma's happiness and her reform which alone can make that happiness possible, a good third of this book will seem irredeemably dull.

Yet sympathetic laughter is never easily achieved. It is much easier to set up a separate fool for comic effects and to preserve your heroine for finer things. Sympathetic laughter is especially difficult with characters whose faults do not spring from sympathetic virtues. The grasping but witty Volpone can keep us on his side so long as his victims are more grasping and less witty than he, but as soon as the innocent victims, Celia and Bonario, come on stage, the quality of the humor changes; we no longer delight unambiguously in his triumphs. In contrast to this, the great sympathetic comic heroes often are comic largely because their faults, like Uncle Toby's sentimentality, spring from an excess of some virtue. Don Quixote's madness is partly caused by an excess of idealism, an excess of loving concern for the unfortunate. Every crazy gesture he makes gives further reason for loving the well-meaning old fool, and we can thus laugh at him in somewhat the same spirit in which we laugh at our own faults—in a benign, forgiving spirit. We may be contemptible for doing so; to persons without a sense of humor such laughter often seems a wicked escape. But self-love being what it is, we laugh at ourselves in a thoroughly forgiving way, and we laugh in the same way at Don Quixote: we are convinced that his heart, like ours, is in the right place.

Nothing in Emma's comic misunderstandings can serve for the same effect. Her faults are not excesses of virtue. She attempts to manipulate Harriet not from an excess of kindness but from a desire for power and admiration. She flirts with Frank Churchill out of vanity and irresponsibility. She mistreats Jane Fairfax because of Jane's *good* qualities. She abuses Miss Bates because of her own essential lack of "tenderness" and "good will."

We have only to think of what Emma's story would be if seen through Jane Fairfax' or Mrs. Elton's or Robert Martin's eyes to recognize how little our sympathy springs from any natural view, and to see how inescapable is the decision to use Emma's mind as a reflector of events—however beclouded her vision must be. To Jane Fairfax, who embodies throughout the book most of the values which Emma discovers only at the end, the early Emma is intolerable.

But Jane Austen never lets us forget that Emma is not what she might appear to be. For every section devoted to her misdeeds—and even they are seen for the most part through her own eyes—there is a section devoted to her self-reproach. We see her rudeness to poor foolish Miss Bates, and we see it vividly. But her remorse and act of penance in visiting Miss Bates after Knightley's rebuke are experienced even more vividly. We see her successive attempts to mislead Harriet, but we see at great length and in high color her self-castigation (chaps. xvi, xvii, xlviii). We see her boasting proudly that she does not need marriage, boasting almost as blatantly of her "resources" as does Mrs. Elton (chap. x). But we know her too intimately to take her conscious thoughts at face value. And we see her, thirty-eight chapters later, chastened to an admission of what we have known all along to be her true human need for love. "If all took place that might take place among the circle of her friends, Hartfield must be comparatively deserted; and she left to cheer her father with the spirits only of ruined happiness. The child to be born at Randalls must be a tie there even dearer than herself; and Mrs. Weston's heart and time would be occupied by it. . . . All that were good would be withdrawn" (chap. xlviii).

Perhaps the most delightful effects from our sustained inside view of a very confused and very charming young woman come from her frequent thoughts about Knightley. She is basically right all along about his pre-eminent wisdom and virtue, and she is our chief authority for taking *his* authority so seriously. And yet in every thought about him she is misled. Knightley rebukes her; the reader knows that Knightley is in the right. But Emma?

> Emma made no answer, and tried to look cheerfully unconcerned, but was really feeling uncomfortable, and wanting him very much to be gone. She did not repent what she had done; she still

> thought herself a better judge of such a point of female right and refinement than he could be; but yet she had a sort of habitual respect for his judgment in general, which made her dislike having it so loudly against her; and to have him sitting just opposite to her in angry state, was very disagreeable [chap. viii].

Even more striking is the lack of self-knowledge shown when Mrs. Weston suggests that Knightley might marry Jane Fairfax.

> Her objections to Mr. Knightley's marrying did not in the least subside. She could see nothing but evil in it. It would be a great disappointment to Mr. John Knightley [Knightley's brother]; consequently to Isabella. A real injury to the children—a most mortifying change, and material loss to them all;—a very great deduction from her father's daily comfort—and, as to herself, she could not at all endure the idea of Jane Fairfax at Donwell Abbey. A Mrs. Knightley for them all to give way to!—No, Mr. Knightley must never marry. Little Henry must remain the heir of Donwell [chap. xxvi].

Self-deception could hardly be carried further, at least in a person of high intelligence and sensitivity.

Yet the effect of all this is what our tolerance for our own faults produces in our own lives. While only immature readers ever really identify with any character, losing all sense of distance and hence all chance of an artistic experience, our emotional reaction to every event concerning Emma tends to become like her own. When she feels anxiety or shame, we feel analogous emotions. Our modern awareness that such "feelings" are not identical with those we feel in our own lives in similar circumstances has tended to blind us to the fact that aesthetic form can be built out of patterned emotions as well as out of other materials. It is absurd to pretend that because our emotions and desires in responding to fiction are in a very real sense disinterested, they do not or should not exist. Jane Austen, in developing the sustained use of a sympathetic inside view, has mastered one of the most successful of all devices for inducing a parallel emotional response between the deficient heroine and the reader.

Sympathy for Emma can be heightened by withholding inside views of others as well as by granting them of her. The author knew, for example, that it would be fatal to grant any extended inside view of Jane Fairfax. The inadequacies of impressionistic criticism are nowhere revealed more clearly than in the suggestion often made about such minor characters that their authors would have liked to make them vivid but didn't know how.[5] Jane Austen knew perfectly well how to make such a character vivid; Anne in *Persuasion* is a kind of Jane Fairfax turned into heroine. But in *Emma,* Emma must shine supreme. It is not only that the slightest glance inside Jane's mind would be fatal to all of the author's plans for mystification about Frank Churchill, though this is important. The major problem is that any extended view of her would reveal her as a more sympathetic person than Emma herself. Jane is superior to Emma in most respects except the stroke of good fortune that made Emma the heroine of the book. In matters of taste and ability, of head and of heart, she is Emma's superior, and Jane Austen, always in danger of losing our sympathy for Emma, cannot risk any degree of distraction. Jane could, it is true, be granted fewer virtues, and *then* made more vivid. But to do so would greatly weaken the force of Emma's mistakes of heart and head in her treatment of the almost faultless Jane.

Control of Judgment

But the very effectiveness of the rhetoric designed to produce sympathy might in itself lead to a serious misreading of the book. In reducing the emotional distance, the natural tendency is to reduce—willy-nilly—moral and intellectual distance as well. In reacting to Emma's faults from the inside out, as if they were our own, we may very well not only forgive them but overlook them.[6]

There is, of course, no danger that readers who persist to the end will overlook Emma's serious mistakes; since she sees and reports those mistakes herself, everything becomes crystal clear at the end. The real danger inherent in the experiment is that readers will overlook the mistakes as they are committed and thus miss much of the comedy that depends on Emma's distorted view from page to page. If readers who dislike Emma cannot enjoy the preparation for the marriage to Knightley, readers who do not recognize her faults with absolute precision cannot enjoy the details of the preparation for the comic abasement which must precede that marriage.

It might be argued that there is no real problem, since the conventions of her time allowed for reliable commentary whenever it was needed to place Emma's faults precisely. But Jane Austen is not operating according to the conventions, most of which she had long since parodied and outgrown; her technique is determined by the needs of the novel she is writing. We can see this clearly by contrasting the manner of *Emma* with that of *Persuasion,* the next, and last-completed work. In *Emma* there are many breaks in the point of view, because Emma's beclouded mind cannot do the whole job. In *Persuasion,* where the heroine's viewpoint is faulty only in her ignorance of Captain Wentworth's love, there are very few. Anne Elliot's consciousness is sufficient, as Emma's is not, for most of the needs of the novel which she dominates. Once the ethical and intellectual framework has been established by the narrator's introduction, we enter Anne's consciousness and remain bound to it much more rigorously than we are bound to Emma's. It is still true that whenever something must be shown that Anne's consciousness cannot show, we move to another center; but since her consciousness can do much more for us than Emma's, there need be few departures from it.

The most notable shift for rhetorical purposes in *Persuasion* comes fairly early. When Anne first meets Captain Wentworth after their years of separation that follow her refusal to marry him, she is convinced that he is indifferent. The major movement of *Persuasion* is toward her final discovery that he still loves her; *her* suspense is thus strong and inevitable from the beginning. The reader, however, is likely to believe that Wentworth is still interested. All the conventions of art favor such a belief: the emphasis is clearly on Anne and her unhappiness; the lover has returned; we have only to wait, perhaps with some tedium, for the inevitable outcome. Anne learns (chap. vii) that he has spoken of her as so altered "he should not have known her again!" "These were words which could not but dwell with her. Yet she soon began to rejoice that she had heard them. They were of sobering tendency; they allayed agitation; they composed, and consequently must make her happier." And suddenly we enter Wentworth's mind for one time only: "Frederick Wentworth had used such words, or something like them, but without an idea that they would be carried round to her. He had thought her wretchedly altered, and, in the first moment of appeal, had spoken as he felt. He had not forgiven Anne Elliot. She had used him ill"—and so he goes on, for five more paragraphs. The necessary point, the fact that Frederick believes himself to be indifferent, has been made, and it could not have been made without some kind of shift from Anne's consciousness.

At the end of the novel, we learn that Wentworth was himself deceived in this momentary inside view: "He had meant to forget her, and believed it to be done. He had imagined himself indifferent, when he had only been angry." We may want to protest against the earlier suppression as unfair, but we can hardly believe it to be what Miss Lascelles calls "an oversight."[7] It is deliberate manipulation of inside views in order to destroy our conventional security. We are thus made ready to go along with Anne in her long and painful road to the discovery that Frederick loves her after all.

The only other important breaks in the angle of vision of *Persuasion* come at the beginning and at the end. Chapter one is an excellent example of how a skilful novelist can, by the use of his own direct voice, accomplish in a few pages what even the best novelist must take chapters to do if he uses nothing but dramatized action. Again at the conclusion the author enters with a resounding reaffirmation that the Wentworth-Elliot marriage is as good a thing as we have felt it to be from the beginning.

> Who can be in doubt of what followed? When any two young people take it into their heads to marry, they are pretty sure by perseverance to carry their point, be they ever so poor, or ever so imprudent, or ever so little likely to be necessary to each other's ultimate comfort. This may be bad morality to conclude with, but I believe it to be truth; and if such parties succeed, how should a Captain Wentworth and an Anne Elliot, with the advantage of maturity of mind, consciousness of right, and one independent fortune between them, fail of bearing down every opposition?[8]

Except for these few intrusions and one in chapter xix, Anne's own mind is sufficient in *Persuasion,* but we can never rely completely on Emma. It is hardly surprising that Jane Austen has provided many correctives to insure our placing her errors with precision.

The chief corrective is Knightley. His commentary on Emma's errors is a natural expression of his love; he can tell the reader and Emma at the same time precisely how she is mistaken. Thus, nothing Knightley says can be beside the point. Each affirmation of a value, each accusation of error is in itself an action in the plot. When he rebukes Emma for manipulating Harriet, when he attacks her for superficiality and false pride, when he condemns her for gossiping and flirting with Frank Churchill, and finally when he attacks her for being "insolent" and "unfeeling" in her treatment of Miss Bates, we have Jane Austen's judgment on Emma, rendered dramatically. But it has come from someone who is essentially sympathetic toward Emma, so that his judgments against her are presumed to be temporary. His sympathy reinforces ours even as he criticizes, and her respect for his opinion, shown in her self-abasement after he has criticized, is one of our main reasons for expecting her to reform.

If Henry James had tried to write a novel about Emma, and had cogitated at length on the problem of getting her story told dramatically, he could not have done better than this. It is possible, of course, to think of *Emma* without Knightley as *raisonneur,* just as it is possible to think of *The Golden Bowl,* say, without the Assinghams as *ficelles* to reflect something not seen by the Prince or Princess. But Knightley, though he receives less independent space than the Assinghams and is almost never seen in an inside view, is clearly more useful for Jane Austen's purposes than any realistically limited *ficelle* could possibly be. By combining the role of commentator with the role of hero, Jane Austen has worked more economically than James, and though economy is as dangerous as any other criterion when applied universally, even James might have profited from a closer study of the economies that a character like Knightley can be made to achieve. It is as if James had dared to make one of the four main characters, say the Prince, into a thoroughly good, wise, perceptive man, a thoroughly clear rather than a partly confused "reflector."

Since Knightley is established early as completely reliable, we need no views of his secret thoughts. He has no secret thoughts, except for the unacknowledged depths of his love for Emma and his jealousy of Frank Churchill. The other main characters have more to hide, and Jane Austen moves in and out of minds with great freedom, choosing for her own purposes what to reveal and what to withhold. Always the seeming violation of consistency is in the consistent service of the particular needs of Emma's story. Sometimes a shift is made simply to direct our suspense, as when Mrs. Weston suggests a possible union of Emma and Frank Churchill, at the end of her conversation with Knightley about the harmful effects of Emma's friendship with Harriet (chap. v). "Part of her meaning was to conceal some favourite thoughts of her own and Mr. Weston's on the subject, as much as possible. There were wishes at Randalls respecting Emma's destiny, but it was not desirable to have them suspected."

One objection to this selective dipping into whatever mind best serves our immediate purposes is that it suggests mere trickery and inevitably spoils the illusion of reality. If Jane Austen can tell us what Mrs. Weston is thinking, why not what Frank Churchill and Jane Fairfax are thinking? Obviously, because she chooses to build a mystery, and to do so she must refuse, arbitrarily and obtrusively, to grant the privilege of an inside view to characters whose minds would reveal too much. But is not the mystery purchased at the price of shaking the reader's faith in Jane Austen's integrity? If she simply withholds until later what she might as well relate now—if her procedure is not dictated by the very nature of her materials—why should we take her seriously?

If a natural surface were required in all fiction, then this objection would hold. But if we want to read *Emma* in its own terms, the real question about these shifts cannot be answered by an easy appeal to general principles. Every author withholds until later what he "might as well" relate now. The question is always one of desired effects, and the choice of any one effect always bans innumerable other effects. There is, indeed, a question to be raised about the use of mystery in *Emma,* but the conflict is not between an abstract end that Jane Austen never worried about and a shoddy mystification that she allowed to betray her. The conflict is between two effects both of which she cares about a good deal. On the one hand she cares about maintaining some sense of mystery as long as she can. On the other, she works at all points to heighten the reader's sense of dramatic irony, usually in the form of a contrast between what Emma knows and what the reader knows.

As in most novels, whatever steps are taken to mystify inevitably decrease the dramatic irony, and, whenever dramatic irony is increased by telling the reader secrets the characters have not yet suspected, mystery is inevitably destroyed. The longer we are in doubt about Frank Churchill, the weaker our sense of ironic contrast between Emma's views and the truth. The sooner we see through Frank Churchill's secret plot, the greater our pleasure in observing Emma's innumerable misreadings of his behavior and the less interest we have in the mere mystery of the situation. And we all find that on second reading we discover new intensities of dramatic irony resulting from the complete loss of mystery; knowing what abysses of error Emma is preparing for herself, even those of us who may on first reading have deciphered nearly all the details of the Churchill mystery find additional ironies.

But it is obvious that these ironies could have been offered even on a first reading, if Jane Austen had been willing to sacrifice her mystery. A single phrase in her own name—"his secret engagement to Jane Fairfax"—or a short inside view of either of the lovers could have made us aware of every ironic touch.

The author must, then, choose whether to purchase mystery at the expense of irony. For many of us Jane Austen's choice here is perhaps the weakest aspect of this novel. It is a commonplace of our criticism that significant literature arouses suspense not about the "what" but about the "how." Mere mystification has been mastered by so many second-rate writers that her efforts at mystification seem second-rate.

But again we must ask whether criticism can be conducted effectively by balancing one abstract quality against another. Is there a norm of dramatic irony for all works, or even for all works of a given kind? Has anyone ever formulated a "law of first and second readings" that will tell us just how many of our pleasures on page one should depend on our knowledge of what happens on page the last? We quite properly ask that the books we call great be able to stand up under repeated reading, but we need not ask that they yield identical pleasures on each reading. The modern works whose authors pride themselves on the fact that they can never be read but only re-read may be very good indeed, but they are not *made* good by the fact that their secret pleasures can only be wrested from them by repeated readings.

In any case, even if one accepted the criticism of Jane Austen's efforts at mystification, the larger service of the inside views is clear: the crosslights thrown by other minds prevent our being blinded by Emma's radiance.

The Reliable Narrator and the Norms of Emma

If mere intellectual clarity about Emma were the goal in this work, we should be forced to say that the manipulation of inside views and the extensive commentary of the reliable Knightley are more than is necessary. But for maximum intensity of the comedy and romance, even these are not enough. The "author herself"—not necessarily the real Jane Austen but an implied author, represented in this book by a reliable narrator—heightens the effects by directing our intellectual, moral, and emotional progress. She performs, of course, most of the functions described in chapter vii. But her most important role is to reinforce both aspects of the double vision that operates throughout the book: our inside view of Emma's worth and our objective view of her great faults.

The narrator opens *Emma* with a masterful simultaneous presentation of Emma and of the values against which she must be judged: "Emma Woodhouse, handsome, clever, and rich, with a comfortable home and happy disposition, seemed to unite some of the best blessings of existence; and had lived nearly twenty-one years in the world with very little to distress or vex her." This "seemed" is immediately reinforced by more directly stated reservations. "The real evils of Emma's situation were the power of having rather too much her own way, and a disposition to think a little too well of herself; these were the disadvantages which threatened alloy to her many enjoyments. The danger, however, was at present so unperceived, that they did not by any means rank as misfortunes with her."

None of this could have been said by Emma, and if shown through her consciousness, it could not be accepted, as it must be, without question. Like most of the first three chapters, it is nondramatic summary, building up, through the ostensible business of getting the characters introduced, to Emma's initial blunder with Harriet and Mr. Elton. Throughout these chapters, we learn much of what we must know from the narrator, but she turns over more and more of the job of summary to Emma as she feels more and more sure of our seeing precisely to what degree Emma is to be trusted. Whenever we leave the "real evils" we have been warned against in Emma, the narrator's and Emma's views coincide: we cannot tell which of them, for example, offers the judgment on Mr. Woodhouse that "his talents could not have recommended him at any time," or the judgment on Mr. Knightley that he is "a sensible man," "always welcome" at Hartfield, or even that "Mr. Knightley, in fact, was one of the few people who could see faults in Emma Woodhouse, and the only one who ever told her of them."

But there are times when Emma and her author are far apart, and the author's direct guidance aids the reader in his own break with Emma. The beautiful irony of the first description of Harriet, given through Emma's eyes (chap. iii) could no doubt be grasped intellectually by many readers without all of the preliminary commentary. But even for the most perceptive its effect is heightened, surely, by the sense of standing with the author and observing with her precisely how Emma's judgment is going astray. Perhaps more important, we ordinary, less perceptive readers have by now been raised to a level suited to grasp the ironies. Certainly, most readers would overlook some of the barbs directed against Emma if the novel began, as a serious modern novelist might well begin it, with this description:

> [Emma] was not struck by any thing remarkably clever in Miss Smith's conversation, but she found her altogether very engaging—not inconveniently shy, not unwilling to talk—and yet so far from pushing, shewing so proper and becoming a deference, seeming so pleasantly grateful for being admitted to Hartfield, and so artlessly impressed by the appearance of every thing in so superior a style to what she had been used to, that she must have good sense and deserve encouragement. Encouragement should be given. Those soft blue eyes . . . should not be wasted on the inferior society of Highbury. . . .

And so Emma goes on, giving herself away with every word, pouring out her sense of her own beneficence and general value. Harriet's past friends, "though very good sort of people, must be doing her harm." Without knowing them, Emma knows that they "must be coarse and unpolished, and very unfit to be the intimates of a girl who wanted only a little more knowledge and elegance to be quite perfect." And she concludes with a beautiful burst of egotism: "*She* would notice her; she would improve her; she would detach her from her bad acquaintance, and introduce her into good society; she would form her opinions and her manners. It would be an interesting, and certainly a very kind undertaking; highly becoming her own situation in life, her leisure, and powers." Even the most skilful reader might not easily plot an absolutely true course through these ironies without the prior direct assistance we have been given. Emma's views are not so outlandish that they could never have been held by a female novelist writing in her time. They cannot serve effecitvely as signs of *her* character unless they are clearly disavowed as signs of Jane Austen's views. Emma's unconscious catalogue of her egotistical uses for Harriet, given under the pretense of listing the services *she* will perform, is thus given its full force by being framed explicitly in a world of values which Emma herself cannot discover until the conclusion of the book.

The full importance of the author's direct imposition of an elaborate scale of norms can be seen by considering that conclusion. The sequence of events is a simple one: Emma's faults and mistakes are brought home to her in a rapid and humiliating chain of rebukes from Knightley and blows from hard fact. These blows to her self-esteem produce at last a genuine reform (for example, she brings herself to apologize to Miss Bates, something she could never have done earlier in the novel). The change in her character removes the only obstacle in the way of Knightley's proposal, and the marriage follows. "The wishes, the hopes, the confidence, the predictions of the small band of true friends who witnessed the ceremony, were fully answered in the perfect happiness of the union."

It may be that if we look at Emma and Knightley as real people, this ending will seem false. G. B. Stern laments, in *Speaking of Jane Austen,* "Oh, Miss Austen, it was *not* a good solution; it was a bad solution, an unhappy ending, could we see beyond the last pages of the book." Edmund Wilson predicts that Emma will find a new protégée like Harriet, since she has not been cured of her inclination to "infatuations with women." Marvin Mudrick even more emphatically rejects Jane Austen's explicit rhetoric; he believes that Emma is still a "confirmed exploiter," and for him the ending must be read as ironic.[9]

But it is precisely because this ending is neither life itself nor a simple bit of literary irony that it can serve so well to heighten our sense of a complete and indeed perfect resolution to all that has gone before. If we look at the values that have been realized in this marriage and compare them with those realized in conventional marriage plots, we see that Jane Austen means what she says: this will be a happy marriage because there is simply nothing left to make it anything less than perfectly happy. It fulfils every value embodied in the world of the book—with the possible exception that Emma may never learn to apply herself as she ought to her reading and her piano! It is a union of intelligence: of "reason," of "sense," of "judgment." It is a union of virtue: of "good will," of generosity, of unselfishness. It is a union of feeling: of "taste," "tenderness," "love," "beauty."[10]

In a general way, then, this plot offers us an experience superficially like that offered by most tragicomedy as well as by much of the cheapest popular art: we are made to desire certain good things for certain good characters, and then our desires are gratified. If we depended on general criteria derived from our justified boredom with such works, we should reject this one. But the critical difference lies in the precise quality of the values appealed to and the precise quality of the characters who violate or realize them. All of the cheap marriage plots in the world should not lead us to be embarrassed about our pleasure in Emma and Knightley's marriage. It is more than just the marriage: it is the *rightness* of *this* marriage, as a conclusion to all of the comic wrongness that has gone before. The good for Emma includes both her necessary reform and the resulting marriage. Marriage to an intelligent, amiable, good, and attractive man is the best thing that can happen to this heroine, and the readers who do not experience it as such are, I am convinced, far from knowing what Jane Austen is about—whatever they may say about the "bitter spinster's" attitude toward marriage.

Our modern sensibilities are likely to be rasped by any such formulation. We do not ordinarily like to encounter perfect endings in our novels—even in the sense of "perfectedness" or completion, the sense obviously intended by Jane Austen. We refuse to accept it when we see it: witness the many attempts to deny Dostoevski's success with Alyosha and Father Zossima in *The Brothers Karamazov*. Many of us find it embarrassing to talk of emotions based on moral judgment at all, particularly when the emotions have any kind of affirmative cast. Emma herself is something of a "modern" in this regard throughout most of the book. Her self-deception about marriage is as great as about most other important matters. Emma boasts to Harriet of her indifference to marriage, at the same time unconsciously betraying her totally inadequate view of the sources of human happiness.

> If I know myself, Harriet, mine is an active, busy mind, with a great many independent resources; and I do not perceive why I should be more in want of employment at forty or fifty than one-and-twenty. Woman's usual occupations of eye and hand and mind will be as open to me then, as they are now; or with no important variation. If I draw less, I shall read more; if I give up music, I shall take to carpet-work.

Emma at carpet-work! If she knows herself indeed.

> And as for objects of interest, objects for the affections, which is, in truth, the great point of inferiority, the want of which is really the great evil to be avoided in *not* marrying [a magnificent concession, this] I shall be very well off, with all the children of a sister I love so much, to care about. There will be enough of them, in all probability, to supply every sort of sensation that declining life can need. There will be enough for every hope and every fear; and though my attachment to none can equal that of a parent, it suits my ideas of comfort better than what is warmer and blinder. My nephews and nieces!—I shall often have a niece with me [chap. x].

Without growing solemn about it—it is wonderfully comic—we can recognize that the humor springs here from very deep sources indeed. It can be fully enjoyed, in fact, only by the reader who has attained to a vision of human felicity far more profound than Emma's "comfort" and "want" and "need." It is a vision that includes not simply marriage, but a kind of loving converse not based, as is Emma's here, on whether the "loved" person will serve one's irreducible needs.

The comic effect of this repudiation of marriage is considerably increased by the fact that Emma always thinks of marriage for others as *their* highest good, and in fact unconsciously encourages her friend Harriet to fall in love with the very man she herself loves without knowing it. The delightful denouement is thus what we want not only because it is a supremely good thing for Emma, but because it is a supremely comic outcome of Emma's profound misunderstanding of herself and of the human condition. In the schematic language of chapter v, it satisfies both our practical desire for Emma's well-being and our appetite for the qualities proper to these artistic materials. It is thus a more resounding resolution than either of these elements separately could provide. The other major resolution of the work—Harriet's marriage with her farmer—reinforces this interpretation. Emma's sin against Harriet has been something far worse than the mere meddling of a busybody. To destroy Harriet's chances for happiness—chances that depend entirely on her marriage—is as close to viciousness as any author could dare to take a heroine designed to be loved. We can laugh with Emma at this mistake (chap. liv) only because Harriet's chance for happiness is restored.

Other values, like money, blood, and "consequence," are real enough in *Emma,* but only as they contribute to or are mastered by good taste, good judgment, and good morality. Money alone can make a Mrs. Churchill, but a man or woman "is silly to marry without it." Consequence untouched by sense can make a very inconsequential Mr. Woodhouse; untouched by sense or virtue it can make the much more contemptible Mr. and Miss Elliot of *Persuasion.* But it is a pleasant thing to have, and it does no harm unless, like the early Emma, one takes it too seriously. Charm and elegance without sufficient moral force can make a Frank Churchill; unschooled by morality it can lead to the baseness of Henry Crawford in *Mansfield Park* or of Wickham in *Pride and Prejudice.* Even the supreme vitures are inadequate in isolation: good will alone will make a comic Miss Bates or a Mr. Weston, judgment with insufficient good will a comic Mr. John Knightley, and so on.

I am willing to risk the commonplace in such a listing because it is only thus that the full force of Jane Austen's comprehensive view can be seen. There is clearly at work here a much more detailed ordering of values than any conventional public philosophy of her time could provide. Obviously, few readers in her own time, and far fewer in our own, have ever approached this novel in full and detailed agreement with the author's norms. But they were led to join her as they read, and so are we.

Explicit Judgments on Emma Woodhouse

We have said in passing almost enough of the other side of the coin—the judgment of particular actions as they relate to the general norms. But something must be said of the detailed "placing" of Emma, by direct commentary, in the hierarchy of values established by the novel. I must be convinced, for example, not only that tenderness for other people's feelings is an important trait but also that Emma's particular behavior violates the true standards of tenderness, if I am to savor to the full the episode of Emma's insult to Miss Bates and Knightley's reproach which follows. If I refuse to blame Emma, I may discover a kind of intellectual enjoyment in the episode, and I will probably think that any critic who talks of "belief" in tenderness as operating in such a context is taking things too seriously. But I can never enjoy the episode in its full intensity or grasp its formal coherence. Similarly, I must agree not only that to be dreadfully boring is a minor fault compared with the major virtue of "good will," but also that Miss Bates's exemplification of this fault and of this virtue entitle her to the respect which Emma denies. If I do not—while yet being able to laugh at Miss Bates—I can hardly understand, let alone enjoy, Emma's mistreatment of her.

But these negative judgments must be counteracted by a larger approval, and, as we would expect, the novel is full of direct apologies for Emma. Her chief fault, lack of good will or tenderness, must be read not only in relationship to the code of values provided by the book as a whole—a code which judges her as seriously deficient; it must also be judged in relationship to the harsh facts of the world around her, a world made up of human beings ranging in degree of selfishness and egotism from Knightley, who lapses from perfection when he tries to judge Frank Churchill, his rival, down to Mrs. Elton, who has most of Emma's faults and none of her virtues. In such a setting, Emma is easily forgiven. When she insults Miss Bates, for example, we remember that Miss Bates lives in a world where many others are insensitive and cruel. "Miss Bates, neither young, handsome, rich, nor married, stood in the very worst predicament in the world for having much of the public favour; and she had no intellectual superiority to make atonement to herself, or frighten those who might hate her, into outward respect." While it would be a mistake to see only this "regulated hatred" in Jane Austen's world, overlooking the tenderness and generosity, the hatred of viciousness is there, and there is enough vice in evidence to make Emma almost shine by comparison.

Often, Jane Austen makes this apology-by-comparison explicit. When Emma lies to Knightley about Harriet, very close to the end of the book, she is excused with a generalization about human nature: "Seldom, very seldon, does complete truth belong to any human disclosure; seldom can it happen that something is not a little disguised, or a little mistaken; but where, as in this case, though the conduct is mistaken, the feelings are not, it may not be very material.—Mr. Knightley could not impute to Emma a more relenting heart than she possessed, or a heart more disposed to accept of his."

The Implied Author as Friend and Guide

With all of this said about the masterful use of the narrator in *Emma,* there remain some "intrusions" unaccounted for by strict service to the story itself. "What did she say?" the narrator asks, at the crucial moment in the major love scene. "Just what she ought, of course. A lady always does.—She said enough to show there need not be despair—and to invite him to say more himself." To some readers this has seemed to demonstrate the author's inability to write a love scene, since it sacrifices "the illusion of reality."[11] But who has ever read this far in *Emma* under the delusion that he is reading a realistic portrayal which is suddenly shattered by the unnatural appearance of the narrator? If the narrator's superabundant wit is destructive of the kind of illusion proper to this work, the novel has been ruined long before.

But we should now be in a position to see precisely why the narrator's wit is not in the least out of place at the emotional climax of the novel. We have seen how the inside views of the characters and the author's commentary have been used from the beginning to get the values straight and to keep them straight and to help direct our reactions to Emma. But we also see here a beautiful case of the dramatized author as friend and guide. "Jane Austen," like "Henry Fielding," is a paragon of wit, wisdom, and virtue. She does not talk about her qualities; unlike Fielding she does not in *Emma* call direct attention to her artistic skill. But we are seldom allowed to forget about her for all that. When we read this novel we accept her as representing everything we admire most. She is as generous and wise as Knightley; in fact, she is a shade more penetrating in her judgment. She is as subtle and witty as Emma would like to think herself. Without being sentimental she is in favor of tenderness. She is able to put an adequate but not excessive value on wealth and rank. She recognizes a fool when she sees one, but unlike Emma she knows that it is both immoral and foolish to be rude to fools. She is, in short, a perfect human being, within the concept of perfection established by the book she writes; she even recognizes that human perfection of the kind *she* exemplifies is not quite attainable in real life. The process of her domination is of course circular; her character establishes the values for us according to which her character is then found to be perfect. But this circularity does not affect the success of her endeavor; in fact it insures it.

Her "omniscience" is thus a much more remarkable thing than is ordinarily implied by the term. All good novelists know all about their characters—all that they need to know. And the question of how their narrators are to find out all that *they* need to know, the question of "authority," is a relatively simple one. The real choice is much more profound than this would imply. It is a choice of the moral, not merely the technical, angle of vision from which the story is to be told.

Unlike the central intelligences of James and his successors, "Jane Austen" has learned nothing at the end of the novel that she did not know at the beginning. She needed to learn nothing. She knew everything of importance already. We have been privileged to watch with her as she observes her favorite character climb from a considerably lower platform to join the exalted company of Knightley, "Jane Austen," and those of us readers who are wise enough, good enough, and perceptive enough to belong up there too. As Katherine Mansfield says, "the truth is that every true admirer of the novels cherishes the happy thought that he alone—reading between the lines—has become the secret friend of their author."[12] Those who love "gentle Jane" as a secret friend may undervalue the irony and wit; those who see her in effect as the greatest of Shaw's heroines, flashing about her with the weapons of irony, may undervalue the emphasis on tenderness and good will. But only a very few can resist her.

The dramatic illusion of her presence as a character is thus fully as important as any other element in the story. When she intrudes, the illusion is not shattered. The only illusion we care about, the illusion of traveling intimately with a hardy little band of readers whose heads are screwed on tight and whose hearts are in the right place, is actually strengthened when we are refused the romantic love scene. Like the author herself, we don't care about the love scene. We can find love scenes in almost any novelist's works, but only here can we find a mind and heart that can give us clarity without oversimplification, sympathy and romance without sentimentality, and biting irony without cynicism.

NOTES

[1] "The Lesson of Balzac," *The Question of Our Speech* (Cambridge, 1905), p. 63. A fuller quotation can be found in R. W. Chapman's indispensable *Jane Austen: A Critical Bibliography* (Oxford, 1955). Some important Austen items published too late to be included by Chapman are: (1) Ian Watt, *The Rise of the Novel* (Berkeley, Calif.,

1957); (2) Stuart M. Tave, review of Marvin Mudrick's *Jane Austen: Irony as Defense and Discovery* (Princeton, N.J., 1952) in *Philological Quarterly,* XXXII (July, 1953), 256–57; (3) Andrew H. Wright, *Jane Austen's Novels: A Study in Structure* (London, 1953), pp. 36–82; (4) Christopher Gillie, "*Sense and Sensibility:* An Assessment," *Essays in Criticism,* IX (January, 1959), 1–9, esp. 5–6; (5) Edgar F. Shannon, Jr., "*Emma:* Character and Construction," *PMLA,* LXXI (September, 1956), 637–50.

[2] See, for example, Mudrick, *op. cit.,* pp. 91, 165; Frank O'Connor, *The Mirror in the Roadway* (London, 1957), p. 30.

[3] "A heroine whom no one but myself will much like" (James Edward Austen-Leigh, *Memoir of His Aunt* [London, 1870; Oxford, 1926], p. 157).

[4] The best discussion of this problem is Reginald Farrer's "Jane Austen," *Quarterly Review,* CCXXVIII (July, 1917), 1–30; reprinted in William Heath's *Discussions of Jane Austen* (Boston, 1961). For one critic the book fails because the problem was never recognized by Jane Austen herself: Mr. E. N. Hayes, in what may well be the least sympathetic discussion of *Emma* yet written, explains the whole book as the author's failure to see Emma's faults. "Evidently Jane Austen wished to protect Emma. . . . The author is therefore in the ambiguous position of both loving and scorning the heroine" ("'Emma': A Dissenting Opinion," *Nineteenth-Century Fiction,* IV [June, 1949], 18, 19).

[5] A. C. Bradley, for example, once argued that Jane Austen intended Jane Fairfax to be as interesting throughout as she becomes at the end, but "the moralist in Jane Austen stood for once in her way. The secret engagement is, for her, so serious an offence, that she is afraid to win our hearts for Jane until it has led to great unhappiness" ("Jane Austen," in *Essays and Studies, by Members of the English Association,* II [Oxford, 1911], 23).

[6] I know of only one full-scale attempt to deal with the "tension between sympathy and judgment" in modern literature, Robert Langbaum's *The Poetry of Experience* (London, 1957). Langbaum argues that in the dramatic monologue, with which he is primarily concerned, the sympathy engendered by the direct portrayal of internal experience leads the reader to suspend his moral judgment. Thus, in reading Browning's portraits of moral degeneration—e.g., the duke in "My Last Duchess" or the monk in "Soliloquy of a Spanish Cloister"—our moral judgment is overwhelmed "because we prefer to participate in the duke's power and freedom, in his hard core of character fiercely loyal to itself. Moral judgment is in fact important as the thing to be suspended, as a measure of the price we pay for the privilege of appreciating to the full this extraordinary man" (p. 83). While I think that Langbaum seriously underplays the extent to which moral judgment remains even after psychological vividness has done its work, and while he perhaps defines "morality" too narrowly when he excludes from it such things as power and freedom and fierce loyalty to one's own character, his book is a stimulating introduction to the problems raised by internal portraiture of flawed characters.

[7] *Jane Austen and Her Art* (Oxford, 1939), p. 204.

[8] It seems to be difficult for some modern critics, accustomed to ferreting values out from an impersonal or ironic context without the aid of the author's voice, to make use of

reliable commentary like this when it is provided. Even a highly perceptive reader like Mark Schorer, for example, finds himself doing unnecessary acrobatics with the question of style, and particularly metaphor, as clues to the norms against which the author judges her characters. In reading *Persuasion,* he finds these clues among the metaphors "from commerce and property, the counting house and the inherited estate" with which it abounds ("Fiction and the Matrix of Analogy," *Kenyon Review* [Autumn, 1949], p. 540). No one would deny that the novel is packed with such metaphors, although Schorer is somewhat overingenious in marshaling to his cause certain dead metaphors that Austen could not have avoided without awkward circumlocution (esp. p. 542). But the crucial question surely is: What precisely are these metaphors of the countinghouse doing in the novel? *Whose* values are they supposed to reveal? Accustomed to reading modern fiction in which the novelist very likely provides no direct assistance in answering this question, Schorer leaves it really unanswered; at times he seems almost to imply that Jane Austen is unconsciously giving herself away in her use of them (e.g., p. 543).

But the novel is really very clear about it all. The introduction, coming directly from the wholly reliable narrator, establishes unequivocally and without "analogy" the conflict between the world of the Elliots, depending for its values on selfishness, stupidity, and pride—and the world of Anne, a world where "elegance of mind and sweetness of character" are the supreme values. The commercial values stressed by Schorer are only a selection from what is actually a rich group of evils. And Anne's own expressed views again and again provide direct guidance to the reader.

[9] The first two quotations are from Wilson's "A Long Talk about Jane Austen," *A Literary Chronicle: 1920-1950* (New York, 1952). The third is from *Jane Austen,* p. 206.

[10] It has lately been fashionable to underplay the value of tenderness and good will in Jane Austen, in reaction to an earlier generation that overdid the picture of "gentle Jane." The trend seems to have begun in earnest with D. W. Harding's "Regulated Hatred: An Aspect of the Work of Jane Austen," *Scrutiny,* VIII (March, 1940), 346-62. While I do not feel as strongly aroused against this school of readers as does R. W. Chapman (see his *A Critical Bibliography,* p. 52, and his review of Mudrick's work in the *T.L.S.* [September 19, 1952]), it seems to me that another swing of the pendulum is called for: when Jane Austen praises the "relenting heart," she means that praise, though she is the same author who can lash the unrelenting heart with "regulated hatred."

[11] Edd Winfield Parks, "Exegesis in Austen's Novels," *The South Atlantic Quarterly,* LI (January, 1952), 117.

[12] *Novels and Novelists,* ed. J. Middleton Murry (London, 1930), p. 304.

Pastoral Poetry: The Vitality and Versatility of a Convention

Hallett Smith

The Elizabethan poet usually began, as Virgil had done, by writing pastoral poetry. And, since many poets begin and not all of them continue, the proportion of pastoral to the whole literary production of the Elizabethan period is fairly high. There have been many attempts to account for this prominence of the shepherd in the literature of an age of sea dogs and explorers, of courtiers and usurers, of magnificent Leicester, dashing Essex, and staid Burleigh.

One critic maintains that pastoral is always a vehicle for something else: "The pastoral, whatever its form, always needed and assumed some external circumstance to give point to its actual content. The interest seldom arises directly from the narrative itself."[1] Another commentator shakes his head over the whole pastoral tradition and seems to think that in the Elizabethan period it is merely a literary fad which got out of hand. "The exquisitely artificial convention of the pastoral poetry of the late sixteenth century and its stylized vocabulary, at times so dazzling and yet so often monotonous, gave little scope for original expression."[2] A more sensitive critic finds the reason for the popularity of pastoral in artistic considerations: "It was the peculiarly combined satisfaction of freedom and formalism which attracted so many Elizabethans to pastoral."[3] Probably the most commonly held view is that pastoral is merely escape literature, especially attractive at a time when populations are shifting, life is becoming more complex, and the townsman dreams nostalgically of life in the country.

It is certainly true that pastoral was a convention. Shepherds thronged in the entertainments for royalty, in the pageants and devices like those presented at Kenilworth in 1575 and in the royal entertainments of 1578. These shows are in part literature, and they had their influence on works which were more purely literature.[4] But to establish the occasion, and even the fashion, of a work of art is not to explain its significance. The more conventional it is, the more likely it is to have some central core of meaning from which individual treatments may originate. "Originality" cannot be estimated until we know what the convention meant to the writers working in it.

Whatever may be said of other times and places, Elizabethan England saw a meaning in pastoral. This meaning was, or constituted, a positive ideal. It was an ideal of the good life, of the state of content and mental self-sufficiency which had been known in classical antiquity as *otium*. The revival of this ideal is a characteristic Renaissance achievement; it would have been impossible in the Middle Ages, when time spent in neither work nor communion with God was felt to be sinful. By projecting this ideal, poets of the age of Shakespeare were able to criticize life as it is and portray it as it might be. Their shepherds are citizens of the same Arcadia as that inhabited by the shepherds of Milton and Matthew Arnold.

The Elizabethan mind took over its conception of pastoral from many sources. The most general and the most obvious of these sources was the Bible. In Genesis, the first great event after the fall of man is one which involves a shepherd; it is the story of Cain and Abel. What it meant to the Elizabethans is explained by Bacon:

> We see (as the Scriptures have infinite mysteries, not violating at all the truth of the story or letter), an image of the two estates, the contemplative state and the active state, figured in the two persons of Abel and Cain, and in the two simplest and most primitive trades of life; that of the shepherd, (who, by reason of his leisure, rest in a place, and living in view of heaven, is a lively image of a contemplative life,) and that of the husbandman: where we see again the favour and election of God went to the shepherd, and not to the tiller of the ground.[5]

Moreover, David, perhaps the most romantic figure in the Old Testament, was a shepherd, as well as being the principal poet and singer of songs among the ancient Hebrews. Of his psalms, the twenty-third was of course a special favorite. It reflected not only the atmosphere of green pastures but also the doctrine of content as the greatest of God's blessings. "The Lord is my shepherd; I shall not want" was explained by the preachers as a pastoral metaphor expressing the truth of Christian content.[6]

In the New Testament there is the central pastoral imagery of Christ the Good Shepherd, and of course the episode of the shepherds hearing from heaven the good tidings of Christ's birth. As Michael Drayton wrote, "In the Angels Song to Shepheards at our Saviours Nativitie Pastorall Poesie seemes consecrated."[7]

Characteristically, the Renaissance mixed examples of the shepherd from Greek and Roman tradition and history with those from the Bible. In Mantuan's seventh eclogue, Moses and Apollo are mentioned in pastoral roles.[8] Paris, the son of Priam, King of Troy, was the most famous of all classical shepherds because from his actions sprang the whole epic narrative of the siege of Troy. Besides Paris, James Sandford's translation of Cornelius Agrippa (1569) cites Romulus and Remus, Anchises, and the emperor Diocletian as shepherds. Thomas Fortescue's translation from Pedro Mexía, *The Foreste* (1586), adds Galerius and Tamburlaine. A shepherd in Drayton's "Dowsabell," is described as resembling Tamburlaine in looks and Abel in temper.[9]

The Elizabethan attitude toward Paris reveals much of the meaning and significance of pastoral in the poetry of the age. The story of Paris is of course one of the great stories: how a king's son, living as a shepherd, is in love with the nymph Oenone; how he is chosen to be umpire among the three goddesses, Juno, Venus, and Pallas Athena, to decide which of them deserves the golden apple inscribed "For the fairest"; how he decides in favor of Venus and is given as a reward the love of the most beautiful of women, Helen; how he deserts Oenone, brings Helen to Troy, and precipitates the Trojan War with all of its consequences—this plot is surely one of the great achievements of the Western imagination.

Dramatic treatments of the story of Paris are mentioned by Saint Augustine;[10] the subject is inherently dramatic, both for the power of the rival claims of the goddesses and for the world-shaking consequences of Paris' choice. The death of Hector and Achilles, the destruction of Troy, the wanderings of Ulysses and of Aeneas, the founding of Rome (and of Britain, too, as the Elizabethans thought), all resulted from this one simple decision by a shepherd on the hills of Ida.

Purely as plot, then, the story of the shepherd's choice had color and vitality. But it was also symbolic, and an understanding of what was represented to the Elizabethan mind by the offers of Juno, Pallas, and Venus while Paris was trying to make up his mind is essential to an appreciation of poetic treatments of the myth. From classical times on down, the principal myths had been interpreted morally, if not allegorically, and the Judgment of Paris was one which lent itself to such treatment in a very natural way. Athenaeus says, in the *Deipnosophistae*,

"And I for one affirm also that the Judgment of Paris, as told in poetry by the writers of an older time, is really a trial of pleasure against virtue. Aphrodite, for example—and she represents pleasure—was given the preference, and so everything was thrown into turmoil."[11]

Fulgentius, Bishop of Carthage, also moralized the myth of the Judgment of Paris. The three goddesses, he says, represent the three ways of life: the active, the contemplative, and the voluptuous. Jove himself, continues Fulgentius, could not make judgment among the three contending goddesses or the ways of life they represent; it is essentially a human dilemma. A shepherd, in Fulgentius' opinion, is the most suitable of all men to be the judge, though of course, according to the bishop, Paris made a foolish choice. Spenser agrees, and in the July eclogue of *The Shepheardes Calender* goes out of his way to condemn Paris:

> For he was proude, that ill was payd,
> (no such mought shepheards bee)
> And with lewde lust was ouerlayd:
> tway things doen ill agree.[12]

To the Renaissance, Paris' mistake was intended as a powerful warning. Italian treatises on nobility considered the Judgment of Paris story to represent the choice which must actually be made by the young man deciding upon a course of life.[13]

In the most popular of the pastoral romances, the Judgment of Paris is a subject for debate; in Montemayor's *Diana*, for example, Delia and Andronius spend the greater part of a night in arguing the question whether Paris gave the apple to the right goddess or not and whether the inscription on it referred to physical or mental beauty.[14] The shepherds and shepherdesses in Elizabethan pastoral poetry often allude to the Paris story or compare themselves with figures in it. An example is from "Phillidaes Loue-Call to her Coridon, and his replying," by "Ignoto" in *England's Helicon;*[15] another is Willye's compliment to Cuddie, the umpire of the singing match in Spenser's August eclogue:

> Neuer dempt more right of beautye I weene,
> The shepherd of Ida, that iudged beauties Queene.[16]

Drayton's Rowland, on the other hand, compares himself to the deserted Oenone.[17]

Whatever the faults of Paris' decision, the son of Priam remained, for the Elizabethan, the archetype of the shepherd. Spenser's Sir Calidore, when he takes off his armor and puts on shepherd's weeds in order to woo Pastorella, suggests the obvious model, "Phrygian Paris by Plexippus brooke."[18]

The Judgment of Paris had of course been treated in medieval love allegories such as Froissart's *L'Espinette Amoureuse,* Machaut's *Le Dit de la Fontaine Amoureuse,* and Lydgate's *Reson and Sensuallyte;* there had been continental dramas on the subject in the fifteenth and early sixteenth centuries; and most important of all for the English pastoral, the Paris story was a common subject of the pageants—for Queen Margaret at Edinburgh in 1503, for the coronation of Anne Boleyn in 1533, and at a marriage masque in 1566.[19] It also appeared in the emblem-books. In Whitney's *Choice of Emblemes* the account of the Judgment is much abbreviated, but full justice is done to the interpretation.[20]

It is obvious, then, that the major Elizabethan treatment of the Paris story, George Peele's play *The Arraignment of Paris* (1584), is in a well-established tradition. It is in dramatic form, but it is so important as an indication of the significance of pastoral in the Elizabethan mind that it must be discussed briefly here.

In the temptation scene, when the three goddesses in turn offer their rewards to Paris, they are more abstract than personal. Juno offers the shepherd "great monarchies, Empires, and kingdomes, heapes of massye golde, scepters and diadems," symbolized theatrically by the appearance of a golden tree, the fruit of which is diadems. Pallas offers fame, wisdom, honor of chivalry and victory, "but yf thou haue a minde to fly aboue." The reward is symbolized by nine knights in armor treading a warlike Almain. Venus offers Paris the services of Cupid, kisses from herself, and finally (here the reward and the symbol become the same thing) Helen.[21] Paris is constantly a symbolic figure; he is suggestive. I do not mean that the artist had nothing to do with this suggestiveness and that the audience could be counted upon to do it all. A sixteenth-century Italian treatise on painting makes clear the artist's obligation in the matter and uses Paris as an example:

> Hence then the painter may learne how to expresse not onely the proper and naturall motions, but also the accidentall; wherein consisteth no small part of the difficulty of the Arte, namelie in representing diversities of affections and passions in one bodie: A thing much practized, by the ancient Painters (though with greate difficulty) who ever indevored to leaue no iotte of the *life* vnexpressed.
>
> It is recorded that *Euphranor* gaue such a touch to the counterfeit of *Paris,* that therein the behoulder might at once collect, that

hee was *Vmpire* of the three *Goddesses,* the *Courter of Helena,* and the slaier of *Achilles.*[22]

But Paris, with the alternatives clearly before him, chooses Venus. When he defends himself before the court of the gods, in Peele's play, he speaks first as a man, blaming his fault, if any, on the judgment of his eye. Then he adds a *reason:* that it was only for beauty he gave the ball, and if other virtues had been concerned he would have chosen Pallas or Juno. Furthermore, he says, he was tempted more than man ever was, and as a shepherd he was relatively immune to offers other than that of Venus.[23] The simplicity of the shepherd's conditions makes for an invulnerability to appeals in the name of wealth or of chivalry. It is only beauty, of the three ideals represented by the goddesses, which has any significant power in a pastoral life.

Paris is the judge precisely because the conditions of the pastoral life provide the greatest independence, the greatest security. The shepherd is not motivated by ambition or by greed. Free from these two common human passions, he enjoys "content," or the good life. Elizabethan pastoral poetry is essentially a celebration of this ideal of content, of *otium.* The comtemplative state enjoyed a freedom, not only from ambition or greed, but from the vicissitudes of fortune. The popular tradition of the fall of princes, represented in Elizabethan literature by the *Mirror for Magistrates* and the poems added to it, had stressed ominously the dangers in the turn of Fortune's wheel. Kings and princes, the high and mighty, were exhibited in tragic circumstances, the victims of their own high position, their ambition, or their greed. The poetic tragedies of the *Mirror* therefore supported, negatively, the same ideal celebrated by pastoral. Occasionally the warning in a *Mirror* tragedy concludes with a direct endorsement of the quiet life of content. In one of the tragedies in Blenerhasset's *Mirror,* for example, the herdsman who kills Sigebert and is hanged for it concludes with the lesson:

And happy he, who voyde of hope can leade
A quiet lyfe, all voyde of Fortunes dread.

This makes the following Induction deal with the question of why it is that formerly the wisest men were content to be shepherds, but now "in these our dayes, non bee Heardmen but fooles, and euery man though his witte be but meane, yet he cannot liue with a contented mind, except he hath the degree of a Lorde."[24]

In order to respond adequately to the appeal of the Elizabethan ideal of the mean estate, content, and *otium,* it is necessary to feel the force of its opposite, a form of ambition which the sixteenth century called most commonly the aspiring mind. Marlowe's Tamburlaine is of course the great representative of the aspiring mind, as he is its philosopher:

> Nature that fram'd vs of foure Elements,
> Warring within our breasts for regiment,
> Doth teach vs all to haue aspyring minds.[25]

But there are many other examples of the concept in Elizabeth England. Mr. Secretary Walsingham, summing up the personal charges against Mary Queen of Scots, said that she had an aspiring mind;[26] and Queen Elizabeth herself, writing a poem about Mary, included the line

> But clowds of tois vntried, do cloake aspiring mindes.[27]

Blue, as the color of the sky, was symbolic of the aspiring mind, according to Lomazzo:

> Persius sat. 1. speaking of Blew garments, sheweth that they belong only to such persons, as aspire vnto high matter: and Cicero vsed sometimes to weare this color, giuing men thereby to vnderstand, that he bare an aspiring minde.[28]

There were many other Roman examples of the aspiring mind; a typical one is Pompey.[29] That the aspiring mind was a dangerous and possibly sinful state is made clear by Du Bartas, who contrasts it to the attitude of the angels.[30] The first example of the aspiring mind, according to Du Bartas, was in the hunter, Nimrod, "that was the first Tyrant of the world, after the time of Noah, the first Admiral of the worlde: his aspiring minde & practises in seeking the peoples fauour, his proud and subtle attempt in building the Tower of Babel, & Gods iust punishment thereof in confounding the language of the builders."[31]

The central meaning of pastoral is the rejection of the aspiring mind. The shepherd demonstrates that true content is to be found in this renunciation. Sidney expresses the preference in terms of a contrast between pastoral and court life:

> Greater was that shepheards treasure,
> Then this false, fine, Courtly pleasure.[32]

In the pastoral episode in Book VI of *The Faerie Queene,* Sir Calidore envies the apparent happiness of the shepherds; he comments that their life seems free from the "warres, and wreckes, and wicked enmitie" which afflict the rest of the world.[33] In reply to this, the sage old Meliboee then answers with an analysis of the pastoral existence which is in effect a definition of "the good life." It consists of four elements: (1) being content with what you have, however small it is—this is the way taught by nature (contrast Tamburlaine's statement that nature teaches us to have aspiring minds); (2) enjoying freedom from envy of others and from excessive care for your own possessions (the flocks multiply without your doing much about it); (3) avoiding the dangers of pride and ambition and also the insomnia that plagues those who hold positions of responsibility (see the testimony of Shakespeare's kings in *2 Henry IV*, III, i, 1-31, and IV, v, 20-27; *Henry V*, IV, i, 266-290); (4) doing what you like. Old Meliboee does not speak from provincial ignorance, either. He once spent ten years at court, but returned to the pastoral life from choice.

The question of the moral validity of pastoral life when compared with life at court is not difficult to answer: the long tradition of dispraise of the court is always, by implication or by direct statement, an endorsement of the pastoral life. But there is a more difficult question when the alternatives are the quiet, retired life of the shepherd on the one hand or a mission of chivalric and honorable achievement on the other. The pastoral romance, both in Sidney and in his sources like Montemayor's *Diana,* mingles pastoral and heroic elements. The question of the relative value of the two kinds of life is naturally raised. The pastoral sojourn of Erminia in the seventh book of Tasso's *Jerusalem Delivered* is used as a contrast to the heroic actions of the main part of the poem. It is also obvious that pastoral and heroic put a different light upon the feelings of love; these might or might not be a detriment to the heroic life, but they are sanctioned in the world of pastoral.

The commentators on the sixth book of Spenser's *Faerie Queene* have been at odds over the meaning of the pastoral interlude there, the Pastorella episode. T. P. Harrison says, "Spenser obviously censures Sir Calidore's pastoral aberration; yet he, like Sidney, is inclined to paint the rural picture sympathetically."[34] The opposite view is expressed by C. S. Lewis:

> The greatest mistake that can be made about this book is to suppose that Calidore's long delay among the shepherds is a pastoral truancy from Spenser's moral intention . . . Courtesy, for the poet, has very little connection with court. It grows "on a lowly stalke"; . . . according to Spenser, courtesy, in its perfect form, comes by nature; moral effort may produce a decent substitute for everyday use, which deserves praise, but it will never rival the real courtesy of those who

so goodly gracious are by kind
That every action doth them much commend.[35]

Lewis is certainly right about Spenser's endorsement of the pastoral life, or his justification of Sir Calidore, for the opening stanzas of Canto x make it clear.[36] Spenser's own words do not, however, support conclusively the suggestion that courtesy is wholly natural. When in the beginning of Canto xii the poet makes a kind of apology for the wandering structure of the narrative, he is careful to defend the idea behind it.[37] The pastoral environment is a further test and demonstration of Sir Calidore's courtesy, but it is not its source. Calidore treats his shepherd rival, Coridon, with great generosity and magnanimity.[38] The pastoral ideal, then, is reconcilable somehow with the code of chivalry and honor, even though its emphasis is different. As the climax and goal of a life of heroic effort there is a state of heavenly contemplation not too different from the state of mind of the pastoral ideal. But this state may be reached only after the knightly quest is achieved as we see in the tenth canto of Spenser's Book I.

Closer to pastoral is the Horatian praise of the country gentleman's life, of which there are many examples in Elizabethan poetry. Wyatt's first satire, a translation of Alamanni, and Thomas Lodge's "In Praise of the Countrey Life," a translation of Desportes, are typical. This type of poetry, like pastoral, proclaims the moral and emotional advantages of the country over the court. Lodge, for example, sings:

Amidst the pallace braue puft vp with wanton showes
Ambicions dwell, and there false fauors finde disguise,
There lodge consuming cares that hatch our common woes:
Amidst our painted feelds the pleasant Fayrie lies,
And all those powers diuine that with vntrussed tresses,
Contentment, happie loue, and perfect sport professes.[39]

This kind of thing moves in the direction of satire, and it will be considered again later in connection with the other elements of satire in the pastoral.

The theme of the Golden Age is one of the great commonplaces of Elizabethan literature.[40] The creation of an Arcadia which is primitive and pastoral, which may be identified with the early period before the birth of Jupiter, and which finally is a country located not so much in central Greece as in some Utopian space, is a result of the work of Polybius, Ovid, and Virgil.[41] There are many sources in antiquity for the theme; it was especially popular among the Stoics, and it was congenial to Stoic thought because it explained the Law of Nature as a survival from the Golden Age.[42] Accordingly, the best example of it may be chosen from Seneca:

> 'Twas in such wise, methinks, they lived whom the primal age produced, in friendly intercourse with gods. They had no blind love of gold; no sacred boundary-stone, judging betwixt peoples, separated fields on the spreading plain; not yet did rash vessels plough the sea; each man knew only his native waters.[43]

Spenser in the Proem to Book V of *The Faerie Queene* follows the convention of idealizing the Golden Age,[44] even though his friend Harvey was of the newer school of Jean Bodin, which thought that the earliest periods of history were the worst and that something like progress had taken place.

The first information given the audience about the pastoral atmosphere in Shakespeare's *As You Like It* compares pastoral life to the Golden Age; the wrestler Charles, informing Oliver, and at the same time the audience, of the circumstances of the banished Duke, says:

> They say he is already in the Forest of Arden, and a many merry men with him; and there they live like the old Robin Hood of England; they say many young gentlemen flock to him every day, and fleet the time carelessly, as they did in the golden world.[45]

The identification of the pastoral life with the conditions of the Golden Age was natural enough. One was a criticism of life by means of adopting the point of view of its simplest and purest elements; the other was a criticism of the present way of life by describing an ideal past.

It is also true that pastoral was considered the earliest form of poetry and would therefore be the natural expression of the earliest blissful age.[46] Not all English opinion agreed with this conventional account, however. George Puttenham, bearing in mind the humanistic use of eclogues for satire, considers that the form cannot be primitive.[47] He insists that the eclogue is a sophisticated form, but he concedes that the pastoral lyric does come down from "the first idle wooings," "the first amorous musicks." The Golden Age, associated with pastoral as we have seen, was supposed to have been an age of free love.[48] It is so celebrated in a song from Tasso's *Aminta* which Samuel Daniel translated under the title "A Pastorall."[49] And since the shepherd is insensitive to the claims of power and wealth, as Paris was, it is sometimes emphasized in pastoral that his susceptibility to love is a cruel bondage. As Montemayor puts it:

> The shepherd busied not his thoughts in the consideration of the prosperous and preposterous successe of fortune, nor in the mutabilitie and course of times, neither did the painfull diligence and aspiring minde of the ambitious Courtier trouble his quiet rest: nor the presumption and coye disdaine of the proude and nice Ladie (celebrated onely by the appassionate vowes and opinions of her amorous sutours) once occur to his imaginations. And as little did the swelling pride, and small care of the hawtie priuate man offend his quiet minde. In the field was he borne, bred and brought vp: in the field he fed his flockes, and so out of the limits of the field his thoughts did neuer range, vntill cruell loue tooke possession of his libertie, which to those he is commonly woont to doe, who thinke themselues freest from his tyrannie.[50]

Love in a pastoral environment is first exploited in the second-century Greek romance *Daphnis and Chloe,* written by someone whose name was perhaps Longus. It is the only one of the Greek romances which is pastoral in character, and it is the great forerunner of the Renaissance pastoral romances—those of Sannazarro, Montemayor, and their many imitators. It plays with the adventures in love of two perfectly simple and naïve pastoral people; their innocence of sex along with their captivation by it is presented with amused sophistication by the author for an equally sophisticated reader. S. L. Wolff well describes the peculiar salacious quality of the romance: "Longus with all his art did not—or rather did not try!—to take his emphasis off the teasing succession of Daphnis and Chloe's attempts, and place it wholly or even preponderantly upon their idyllic simplicity, their idyllic environment. *They* are simple enough, but *we* are not; and Longus knows it."[51]

There was an Elizabethan translation of *Daphnis and Chloe,* by Angel Day from the French of Jacques Amyot, in 1587. Day's version does not include the more salacious parts of the Greek romance, substituting instead pastoral lyrics and inserting a pastoral praise of Queen Elizabeth under the title "The Shepheardes Holidaye." Day's language is often colloquial and vivid, especially in descriptive scenes, but his tone is softened and sobered; the conscious absurdity and the conscious aphrodisiac quality of the original are quite lacking.[52] The great translation of *Daphnis and Chloe* into English is not Day's but that of George Thornley in the mid-seventeenth century.

The innocent and naïve, but pagan, lover immediately calls to mind such figures as Shakespeare's Adonis and Marlowe's Hero and Leander. Marlowe especially may have been influenced by Longus, but the significant point here is that pastoral is touching the boundary of still another literary genre, that of Ovidian-mythological poetry. In the Ovidian tradition sexuality was of course an important element, and the shepherds of pastoral, if made creatures of myth (and Paris could be treated as a mythology or pastoral) became suitable subjects for the Ovidian love poem.

The general tendency of English pastoral literature was to subdue the sexual element and make the love scenes romantic and innocent. The innocence of rustic lovers is not exploited for the superior feeling of more worldly readers; what humor there is develops from gentle satire of rude and boorish characters. A conventional comic device is the detailed description of a costume which is inappropriate or absurd.[53] The love is generally idyllic, lending itself to lyrical treatment, fitting in with the idealized setting, timeless and remote.

The element of love in pastoral romance works in two directions—toward lyric simplicity, as I have said, and toward plot complication. The events of pastoral plot usually come from outside and are not the result of the lovers' characters. Brigands, unscrupulous rivals, uncoöperative parents all provide motion and direction for the plot. The oracle, the exposed child, the changeling motif supply a frame for the beginning and conclusion of the story. Essentially, however, there is nothing complex about the course of love itself in the pastoral plot. Fortune and villains provide the difficulties; they do not lie in the nature of love itself. Love expressed as emotion (rather than as plot) is simple and lyric; love used as plot entanglement (not as feeling) is involved and complicated.

Pastoral emphasizes the irrationality of love. That is, it agrees with the general Elizabethan view. Lovers are subject to the whims of fortune (although Fortune is kinder in Arcadia than elsewhere), but there is no blame imputed to anyone for falling in love. It is irrational but unavoidable. The lyric, then, accepts the fate of love but complains at its sorrows just as it rejoices at its pleasures. "Since that in love there is no sound/ Of any reason to be found" is a basic assumption.[54]

Love is simple in essence, but the variety and complexity of its consequences make for a total paradox. Though there is no jot of reason in love, the lover invariably reasons about it. Pastoral provides amply for this paradox. It utilizes for the purpose various devices which taken out of their context seem absurd. The most common perhaps is the "cross-eyed Cupid" situation, in which A loves B, B loves C, C loves D, and D loves A. It is used in Montemayor,[55] and of course it is a device in Lodge's *Rosalynde* and Shakespeare's *As You Like It,* as well as in the woodland part of *A Midsummer Night's Dream.* The paradox is that love itself is so simple; the lyric and plot elements of pastoral romance work together to enforce the contrast between simplicity and complexity.

Another aspect of pastoral love is the contrast between the direct, personal, subjective expression of the feeling and the same feeling seen in some other way, reflected, as in a mirror. In Book XI of the *Diana* Syrenus hears three nymphs singing his own farewell song to Diana—a song which one of them got from a shepherd who heard it long ago and memorized it. A similar effect is produced by having a pastoral lover hang his poems on trees, to be read or recited by others, sometimes in his hearing. There is an absence of self-consciousness in both these devices which makes the paradoxical effect possible. The naïveté of the whole pastoral convention is being utilized.

The ancestry of much pastoral poetry has something to do with its quality. The primitive song-and-dance games of the countryside, which often kept the color of their native surroundings, were in large part wooing ceremonies or complaints of the rejected lover who wore willow at the wedding and was expected to display his sorrows to heighten the merriment of the occasion. There were also celebrations of the beauty of the shepherdess who was crowned queen of the May. These popular customs were beginning to die out in Elizabethan times, or rather to be relegated to the use of children. But the courtly vogue, picking them up, made of them something both sophisticated and naïve. There is an awareness on the part of the Elizabethan poet of pastoral that he is exploiting a quality which works in two ways.[56]

This combination of "distance" and familiarity, of formalism and freedom, gives the Elizabethan love lyric and the song of good life their characteristic tone. Their "Elizabethanness," that quality which makes them popular in the anthologies, which permits enjoyment of them without any concern for the authorship, derives from this suspension.

If we turn to the greatest storehouse of Elizabethan pastoral lyric, the anthology published in 1600 called *England's Helicon*,[57] we may examine the concrete results of the fashion. The compiler of this anthology had under survey the whole body of Elizabethan literature, from *Tottel's Miscellany* on down to the end of the century. He selected poems from translated pastoral romances (Montemayor's *Diana* translated by Bartholomew Yong), from original romances in English (Sidney's *Arcadia*, Greene's *Menaphon*, and Lodge's *Rosalynde*), from the songbooks of Byrd and Morley and Dowland, from plays, from other anthologies (*The Passionate Pilgrim*, 1599), and from manuscripts. His volume has remained popular from 1600 to the present time, and his modern editor says it would be hard for anyone to compile a better anthology of the period without lavish use of Shakespeare and Jonson.[58]

I shall consider the poems in the volume under several headings, without suggesting that these headings constitute rigid "types" or kinds. For purposes of clarity it is easier to talk about pastoral lyrics as complaints, invitations, palinodes, love dialogues, blazons, and dance songs than to group them all together.

More of the poems in *England's Helicon* are complaints than any other kind. Most commonly the shepherd himself is the speaker, although sometimes the complaint is "framed" within the poem as something overheard by the speaker. This latter is an old medieval device, familiar in such poems as Chaucer's *Book of the Duchesse.* The cause of the shepherd's complaint is of course always unrequited love, or a mistress who has proved fickle, and his sorrow is almost always reflected in the change made not only upon himself but also upon his flocks, his dog, upon nature itself. No. 35 (which had already appeared in Weelkes' *Madrigals,* 1957, and *The Passionate Pilgrim,* 1599) begins:

My Flocks feede not, my Ewes breede not,
My Rammes speede not, all is amisse:
Loue is denying, Faith is defying,
Harts renying, causer of this.[59]

This kind of complaint serves, of course, as a description of the values in pastoral life by bewailing their loss. The emphasis is not so much sentimental, in that sympathy is asked for the lovelorn shepherd, as it is pictorial, in which the "merry jigs," the clear wells, and the happy herds are thrown into strong relief by having their basic attributes reversed.

Quite frequently some object of comparison is found, so that the rhetorical expression of the shepherd's grief can be saved for a climax. This principle of economy is apparent in a fine lyric by Thomas Lodge:

A Turtle sate vpon a leauelesse tree,
Mourning her absent pheare,
With sad and sorrie cheare.[60]

The contrast of bitter and sweet is the complaining shepherd's constant theme; sometimes it is expressed more lavishly, as by Lodge in a poem which he himself described as Italianate in manner.[61]

Sometimes the shepherd's complaint takes the form of a narrative and is elaborated in such a way as to make the effect of a pageant or little drama. In this case the pastoral element is likely to be mere stage setting for the central situation, which derives from medieval allegory or Anacreontic cupid-lore. A good example is No. 126 in *England's Helicon,* by Michael Drayton.[62]

Fifteen of the poems in this pastoral anthology are by Sidney; all are taken from the 1598 folio volume containing the *Arcadia, Astrophel and Stella,* and miscellaneous poems. Actually, fewer than half of the Sidney poems in the *Helicon* are pastoral when taken out of context, but Sidney's name gave prestige to the volume and he was thought of as a writer who had lent seriousness and dignity to the pastoral mode. Thomas Wilson, for example, confessed to a certain embarrassment about his translation of Montemayor's *Diana:* "Soe it may bee said of mee that I shewe my vanitie enough in this litle, that after 15 yeares painfully spent in Vniversitie studies, I shold bestow soe many ydle howres, in transplanting vaine amorous conceipts out of an Exotique language." But his justification was that however vain and frivolous the *Diana* seem, Sir Philip Sidney "did very much affect and imitate the excellent Author there of."[63]

The best known of Sidney's poems in the volume is "Ring out your belles, let mourning shewes be spread," a more elaborate and subtle poem than Drayton's "Antheme" and of the same type; but there is nothing specifically pastoral about the poem. Sidney's characteristic touch and his skill in conveying a mood by indirection are best exemplified in No. 5, called "Astrophell the Sheep-heard, his complaint to his flocke." It begins in the usual mood of the forlorn shepherd, telling his merry flocks to go elsewhere to feed so they may have some defense from the storms in his breast and the showers from his eyes. The poet leaves us uncertain how to interpret this extravagant feeling until the shepherd states to the sheep the extent of his love, in terms the sheep could understand:

> Stella, hath refused me,
> Stella, who more loue hath proued
> In this caitiffe hart to be,
> Then can in good eawes be moued
> Towards Lambkins best beloued.[64]

Sidney is pushing homely pathos to the point at which it is felt as humor also, and the comic tone is underlined two stanzas later:

> Is that loue? Forsooth I trow,
> if I saw my good dogge greeued:
> And a helpe for him did know,
> my loue should not be beleeued:
> but he were by me releeued.

Finally, at the conclusion, the identification of the shepherd's emotions with his pastoral environment, a stock feature of the mode, is used for comic purposes. The complaints of the shepherd-lover are whimsically identified with the bleatings of his sheep.

Parody is not the most difficult art. The "distance" between pastoral and reality (which Panofsky says is intimately connected with that other Renaissance invention, perspective) can easily be foreshortened or flattened out so as to make a fantastic effect. But it is not so easy to make the pathetic and absurd felt at once, as partners in the result. This Sidney was able to do. As Theodore Spencer accurately expresses it, "The pastoral setting, the traditional tone of lament, the rigorous form of the verse have been revitalized not merely by Sidney's superb technique, but by the fact that he has put into them something more than the purely conventional emotion."[65]

The other kind of pastoral complaint besides that of the rejected shepherd is of course that of the betrayed or abandoned sherpherdess. She is the Oenone of the Judgment of Paris story. In *England's Helicon* Oenone's complaint from Peele's *Arraignment* is No. 149, the next to the last poem in the book. There are half a dozen other nymph's complaints in the volume, of which the most interesting are Selvagia's song from the *Diana*, as translated by Bartholomew Yong (No. 103), with its graceful return at the end to the chorus of the beginning,

It is not to liue so long,
as it is too short to weepe,

and No. 118, "Lycoris the Nimph, her sad Song," from Thomas Morley's *Madrigals to Four Voices* (1594).[66] The varied line length of the second poem and the feminine rhymes suggest the fragility of the nymph and the insecurity she feels. And the poem progresses very prettily from idyllic description to rhetorical exclamation to the final taunt and pout, conveyed by the strikingly simple and direct language of the last two lines. Its sudden transitions of mood are characteristic of the poem-for-music.

Some half dozen of the poems in *England's Helicon* are invitations, a few of them the most attractive and famous poems in the volume. At its best, the invitation poem is simple in language and in versification, preferring short lines and a direct rhetoric. The strategy of the shepherd is to call attention to the beauty and innocence of the pastoral setting and to use these qualities as arguments naturally reinforcing his simple desires:

Faire Loue rest thee heere,
Neuer yet was morne so cleere,

Sweete be not vnkinde,
Let me thy fauour finde,
Or else for loue I die.

This (No. 74) is Drayton, who well understands the Elizabethan art of securing a beauty and simplicity which seems almost impersonal. Passion and thought are carefully strained out; the poem must be self-contained and must cast no oblique lights. The humorous and the sentimental attributes of the complaint are entirely lacking. The *aubade* and the May-morning song are cousins to it, but the clearest and simplest form for this state of mind is the pastoral lyric of invitation.

Come away, come sweet Loue,
The golden morning breakes:
All the earth, all the ayre,
Of loue and pleasure speaks.

This is an anonymous poem, taken from Dowland's *First Booke of Songes or Ayres* (1597). I have cited these two poems of invitation to show that the most famous of them, Marlowe's "The passionate Sheepheard to his loue" (No. 137), is not alone in its class, even though it is superior to all of its kind.[67] The greatness of Marlowe's poem consists in the completeness of his pastoral picture and its total identification with the state of mind which the pastoral lyric of invitation is intended to induce. It includes gowns, shoes, beds of roses, cap, kirtle, slippers, and belt, all rural and simple, but rich and fine; more significantly it includes the entertainments fit for the contented mind: to see the shepherds feed their flocks, to listen to the music of the shallow rivers, and best of all to watch the shepherd swains dancing and singing. These are delights to move *the mind* (as the last stanza in the *Helicon* version specifies), and there is of course no ground for refusal to this invitation—except the one given in the answer ascribed to Ralegh, that the pastoral picture assumes a youthful, single-hearted, timeless world; deny this premise and you destroy the force of the whole thing. Just so, in Spenser's garden of Adonis, there is no disturbing element but Time:

But were it not, that Time their troubler is,
All that in this delightfull gardin growes
Should happy bee, and have immortall blis:
For here all plenty and all pleasure flowes,
And sweete Love gentle fitts emongst them throwes,
Without fell rancor or fond gealosy:
Franckly each paramor his leman knowes,

Each bird his mate, ne any does envy
Their goodly meriment and gay felicity.[68]

The extreme popularity of Marlowe's poem caused many parodies and imitations of it, one of which is given in the *Helicon* as No. 139; to some extent these parodies show that the original poem ceased to be felt as a pastoral invitation. Modern criticism can more readily approach the famous poem from the point of view of its contemporaries if it takes into account the whole pastoral mode and the special nature of the lyric of invitation.

The palinode, a song in rejection of love, is represented in *England's Helicon* by a few examples. One of them, No. 54, is a definition of love put in such terms as to warn the inexperienced away from it. The poem is an example of those which were not originally pastoral but were doctored by the editor of *England's Helicon* to make them fit the pastoral character of his anthology. Lifting it from *The Phoenix Nest* (1593), the editor added speech tags for two shepherds, Melibeus and Faustus, and substituted phrases like "Sheepheard, what's" for "Now what" and "good Sheepheard" for "I praie thee." A better example of the rejection of love is the well-known ballet of William Byrd, "Though Amarillis daunce in greene" (No. 110). It has a pastoral and rustic atmosphere, since the chorus to each stanza is the humorously resigned exclamation, "Hey hoe, chill loue no more," and the second stanza begins "My Sheepe are lost for want of foode." It is interesting that there is so little of the rejection of love in the anthology. Perhaps a reason is that in the pastoral romances no shepherd ever cures himself of love by philosophy; it can be done only by magic or a drug. Therefore there is no tradition within this mode of a rejection of love, as there is in others. The Ovidian *remedia amoris* or the Platonic "Leave me, O love, which reachest but to dust" has no place in pastoral.[69]

The "blazon," or catalogue of the lady's beauties, is in style if not in origin a pastoral adaptation of one of the main conventions of the Petrarchan sonnet. As such it is subject to the same limitations as those felt by the sonneteers, but perhaps pastoral praise exhausts itself sooner because the comparisons must be those which are possible for a shepherd. Further the naïve quality of the shepherd does not fit with his being an accomplished fine courtier (unless there is allegory, of course; I am here dealing only with the lyric); wit and ingenuity are out of place among sheep-flocks, as Shakespeare points out in *As You Like It.* Accordingly, we get blazons which are effective because of their subdued tone and restraint; they are likely to be plaintive, as for example the one by J. Wotton in *England's Helicon,* No. 41.

The finest and most elaborate blazon in all English pastoral poetry is of course Spenser's praise of Queen Elizabeth in the April eclogue of *The Shepheardes Calendar,* which is printed in *England's Helicon* as No. 6. The comment on this poem has mostly concerned itself with the flattery of royalty and with the versification. Considered purely as a blazon, however, its structure and proportion are very impressive. The style itself is first established, as a "siluer song," and the Muses are invoked for aid. Then comes the justification for the heightened praise: that the lady is "of heauenly race" and therefore without mortal blemish. Within this framework, she is first presented as a picture;[70] the following stanza forms a bridge from her physical beauty to her "heauenly hauiour, her Princely Grace," and this makes possible the association with her of the sun and the moon in the two succeeding stanzas. The summary of this part is the line "Shee is my Goddesse plaine," and we are brought back to the lowly pastoral atmosphere by the shepherd's promise to offer her a milk-white lamb when the lambing season comes. The musical glorification of Eliza then follows, with the Muses trooping to her and playing their instruments, while the Graces (she herself making the fourth) dance and sing. The Ladies of the Lake then come to crown her with olive branches symbolizing peace, and this leads to the lovely flower stanza in which the Queen is again associated with the beauties of earth. As such she is to be attended by the "Sheepheards daughters that dwell on the greene," and we have the pastoral atmosphere reaffirmed. Finally, the attendant maidens are dismissed, with the quaint promise by the shepherd of some plums if they will return when he gathers them.

The most remarkable quality of the poem considered as a pastoral blazon is the firm and sure control the poet exercises over his transitions and the harmonious blending of many motifs. Classic myth, abstract divine qualities, the reality of earth, music, and color—all are here. The poem has an organic motion, wavelike, easy, and natural. Its stability comes from its pastoral inspiration and method.

The gayest pastoral lyrics are the roundelays, jigs, and dance songs, of which *England's Helicon* exhibits a half dozen examples. Spenser is again represented as the most expert maker of this type of poem, thanks to the fact that the editor did not pick up the "Cupid's Curse" roundelay when he was going through Peele's *Arraignment of Paris.* The roundelay from the August eclogue of *The Shepheardes Calendar* is No. 11 in *England's Helicon.* It seems probable that Spenser's poem was written to an already existing tune, "Heigh ho Holiday."[71] Either because of the popularity of the old tune or the success of Spenser's poem, there are several imitations, two of them in the *Helicon:* No. 81 from Lodge's *Rosalynde,* "A Blithe and bonny Country-Lasse," and No. 125 by H. C., "Fie on the sleights that men deuise"[72] These poems were to be sung by two singers, alternating; the editor of *England's Helicon* has removed the speech-tags and has left the indication of how the songs were sung only in the heading to No. 125: "two Nimphes, each aunswering other line for line."

Two shepherds' jigs, "Damaetas Iigge" by John Wotton (No. 28) and "The Sheepheard Dorons Iigge" from Greene's *Menaphon* (1589; No. 32), have the same carefree spirit. The characteristic feeling is that of Wotton's first stanza:

Iolly Sheepheard, Sheepheard on a hill
    on a hill so merrily,
    on a hill so cherily,
  Feare not Sheepheard there to pipe thy fill,
Fill euery Dale, fill euery Plaine:
  both sing and say; Loue feeles no paine.

This atmosphere of merriment and naïveté distinguishes some of the *Helicon* poems which are otherwise hard to classify, such as the pleasant narrative poem of Nicholas Breton's "Phillida and Coridon" (No. 12), which merely relates, in short lines appropriate to the fresh and simple feeling of the poem, a pastoral betrothal.[73] Although this poem reads like a mere pretty narrative, it, too, was originally set to music and as a song in three parts was sung to Queen Elizabeth by three musicians "disguised in auncient Countrey attire" as she opened the casement of her gallery window about nine o'clock on a September morning. According to the account published in 1591, the song pleased Her Highness so much, both in words and music, that she commanded a repeat performance and graced it highly "with her chearefull acceptance and commendation."[74]

The royal progress was, incidentally, one of the important sources of pastoral poetry and pageant. In the next year, 1592, the Queen was again entertained with a shepherd's speech at Sudeley, and she would have seen a pastoral play except that the Cotswold weather prevented its production.[75] In 1599 when Elizabeth visited Wilton, she was entertained by a song in praise of Astrea, sung by two shepherds, Thenot and Piers, the words written by her hostess, the Countess of Pembroke.[76] Whether the progress was primarily responsible or not, much of the glorification of Her Majesty took a pastoral form. In fact,

William Empson thinks that "it was this Renaissance half-worship of Elizabeth and the success of England under her rule that gave conviction to the whole set of ideas."[77]

Sometimes the shepherd's complaint was transformed into a song, and, when the naïveté was emphasized and the chorus lines made prominent, something like a comic tone tempered the declaration of love. An example is *Helicon* No. 68, by H. C.

England's Helicon contains several examples of the song of good life to which we have already referred. The editor was no doubt aware that some of his readers would tire of love songs, and he may have been as willing to please them as is the clown Feste in *Twelfth Night,* when he asks the two tippling knights, who have demanded a song, "Would you have a love-song, or a song of good life?" Feste, as a professional entertainer, knows the conventional types of song well enough, though the commentators have not done much to illuminate the passage.

Examples of the good-life song in *Helicon* are No. 10 by Lodge, a piece preferring the shepherd's life to that of kings and worldlings, and No. 104, taken from a songbook of Byrd's. The second poem in *England's Helicon,* mainly a blazon of the shepherd's mistress, begins with two stanzas on the good life, in which it is claimed that

Good Kings haue not disdained it,
  but Sheepheards haue beene named:
A sheepe-hooke is a Scepter fit,
  for people well reclaimed.
The Sheepheards life so honour'd is and praised:
That Kings lesse happy seeme, though higher raised.[78]

The pastoral lyric concerns itself largely, as we have seen, with love and the good life. It is less psychologically and rhetorically complex than the Petrarchan sonnet, less troubled by the sexual paradox than the poetry of the Ovidian-mythological tradition. A few more comments on its treatment of love may be useful. In general, love in the pastoral world is thought of as innocent, chaste, childlike. The final lines of No. 147 in *England's Helicon* (by "Shepherd Tonie") are representative:

Take hands then Nimphes & Sheepheards all,
And to this Riuers musiques fall
Sing true loue, and chast loue
  begins our Festiuall.

So general is this atmosphere that one wonders if the edtior of the great pastoral anthology realized that one of the poems he took from

Yonge's *Musica Transalpina* (Nos. 131 and 132) exploits a *double entendre* on the word "die." It is curious indeed to encounter here a poem not very far in intention from Dryden's song, "Whil'st Alexis lay prest," in *Marriage à-la-Mode.*

There is little in common between Elizabethan pastoralism and the transparent pretense of Restoration shepherds and shepherdnesses. The Elizabethan view of pastoral is at once more serious and more gay. It emphasizes the value of *otium* and the mean estate, and, possibly because a realization of that value produces a legitimate feeling of freedom, Elizabethan pastoral gaiety is natural, untainted, and harmonious:

> Harke iollie Sheepheards,
>   harke yond lustic ringing:
> How cheerfully the bells daunce,
>   the whilst the Lads are springing?
>
> Goe we then, why sit we here delaying:
> And all yond mery wanton lasses playing?
>   How gailie Flora leades it,
>   and sweetly treads it!
>   The woods and groaues they ring,
>   louely resounding:
>   With Ecchoes sweet rebounding.

This is the note on which the reader of *England's Helicon* in 1600 closed the book.[79]

NOTES

[1] W. W. Greg, *Pastoral Poetry and Drama* (London, 1906), p. 67.

[2] Anonymous review of *England's Helicon,* ed. Hyder E. Rollins, 2 vols. (Cambridge: Harvard University Press), in *TLS,* April 11, 1935, p. 240.

[3] Kathleen Tillotson in *The Works of Michael Drayton,* ed. J. W. Hebel, 5 vols. (Oxford, 1931–1941), V, 4.

[4] See, for example, Thomas Blenerhasset's *Revelation of the True Minerva,* ed. J. W. Bennett (New York, 1941), and I. L. Schulze, "Blenerhasset's *A Revelation,* Spenser's *Shepheardes Calender,* and the Kenilworth Pageants," ELH, XI (1944), 85–91.

[5] *Sir Francis Bacon, Works,* ed. James Spedding, R. L. Ellis, and D. D. Heath, 15 vols. (Boston, 1860–1864), VI, 138.

[6] See, for example, *Davids Pastorall Poeme: or Sheepeheards Song. Seven Sermons, on the 23. Psalme of Dauid,* by Thomas Jackson (1603).

[7] "To the Reader of his Pastorals" in *Works,* ed. Hebel, II, 517.

[8] *The Eclogues of Baptista Mantuanus,* ed. W. P. Mustard (Baltimore, 1911), p. 97. Translations or

adaptations of this passage are in Alexander Barclay's fifth eclogue (before 1530), lines 469–492; in Turbervile's translation (1567), sig. K2^{v}; in Spenser's July eclogue in *The Shepheardes Calender* (1579), lines 131–160; and in Francis Sabie's *Pan's Pipe* (1595), sigs. D2^{v}–D3^{r}.

[9] *Works,* ed. Hebel, I, 89.

[10] *De civitate Dei,* XVIII, 10.

[11] *The Deipnosophists,* XII, 510 c, trans. C. B. Gulick, Loeb Classical Library, 7 vols. (1922–1949), V, 295.

[12] The same point had been emphasized by Horace in *Epistles,* II, 10. The idea was also familiar to Renaissance Platonists and was elaborated by Ficino, for example, in his commentary on Plato's *Philebus.* See P. O. Kristeller, *The Philosophy of Marsilio Ficino* (New York, 1943), pp. 358–359.

[13] The passage in G. B. Nenna's treatise is so typical, and the reputation of his book in England is so amply attested to by Edmund Spenser, Samuel Daniel, George Chapman, and Angel Day, that it must be quoted: "Now let vs consider what fruit may be gathered by the shadowe of fables, especially of this which I euen now recited. For indeed vnder those vailes we may receiue no lesse pleasant then profitable instruction . . . After that a man is once framed, and that he hath attained to that age, that hee beginneth nowe to discourse within himselfe, what kinde of life hee were best to followe as the most noble in account amongst men: whether that which is grounded vppon knowledge, which the Philosophers were wont to cal a contemplatiue kind of life: or otherwise, yt which guideth a man that addicteth himself only to worldly matters, which they terme actiue: or else that which consisteth wholy in pleasure, which they name delightfull. Then straightwaie discord entreth: of which three sortes of liues, Soueraigne Iupiter will not giue sentence which is the best, least that in approuing the one, he should condemne the other two; and so the life of man should rather be constrained then free, but hee leaueth them to the judgement of man, to the end that he may as pleaseth him, tie himselfe to that kind of life that shall best like him; it may be, shewing vs thereby, the free choice which is granted to vs by him. Of the which notwithstanding he that is caried away to follow the delightfull kind of life, doth bring vnto him selfe vnspeakeable detriment" (*Nennio, or a Treatise of Nobility,* trans. William Jones, 1595, sig. H3^{v}).

[14] Trans. Bartholomew Yong (1598), p. 53.

[15] Rollins ed., I, 70.

[16] Lines 137–138.

[17] *Idea The Shepheards Garland* (1593), Eclogue IX, lines 55–60.

[18] *Faerie Queene,* VI, ix, xxxvi.

[19] See C. R. Baskervill, "Early Romantic Plays in England," *MP,* XIV (1916–17), 483; T. S. Graves, "*The Arraignment of Paris* and Sixteenth Century Flattery," *MLN,* XXVIII (1913), 48–49; A. H. Gilbert, "The Source of Peele's *Arraignment of Paris,*" *MLN,* XLI (1926), 36; and Douglas Bush, *Mythology and the Renaissance Tradition in English Poetry* (Minneapolis, 1932), pp. 51–52.

[20] Ed. of 1586, p. 83.

[21] Sig. C^{r}.

[22] G. P. Lomazzo, *A Tracte Containing the Artes of Curious Paintinge,* trans. Richard Haydocke (1598), sig. Bb6^{r}.

[23] Sig. D4^{r}.

[24] *Parts Added to the Mirror for Magistrates,* ed. L. B. Campbell (Cambridge, England, 1946), pp. 462–463.

[25] Lines 869–871. For evidence

that Tamburlaine was a symbol of this Renaissance spirit before he appeared in Marlowe's play, see my "Tamburlaine and the Renaissance," *Elizabethan Studies in Honor of George F. Reynolds* (Boulder, Colo., 1945), pp. 128–129.

[26] Conyers Read, *Mr. Secretary Walsingham and the Policy of Queen Elizabeth,* 3 vols. (Oxford, 1925), I, 69.

[27] George Puttenham, *The Arte of English Poesie,* ed. Gladys D. Willcock and Alice Walker (Cambridge, England, 1936), p. 248.

[28] *The Artes of Curious Paintinge,* trans. Haydocke, p. 122.

[29] *Fennes Frutes* (1590), sig. E3ᵛ.

[30] *The First Day of the Worldes Creation,* trans. Joshua Sylvester (1595), sig. El'.

[31] *Babilon,* trans. William L'Isle (1595), sig. A3ᵛ.

[32] "Disprayse of a Courtly life," first published in *A Poetical Rhapsody* (1602), ed. Hyder E. Rollins, 2 vols. (Cambridge: Harvard University Press, 1931, 1932), I, 9–12.

[33] VI, IX, xix.

[34] "The Relations of Spenser and Sidney," *PMLA,* XLV (1930), 720.

[35] *The Allegory of Love* (Oxford, 1936), pp. 350–353.

[36] VI, x, iii.

[37] VI, XII, ii.

[38] VI, IX, xlv.

[39] "Sonnets" appended to *Scillaes Metamorphosis* (1589), sig. D4ʳ.

[40] For the general background, see A. O. Lovejoy and George Boas, *Primitivism and Related Ideas in Antiquity* (Baltimore, 1935); Paul Meissner, "Das goldene Zeitalter in der Englischen Renaissance," *Anglia,* LIX (1935), 351–367; E. Lipsker, *Der Mythos vom goldenen Zeitalter in den Schäferdichtungen Italiens, Spaniens und Frankreichs zur Zeit der Renaissance* (Berlin, 1933).

[41] Erwin Panofsky, "Et in Arcadia Ego," *Philosophy and History,* ed. Raymond Klibansky and H. J. Paton (Oxford, 1936), pp. 225–227.

[42] See L. I. Bredvold, "The Naturalism of Donne in Relation to Some Renaissance Traditions," *JEGP,* XXII (1923), 471–502.

[43] *Hippolytus,* in *Seneca's Tragedies,* trans. F. J. Miller, Loeb Classical Library, 2 vols. (1916–17), I, 525–539.

[44] V, Proem, ix.

[45] I, i, 109–114.

[46] For a Renaissance account of this historical side of pastoral, see F. M. Padelford, *Selected Translations from Scaliger's Poetics* (New York, 1905), pp. 21–32.

[47] *The Arte of English Poesie,* ed. Willcock and Walker, pp. 37–39.

[48] The differing attitudes possible on this and other points are noticed by Lois Whitney, "Concerning Nature in *The Countesse of Pembrokes Arcadia,*" *SP,* XXIV (1927), 207–222.

[49] This is the final poem in Daniel's *Works* (1601); it did not, as Grosart asserts, appear in the *Delia* of 1592 (*Complete Works of Samuel Daniel,* ed. A. B. Grosart, 5 vols. [London, Spenser Society, 1885–1896], I, 260).

[50] *Diana,* trans. Yong, sig. A1ᵛ.

[51] *The Greek Romances in Elizabethan Fiction* (New York, 1912), p. 131.

[52] It is impossible to agree with Wolff that "Angel Day's version is pervaded by this indulgent ridicule of rustic wits, manners, speech and dress" (*ibid.,* p. 122, n. 6). Day presents it all quite seriously.

[53] I have pointed out an example of this in Lodge's *Rosalynde.* See *The Golden Hind,* ed. Roy Lamson and Hallett Smith (New York, 1942), p. 665. There is another in Montemayor's *Diana,* trans. Yong, sig. E6ᵛ.

[54] Montemayor, *Diana,* trans. Yong, sig. D5ʳ.

[55] *Diana,* trans. Yong, sig. B6^{r}.

[56] A good account of the popular dance-song background of Elizabethan pastoral is given in C. R. Baskervill, *The Elizabethan Jig* (Chicago, 1929), chap. I.

[57] Edited by H. E. Rollins in two volumes (Cambridge: Harvard University Press, 1935).

[58] Rollins, II, 3–4.

[59] Rollins ed., I, 56.

[60] Rollins ed., I, 58.

[61] Rollins, I, 85, and II, 134.

[62] Rollins, I, 167. This poem was used by Drayton to take the place of a more direct song of complaint which he had published in his second eclogue in *Idea The Shepheards Garland* (1593). The version as given in *England's Helicon* was printed in the 1606 edition of Drayton's eclogues and revised further for publication in 1619 (see *Works,* ed. Hebel, I, 53, and II, 525). Mrs. Tillotson remarks that "the song [as given in *E. H.*] gives a much more detached and playful impression of Rowland's love than the song of *Shepheards Garland*" (*ibid.,* V, 184).

[63] Preface, reproduced in *Revue Hispanique,* L (1920), 372.

[64] I have substituted the correct reading "eawes" of the 1598 folio for the meaningless "by us" of *England's Helicon.*

[65] "The Poetry of Sir Philip Sidney," *ELH,* XII (1945), 267. Spencer is speaking of a poem not included in *England's Helicon,* the double sestina "You goat-herd gods." It is certainly true that a better selection from Sidney's poetry in the 1598 folio could be made than that of the editor of *England's Helicon.*

[66] Rollins' note (*England's Helicon,* II, 173), is possibly misleading when it says that the poem was taken from Morley's book "with very lavish changes." Rollins depends upon E. H. Fellowes' *English Madrigal Verse, 1588–1632* (Oxford, 1913), p. 126, for what he calls "the original." But Dr. Fellowes' text is a reconstruction from the various part-books of Morley, and in his reconstruction Dr. Fellowes is markedly classical. Every variant from Fellowes' text in *England's Helicon* can be found in some one of the part-books. The editor of the *Helicon* simply made a different reconstruction, pruning away the "Aye me's" and the like less rigorously. I grant that he arranged the first line incorrectly for the rhyme. The whole point is of some importance in that it raises the question of what *are* the words that make up a poem when they occur as words to a madrigal. For Fellowes' method of reconstruction, and his triumph in reconstructing a poem by Ben Jonson, see *English Madrigal Verse,* pp. xv-xvii; most Elizabethans, I am convinced, were not as firmly sealed of the tribe of Ben as Dr. Fellowes. Certainly the editor of *England's Helicon* was not.

[67] R. S. Forsythe, in "*The Passionate Shepherd* and English Poetry," *PMLA,* XL (1925), 692–742, provides an elaborate treatment of the imitations of Marlowe's poetry in English and some account of earlier uses of the invitation motif.

[68] *Faerie Queene,* III, vi, xli.

[69] The poem printed by Albert Feuillerat (ed., *The Complete Works of Sir Philip Sidney,* 4 vols. [Cambridge University Press, 1922–1926], II, 344–346) from Harleian MS. 6057, entitled by him "A Remedie for Love" and said in the manuscript to be "An old dittie of Sr Phillipp Sidneyes omitted in the Printed Arcadia," may seem to be a contradiction of this statement. Actually, the poem is a version of the "mock-blazon" on Mopsa which I discuss below, p. 53 [of Smith's book].

[70] The editor of *England's Helicon* apparently liked a more regular line than he found in Spenser. He changes line 6 from "With Damaske roses and Daffadillies set" to "With Daffadils and Damaske Roses set."

[71] See Bruce Pattison, "The Roundelay in the August Eclogue of *The Shepheardes Calender*," *RES*, IX (1933), 54–55, and his *Music and Poetry in the English Renaissance* (London, 1948), pp. 173–174.

[72] This poem, although Rollins (*England's Helicon*, II, 178) says it is known only in the *Helicon*, appears in Thomas Deloney's *Garland of Good Will*, 1631 (*Works*, ed. F. O. Mann [Oxford, 1912], pp. 344–346); whether it was in the *Garland* as entered in 1593 and published in 1596, hence before its publication in the *Helicon*, is not known.

[73] Perhaps the closest parallel to Breton's poem is the "Dowsabell" song in Drayton's eighth eclogue of *Idea The Shepheards Garland*, 1593 (see *Works*, ed. Hebel, I, 88–91). But Drayton's poem is much more "naturalized," with English place names and very specific details about the materials of the shepherds' clothing and equipment. It moves the pastoral environment out of Arcadia to the English countryside. This realism no doubt had a comic effect for the Elizabethans, and Drayton uses a comic meter, that of Chaucer's *Sir Thopas*.

[74] *The Honorable Entertainement gieuen to the Queenes Maiestie in Progresse, at Eluetham in Hampshire, by the right Honorable the Earle of Hertford* (1591), sig. D2^v.

[75] *Speeches Delivered to Her Maiestie this Last Progresse, at the Right Honorable the Lady Rvssels, at Bissam, the Right Honorable the Lorde Chandos at Sudley, at the Right Honorable the Lord Norris, at Ricorte* (Oxford, 1592), sigs. B–C^r.

[76] Printed as No. 4 in Davison's *A Poetical Rhapsody* (1602), ed. Rollins, I, 15.

[77] *English Pastoral Poetry* (New York, 1938; American edition of *Some Versions of Pastoral*), p. 34. For a discussion of Elizabeth in this role and a survey of the many relevant works, see E. C. Wilson, *England's Eliza* (Cambridge: Harvard University Press, 1939), chap. IV, "Fayre Elisa, Queene of Sheperdes All."

[78] I have found about forty-five additional Elizabethan poems which would be called "poems of good life."

[79] Part II of Professor Smith's chapter goes on to a critical examination of the pastoral eclogue [editor's note].

APPENDIX

Form and Matter in the Publication of Research

R. B. McKerrow

May I as one who has had occasion both as a publisher and an editor to read a very considerable number of books and articles embodying the results of research into English literary history plead for more attention to *form* in the presentation of such work?

I do not know whether advancing age has made me thicker in the head than I used to be or whether I have merely become more impatient—there is so much that one still wants to do and constantly less and less time in which to do it—but it certainly seems to me that there has been a tendency in recent years for the way in which the results of research are set out to become progressively less efficient, especially among the younger students, both in England and in America. And when I say "less efficient" I am not thinking of any high qualities of literary art, but of the simplest qualities of precision and intelligibility. Indeed, I have sometimes wondered whether the fate of "English studies" will not eventually be to be smothered in a kind of woolly and impenetrable fog of wordiness that few or none will be bothered to penetrate.

It may perhaps surprise some readers of *R.E.S.* if I tell them that I have several times been compelled to refuse articles offered to me which seemed, from the evidence of the footnotes, to have been the product of real research, for no other reason than that after several readings I have completely failed to discover the point or points which the author was trying to make. In one or two cases this has perhaps been due to the author's inability to express himself in English at all, but in others the trouble has seemed to be rather due to a complete ignorance of the way in which he should present his material. Being himself fully cognizant of the point at issue and with the way in which his research corrects or supplements views currently held on his subject, the author has apparently assumed that all would become clear to his readers by the mere recital of his investigations without any commentary on the results as they appear to him. But such a mere recital of an investigation will only convey what is intended by the author to a person with the same knowledge and mental outlook as the author himself, and to anyone else may be almost meaningless.

Articles of which I have been unable to make out the point at all I have necessarily rejected, generally after trying them on a friend or two, lest I were at the time more than usually dense; but I must confess to having printed in *R.E.S.* a certain number of articles which I regarded as definitely bad work. These were some which contained good research which I was assured would be useful to those with knowledge of the subject and willing to spend time and effort in puzzling out the bearing of the new matter, but of little if any use to others. Such articles cannot, of course, be lightly rejected. The pity is they could so easily, by a writer of adequate training in presenting his facts, or with sufficient imagination to enable him to dispense with such training, have been made really interesting contributions to knowledge which would have appealed to a wide circle of readers, instead of only being absorbed with difficulty and distaste by the few.

For it is imagination which is, before all else, necessary in presenting a piece of research. It is not to be considered as, so to say, an emanation of the author's brain which has been allowed to escape into the void, a mere fragment of knowledge detached from its originator, but one which is intended to become part of the knowledge of others, and in order that it may do this it must be so shaped and adapted that it may fit with ease and certainty on to the knowledge of others, those others being of course the likely readers.

New facts, skilfully prepared for our easy assimilation, for forming part of our existing aggregate of knowledge, are invariably welcomed, even when the subject is not one in which we are normally much interested, when a badly presented bit of what should be our own special subject may completely fail to make any impression on our consciousness.

We ought, I think, at the start to realize that no readers whom we are likely to have will be nearly as much interested in our views or discoveries as we ourselves are. Most of them will be people who are a little tired, a little bored, and who read us rather out of a sense of duty and a wish to keep up with what is being done than because they have any real interest in the subject; and in return for our reader's complaisance it is our duty as well as our interest to put what we have to say before him with as little trouble to him as possible. It is our duty because we ought to be kind to our fellow creature; it is our interest because if the view that we wish to put before him is clearly and competently expressed, so that he understands without trouble what we are trying to say, he will be gratified at the smooth working of his own intelligence and will inevitably think better of our theory and of its author than if he had had to puzzle himself over what we mean and then in the end doubt whether he had really understood us, so raising in himself an uneasy doubt whether his brains are quite what they used to be!

Now I suggest that if we analyse almost any piece of research which seems to us thoroughly workmanlike and satisfactory from all points of view, we shall almost always find that it falls into five parts in the following order.

1. The *introduction,* in which the author briefly states the present position of research on his subject and the views currently held on it.
2. The *proposal,* in which he describes in outline what he hopes to prove.
3. The *boost,* in which he proceeds to magnify the importance of his discovery or argument and to explain what a revolution it will create in the views generally held on the whole period with which he is dealing. This is, as it were, a taste of sauce to stimulate the reader's appetite.
4. The *demonstration,* in which he sets forth his discovery or argument in an orderly fashion.
5. The *conclusion,* or *crow,* in which he summarizes what he claims to have shown, and points out how complete and unshakeable is his proof.

Of course I am not serious in this! It is not to be supposed necessary that we should *formally* divide our research articles in this way, but it is a real and practical division and there are few research articles which would not be improved by the adoption of such a framework, at least under the surface.

The following points might, I believe, be worth much more serious consideration than seems frequently to be given to them.

1. The subject of a research article should always be a unity. The paper should always deal either with a single subject or with a well-

defined group of subjects of the same general character. Thus a particular literary work might be dealt with in all its aspects, or any one aspect might be dealt with, say, its origin, its date, its popularity, or what not, or its author's life or any one period or incident of it. On the other hand it is seldom well to mix two pieces of research on different scales, an account of a man's works as a whole and of a particular one of his works dealt with in much greater detail. Similarly, an article in which an attempt is made both to give new discoveries in an author's biography and a correction in the bibliography of one of his books will almost certainly turn out an unreadable muddle. These various kinds of discovery may often arise as the result of a single piece of research, but it is much better to put them forward in quite independent articles. Opportunity may always be found to insert a cross-reference from one to the other in order to ensure that students do not overlook the author's other discoveries.

2. Give your book or article a name which tells at once what it is all about. Facetious and cryptic titles should be utterly eschewed. At best they annoy, and at worst they tend to be forgotten and to render the work under which they are concealed untraceable. Fancy names, pastoral and the like, should never be used, however familiar they may be to students versed in the literature of a particular period. Thus Katherine Philips may have been well known to students of her time as the "Matchless Orinda," but one who writes about her by the latter name risks his work being entered in indexes under headings where it will be missed by scholars searching for her under her family name.

3. Remember that though the great majority of your readers are likely to have a considerable knowledge of English Literature as a whole and an expert knowledge of a certain part of it, only a minority are likely to be experts in your particular period or field. In any case very few indeed can be expected to possess the minute knowledge of it which you who have just been devoting all your time to the study of it have or ought to have. (Indeed, if you do not know *much* more than others, why are you writing about it?) Keep this in mind in the whole of your writing and *adjust what you say to the knowledge which you may reasonably expect your readers to have.* This is really the whole secret of exposition, and it is so simple that it seems incredible that writers of research articles should so often be ignorant of it. But they are, they are! If you have a young brother or sister of, say, fifteen years old or so, think that you have him or her before you and that you are trying to explain the point of your article to them and at the same time to prevent them from thinking what an ass you are to be wasting their time and yours about anything so completely futile. If in

your imagination you see their eyes light up and their faces set with a desire to protest or argue, you will know that whether the thesis of your paper is sound or not its presentation is at least on the right lines!

Naturally the method of presenting an argument must depend on the persons for whom it is intended. You need not in an article in *R.E.S.* explain who Ben Jonson or John Dryden or Cynewulf or Layamon were, but it would be unwise to expect all your readers to have precise knowledge as to their dates or the details of their biography. If these are required for your argument it is easy to give them without the reader being moved to indignation by the feeling that he is being treated like a child. In this connection much offence may often be avoided by the insertion of the little phrases "of course," or "as everyone knows"—*e.g.* "Stephen Hawes, who was of course writing in the earliest years of the sixteenth century, and called Lydgate 'master'" gives information which every reader of *R.E.S.* must have known at some time, but of which a few may need to be reminded in an article concerning the poetical associations of Henry VIII's court.

In your introduction, then, take your reader metaphorically by the hand and lead him gently up to the threshold of your research, reminding him courteously and without any appearance of dogmatism, not with the gestures of a teacher but gently as a comrade in study, of what he ought to know in order to understand what you have to tell him—the object of your research. He will be far better able to appreciate your demonstration if he knows what to look for, and to know what to look for if you tell him at once just what the current views of the matter are and how your own differ from them.

4. So far as possible state your facts in chronological order. When a digression is necessary, make quite clear that it *is* a digression, and when you reach the end of it, make quite clear that you are returning to the main course of the story. And always give plenty of dates, *real* dates, not the kind of dates of which many of the historical people seem to be so fond—"about two years before the conclusion of the events which we have described" or "later in the same year," which after reading several earlier pages turns out to be the year in which "the king" attained his majority, necessitating further research to discover what king and in what year and what part of the year he was born and what "majority" meant at the time. But enough! We have all suffered. Keep on remembering that though *you* are perhaps completely familiar with all aspects of your subject, your reader may not be.

5. State your facts as simply as possible, even boldly. No one wants flowers of eloquence or literary ornaments in a research article. On the

other hand do not be slangy, and, especially if you are writing for *R.E.S.*, do not use American slang. We may be interested in it, but we may not always understand it. Only a few days ago I had to beg the author of an excellent article which I was printing to substitute some phrase more intelligible to us over in England for a statement that certain evidence—"is not quite enough to convict of actual skulduggery (and the aroma of high-binding will not down) . . ."

6. Never be cryptic nor use literary paraphrases. Needless mysteries are out of place in research articles. There are plenty of them there already. If they think that you are trying to be superior, most readers will stop reading at once.

7. Do not try to be humorous. Humour is well enough in its place, but nothing more infuriates a man who is looking for a plain statement of facts than untimely humour, especially if he does not know whether the writer is really trying to be humorous or not, a point which some would-be humorists fail to make clear.

8. Do not use ambiguous expressions. The worst of these are perhaps phrasing containing the word "question." If you say "there is no question that Ben Jonson was in Edinburgh in 1618" most people, perhaps all, will take you to mean that he *was* there in that year; and the same if you say "that Jonson was in Edinburgh in 1618 is beyond question" or "does not admit of question." If, however, you say that "there is no question, of Jonson having been in Edinburgh in 1618," most people, though I think not all, will take you to mean that he was *not* there in that year. But there is certainly no question that it would be better to use a phrase the meaning of which is not open to question.

Avoid also the word "doubtless," which has been defined as "a word used when making a statement for the truth of which the speaker is unaware of any evidence."

Do not overtask such expressions as "it is generally admitted that," "there can be no doubt that," "it is well known that" unless you can shift your responsibility on to at least one other person by giving a reference.

9. Always be precise and careful in references and quotations, and never fear the charge of pedantry. After all, "pedant" is merely the name which one gives to anyone whose standard of accuracy happens to be a little higher than one's own!

10. Do not treat the subjects of your research with levity. Above all avoid that hateful back-slapping "heartiness" which caused certain nineteenth-century Elizabethans to refer to "Tom Nash," "Bob Green,"

"Will Shakespeare" and so on, with its horrible flavour of modern gutter journalism which refers in this way to film stars, long-distance fliers, and the like. These Elizabethans had certain qualities which have made it seem worth while to keep their memories green for more than 300 years, and on this account, if for no other, they should be given the courtesy which is their due.

11. Above all, whatever inner doubts you may have as to whether the piece of research upon which you have been spending your time was really worth while, you must on no account allow it to appear that you have ever thought of it otherwise than of supreme importance to the human race! In the first place, unless you yourself believe in what you are doing, you will certainly not do good work, and, secondly, if your reader suspects for a moment that you do not set the very highest value on your work yourself he will set no value on it at all. He will on the other hand be full of fury that you should have induced him to waste his precious time in reading stuff that you do not believe in yourself, an attitude which will completely prevent him from appreciating any real and evident merit which there may be in it. After all, one can never be certain of the value of one's own work. Often in scientific research a discovery which in itself seemed most trivial has led to results of the utmost importance, and though sensational occurrences of this kind may be rarer in literary research than in science, it is still true that what is merely a side-issue in one research may give rise, when critically examined, to results of quite unexpected value.

As a general rule the interest and importance of a piece of research lies either in the facts disclosed or the methods by which they have been brought to light—or in both. To these prior considerations the manner of presentation may indeed be subordinate. Nevertheless good presentation may help enormously in the effective value of good research, while bad presentation may rob it of the recognition which is its due.

Suggested Reading

Bibliography

W. W. Greg, "The Bakings of Betsey," *The Library*, 3d ser., II (1911), 225-259.

Charlton Hinman, *The Printing and Proof-Reading of the First Folio of Shakespeare*, Oxford, 1963.

Textual Criticism

Fredson Bowers, "Textual Criticism," in *Aims and Methods of Scholarship in the Modern Languages and Literature*, ed. James Thorpe, New York, 1963.

Paul Maas, *Textual Criticism*, Oxford, 1958.

Authorship and Dating

"The Case for Internal Evidence," *Bulletin of the New York Public Library*, 1957-1960; a series of articles about methods of proving authorship.

Jacques Barzun and Henry F. Graff, "Verification," in *The Modern Researcher*, New York, 1957.

Biography

W. J. Bate, *John Keats*, Cambridge, Mass., 1963.

James Clifford, ed., *Biography as an Art; Selected Criticism, 1560-1960*, New York, 1960.

Sources and Analogues

Ernst Robert Curtius, *European Literature and the Latin Middle Ages*, trans. Willard R. Trask, New York, 1953.

John Livingston Lowes, "Loveris Maladye of Hereos," *Modern Philology,* XI (1913-14), 491-546.

History of Ideas and the Concept of Period

M. H. Abrams, *The Mirror and the Lamp: Romantic Theory and the Critical Tradition,* New York, 1953.

Ronald S. Crane, "On Writing a History of English Criticism, 1650-1800," *University of Toronto Quarterly,* XXII (1953), 376-391.

A. O. Lovejoy, *Essays in the History of Ideas,* Baltimore, 1948.

Style

Leo Spitzer, *Linguistics and Literary History: Essays in Stylistics,* Princeton, 1948.

Richard M. Ohmann, *Shaw: The Style and the Man,* Middletown, Conn., 1962.

Historical Interpretation

Helen Gardner, *The Business of Criticism,* London, 1959.

A. S. P. Woodhouse, "The Historical Criticism of Milton," *PMLA,* LXVI (1951), 1033-1044.

Marc Bloch, *The Historian's Craft,* trans. Peter Putnam, New York, 1953.

K. R. Popper, *The Poverty of Historicism,* London, 1957.

Form and Convention

Kenneth Burke, *The Philosophy of Literary Form,* rev. ed., New York, 1957.

Moody Prior, "Poetic Drama: An Analysis and a Suggestion," *English Institute Annual, 1949,* 1950.

Yvor Winters, "Problems for the Modern Critic of Literature," *Hudson Review,* IX (1956), 325-386.

Scholarly Prose

Richard D. Altick, "The Philosophy of Composition," in *The Art of Literary Research,* New York, 1963.

Graduate Study and the Profession

Ronald S. Crane, "History Versus Criticism in the University Study of Literature," *The English Journal* (College Edition), XXIV (1935), 645-666.

Stuart P. Sherman, "Professor Kittredge and the Teaching of English," *The Nation,* September 11, 1913; reprinted in *Great Teachers,* ed. Houston Peterson, New Brunswick, New Jersey, 1946.

Notes on Authors

The late R. C. Bald was Professor of English at the University of Chicago. He edited Elizabethan plays and studied literary friendships of the romantic poets as well as the printing of seventeenth-century books. At the time of his death he was completing a full-length biography of John Donne.

Fredson Bowers, Chairman of the English Department at the University of Virginia, has written influential books on bibliography and textual studies, numerous critical articles, and studies of literary history. His book reviews have a devastating thoroughness. Having edited the dramatic works of Thomas Dekker, he is now preparing editions of Marlowe, Beaumont and Fletcher, Hawthorne, and Stephen Crane.

Sir Walter Greg's *A Bibliography of the English Printed Drama to the Restoration* (1939-1959) capped a lifetime of original research in Elizabethan literature. As Librarian of Trinity College, Cambridge, Editor for the Malone Society, and regular contributor to *The Library,* he shaped the thought of two generations of scholars.

Bruce Harkness, Associate Dean of the College of Liberal Arts and Sciences, University of Illinois, is a student of modern fiction and an authority on Joseph Conrad.

S. Schoenbaum is currently editing the plays of Thomas Middleton. His revision of Alfred Harbage's *Annals of English Drama* and his teaching at Northwestern University have earned him a reputation for soundness and accuracy.

G. E. Bentley, Jr., who teaches at the University of Toronto, is completing an edition of Blake's manuscripts for the Clarendon Press, the first volume of which set new standards for impressive facsimiles of literary documents.

Donald C. Baker, Associate Professor of English at the University of Colorado, has written articles on Chaucer and other Middle English authors.

Leon Edel, author of a multi-volume life of Henry James, is Professor of English at New York University. He has also written on the modern psychological novel.

Richard Ellmann of Northwestern University is noted for his detailed and imaginative studies of Yeats and Joyce.

Harrison Hayford of the English Department at Northwestern University is co-editor of the definitive edition of *Billy Budd.*

A. J. Smith, who teaches in the University of Swansea, Wales, has written extensively on Donne's poetry.

James B. Colvert of the University of Virginia is preparing a book on the art of Stephen Crane and is editor of a forthcoming edition of Crane's works.

The late F. P. Wilson was general editor of the Oxford History of English Literature, Merton Professor of English, and author of studies of English prose and drama.

Don Cameron Allen, Sir William Osler Professor of English in Johns Hopkins University and editor of *ELH,* has published important books on seventeenth-century poetry and prose. His learning ranges over all of European literature and thought of the Middle Ages and the renaissance.

Morton W. Bloomfield, who teaches at Harvard University, has written on *Piers Plowman* and the history of English. His articles in *Speculum, Modern Philology,* and *PMLA* have stimulated a wide interest in medieval literature.

F. O. Matthiessen, through his classes at Harvard, his books on T. S. Eliot and Henry James, and his studies of classic American authors, was one of the most effective teachers in America.

Graham Hough's versatility enables him to write authoritatively on almost anyone from Spenser to D. H. Lawrence. He is a fellow of Christ's College and University Lecturer at Cambridge.

Ernest Tuveson, Professor of English in the University of California at Berkeley, is an expert on eighteenth-century thought; his principal work is *The Imagination as a Means of Grace: Locke and the Aesthetics of Romanticism,* 1960.

Frank Kermode's *The Romantic Image* influenced the study of twentieth-century literature by emphasizing the continued force of the romantic tradition. His reviews and articles collected in *Puzzles and Epiphanies* (1962) have freshness and trenchancy. He is Professor of English Literature in the University of Bristol.

R. S. Crane, Distinguished Service Professor Emeritus in the University of Chicago, has done important work on Bacon, Locke, Shaftesbury, Hume, and Goldsmith; his studies of literary theory in *The Languages of Criticism and the Structure of Poetry* (1953) have been widely read.

William Arrowsmith, Professor of Classics at the University of Texas, is editor and chief translator of *The Complete Greek Comedy.*

Wayne C. Booth's *Rhetoric of Fiction* won the Christian Gauss award for 1961. He is Dean of the College at the University of Chicago and has contributed regularly to the *Carleton Miscellany.*

Hallett Smith, Professor of English at California Institute of Technology, has exerted a steady influence upon Elizabethan studies through his critical writing and his well-balanced anthologies.

R. B. McKerrow edited the *Review of English Studies* and the works of Thomas Nashe; he was a pioneer in modern bibliography.